The Twelve Wild Swans

The Twelve Wild Swans

A Journey to the Realm of Magic, Healing, and Action

Rituals, Exercises, and Magical Training
in the Reclaiming Tradition

Starhawk and Hilary Valentine

HarperOne
An Imprint of HarperCollins*Publishers*

HarperOne

HarperCollins books may be purchased for educational, business, or sales promotional use. For information, please e-mail the Special Markets Department at SPsales@harpercollins.com.

HarperCollins Web site: http://www.harpercollins.com

HarperCollins®, ▦®, and HarperOne™ are trademarks of HarperCollins Publishers.

FIRST HARPERCOLLINS PAPERBACK EDITION PUBLISHED IN 2001

Library of Congress Cataloging-in-Publication Data

Starhawk
    The twelve wild swans: a journey to the realm of magic, healing, and action / Starhawk and Hilary Valentine. — 1st ed.
    p. cm.
    ISBN: 978–0–06–251669–5
1. Witchcraft. 2. Goddess religion. 3. Magic. I. Valentine, Hilary. II. Title.
BF1566S.7713   2001
299—dc21   00–039547

HB 03.24.2020

To the teachers, students, and organizers of Reclaiming,
and to our loving and supportive partners,
Michael and David

Contents

Exercises

Acknowledgments

This book is a collective work, a compilation of insights, exercises, and rituals developed by all of us who have taught in the Reclaiming tradition. We thank everyone who has contributed to this book. Some are named in the text or the resources, but in reality everyone in our extended community has contributed to the development of this material. We thank our students, too, for we learn from you as much as we teach.

Many people have previously attempted to write some version of this book. We thank Rose May Dance, M. Macha Nightmare, Diane Baker, Beverly Frederick, Doug Orton, and all the others whose attempts laid the groundwork for this. Sharon Jackson's research and insights into the story were invaluable. And we are deeply grateful for Marie Cantlon's editorial suggestions at an early stage.

There are many people who work tirelessly in Reclaiming in capacities other than teaching, who organize rituals, Witchcamps, and events, who produce the *Quarterly*, maintain the Web page, keep the books, take notes at the meetings, and generally do all the hundreds of tasks that keep our community growing and thriving. We are deeply grateful for their work and for the dedication, imagination, and courage of those who have taken their magic into political activism.

We also want to thank our wonderful editors, Liz Perle and David Hennessy, for their caring work and support, and the entire team at Harper San Francisco, including Terri Leonard, Liza Hetherington, and Calla Devlin. Our agent, Ken Sherman, is always a stalwart advocate.

Finally, we thank our partners and families for loving us through this process.

STARHAWK
HILARY VALENTINE
MAY 2000

Introduction

Embarking

Once upon a time, there was an island, a misty, secluded spot only half in this world, where priestesses, heroes, heras, and mages would go to be trained in magic. Called Avalon, Mona, the Isle of Women, its hidden groves would shelter the wise as they learned the language of birds and the speech of nature, the arts of sensing and shaping unseen energies, of moving at will through the spectrum of consciousness, of bending reality and shifting fate. The teachings of this place would be conveyed not through courses and tests but through transformative personal journeys that would change initiates as they faced challenges and grew in spiritual depth, integrity, and strength.

Avalon no longer exists in today's world. The teachings of Witches and mages were for centuries condemned as heresy or ridiculed as superstition. Ancient knowledge was lost, forgotten, or superseded by the teachings of science and technology. Deep forests that were gateways to the Otherworld have been clear-cut; oracular caves have been replaced by Internet search engines.

Yet magic has reawakened in today's high-tech world. The last half of the twentieth century saw a renewal of the ancient spiritual traditions of the Great Goddess. Women and men who sought new models of spiritual empowerment and craved an earth-honoring spirituality respectful of nature created new constellations of religious movements. Earth-based spirituality, feminist spirituality, Paganism, Gaia theory, Wicca, Witchcraft—hundreds of new/old traditions have arisen that reflect a diversity of approaches to the same basic understanding: that this earth—indeed, this cosmos—is a living being and that the interwoven web of life is sacred.

All magic arises from this basic understanding that everything is interconnected and interdependent. Magic has been defined by Western occultist Dion Fortune as "the art of changing consciousness at will." Ritual, meditation, trance, prayer—indeed, all the techniques outlined in this book—are the tools of that art.

Over the last decades, those of us involved in the Goddess movement have learned much about magic through the process of creating and exploring ritual. And we have created our own Avalons: places and structures for teaching and training others, drawing on our experiments and the wisdom of our life experiences.

This book is an invitation to the isle of magic. In it we have attempted to document some of the exercises, processes, and training materials that our community has developed over the past twenty years and to put them in a form that can lead learners through a transformational journey. While many resources exist that give an introduction to magic, this book moves beyond beginning work to include advanced techniques for both individuals and groups.

The community we speak of is called *Reclaiming*. We are part of the larger movement, called *feminist spirituality*, that critiques the patterns of domination embedded in patriarchal religions and reenvisions a spirituality that can liberate women and men. For us, that new vision is rooted in the Goddess, the earth being who embodies the cycles of birth, growth, death, decay, and renewal in nature and in our human lives.

We are Pagans: we practice an earth-based spirituality rooted in respect for nature. We are Witches: our roots are in the initiatory Goddess traditions that arose in Europe and the Middle East, although our practice is strongly shaped by the multicultural traditions of this land. We make a powerful, personal commitment to the Goddess as we understand her, and we are willing to identify with the victims of the Witch persecutions and to work to counter the negative stereotypes associated with the word *Witch*. We are feminists: we believe that neither women nor men can be truly free until the unequal power relations between genders are broken down. Our analysis of power extends to the relations between races, classes, between humans and the earth; we see all forms of domination as interconnected and destructive.

Feminist spirituality, Goddess religion, Paganism, earth-based spirituality, and Witchcraft are like circles that overlap in many areas and retain some distinct differences. There are Pagans who don't define themselves as Witches, and Witches who don't define themselves as feminists. There are feminists in Christian, Jewish, and Buddhist traditions who don't identify with the Goddess. Our self-definition affects our practice and teaching of magic. We teach and work in a nonhierarchical structure, and we use our awakened abilities within an ethical framework that acknowledges the inter-connectedness of all beings.

At the core of the Reclaiming tradition is the insight that spiritual practice, personal healing, and political activism are the three legs of the cauldron in which wisdom and magic are brewed. If we truly experience all life as inter-connected, then we must be concerned with what happens to the rain forests of Brazil and the topsoil of Iowa, to the child suffering in a sweatshop in Asia as well as the homeless child on our city streets. And that concern needs to be expressed not just through prayer and meditation, as powerful as they might be, but through concrete action in the world.

To act effectively, whether that means offering service in our communities or working for political change, we need the personal strength that comes when we have learned to know ourselves. Healing ourselves is part of healing the earth.

Activism and service are sustained by our deep connection to the greater cycles and powers around us. Magic and ritual help us create communities of support and find inspiration and strength when we most need it. In November 1999, I, Starhawk, was in jail for five days for protesting the meeting of the World Trade Organization in Seattle. Most of the strong, beautiful, and empowered women in my cell block were under twenty-five. In one of our dis-cussions, Lucy, a trainer and organizer who at thirty-one was an "old lady" in the group, remarked that the average "life span" of an activist was three years before burnout. So why was I there, at forty-eight, a little fat and creaky from sitting on concrete floors and mixing it up with the cops? Because for the more than thirty years that I've been active politically, I've had rituals to sustain me, close friends to support me and participate with me, and a deep, personal con-nection to the great powers of love and freedom that inspire us to work for change.

The Reclaiming tradition was born out of the convergence of magic and activism. Twenty years ago, when my first book, *The Spiral Dance*, was pub-lished, a group of us who had connected around the bridging of politics and spirituality created a ritual to celebrate Halloween that incorporated art, music, and dance on a scale new to us. We went on to help organize an anti-nuclear march that brought ritual, street theater, art, and music to a political protest. My women's coven began teaching classes together, and because we felt we had worked through a number of power issues successfully, we co-taught to model a shared flow of power. A small nucleus of community devel-oped from those classes, and in 1981 many of us participated in the blockade at the Diablo Canyon nuclear power plant, built on an earthquake fault in central California. When we returned home, we formed the Reclaiming Collective.

The blockade left an indelible imprint on the development of our community. We learned a decentralized model of power, in which small, covenlike groups called *affinity groups* made decisions by consensus. Larger strategies and major decisions were coordinated by spokescouncils made up of representatives from the smaller groups. Real care was taken to listen to each person's voice and hear each person's concerns. Most of all, we learned that power does not have to be vested in one charismatic leader, that it can truly be spread throughout the larger group.

Our understanding of power and our approach to teaching are expressed in the Reclaiming Principles of Unity:

Reclaiming Principles of Unity

"My law is love unto all beings . . . "
The Charge of the Goddess

The values of the Reclaiming tradition stem from our understanding that the earth is alive and all of life is sacred and interconnected. We see the Goddess as immanent in the earth's cycles of birth, growth, death, decay, and regeneration. Our practice arises from a deep spiritual commitment to the earth, to healing, and to the linking of magic with political action.

Each of us embodies the divine. Our ultimate spiritual authority is within, and we need no other person to interpret the sacred to us. We foster the questioning attitude and honor intellectual, spiritual, and creative freedom.

We are an evolving, dynamic tradition and proudly call ourselves Witches. Honoring both Goddess and God, we work with female and male images of divinity, always remembering that their essence is a mystery that goes beyond form. Our community rituals are participatory and ecstatic, celebrating the cycles of the seasons and our lives, and raising energy for personal, collective, and earth healing.

We know that everyone can do the life-changing, world-renewing work of magic, the art of changing consciousness at will. We strive to teach and practice in ways that foster personal and collective empowerment, to model shared power, and to open leadership roles to all. We make decisions by consensus, and balance individual autonomy with social responsibility.

Our tradition honors the wild, and calls for service to the earth and the community. We value peace and practice nonviolence, in keeping with the Rede "Harm none, and do what you will." We work for all forms of justice: environmental, social, political, racial, gender, and economic. Our feminism includes a radical analysis of power, seeing all systems of oppression as interrelated, rooted in structures of domination and control.

We welcome all genders, all races, all ages and sexual orientations, and all those differences of life situation, background, and ability that increase our diversity. We strive to make our public rituals and events accessible and safe. We try to balance the need to be justly compensated for our labor with our commitment to make our work available to people of all economic levels.

All living beings are worthy of respect. All are supported by the sacred elements of air, fire, water, and earth. We work to create and sustain communities and cultures that embody our values, that can help to heal the wounds of the earth and her peoples, and that can sustain us and nurture future generations.

The commitment to a model of shared power has influenced our teaching, our approach to ritual and magical training, and our organizational structures. Our Avalon would not be directed by one High Priestess: it would be governed by a council. Our novices would not be expected to blindly obey authority, but to understand and keep the agreements and disciplines of community life. Hilary and I are cowriting this book for the same reason we co-teach in Reclaiming: to model shared power.

We recognize three kinds of power in ourselves and in human societies. *Power-over*, or domination—the ability of an individual or group to impose force or sanctions, or to control the resources of others—is one we are all familiar with and face in most areas of our lives, from school to work. *Power from within* is a very different kind of power, more akin to creativity than force. The root meaning of the word *power* is "ability," and power from within is our ability to do, to say, to make, to act, to imagine, to dream, to make our dreams real. Power from within is not limited: if you have the power to paint a beautiful landscape, it doesn't limit my power to do the same. In fact, I might learn from watching you, and find my own power from within enhanced. Our magical training fosters and nurtures power from within. We call this process *gathering power*, or *empowerment*.

The third kind of power, *power-with*, is relational, the influence or status we might have among a group of equals. When we become leaders, teachers, or activists, we must become aware of power-with and learn to work with it consciously.

The training we offer takes many forms: weekly classes co-taught by at least two teachers in our home communities, weekend workshops or seminars, individual apprenticeships, long-term training, and the weeklong intensives we call *Witchcamps*, where a team of up to twelve teachers creates a program for a large body of students that includes both smaller, focused classes and large group rituals that explore a theme.

This book is in part the story of our community, and you will be introduced to many of the characters we've worked with and been inspired by over the years.

The material we draw on has been developed and used by a web of teachers that now stretches across North America and Europe. We have tried to record here at least some of what we've learned over the last twenty years of practice.

If you could travel to that magic isle of Avalon, you might find on it somewhere a library filled with ancient leather-bound books of lore, herbals scented with lavender and rosemary, spell books fragrant with incense, Books of Shadows kept by Witches to record their magical work. Imagine that this book comes from that library. Take it down from the shelf, breathe its spicy scent, and settle yourself into a cozy nook. Mysteries await you. Prepare to explore the magic realms.

A Map of the Magic Isle: Finding Your Way Through This Book

Magic is not linear. A magic isle would be crisscrossed not by straight roads but by winding and circular trails that meet in unexpected places and double back on each other. Because this book outlines an initiatory journey, its structure is also spiraling and complex. However, we hope to provide you with clear signposts and a good map to guide your way.

We've chosen one of our favorite stories, "The Twelve Wild Swans," as the theme for this book. It's not a comfortable story, and the work that arises from it may be very challenging. But it contains within it the instructions for a transformative journey.

"The Twelve Wild Swans" is an old, old story. It is found all over Europe in hundreds of versions, from Scandinavia to Italy, and shares elements with other tales ranging from Eastern Europe to Ireland. Rich with symbolism and emotion, the story serves as a powerful connecting thread for training in ritual and magic.

In the Goddess tradition, we have no sacred text other than nature herself. We have no Bible, no Koran, no Bhagavad Gita, no official compilation of myth and story. What remains of the stories our ancestors told are passed down to us as fairy tales and folk tales. These tales have been told for centuries around the fire at night, as entertainment. While some storytellers may have repeated them word for word as they learned them, others felt free to embroider and add what they considered improvements. Some may have remembered every detail; others took a half-forgotten tale and reconstructed it, perhaps mixing in details from some other story. When politics and religion changed form and heresy was redefined, dangerous aspects of the stories were hidden or given a Christian gloss.

Working with these tales involves a process of uncovery. It's as if we're trying to sail an old, old ship so encrusted with barnacles and seaweed that the true shape of the keel can only barely be discerned.

When we start the scraping-away process, we face the temptation of simply removing all the elements that make us uncomfortable or that don't fit our current picture of how things should be. But often the power in the story arises from those aspects that make us uneasy. How do we distinguish the barnacles from the underlying carving that has been obscured?

In the Reclaiming tradition, we approach the stories in a unique way. We do not analyze them for archetypal elements, in Jungian fashion. We do not take the characters, Goddesses, or Gods as role models for how we should be as women or as men, nor do we see the tales as morality plays.

Instead, we look for the true form of the ship. We find clues in the colors, symbols, and actions and their historical associations. When we encounter an aspect of the story that seems problematic, we welcome it as an opportunity to work fully with the material it evokes through meditation, reflection, and ritual. As we do so, the story evolves and transforms. We may never know what the original intention of the first tellers was, but we can know what our intentions are and how the tale can work for us.

"The Twelve Wild Swans" has been used many times as a theme in Reclaiming Witchcamps, and we've poked and prodded at the incrustations many times. The version we've chosen for this book is our own retelling and includes the aspects we've found most rewarding our probes. Many other versions exist, and the bibliography includes references to other retellings and interpretations.

At first glance, the tale can be mistaken for yet another story of a woman sacrificing herself for men, yet another lesson to women to keep silent instead of raising our voices loud. In Reclaiming, we welcome the chance to explore these issues, challenge the stereotypes, and transform the pain and rage they evoke. But we also find in this story a profound guide through the process of growth and empowerment.

The power of "The Twelve Wild Swans" comes precisely from its disquieting elements. Rose sets out to rescue her brothers. Is this a reversal of the old male/hero/rescuer stereotype, or a perpetuation of the dreary old role of woman sacrificing for men, or something else entirely? Rose is enjoined to keep silent during her painful task. Is this another incidence of oppression, or a teaching about power?

Over the years of scraping away at this story, we've found the keen hull of an initiation tale—not in the sense of a formal initiation into a tradition, but initiation as a rite of passage leading to a fuller state of being. Every initiation begins with a challenge, a task that we take on. It becomes a journey that requires leaving a comfortable state of being for danger and risk. On the way, if we're lucky and worthy, helpers and guides appear. They may offer us still more tests and challenges. If we face them successfully, we grow in power—not power over others, but power from within, creative, magical, and healing power.

Encoded in "The Twelve Wild Swans" is a set of instructions for becoming a healer, a shaman, an artist, a Witch: one who can walk between the worlds and retrieve lost souls, one who can restore balance and justice to a world made ill.

That process is never easy. Gathering personal power requires dedication, focus, courage, and, yes, even sacrifice. We are required to think in new and complex ways. Issues are no longer clear-cut, and simple formulas will not guide us. Empowerment demands self-healing, but not mere self-interest. We must learn to tell the difference. Silence can be a mark of oppression or a source of strength. We must learn when to contain our power and when to express it, how to offer service to the great powers of life and death and to our communities without falling into servitude.

As we undertake the journey the story lays out for us, we have the opportunity to wrestle with all the uncomfortable questions. As we move through the various paths laid out in this book, we will tell the story in parts, decoding each as we go along. As we practice the meditations, exercises, and rituals, our insights will deepen. In the end, the story becomes our own.

In our Reclaiming Witchcamps, we often take a myth or fairy tale to serve as our weeklong theme. Breaking it into parts, we create a sequence of evening rituals that illuminate the issues raised by each section and provide a journey of personal and collective empowerment. In the mornings, campers have a choice of several different "paths" in which they can do focused work in smaller groups.

We've modeled this book on the structure of a Witchcamp. Each of the seven chapters of this book contains a piece of the story, with commentary. Each chapter also suggests work in three possible paths that lead us through the realms of magic, healing, and action.

The *Elements Path* contains the basic skills and tools necessary to work magic and create ritual. It's the path to start with if you are new to Witchcraft and magic. Even if you are experienced at ritual, the Elements Path can provide a good review of your skills and understandings and the coherent sequence of training that many of us never received. It teaches what we need to know to establish the first leg of the cauldron, that of personal spiritual practice and magic.

The *Inner Path* is the second leg of the cauldron and focuses on personal healing. Our story is a rich source of material that can help us face and transform the wounded places within that block our power, joy, and ability to love. Magic gives us tools for self-knowledge and change.

The *Outer Path* helps us take our power out into the world, to offer service to our communities, and to find the strength, courage, and faith we need to confront the larger structures of domination that shape our society. We may become teachers, healers, organizers, ritual makers, activists. As soon as we step into these roles, we face new challenges and need new tools and understandings.

You will hear Starhawk's voice in this introduction as well as in the comments on the stories and in the Outer Path, Hilary's voice in the Elements Path and the Inner Path. Part of the Reclaiming tradition is that teachers share something of their personal experiences and join their students in working through the material presented. Hilary will share her personal stories in the Elements Path and the Inner Path: she is the "I" of those paths. In the introduction and the Outer Path, *I* refers to Starhawk.

Think of this book as your sourcebook for planning your own transformative journey of growth and healing. As an individual or a group, you can make your way through this book in several different ways. You can simply read it, noting which parts of it affect you strongly and which seem irrelevant. You can work through one of the paths in a series of seven or more sessions, either in a group or alone with your journal. Or you can work through the book three times, following each path in turn. These are the primary ways we've designed the book to be used. However, you might also choose a particular section of the story that moves you and do the work for that section associated with all three paths. Finally, you can use it as a resource, picking and choosing from the material to take what you need at any given time.

For individuals, this book can be a self-study manual. We recommend keeping a journal, a Book of Shadows, and we will suggest ways to use it as we go along. We will also be clear about which rituals and exercises are best done with a partner or with some outside source of support.

A circle, coven, or study group can also use this book as a guide. Participants could take turns facilitating sessions and pass the leadership around the circle.

And this book is also meant as a sourcebook for those of you who are teaching and creating rituals in your own communities. You are welcome to use the material as it is presented here or to change it, adapt it, and make it your own. We do ask that you credit this book as your source. And we ask that you not call yourself a "Reclaiming" teacher unless you are part of and accountable to a teaching group based in a Reclaiming-affiliated community. If you receive money for your teaching work based on this book, we ask that you contribute some or give some equivalent energy back to your local community or to some of the groups listed in the "Resources" section in the back of this book.

Putting out a book like this is in some ways an act of faith. By putting this material in print, we let go of our control over it. We have no way of monitoring how people will use it or of assuring the level of integrity, skill, or responsibility of those who may teach from this source. We can include cautions, suggestions, and safeguards, but we cannot make people heed them. We encourage students to follow their intuition and heart in choosing teachers. No responsible teacher will force or manipulate you into doing something that does not feel right or that goes against your sense of ethics or personal boundaries. You always have the right to say no. You have the right and the ability to change any suggestions, rework the imagery of any meditation, and pop out of trance if its direction isn't right for you in that moment.

Letting go of control is never easy. But making this material available is in keeping with one of Reclaiming's core principles: that everyone has the ability to make magic, that nobody "owns" the keys to the deep realms of power, that we can each take responsibility for our own learning and growth, and that we all learn by experimentation and by sometimes making mistakes. For me, one of the greatest rewards over twenty years of teaching and writing about these issues has been to see other people bring their own creativity to the material and develop it in ways I would never have imagined. Sharing power means also opening up to sources of inspiration and vision that no one person could ever tap.

Finally, we use a few conventions we'd like to clarify before we begin. The material in this book can be used by women and by men, in same-sex groups or mixed groups. We use the word *priestess* to refer to either a woman or a man who takes on a leadership role in a ritual. Also, to avoid endlessly writing out "he or she," we sometimes simply use "she" just as a counterbalance to centuries of male domination. But unless something is specifically designated for women or for men only, you may assume that all genders are included.

When we ask you to do something "in sacred space," we mean you should first ground, cast a circle, invoke the elements, Goddess, and God—and that you should "devoke" and open the circle when you are done. Directions for all of these actions can be found in the Elements Path in chapter 1, and more elaborated discussion can be found in Starhawk's *The Spiral Dance*.

In many exercises, we have included specific suggestions for working either in a group or individually. We trust that you will feel free to adapt any of the material to your own needs and circumstances.

We introduce other teachers and certain key techniques the first time they appear. We try to provide references as needed, but if you are browsing through the book or working through the paths out of order, please do use the index if you find yourself wondering, "Now, who is that?"

We include many meditations and trances in this book. Sometimes we write out a fairly complete transcription; at other times we simply indicate a rough outline for a guided journey. When we are teaching or leading ritual, we never read trances or memorize them verbatim. Instead, we suggest you read the trance over several times to yourself and fix in your own mind the landmarks of the journey. Let yourself be influenced by the rhythm and language we've provided, but improvise. Let the journey come alive, and know that it will be different each time you guide it.

We hope this book will be useful and inspiring to all those embarking upon the study, practice, or teaching of magic and will be a resource for personal and world healing.

The mists part; the barge awaits. Tune your ears to the voices of the Otherworld, and gather your courage. The journey begins.

The Twelve
Wild Swans

Once upon a time, far, far away across the sea, there lived a queen who had twelve strong young sons, but no daughter. One winter's day, as she sat at her window sewing, she looked out to see a raven, pecking at the bloody snow where the butcher had killed a calf. "Oh," she yearned, "if only I could have a little daughter with skin as white as that snow, lips as red as the blood, and hair as black as the raven. I would even exchange my twelve sons for such a daughter." In that moment, an Old Woman appeared, bent over on a stick, dressed all in black. "That is an ill wish," said the Old Woman. "And to punish you, it shall be granted." And she disappeared as quickly as she had come.

Sure enough, the queen conceived a child. Although her twelve sons were placed in a locked room under the strongest guard, at the moment of the baby girl's birth, they turned into swans and flew out of the open window, never to be seen again. The king and queen named the little girl Rose, and Rose grew up alone in the castle. She was never told of the existence of her brothers or of how they had come to be lost. But as she grew, the child felt lonely, and she was aware of the shadow of some mystery or secret. She became more and more curious. She took to asking all sorts of questions of the most unlikely people, and so it was that one day as Rose approached womanhood, she finally heard the whole story from her old nurse, who had known her brothers well and still grieved for them.

As soon as Rose heard the nurse's story, she knew what she must do. "No matter what the cost," she vowed, "I'll find my brothers and break the spell that binds them." She bade farewell to her parents and walked out of the castle gate with only the clothes she was wearing and a loaf of bread.

She found herself in the wildwood, and she was lost at once. Her soft princess hands and her delicate princess clothes were soon scratched, torn, and dirty, but Rose continued on her way until she found a little stream. Here she stopped to rest for a bit, to drink and wash and eat some of her bread. As she rested, an Old Woman suddenly appeared. "May I have a bit of your bread, child? I'm so hungry . . . "

Although she had little to offer, Rose shared her meal with the Old Woman, and as they talked and ate, Rose poured out her story. "My dear girl," said the Old Woman, "if you follow this river to its end, it will take you to the ocean. Swans live there, by the side of the sea. Perhaps there you will find your brothers."

Rose followed the Old Woman's advice, and when she arrived at the seaside, she found a little hut with twelve narrow beds inside. Sure that she was soon to be reunited with her brothers, Rose waited by the hut. The sun began to set, and in its last rosy light, twelve great swans swooped out of the sky. As their feet touched the earth, the sun set, and before Rose's astonished eyes the swans turned into handsome young men. "I am your sister!" cried Rose.

Her brothers stared at her, horrified. "What have we done!" they cried. "We have vowed to kill the first young girl we meet, because our misfortune came to us through a girl!" Rose shrank back from them, but in this moment the Old Woman appeared again. She faced the frightened, angry brothers: "Break that wicked vow, which you never should have made. Can't you see? This is your own dear sister. Only through her can you be restored." And she disappeared as quickly as she had come.

All through that night, Rose and her brothers talked and planned. The next day was Midsummer Day, the longest day of the year. Only at this time could the swan brothers travel across the sea to the magical land of the powerful fairy called the Fata Morgana. The long daylight hours allowed them enough time in swan form to cross the trackless ocean safely. Otherwise they would turn to men as the sun set and plunge helplessly into the gray and heaving sea. Now they planned to bring Rose with them. During the short night, the thirteen wove a strong basket of willow in which Rose could ride while the swan brothers carried her on a journey Beyond.

As dawn broke, the brothers changed shape, and all of them grasped the basket with their bills, lifting Rose into the sky. They flew and flew, until it seemed their strength must fail, but as twilight came on they spied a huge rock jutting out of the surf, and here they landed just as they began to shape-shift. With Rose in the middle, the brothers huddled on the rock through the short night as the surf broke and crashed around them. When dawn came, they rose again into the sky. They beat with their great powerful wings ever closer to the land of the Fata Morgana.

As another long day came to an end, they saw the coastline of a strange new land open below them. As they began to dip down toward the earth, Rose spied a glittering fairy castle in the clouds. "What is that beautiful palace?" she cried. "That is the castle of the Fata Morgana," answered her brothers, "where no mortal may come."

In the green hills of the coast lay a cave, where the swan brothers lived when they were in this land. Here they landed, glad to be safe on the green earth again. As the sun set, they assumed their human shapes and went into the cave to rest from their journey on beds of soft and fragrant boughs. As Rose slept, she dreamed, and in her dream she entered the fairy castle.

Through doors and hallways both strange and strangely familiar, Rose walked in search of the Fata Morgana. The castle seemed to glow with a transparent inner light, the color of darkness if darkness could shine. When Rose found the throne room and approached the Dark Fairy herself, Rose saw that she, too, was shining, lit up from within. It seemed that the Fata Morgana knew Rose's question without words, and at a slight movement of the fairy's hand, a vision opened up in Rose's mind. She saw that she must make twelve shirts from wild nettles, one for each of her brothers. If she could complete this task in solemn silence, neither speaking, laughing, nor crying, when she threw the shirts over her brothers they would be restored to their human forms, and the spell would be broken. The vision faded, and the face of the Dark Fairy was clear again before her. "It will not be easy," she said. "It is up to you. Do you say yes or no?" "Yes," said Rose quietly, and it was the last word to fall from her lips for many years.

Rose awoke, safe among her brothers in the green cave. She rose at once and went into the woods to gather nettles. She worked in silence, harvesting, soaking, pulling out the fibers, spinning thread, weaving cloth, and cutting and sewing the shirts. When the nettles stung her, she did not cry out. When she and her brothers sat together around the fire at night, eating and talking, she did not laugh or tell tales with them. The brothers knew somehow that her task was for their benefit, and they became accustomed to the fact that she no longer spoke. And so they all lived for a time in peace.

But one day as Rose sat outside the green cave, spinning her thread, who should ride by but the king of that land. He was struck by her mystery, her purpose, and her beauty, and he fell in love with her at once. She was also of an age for love, and so she gathered up all her things and, mounting the horse before him, rode back into the world of men. They loved each other well and would have been very happy had it not been for the jealousy of his mother, who feared this strange, speechless young woman with her odd ways.

Since Rose no longer lived in the forest, when she needed more nettles for her work, she had to harvest them from the churchyard. Here among the gravestones there grew a great healthy stand of nettles. Although she feared the Lamia—snake-bodied women who fed on the bodies of the dead—she feared being questioned more, and so she harvested her nettles at night. The king's mother watched her secretly, and in the morning she went before the king. "A witch!" she cried. "That's who you've married and brought among us. What would an honest woman be doing in a graveyard at night? Why doesn't she explain herself?" The king defended his love and refused to listen to the accusations, but the whispers grew behind Rose's back.

A year passed, and to her joy, Rose gave birth to a beautiful little baby. But while the new mother slept, the jealous old queen stole the baby and threw it off the castle walls into the waiting mouth of a huge wolf. Then she killed a puppy and marked the young mother's mouth with blood. "Alas!" she raised the alarm, "the witch has eaten her own child."

Again the king defended Rose, but the whispers behind her back grew even stronger. She could not speak to defend herself or to let loose her terrible sorrow at the loss of her beloved child. She spun and wove and sewed with more determination than ever, but her eyes filled again and again with unshed tears. Now she knew what the Dark Fairy had meant: "It will not be easy."

Another year passed, and again Rose was brought to childbed. Another beautiful baby was born, to the rejoicing of Rose and the young king. But again the old queen stole the child and threw it into the waiting jaws of the wolf, marking the mother's mouth with puppy blood. This time the king could not overrule his frightened counselors and his terrified populace. There was too much evidence, too much suspicion and rumor, and the people demanded that the witch be burned. Rose was thrown into the dungeon, along with her handiwork (which no one wanted to touch). All that long night, while the people erected a stake and prepared a great bonfire ready to burn her, Rose sewed and sewed. She was almost done with the last shirt.

At dawn, the executioner's cart came for her and carried her to the stake. Still her fingers flew at her work, and she neither spoke nor wept. She was tied to the stake, and the fire was thrust in under her. As the flames began to leap about her, there came a great rush of wings out of the sky. Twelve swans swooped into the square over the stake, beating out the flames with their wings. As each landed, Rose threw a shirt over him, and each was transformed into a strong and handsome man. They boldly surrounded her, keeping the people back, as the burning wood burst into green leaf and blooming roses instead of flame. "I am innocent," cried Rose, and she fell down as if dead.

The young king stepped through the people and plucked a single rose from the pyre. As he laid it on Rose's breast and gathered her up, she sighed and awoke. At that moment, the crowd parted again for the Old Woman leading a little child and carrying a baby snugly wrapped. She had been the wolf that had snatched up the babies, and she had raised them safe and sound until they could be restored to their parents. "Here are your beautiful babies," she said to Rose and the king. "Care for them well." And so, they lived happily ever after. But the last shirt was not finished; it lacked the final sleeve. And so it was that Rose's youngest brother was left to live out his life with one human arm and one swan wing.

ONE

Leaving the Castle

Comments on the Story

A queen makes an ill wish: she would trade her twelve strong sons for one daughter. The girl is born; the sons are transformed into swans and fly away. Rose grows up in ignorance of their existence but with a gnawing sense of something amiss. When she finally learns the fate of her brothers, she decides she must find them and save them. And so she leaves the castle and sets out on her quest.

When we approach this story as a guide through an initiatory journey of empowerment, we recognize that nothing in it is quite what it appears to be. Our queen is more than a queen, and the daughter she wishes for is more than an ordinary daughter. The clue is found in that classic fairy-tale formula of "hair black as the raven's wing, lips as ruby red as blood, skin as white as snow." The red, the white, and the black are the colors of the Goddess—the young moon, full moon, and old moon, respectively. They are also the colors of the cycle of life. According to archaeologist Marija Gimbutas, in the Goddess cultures of old Europe white was the color of death, of ice and bone and the snows of winter; black was the color of earth, of the darkness of the womb, of gestation; red was the color of blood, birth, menstruation, and life.

The queen wishes for a daughter who will embody the Goddess herself, the full cycle of birth, growth, death, and rebirth. Our queen-priestess needs an heir, someone to whom she can pass on her power and knowledge of the mysteries unique to women. We might think that twelve fine, strong sons would be enough for any woman, but without a daughter, the cycle is not complete.

The sons in this story are not ordinary sons. They are twelve—the number of months in the solar year, the signs of the zodiac. Our queen is the mother of time itself. Rose, her daughter, will be the thirteenth moon that completes the lunar cycle.

The queen makes an ill wish. She would trade all twelve of her sons for a daughter. In the manner of fairy tales, her wish is granted.

The practice of magic rests on the power of the word. We say it will be so: we make it so. The more personal power or structural power we have, the more weight our words carry and the more we must be responsible for them. We make a thousand ill wishes every day, harbor hundreds of impulses that we quickly suppress. But a queen, a person of power, must be wary of what she allows herself to voice. The worst danger in magic is that we may get what we ask for.

The Old Woman who appears is the Crone incarnate, guide and teacher who practices "tough love." She teaches not by imposing punishments but by making us face the consequences of our actions. And so Rose is born, and the brothers, in spite of all efforts to protect them, are transformed into swans.

Rose grows surrounded by secrets and evasions—as do so many of us. While she may be the living representative of the Goddess, she takes on individual form and personality. When we work with the story, we become Rose, facing her challenges and undergoing her transformations.

Rose senses that something is wrong, something is missing. She doesn't know what, but she knows that her world is not complete. Her distress, her uneasiness, is the beginning of her quest. An initiation journey often begins with the perception that something is wrong. We undertake a process of transformation because we want more than what is given. We sense that some loss requires restitution; some balance must be restored.

So Rose asks uncomfortable questions, until finally she is answered with the truth. In this she functions as a model feminist heroine. But as soon as she learns the truth, she accepts responsibility for restoring her brothers. While most of us, faced with her situation, would weep, cry, engage a therapist, or form a support group for Adult Siblings of Avians, Rose simply determines to rectify the situation.

This is one of the most challenging points in the story. Rose didn't ask to be born, and she never consented to having her brothers changed into swans. This whole mess is not her fault. Yet she knows intuitively that only she can heal it.

Rose has come to the same starting point each of us must reach when we begin a magical journey. Like Rose, we all live in a world in which many things are wrong. The Goddess tradition does not preach perfection. The universe may be perfect in its inception, that instant before the big bang when all existed as one incredibly tiny, multidimensional point of perfect symmetry. But that perfection isn't much help to us on a day-to-day level. And ever since then, things have been unfolding with a high degree of randomness and a certain amount of chaos, with plenty of room for mistakes to be made. We honor that imperfection, because it is that very quality of randomness that allows for freedom, for creativity and spontaneity. But the price we pay for living in an exuberant, unpredictable, surprising universe is about the same as for attending a wild, unpoliced party where you can crank the music up loud and smash your glassware in the fireplace: there's a certain amount of cleaning up to do.

We each inherit many, many ills we did not create. The path to personal power requires that we know what we are called to heal and what we are not called to fix. In our personal lives, we did not create the families we were born into. We did not build the castle, nor did we contribute to its design. We may or may not be able to heal its ills. Sometimes trying to heal our families may simply embed us more deeply in their destructive patterns.

To gain the insight we need, we must step outside the castle walls, out of our usual frame of experience. Magic teaches us to create portals, to open doors and dare the wilderness.

Collectively, too, we live in a castle not of our own design, full of secrets and inherited ills. None of us alive today created our heritage of sexism, racism, poverty, social injustice, war, or environmental degradation. Sometimes these conditions may oppress us personally; at other times we may benefit from them directly or indirectly. We can respond with rage, with guilt, with grief or paralysis, but none of these will help matters much. Only Rose's response, the willing undertaking of responsibility, can lead to healing.

Women may be rightfully resentful of the many times we are expected to clean up after others. Youth may be enraged at the environmental, economic, and social messes they inherit. Working with this story in Germany, we touched the deep pain and anger felt by many postwar Germans about their country's Nazi heritage, the guilt the younger generation inherits over the genocide perpetrated before they were born.

Nonetheless, as women and men of conscience at the beginning of the twenty-first century, we are called to become Rose, to develop those qualities of courage and responsibility that can lead to healing. And so the brothers become the endangered redwoods, the homeless person on the street, the war victim crying in a far-off land, and the unresolved pain in our own homes and hearts.

A journey of initiation must be undertaken willingly; it cannot be imposed from without. Rose voluntarily takes on her task; no one requires it of her or even suggests it to her. In fact, others do their best to talk her out of it. But her deepest intuition tells her that this task is hers and hers alone. Only she can save her brothers.

We live today in a castle that has expelled many wild swans, many values that might open the heart to the wild and take us soaring on the wind. The work of this beginning chapter is, first, to recognize that something beyond the castle exists—that something, someone, is missing. We must be willing to keep asking questions until we find out what or who that is. If we choose to take on the task of healing, we will need the skills of magic, which can open a doorway in the walls that enclose us.

We cannot rectify every mistake or heal every wound. The work of this chapter in the story is to learn to hear the deep call within, to recognize, as Rose does, what challenges do belong to us. When we answer the call with courage and responsibility, we begin a process that will transform us as deeply as it changes the world around us.

The Elements Path

Rose grew up alone in her parents' castle, but she sensed that some secret was being kept from her. She longed for something without knowing what she was missing. No one told her that before her birth she had already lost her twelve brothers.

These feelings are only too familiar to women and men today. As our lives become more hectic and hurried, more fragmented and isolated, we long for something without knowing what it is. We may feel that something is being kept from us, something that should be our birthright, but we have little idea of what it could be.

Like Rose, we need to find the determination and courage to ask over and over about this elusive feeling. Something is missing! We need to trust our deep sense that something is not right. Here is a bit of the story of what happened before we were born.

Before We Were Born

For thousands of years, until the very recent past, our ancestors lived in a constant deep intimacy with nature. Every moment of their daily lives involved the animals and plants that provided their food, the weather, and the seasons. They were deeply connected to each other, too, in villages and tribes where a few families depended on one another for generation after generation with little change.

Although languages and customs have varied widely from region to region, there are certain parts of life that all nature-based human cultures share. All over the world, people have felt that nature herself was a great Goddess. She was the source of our birth, our sustainer in life, provider of food, water, warmth, and shelter. Her dark arms stretched out to welcome us home at death. She showed herself to us in the beauty and wonder but also the hardship and terrors of the life of nature and our human lives. She was the triple Goddess of life, death, and rebirth.

Her delight was the sex and fertility of humans and animals, blossom and bee. She was our mother, and also the mother of the animals and plants. She was the mother of the elements, too—the great rocks and winter storms, rainbows, little creeks, manure piles, and skeletons. Thus we were relatives of all creation, living always in a great, interconnected web of life.

The elders and the wise women and men of the ancestral villages had special spiritual responsibilities. It was their job to keep peace between the people and the local spirits that held the power of weather patterns and plant and animal lives. The harmony between the visible and invisible worlds needed care and attention. Respect had to be offered to the food plants and to hunted and domestic animals. The cycles of sun and moon had to be observed and celebrated. The natural cycles of human life were also honored, with ceremonies for births, puberty, marriage, elderhood, and death.

The midwives and healers, the smiths, the poets and storytellers all had their roles to play in keeping the balance between the people and Mother Nature. When something slipped out of alignment, it had to be bent and woven back into the flow and harmony of nature. Knowledge of how to do that bending and weaving was the province of the wise—the art and craft of magic. *Wicca, Witchcraft, Witch.* These words come from the same roots as *wicker,* as in wicker furniture, which is made of willow twigs woven and bent together into a pattern.

This ancient nature-based way of life was already coming to an end in Europe when written history began. We will never know exactly what brought about the changeover to the monotheistic Sky Father religions. But God became male, and He now ruled from a distant place. Evil was said to come into the world through women, and women no longer held spiritual authority. Nature herself became something to be conquered and controlled rather than revered. Human nature was described as sinful, and sex as shameful. The sounds of axes were heard in the sacred groves.

In some places the new and old coexisted for a time. Elements of the old nature religion were simply adopted into the new ways and renamed. For example, Brigid, the triple Goddess of Ireland, goddess of forge, poetry, and healing, became Saint Brigid. The old winter solstice rituals for the sun's birth became Christmas, the Son's birth. The practitioners of the old ways came to be called *pagan* (from the plain) or *heathen* (from the heath). But eventually all over Europe the old ways were driven into secrecy in the woods and caves. Finally they became illegal, and the last of the old practitioners who could be found were burned, drowned, or hanged in inquisitions and witch-hunts.

The native European nature-based religions and the people who lived by them met the same fate as other native peoples all over the world. Their nature-based village ways, and the spiritual practices that went with them, were finally destroyed and forgotten. All that remained were nursery rhymes and fairy stories, May baskets, Yule logs, "The Farmer in the Dell," and "Hi-Ho the Derry-O."

> *There was an old woman tossed up in a basket*
> *Seventeen times as high as the moon.*
> *And where she was going, I couldn't but ask it,*
> *For in her hand she carried a broom.*
> *"Old woman, old woman, old woman," quoth I,*
> *"Oh whither, oh whither, oh whither so high?"*
> *"To sweep the cobwebs out of the sky."*
> *"May I go with you?" "Yes, bye and bye."*
>
> —MOTHER GOOSE

Finding Our Lost Brothers

In Rose's story, she lost her twelve brothers before she was even born, through no fault of her own. We, too, have suffered a terrible loss long before we were born, a loss that leaves us lonely and uneasy in our castles. As our species has utterly dominated every animal and plant species, we've also lost our sense of interconnectedness and intimacy with nature. As we've dammed every river, paved over every meadow, and built highways through every mountain pass, we've lost our sense of belonging to this earth and our right place on it. We've lost the free flow of our passion, our sense of magic and awe. The wise women of old whose job it was to keep peace between us and the nature spirits are long gone. We can't name our sickness, nor do we know what our medicine could be.

And yet, in this generation, the Goddess is arising. In dreams, through ancient symbols and stories, she speaks to us. Through the symptoms in our bodies and in our families she speaks of what is out of balance. She will tell us the name of our illness and the name of our medicine. But like Rose, we have to ask the right questions over and over. Like Rose, we have to listen to the answers and then take responsibility to act.

In the Elements Path, we will pick up the broken threads left by the great-grandmothers. We will learn how to begin an active practice that honors Mother Nature and invites healing into our lives. We will learn how to create sacred space, how to rely on Mother Nature, and how to begin a right relationship with the elements of air, fire, water, and earth.

Why Do We Create Sacred Space?

Magic has been defined as the art of changing consciousness at will. When we create sacred space—which includes grounding, purifying, casting a circle, and invoking the elements—we are intentionally entering an altered consciousness. But why would we want to change consciousness?

Talking Self/Younger Self

In our daily lives most of us use one kind of consciousness almost exclusively. We drive the car, answer the phone, write checks with a logical, verbal, task-oriented, "grown-up" part of ourselves that in Reclaiming tradition we call *Talking Self*. When we fall asleep, Talking Self falls asleep, too. But we are still conscious in some way, and sometimes we can remember a dream world of vivid sensation, powerful emotion, and a logic wholly unlike that of waking life, a dream world inhabited by *Younger Self*.

We can observe the working of Younger Self's logic in small children, too. From a two-year-old's point of view, the statement "First we have to go to the bank; then we can get ice cream" makes no sense whatsoever. Passion, hunger, will, and ice cream create their own world in which the word *after* simply doesn't make any sense. Ice cream is now.

Artists, too, are aware that creative impulses come from somewhere outside Talking Self. While painting an ominous canvas with a livid orange moon showing the shadow of teeth, the artist knows perfectly well that the "real" moon doesn't have teeth. But in the artistic vision, which feels like a true vision of another world, the moon *is* orange and it *does* have teeth.

Some mystics have searched for access to these other realms with hallucinogenic drugs. Witches everywhere will assure you that these realms can be reached at will, with training and practice. This is what we mean by "the art of changing consciousness at will."

In Reclaiming tradition we honor these other forms of consciousness, which find outlet in artistic impulses, daydreams, "accidents," physical health and energy, and many other nonverbal expressions. So magic is the art of communicating with Younger Self intentionally in ritual, while awake, rather than waiting for a nightmare, accident, or illness to force us to pay attention.

Younger Self may have known for years that a certain job wasn't right for us, but Talking Self may not know until carpal tunnel syndrome sets in.

Deep Self

Connecting with Younger Self may seem like a good idea for general mental and physical health, but it is actually much more. For in Reclaiming tradition, the way to Deep Self lies through Younger Self. *Deep Self* is the part of us that is directly connected to, or even part of, the Goddess. To our normal everyday consciousness, divine power is a distant theory—maybe something we should care about but terribly vague, perhaps old-fashioned, and usually theoretical.

But to Younger Self, divine power is as real as french fries or the tooth fairy. It just *is* a wondrous, sensual fact of living that we can observe anytime by watching a child absorbed in chasing fireflies on a summer night, by remembering a mysterious or vivid dream, or by getting the chills at an unexpected twist in a fairy tale. In these moments, a sense of awe and present power may make the hair on our necks stand up and a trembling sensation run down our spines or the backs of our legs. Deep Self can be directly felt by Younger Self but not by Talking Self.

So in order to recapture the simple, reliable presence of a divine power that can heal any hurt and bring a sad and sick world to rights, we have to learn to release the narrowness and prejudice of Talking Self, who has long believed that magic isn't real.

In the Elements Path we will learn to create sacred space using magic that appeals to Younger Self. We will also study the elements of air, fire, water, and earth one by one and learn some of the magical techniques that correspond to each of them. We will learn to rely on Mother Nature for guidance and to develop our relationship with the Goddess. We will return to the center of our circles with many new skills, prepared to begin creating our own rituals, prepared to pick up the broken threads left by the grandmothers.

Like Rose, we have asked difficult questions. We have found that our uneasy intuition was correct, that something is wrong in the castle. We have found our purpose: to restore justice in our worlds by walking away into the wild, away from the world of Talking Self into the vivid, concrete, magical world of Younger Self. We will make ourselves a doorway out of our old mode of consciousness by creating sacred space.

How Do We Create Sacred Space?

When we create sacred space together before each ritual, or alone at our home altars, we practice a discipline that trains Talking Self to let go of being sensible and logical for a while. We follow the same basic structure each time we want to walk out the door of ordinary consciousness to travel between the worlds.

First, we ground and purify ourselves. Then we cast a circle around ourselves, defining the difference between ordinary time and space and the sacred space we are creating. We invoke the powers of the elements, air, fire, water, and earth, we invoke the center and we invoke the divine powers, calling them to join us in our sacred space.

We do these basic spiritual exercises in a way that appeals to Younger Self. We ground by imagining being a tree. We purify by actually mixing salt and water to make our own little ocean to bathe in. We take a sharp knife and "cut" a circle around us, cutting away the veil of illusion that holds us in our ordinary consciousness. These vivid, sensual practices, which literally act out in the real world with physical objects the states of consciousness that we are trying to create, are at the heart of witchcraft. In this chapter, we will learn each of these skills, and then we will begin our study of the elements by considering the element air.

Creating Sacred Space: Grounding

The first step in creating sacred space is a meditation we call "grounding." Witches and mystics of all religions share a common insight that all the energies of the universe are connected in a single, complex field. So the incredible explosive power of our sun, the great magnetic and gravitational fields of space, and the microscopic explosions along my nerve fibers that make me blink are all part of an enormous, complex dance. The "Tree of Life Meditation," which we use in Reclaiming before rituals, is our way of connecting ourselves consciously with this great dance of energies.

The grounding also serves the same purpose as a lightning rod. In lightning country, houses have lightning rods so that a sudden surge of power can pass harmlessly through the house and into the earth. The electrical systems in our houses are grounded, too, so that a power surge will pass through the house without starting a fire. Houses, and the people in them, can move enormous amounts of energy, as long as it keeps moving through them and doesn't get stuck.

The traditional grounding exercise that we use in Reclaiming before every ritual does much the same thing. It connects us to the enormous sources of energy in the universe and also makes sure there is a clear channel for energy to keep moving through us, from earth to sky and from sky to earth.

Grounding Exercise: The Tree of Life

Stand comfortably, and roll and shake out your hips and shoulders, your knees and neck, so that you are loose and relaxed. Allow your attention to draw together into a glowing point of awareness behind your eyes, inside your skull. Allow this point to drop through your body, through your throat . . . your heart . . . your solar plexus . . . your womb, or your pelvic cavity if you are a man . . . between your legs and down your legs and stream out into the floor or ground below your feet. Like roots, seeking the soil, easily down, down, down . . . through the foundation of the building (if indoors), through the topsoil into the earth . . . past the shards and bones of those who came here before us, past the water table, into the rock, down, down, down . . . Feel the pressure and heat of mother earth's living body, feel the rock begin to move, soften, feel the magma power, the pulsing heart of Mother Earth, beating, warm, incredibly strong . . . Rest here a moment . . . Now begin on your breath to pull the earth's energy back up toward your body, breathe up through the magma . . . breathe through the rock . . . the water table . . . past the bones of the ancient peoples, through the topsoil and into your feet . . . up your legs on a breath . . . into your pelvis, warm, surging up into your belly, breathing, filling your chest, down your arms and into your throat on a breath, becoming a hum, up into your head, opening all the spaces in your head with breath and a humming sound, up and out the top of your head, where your skull was open when you were born . . . reaching up like branches, like antlers into the sky reaching for the sun, the moon, and the starfire shining in the dark and behind the dark, connecting to the luminous, dark powers of the sky . . . Let the sky energy rain back down on your body, feel the energy of earth and sky flowing up and down you, rest in the certainty of as much energy as you'll ever need . . . When you've had enough, kneel down and touch the ground, letting any extra energy flow back, keeping what you need for yourself . . . when you are ready, stand up, fully grounded and ready for magic. . . .

Creating Sacred Space: Purification

After grounding, the next step in creating sacred space is to release any tension, worries, or distractions that might make it difficult to focus on the work at hand. Whether it's something as simple as tension from bad traffic or a difficult workday or something as complex as an ongoing personal conflict with another circle member, we try to "turn over a new leaf" each time we begin ritual.

Purification Exercise: Salt Water

The group chooses one of the participants to make the salt water. You can also do this alone, but it's lots of fun with friends. You will need a clean bowl, a pitcher of fresh water, and a small container of salt. Pour some water into the bowl, enjoying the fresh sound of falling water. Hold your hands over the water, feeling its coolness. Bring to mind lovely, healing waters you have known, springs, creeks, wells. Say a few words to bring these images to the minds of your friends. Say, "Blessed be, creature of water." Hold the container of salt in your hands for a moment, taste a bit of it on your tongue. Bring to mind the salty release of great sex, of a good cry. Imagine a great rain, washing down the continent and rinsing everything into the vast salty sea. Say a few words to bring these images to the minds of your friends. Say, "Blessed be, creature of earth." Sprinkle and stir the salt into the water. I often use my hands, but traditionally witches use their *athalmes*, their special magical knives.

Now set the bowl down in the center of the circle, and begin to release your troubles and tension into it. We often use our hands to stroke and pull the tension out of tight spots in our bodies, throwing handfuls of tight old energy into the bowl. We use our voices, starting with a breath or sigh, growing to a hum, and building to wails and roars, naming our troubles in a way that appeals to Younger Self like "yucky, yucky, icky traffic, get off, get off, get off me . . ." Sometimes others in a group will resonate and pick up on one person's distress, like the time we all ended up chanting "money, money, money" and sticking our tongues out toward the bowl of salt water. Eventually the energy will die down, and the group will calm down together.

In the relaxed silence that follows, we all put a hand under the saltwater bowl and lift it together to the sky. We call on the moon by her phase, new, full, or old, and ask her to change us as she changes, to take our old, tired troubles and fill us with fresh, clean energy and new starts. (Alternatively, you can imagine a drain in the bottom of the bowl, draining all the icky stuff down into the center of the earth, where the heat and pressure of the earth purify it. There's more than one way to skin a cat, as my old mother used to say.) Setting the bowl back down again, we sprinkle one another with the water, asking blessings and healing for one another. "May you be cleansed, may you be purified." Depending on the mood of the group, this may be quite solemn and holy, or it may turn into a water fight, complete with shrieks and giggles.

The "Tree of Life Grounding" and the "Saltwater Purification" are the basic exercises we teach beginners and use most frequently. But they are only the beginning. There are as many ways to ground and purify as there are people creating ritual. We rarely do anything the same way twice. Creativity and a sense of humor lead us in a thousand different directions, and we are constantly experimenting, finding new ways to get Younger Self to come out and play. Rob used to do the shortest grounding ever heard, "Roots down, branches up!" when he was in a hurry. Raven used to pause in a "Tree of Life" when our roots touched the center of the earth and do a purification right then. "Send any old tension and worries down your roots on a breath and a sound, into the hot heart of Mother Earth. She knows what to do with them!"

Creating Sacred Space: Casting a Circle

After grounding and purifying, you will be ready to cast a circle. For your circle to have power, you will need to prepare yourself by meditating on the directions: east, south, west, and north. You will need to do some firsthand observation of Mother Nature in action. She's been busy all around your own front door, by day and by night. Now it's time for you to begin to notice what she's up to.

Exercise: Preparing to Cast a Circle

Start by meditating on the east. Try to get up early enough to be outside at dawn. Find the brightness of the rising sun; that is the east. The east is not an abstract spiritual theory; it's as familiar and practical as breakfast.

Observe where the sun first strikes your neighborhood, your block, the house or building where you live. Open all your senses to the dawn. Do you hear a change in the sounds of birds, frogs, and insects? In the sounds of traffic? Is there a breeze that springs up or dies down at dawn? Take a deep breath. How does the air smell as it changes from darkness to light? Sense for coolness and warmth, dampness, heaviness or lightness of the air. Notice how the dawn invites you to make a fresh start. When you are finished, say, "Blessed be the east."

Over the course of several days, do the same for noontime, sunset, and midnight. Look for the sun standing high in the south at noon, and feel its strongest heat and brightness. Open all your senses to noontime, just as you did to dawn. Notice how the noontime invites you to action. Say, "Blessed be the south."

At sunset, you will be facing west as you watch the setting sun. Once again, open all your senses to the west. Notice how the half-light invites you into the dream world. Say, "Blessed be the west."

Try to find the North Star in the sky at midnight. Facing north, open all your senses to midnight. Notice how the silent dark, the stillness and cold, touch your deep sense of awe. Say, "Blessed be the north."

Take your time with this exercise. Grounding your spiritual practice in your own personal, unhurried observation of Mother Nature will pay rich dividends for you. Becoming a practicing witch is not a race against the clock; it's the work of a lifetime. Soon it will begin to feel easy and natural to find the directions. Try it at the grocery store, at work, or picking up the kids. Wherever you are, your world is bounded by east, south, west, and north. When you can easily and naturally feel your orientation to the directions, you are ready to cast a circle.

Exercise: Casting Your First Circle

Many women and men like to cast their first circles around their bedrooms, but kitchens and favorite outdoor places run a close second. We often cast our circles holding a sharp, double-bladed knife in our strongest hand, but fingertips work just fine, as does a pen, a feather, a stick, or whatever appeals to your Younger Self at the moment.

Ground and purify, say out loud, "Let this circle protect me from all that is harmful, and let in all that is healing." Face the north. Stretch your arms out towards the north, and feel the energy humming in the tips of your fingers or humming through your fingers and your knife. You're alive. I promise there is energy in the tips of your fingers. You may need to adjust your attention to feel the light, living hum of your body going about its wondrous business. If it's difficult to feel, try rubbing the tips of your fingers together, snapping your fingers, clapping your hands. Now feel again.

Next, walk around to the east, feeling your fingertips, or your knife, drawing an arc of energy through the space. Have you ever seen the afterglow when children swing sparklers around on the Fourth of July? Some people "see" magical energies like that, some people sense them as physical sensations like heat or cold, some sense them as though powerfully imagining them. Whichever door to the Otherworld works best for you, walk right through it like Rose.

Now, facing east, allow your own impressions of the east at dawn to flood your imagination and memory. Hold that image as strongly as you can, and say out loud, "By the air that is her breath." Continue around to the south, and when you're facing the south, let your impressions and memories of the noon sun high in the south flood your imagination. Say, "By the fire of her bright spirit." Continue to the west, and let your mind fill with the image of the setting sun at twilight. Say, "By the waters of her living womb." Continue back to the north, and remember the North Star at midnight. Say, "By the earth, which is her body," closing the circle at the exact spot where you started.

Turn and walk back to the center of the space you've marked. Here stretch one hand as high as you can reach, and stretch the other toward the earth. Imagine the arc of energy you drew around the circumference of your circle springing up above and below and all around you into a sphere of glowing energy. Say, "By all that is above, and all that is below, the circle is cast. We are between the worlds. What is between the worlds can change all the worlds." It is done. We have cast a circle.

Creating Sacred Space: Invocation

We cast a circle before a ritual first of all to exclude the ordinary responsibilities and distractions that make it difficult to focus and concentrate. This is very similar to bowing when stepping onto the mat at a martial arts practice or the moment of silence and prayer that opens many twelve-step meetings. We compose our minds and spirits and prepare ourselves to enter another "world" where different rules apply.

The second reason for casting a circle is to contain the energies of the participants so that power can be raised and directed to a purpose. As Starhawk wrote in *The Spiral Dance*, to boil water you need a pot.

A third reason for the circle is that it allows us to intentionally invite in powers that we may find helpful in our work. We call these invitations "invocations," which just means that we are using our voices (*voces* in Latin) to call something "in." Witches in the Reclaiming tradition always begin ritual by inviting the powers of the four elements into the circle.

When we say that there are four elements, we are not referring to the periodic table of the elements that scientists use to describe atoms. We are referring to the ancient science of many earth-based cultures that knew that there were three physical states, air, water, and earth (science would now refer to them as gas, liquid, and solid) and one other state, fire (or energy). We call these the Elements of Life, because they are what we each need for life. Each human being, each animal, and each plant needs clean air, fresh water, healthy soil or food, and an energy source in order to live. Our lives can take place only in the delicate balance of all these. We animals take in oxygen and food and breathe out carbon and excrete nitrogen. Meanwhile, plants feed off nitrogen and breathe in carbon while breathing out oxygen and producing food. The sun warms our planet and sets the great ocean and air currents in motion, the moon pulls the tides, and we swing through the great cycle of our seasons and our weather. No matter how we vote or whether we are rich or poor, none of us can live outside the balance of these elemental cycles.

In our tradition, each element corresponds with one of the cardinal directions: east with air, south with fire, west with water, and north with earth. And we begin each ritual by calling on (invoking) the power of the elements and reminding ourselves of exactly where we stand, amidst the balance of the Elements of Life. Our lives depend on nature, and now in the twenty-first century, the green and living planet we call "nature" depends on us.

Exercise: Invoking the Elements of Life

Face the east in the circle you have made. With your strongest hand, draw an invoking pentacle at the easternmost edge of the circle. The pentacle is

INVOKING PENTACLE   BANISHING PENTACLE

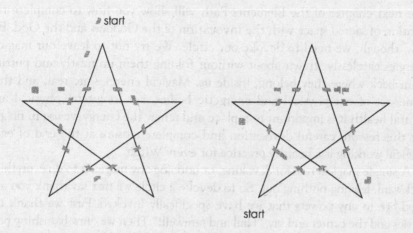

like the air lock in a submarine; it allows the powers that you are specifically inviting to enter your circle without disrupting the protective power of the circle. Say, "East, Powers of Air, I thank you for sustaining my breath. Come springtime, new life, clarity of vision, eye of hawk, be welcome." Or, even better, use words of your own as you develop your own associations with the directions and elements. Walk around to the south, and draw another invoking pentacle. Say, "South, Powers of Fire, I thank you for sustaining the dance of my life. Come hearth-fire, noontime, come heat of sex, transforming anger, come Ever-dancer, be welcome." Walk around to the west, and draw another invoking pentacle. Say, "West, Powers of Water, I thank you for sustaining my blood. Come surging tide, moon-pulled, dissolver, heart's love, whale song, twilight, be welcome." Walk around to the north, and draw another invoking pentacle. Say, "North, Powers of Earth, I thank you for sustaining my body. Great Bear, cave-dweller, winter-sleeper, silent earth and fertile field, midnight, be welcome." Coming back to the center of the circle, call the center. "Center, I thank you for sustaining my spirit. Hub of the Great Wheel, hearth, Orb-weaver in your web, cauldron's brew, be welcome."

In Reclaiming circles, different people often volunteer to call each direction/element. Or the whole group can call the elemental powers together. Some of the most effective invocations I've experienced have been wordless, a slowly building whistle of birdsong and breath in the east, a riot of snapping fingers and clapping rhythm in the south, crashing sound of waves and lonely, longing cries in the west, stamping feet and deep humming tones in the north. These are invocation styles that bring the whole group in, and the power flows strongly. In a trained group there is no need to explain the qualities of each element.

Creating Sacred Space: Devoking

The next chapter of the Elements Path will show you how to complete the creation of sacred space with the invocation of the Goddess and the God. For now, though, we need to devoke our circle. We try not to leave our magical energies carelessly strewn about without folding them up neatly and putting them back where they belong, inside us. Magical energies are real, and they come out of our physical and energetic bodies. For long-term physical and mental health it is important to replace and renew the energy we use in magic. For this reason, careful devocation and complete closure at the end of each magical working is a healthy practice for every Witch.

A simple magical rule for devoking, or undoing any magic, is to do everything backward, leaving nothing out. So to devoke a circle we first say thank you and good-bye to any powers that we have specifically invoked. First we thank the deities and the center and say, "Hail and farewell!" Then we draw banishing pentacles in each of the directions, closing our air locks, as we say good-bye to the earth, the water, the fire, and the air, thanking them specifically for the help we got from them during the ritual. Then we open the circle by saying, "By the earth that is her body, by the waters of her living womb, by the fire of her bright spirit, by the air that is her breath, the circle is open, yet unbroken. May the peace of the Goddess go in our hearts. Merry meet, and merry part, and merry meet again!"

Like Rose, we have asked questions and found out why we were uneasy in our old castles. We have created a doorway out of our old castle, out of our normal consciousness. When we want to walk between the worlds, we can create sacred space and invite Younger Self to come out and play. Now we will begin our study of the elements, by working with the element air.

The Power of the Elements

In Witchcraft, each of the four elements corresponds to a direction, to a magical tool, to colors, and to many plants, stars, and stones. These correspondences add to our magical tool kit, so that if a Witch wants more energy on a certain day, she can drop a tiny gold earring of a lion, calendula petals, a drop of lemon oil, and some whole grains of wheat into a tiny square of orange cloth, hold it up in the sunlight while facing south, and hang it around her neck. She has invoked the power of fire (while reminding herself that if she wants energy she has to eat healthy food), and she will feel it with her all day long.

In the early training of each Witch, she or he learns not only how to ground, purify, and cast a circle, but also how to invoke each element, and she is introduced to the magical techniques that correspond to each. As we work through the story of the Twelve Wild Swans, we will stop along the way and learn about the powers of each element in turn.

Air

Magical techniques that correspond with air include breath control and visualization. The tool of air is the *athalme*, the Witch's black-handled, double-edged knife. The task of air is the creation and protection of boundaries. The power of the wise corresponding to air is "to know."

Breath Exercises

The air we draw in with every breath is a work of art and history, created by Mother Nature. It contains the outbreath of ancient plants and algae, the exhalation of oceans and volcanos, a bit of smoke from last year's forest fires, the exhaust from yesterday's traffic. Our breath is the end-product of myriad natural processes (including human activities). It connects us to all the living and the whole life of nature.

Basic Breath Meditation

Breathe in, knowing that the whole life of nature feeds you. Breathe out, knowing that you feed the whole life of nature. Keep breathing deeply in and out until you feel fully energized and connected to all things. Raise your arms up above your head and breathe out a giant "thank you." Rest for a moment with an open mind, and see what Mother Nature sends back to you. This meditation alone, practiced regularly, will be a wonderful foundation for a personal spiritual practice.

Many Different Breaths

When I was preparing to give birth, the midwives taught me three basic breaths. The first was a simple, slow breath from deep in the belly. This breath was to help keep me calm and centered during the painful intensity of the contractions. The next breath was a quick shallow inbreath, followed by a quick blowing for the outbreath, as though I were blowing out a candle. This breath was to help me control my impulse to push, if it came too early, before I was completely dilated and ready to give birth. The third breath was a deep, powerful, pushing groan, to help get the baby out when it was time.

These simple breath techniques, which are already familiar to many women who have given birth and their partners, show us an important bit of wisdom about our breaths. Different kinds of breath correspond to different physical, emotional, and spiritual states. By changing your breath, you can create change in your body, emotion, and spirit. Try practicing the three breaths of the laboring woman, and see for yourself how each breath makes you feel.

Practice using the first breath to calm and center yourself in difficult moments, the second to control an unwise or untimely impulse, and the third to give you the power to do the impossible (believe me, giving birth seems impossible until it actually happens). You may not want to use the third breath in public unless you are actually moving furniture or practicing the shotput. For some reason people think it's odd when women walk around making sustained groaning sounds from deep in their bellies.

There are many breath techniques besides these three, but these are a wonderful starting place, already familiar to many women. By simply observing your own breath habits and patterns and consciously using your breath to help yourself, you can get to know yourself better and add powerful tools to your spiritual tool belt.

Honoring Air: Giving Back

In the previous exercises we worked on ways we can use air to help us. Now it's only fair to work on some ways that we can help the air. This is the law, the heart of earth-based spirituality. We give to nature, and so we receive. We receive, and then we must give back. Ignorance of this law and disregard for it have painted our species into quite a corner now at the turn of the millennium.

So now it's time to make a start in your own commitment to the air. First you need some information. Where does the air you breathe come from? What is "upstream" from your prevailing winds? What's "downstream" from you? Who breathes your exhaust? Whose are you breathing? Is there one thing you can change in your own life to help keep your air cleaner and healthier? Next time you do the basic breath meditation, commit yourself to making this one small change when you breath out the big "thank you" at the end of the meditation.

Visualization

In addition to breath, another magical technique associated with the air is visualization. When we close our eyes and rest in the blue-black of inner space, odd, glowing afterimages appear as though on a screen in our minds. In dreams, we can "see" a complete and detailed drama that takes place within our minds, and we can even participate and take action there. We can learn to "see" scenes and visions with our inner eye while we are awake, also.

Some people visualize quite easily; others have to practice. Visualizing the outcome we desire, in the greatest detail possible, is the first step in any spell. We sometimes refer to this as "setting an intent."

At the great Reclaiming Halloween celebration in San Francisco every year, we set the intent for our year's work by singing together, "May all the forms of life be saved, may all the colors of our skin be praised, may all the buried streams run free, and the salmon return each year from the sea . . ." These are only a few details of the specific, concrete picture we create for ourselves of the world in which we want to live. The chanting, dancing, and visualizing go on for hours.

For now, let's concentrate on setting an intent for the outcome of the work of the Elements Path. Can you imagine developing a spiritual practice that is both fun and fulfilling? Can you imagine finding a perspective where you are the hero of your own life story, supported by divine power and by the powers of nature? Can you imagine yourself both relaxed and energetic, taking excellent care of yourself physically, emotionally, and spiritually?

Can you imagine yourself filled with purpose, a skillful gardener in Mother Nature's garden, whether that garden is an organic farm, an inner-city soup kitchen, or your own kitchen table? Choose one specific image of yourself involved in a fulfilling spiritual practice, and concentrate on it. Close your eyes, and imagine the scenario in as much concrete detail as you can. Look down at your feet. Where are you? What are you wearing (if anything)? What sounds do you hear? What is the quality of movement in your body? Are you alone or with others? Look around you and above you. What is the weather, the season, the time of day?

If you can clearly imagine a fulfilling spiritual practice for yourself, you have stepped onto the path, like Rose. Maybe something subtle has been amiss in your life as you have been leading it. Maybe you are ready to ask the right questions and take determined action on your own behalf. When Rose knew something important was wrong in her life, she persisted in her questioning until she found out what it was, and then she fearlessly walked away from her life as she had known it.

Like Rose, we have asked hard questions and found out that our lives are out of balance. Not only our twelve brothers, but all our relations, the rocks, the rabbits, the little springs, and the midnight sky, we've lost them all in a culture that has forgotten Mother Nature and our right place in the circle of life. Like Rose, in the Elements Path we have walked away from everything we have known and stepped between the worlds. We've learned to create sacred space for ourselves and begun a right relation with the element of air. In the chapters to follow, we will continue to search together for our lost brothers, building the basics of a spiritual practice based on Mother Nature.

The Inner Path

Rose grew up in a home where something was deeply wrong. A terrible injustice and a terrible loss had happened in this home before she was even born. Those events cast a long shadow over her life. As she grew up, she could feel that something was wrong, although she did not know what it was. She followed her intuition and asked persistent questions until she eventually asked the right person the right question at the right time. Finally she found out what had happened to her brothers; her intuition had been right all along. Now she could take action.

Many women and men today begin to seek a spiritual practice because, like Rose, they find themselves in need of personal healing. Many of us suffer or have suffered from disordered family lives. Sometimes the actions and choices others made before we were even born have affected us deeply. We may find ourselves trained to a way of life based on painful and habitual fears and resentments. Our families may be burdened by secrets of past generations: infidelities, suicides, alcoholism, incest. We may be trying to comfort ourselves in ways that don't work: with food, overwork, unhealthy relationships, money, drugs, or alcohol. We may be dealing with chronic or intractable physical or emotional pain. Or we may simply be failing to thrive, a little sad or bored or hopeless in a life that may seem slightly unreal or trivial.

Even those of us who are lucky enough to have had good health and supportive family relationships may be troubled by the disorder in our larger human family. We may have had to overcome obstacles and work extra hard for our self-esteem because our gender, our skin color and hair, or our class background was disrespected by media, schools, and society. We may feel deeply unsettled as we walk past a homeless woman and her baby, knowing something is deeply wrong with how privilege and responsibility are doled out in our culture. Or we may feel justifiably fearful when we open the newspaper in the morning to read of some insanely violent event between people or nations. These feelings are disturbing and alienating whether or not we think of ourselves as politically involved. The alienation and insecurity of an unhealthy culture affect each of us. We've all grown up in a disturbed extended human family. We all need ongoing healing.

For us, healing means more than seeking relief for a symptom or illness or family problem, although it may include all of these. Healing means becoming *whole*, a unique, powerful, aware, fulfilled person. Healing means becoming the main characters in our own life stories—heras and heroes. It means living passionately, creatively, and joyfully.

Healing also means becoming *part of a whole*, comfortable, connected, and intimate with other people and with nature. We are each a thread in the web of life. For the whole design to prosper, each of us must shine our colors brightly, and the thread that is our personal life story must be both strong and flexible, since it helps to hold the whole pattern.

When Rose finds out the truth about her family history, she walks away from her old life. Like Rose, as we work through the story of the Twelve Wild Swans, we will have an opportunity to walk away from old patterns of thinking and feeling about ourselves. In the Inner Path we will learn some alternatives.

We will practice some of the magical tools that Witches in the Reclaiming tradition use regularly for the development and maintenance of their own inner health, wholeness, intuition, and power. Some of these techniques may be useful to you as we work through this story, layering a spell together for personal healing. And some of these techniques may be ones you choose to adopt or adapt as part of your own spiritual practice for a lifetime.

The exercises in the Inner Path assume that you already know how to create sacred space, keep an altar, move into and out of trance states, that you have some practical experience with your own energy body, and that you have a relationship with the Goddess and the natural world that can support your work. If you feel you're not quite ready, by all means go ahead and read the Inner Path, but please start working with the exercises in the Elements Path first.

Why Do We Work with Fairy Stories?

In Reclaiming, when we seek healing we often work with fairy stories. These stories promise, over and over, that if we set off on the path with nothing but courage, determination, and a kind heart, we will reach our goals no matter how impossible they may seem. The stories promise that in return for our greateartedness, the universe will provide miraculous assistance that can bring about huge, impossible changes for the better. They are full of hope.

In our darkest hour, we will receive mysterious supernatural guidance or sometimes help and advice from plants and animals. We will be sorely tested, but even if we end up working in a filthy pigsty, we may look up at the castle window and see the princess looking down at us with love and longing. Although we may be the lowest scullery maid, we are also perhaps the only one who can bring back the water of life to heal the sick king. There are a million stories, just as there are a million souls searching for fulfillment. But each and every story promises that we can become the main character in our own triumphant life story.

These stories, though, are more than just encouraging and inspiring. They are also templates for soul healing from Europe's ancestral wise women and healers. When the ancient earth-based cultures of Europe were destroyed, these stories remained.

The fairy stories are told from a completely different cultural and psychological perspective than our modern one. In these stories women and men and even little children each have their own powers, cleverness, and magical abilities. The natural world is a great resource that helps those who respect and care for it and punishes the selfish and exploitative. The spirit world of dreams, visions, and magic is walking invisibly beside each character, just a prayer and a breath away, ready to assist those whose hearts are pure. The stories don't recommend a spiritual way of life; instead, they assume a spiritual way of life. There is much we modern people have to learn from the assumptions of these ancient tales.

As we work through Rose's story, we will follow her as a guide into a way of life based on the assumptions of an ancient, earth-based wisdom. She will show us how to walk away from our unhealthy castle, how to trust ourselves to a little stream through the wildwood. She will show us how to face the bitterness and desire for revenge that comes from past injustices. She will set us an example of daring and courage, by stepping into a homemade basket to be lifted into the sky and flown over the sea to the Otherworld. She will show us how to rely on the green world of nature for our strength, and she will show us how to keep to our life purpose through love and loss and attack. Finally, she will be our example as she faces death. Through all her courage, vision, and endurance, the transformation she seeks comes about, miraculously, at the last moment. And here is an opportunity for us.

Because if we learn to live our lives like Rose, we may find that we are able to solve problems that before seemed impossible. With a little practice, we can learn to access and rely on the power of the natural world. We can learn to find guidance in dreams and visions, and we can learn to find inner strength in unexpected places. With these tools we learn from Rose, we can try again to heal a difficulty that has been intractable for years, whether it is an addiction, a difficult relationship with a family member, a physical ailment, or simply an inner pattern of unhappiness. We can try to become the heras and heroes of our own tales and live joyfully and passionately, no matter how distant that goal may seem at the moment. Even if what you long for seems almost impossible, achieving it can hardly be more difficult than turning twelve swans into brothers.

There is a saying in Witchcraft that "a healthy priestess makes all things whole." Just as we cannot be completely happy in an unjust and disordered family or community, so a family or community cannot remain as unjust and disordered if one member heals. We can learn to call on the power of the Goddess and her ancient cultures to change ourselves. And we will inevitably change our surroundings, making our personal worlds and the people we love healthier, happier, and more whole.

The fairy stories are time capsules sent to us from the ancestors of the ancient European earth-based cultures. Their magic can be unlocked today to release the magic and the deep knowing of a culture more compassionate than ours to the true hearts and lives of women and men.

How Younger Self Can Help

As Witches, when we work with a fairy story, we are not trying to analyze or "understand" it. Remember, for us healing comes from Deep Self, and Deep Self communicates through Younger Self. The symbols in the stories are the language of Younger Self, who communicates through sensuality, art, dream, and vivid images; through jokes, "irrational" impulses, and physical sensation. Younger Self lives behind the veil and knows the smells and shapes of all the lost parts of the self. As we follow Rose, searching for her lost brothers, we can find the lost parts of ourselves if we engage playfully and creatively with Younger Self, and if we refrain from trying to force Talking Self's logic into this sensitive communication.

We have lost parts of ourselves because in order to function in a culture that is hostile or indifferent to the whole lives of our human souls, we have learned to hide our true natures: harlequin, mischievous, fierce, tender, animal, changeable, wild, inspired. It simply won't do on the bus, in the office, at the grocery store. And the pieces of ourselves that we mustn't use or show gradually fade behind the veil until we ourselves don't know where to look for them. Then, like Rose, we feel that something is wrong, something is missing, and we don't even know what it is. So we must ask a million questions and finally walk out of the wall of that old castle, with no map, only a fierce determination to restore what was lost and our courage to face the unknown as we seek our true natures.

Every emotion, every vision and dream, every sensation, every desire plays its own part in the ecology of the self. The lost parts of the self are sometimes those that are taboo in our culture and that we each guard carefully in shadow, revealing them to no one and sometimes not even to ourselves. But even these are part of our soul ecology. Just as the worldview of the Witches embraces the thorn and rose, the honey and the bee sting, so as we seek to understand and care for ourselves, we must not divide ourselves into "bad" and "good."

Witches do not seek to control, to repress, to rise above, or to detach from our human desires and our human nature. For us, the Goddess is immanent in the natural world; all beings are holy in all their parts, and this includes our selves. So we seek to know, love, and understand ourselves, *all* of ourselves, to develop patience and compassion, and skill and a sense of humor about ourselves. We seek to learn how to take excellent care of ourselves, as we would of a beloved child, as the Goddess would of us. "For behold, I am the Mother of all things, and my love is poured out upon the earth." (The Charge of the Goddess, *Spiral Dance*, p. 90)

Younger Self will act as our guide as we pass beyond the veil, searching for the lost parts of ourselves. But we must refrain from "analyzing" Younger Self's language of concrete images and powerful sensuality.

Have you ever woken up from a strong or disturbing dream feeling as though the tectonic plates under the house of your spirit have shifted as you slept? Younger Self has spoken in a powerful, sensual voice. And even if you can't remember the dream at all, the feeling on awakening can be as though a powerful force had stirred your pot or thrown open all the doors and windows inside your head.

Then sometimes, if you are of an analytical mind, you might look up the symbols in a book and find out that the hairy spider from the dream is a symbol of the wicked mother. The flowering tree is a symbol of the Goddess. The heaving ocean is a symbol of the unconscious mind. Suddenly the experience that was mysterious and powerful on awakening seems like something that could be decoded with a spy ring from a box of Cracker Jack. All the steam goes out of it like a popped balloon.

By "breaking the code" of the dream, the power of the dream can also be broken. This happens because the power of the dream comes from its appeal to Younger Self. Younger Self can, in turn, bring the infinite power of Deep Self to bear on the problem the dream presents. Deep Self is the part of each of us that is connected to, or even part of, the Goddess. Deep Self speaks to us through Younger Self, and we experience the nearness of Deep Self as a feeling of mystery, of nameless power, even of disorientation. When we "break" the dream's appeal to Younger Self by explaining it logically, we also break the invisible cord to Deep Self, and the sense of power and mystery vanishes.

As Witches, we work with dream and story symbols in a different way. We don't take them apart and analyze them for the benefit of Talking Self, any more than we would cut up a favorite pet to see how it worked. Just as with a beloved animal friend, we want to interact with a story or dream as a living whole, with its own humor, compassion, offer of friendship, and unpredictable energy.

Instead of breaking down the symbols in a story, we try to let the symbols build and become even more detailed and mysterious. We engage Younger Self in sacred space and let our own most personal memories and associations crystallize onto the template of the story. We encourage the fairy story to apply more and more intimately to our own story, until it casts a new light on our old troubles, like sunrise through stained glass.

This is not to say that analyzing dreams and learning about the history of symbols in the Western mystery traditions aren't valuable, important, and even fun. Priestesses do all these things in Reclaiming and sometimes gain priceless insights from intellectual and analytical work.

But we do not expect the deep healing and transformation from analytic modes of consciousness that we do when we are willing to engage Younger Self and enter the wild forest of our own underworlds. Then we can count on help from the power that turns the stars, and we never emerge from such an adventure unchanged. So if you are ready, let's allow ourselves to be Rose for a while. Let's build a Rose altar, do Rose trances and Rose dances, create Rose spells and meditations, get together with our friends and do Rose rituals. Let's live her adventure together, binding our own life stories with hers, learning from her and from the ancestors who told her tale, and letting her transformation bring change into our own lives.

Friends Can Help

Many Witches choose to work on their psychic development in circle with like-minded friends. This is the basic practice of Witchcraft: to meet at the moon's phases, with an intimate circle of no more than thirteen, and make magic together. Just as women have always gotten together for "girls' night out" or sewing circle, or tea or cards or jogging, so we find ourselves benefiting from the support and motivation of like-minded friends as we try to bring the deepening and exercise of our soul-life forward, off the back burner. Spiritual practices in the Goddess tradition can be pursued solitary, but even more momentum for change and healing can be developed by working with others. There are some exercises in the Healing Path that require help from other people or the energy of a group. Our relationships with others, how we work in a group, our abilities to share and care for one another, are sometimes the most important part of healing work. So if it's possible, you may wish to follow the exercises in the Inner Path with a group of friends.

Asking Questions

Rose was the child of a difficult family history, which occurred before she was born. Her intuition told her that all was not as it seemed. She asked a million persistent questions, until she found out what she needed to know about her past and her own purpose. Once she found out what she needed to know, she walked out the door of her old castle, away from her old life, into the wild. Now we will use our intuition to ask a million questions about our own lives, and we will find a doorway out of our own castles. We will gain the courage to walk away into the wild, setting out on an unknown journey.

Let's allow ourselves to be like Rose. Let's give ourselves some time and attention and ask persistent questions about our own inner landscape. Where do we feel the shadow of something out of balance? Where do we need inner healing? Whom or what have we lost through no fault of our own? What is this sense of present absence? How do we even know what questions to ask? Of whom? And when?

Asking the Right Question

In magic, it's very important to ask the right question, because Younger Self takes words very literally, as though they were things. Every Witch has her story about how she learned this the hard way. For example, in San Francisco, finding a parking place is a major challenge every day for those who drive. But if I were casting a spell to never have to look for a parking place again, I would have to be very careful about my words. The easiest way for this to come true would be for someone to steal my truck! Then I would never have to worry about parking again.

So in the same way, when we embark on a journey toward self-healing and transformation in the Inner Path, we have to be careful what we ask for, because we just might get it.

It's particularly important to avoid trying to "improve" the self in a way that is actually quite critical or hostile to the self. I've frustrated myself for years by using magic to try to "correct" a painful and embarrassing habit of mine: nail-biting. But the more I try to use magic to stop this habit, the more entrenched my Younger Self becomes. She says she likes biting her nails, that it's comforting.

Instead of threatening to "improve" my self by taking away her comfort, I need to direct my magic toward discovering powerful and effective ways to comfort myself that are more fun than nail-biting. I received some useful guidance in a recent dream, which suggested that when I'm tired and anxious and start to bite my nails, I could try playing operatic music for myself. Now, I've never listened to operatic music in my life! Talking Self was surprised, perhaps even a bit insulted, by this dream guidance. Those reactions can be a good sign that the guidance actually comes from a deep source. Remember, the transformative power of a working must come through Younger Self from Deep Self.

Taking care when asking the question, or stating the intention of work for inner healing, is very important. Of course, it sometimes takes years of persistently asking the wrong question to find out what might be needed instead. It takes courage and perseverance to keep asking questions. It's scary to ask questions when the answers may involve making difficult changes or taking new risks. But there is a price to be paid for not asking questions, also.

Finding Your Questions

Now it's time to ask some questions of your own. You may already know exactly what you want to work on in your own inner life. There may be some urgent emotional crisis or health problem that you know needs attention. You may be coming to the Inner Path with a general sense of unwellness or disturbance. Or you may feel terrific and want to keep growing and changing because you're curious and excited.

But in Reclaiming, we use magic and enlist the help of Younger Self to choose the questions and develop the intention. So even if you think you know exactly what you want to work for, please try the following exercises. Younger Self may have something to add. There may be some surprises, so bring along your open-mindedness and courage.

Questioning Exercise: A Mysterious or Disturbing Dream

Begin keeping a notebook and pencil or pen by your bedside. When you wake up, whether it's in the middle of the night or in the morning, immediately write down any dreams you remember. It's amazing how quickly the vivid and important details of a dream vanish, sometimes within minutes of getting up out of bed.

If you have trouble remembering your dreams, here are some suggestions. Make yourself a dream pillow with fragrant herbs. Bay, mugwort, and jasmine are among the herbs traditionally associated with prophetic dreaming, but there are many more as well. Pray from the bottom of your heart for a helpful dream. Drink a glass of water before going to bed. When you need to get up in the night to go to the bathroom, you may remember a dream.

After recording several dreams over a period of time, look over what you've found. Do you have a dream that you find particularly mysterious or disturbing? Is one of your dreams part of a series that has repeated itself throughout your life or recently? Does one of the dreams include a detail that seems particularly moving or odd?

If so, your dreams have given you a doorway that you can walk through, if you so choose. Like Rose, you can walk away from the familiar world of your castle, into another world. Ask the Goddess's assistance, and place your notes, or a drawing of your dream, or an object that symbolizes it, in a safe place.

If you are lucky enough to be working with friends in circle, you may wish to spend a night telling dreams. We often set a quiet rhythm as a background for our dreamstories by patting our hands on our knees. When we tell dreams in a group, we speak in the present tense—for example, "I am in a long white hallway . . ." The rhythm, the immediacy of the dream, and its powerful, mysterious images combine to appeal to Younger Self. Sometimes circle sisters may offer gifts and challenges to the dreamer—for example, "I give you a cloak of invisibility, so you can elude the gangsters" or "I challenge you to actually take a walk alone in the woods at night." The dreamer can choose to accept or reject these gifts and challenges.

Questioning Exercise: Using Divination

Many Witches rely on some form of divination to guide and assist them and to give Younger Self a way to speak up. If you are familiar and adept with tarot cards, astrology, runes, or scrying (allowing visions to arise) in crystal, flame, or water, you will know how to do a reading for yourself. If you are new to divination methods, now is a good time to treat yourself to a pack of tarot cards and a good tarot book. I will use the example of the tarot simply because it is the divination tool I use for myself. If you are more comfortable or familiar with some other method of divination, by all means use it.

Create sacred space, and do a reading for yourself. You will find directions in your book. If you are new to the tarot, please spend some time just gazing at the cards and allowing patterns to emerge, before you look each card up in your book. You may want to make some notes of your own impressions and responses before you open your book, because, like the details of a dream, your own gut-level responses to the images in the cards may vanish in the face of the book's expert interpretations.

Now ask yourself which card in the reading is most mysterious or disturbing to you. Which other card in the reading could help you with this mystery or difficulty? Pull these two cards out of the reading, and play with them for a moment. Are you more comfortable with the helpful card covering the mysterious one? Do you like it when the mystery peeks out? Do they belong beside or above one another, or upside down with a potted plant on top of them? Let Younger Self play with the cards, and find what feels right. Then place the cards in a safe place. Like the dream image in the previous exercise, the images in these cards can provide you with a doorway into the Inner Path, away from your old life, and into another world.

Readings and divination of all kinds are especially valuable when done in circle with friends who know you well. Your circle sisters may see clearly a message that is hiding in one of your blind spots about yourself. We often need this kind of outside perspective and reality check.

Questioning Exercise: Physical Sensation, Gesture, or Symptom

We all have habitual gestures, postures, even illnesses that can provide a doorway into our own inner process. Some people pull an ear or twirl their hair; some people throw their hands in the air when pressured, while others make a fist. Some women stand with their shoulders up around their ears; others slump their shoulders forward to hide their breasts. Others bite their nails or get a stomachache if upset. Sometimes, over the years, these gestures, postures, or symptoms have become so habitual that the original emotion and content of the gesture is lost; we no longer know why we do it. But our body remembers. Younger Self remembers and keeps speaking up in nonverbal body language. If you wish, you may choose a particularly mysterious or frequently repeated physical expression as the doorway into the Inner Path. Draw yourself a picture of your gesture, or find an object that symbolizes it for you, and place it in a safe place, like a question for the Goddess. In circle, you may each wish to choose and demonstrate a gesture or posture that is particularly disturbing or mysterious. Chances are, your circle sisters will be able to throw some light on your question.

Questioning: A Regular Practice

Many Witches take time on a regular basis to record dreams, attend to the sensory and postural wisdom of their bodies, and use divination. There are many other intuitive practices that can be used as well. There are body maps, where we draw an outline of ourselves and use art supplies to draw a picture of what we feel in our bodies. There is automatic writing or drawing, where we set a specific time, such as five minutes, and then write or draw continuously, without censoring anything, for the agreed-upon time.

These ongoing self-studies, which awaken intuition, can be recorded in our Book of Shadows. When we talk these intuitive practices over with our circle sisters, we create a reservoir of understanding for ourselves. Our friends can remind us of the dream we had last year and how it relates to a challenge we may face today. Or they can ask, "If you're so excited about your job offer, how come you're twisting your wedding ring, the way you always do when you're upset?" Dreams, images, sensation, and posture are all part of the nonverbal language of Younger Self. When we deepen and rely on intuitive practices to improve the communication between Talking Self and Younger Self, the wisdom of Deep Self can step forward to take a more active role in our lives.

Questioning Creates a Doorway

By now, your questioning has shown you a doorway out of the castle of ordinary consciousness into the world of your own complex inner process. This doorway may be a disturbing image from a card or a dream. It may be a gesture or posture or habit that engages your attention powerfully and that you intuitively know holds some mysterious secrets for your healing process. This disturbing dream, image, or sensation is your personal doorway out of the castle and into the wild, into the work of the Inner Path. Now we will walk away from the rigid, secretive walls of the old castle, as we bind Rose's story together with our own in order to seek personal healing. We are almost ready to seek the courage we need, but first we must look at our own emotional reactions to the disturbing dream or divination or sensation that is propelling us out of our old way of being, out of the "castle."

Walking out the Doorway: Blame

When Rose asks the right question, she finds out that her intuition was correct: all is not right in the castle of her birth. A dreadful injustice, linked with her own life, took place before she was born. This injustice places a terrible burden on Rose. Now, whose fault is that?

When we discover some difficulty or shadow in our inner landscapes, we often long to find a bad guy. The first time I did this kind of magical work in a Reclaiming class, I brought a disturbing dream image to class. In the dream I was flying, and my father was on the ground with a gun that shot flames, trying to shoot me out of the sky. During the course of the six-week class, I actually broke out with quarter-sized painful red spots all over my body—a symptom I had never experienced before and have never experienced since.

Of course I wanted a bad guy to blame, and there was my father, all ready to do the job. It's true that my father was sometimes a violent man. I was a very sensitive (my mother says overly sensitive) little girl. He scared me a lot when I was very little, and I blamed him. But that's as far as I had ever gotten. I was still on the ground covered with burn marks, when what I really wanted was to fly free.

I had to be like Rose. She didn't cause her brothers to be bound in swan form. Her mother was the one who caused this injustice, before Rose was even born. But Rose can't live the life she wants without freeing her brothers. In a way, it doesn't matter whose fault it is. The question is, What is Rose going to do now?

In my case, I had to dare to return to the dream landscape and confront my father there. I had to free myself, so that I could fly. With help from my friends in the class, I was eventually able to drop a net over the flamethrower, so that my father couldn't use it to hurt me anymore.

In our story, Rose has to summon the courage to leave her home and everything she knows to go find her brothers. It's not fair that Rose has to pay the price for her mother's mistake. But it is a universal human condition. We each experience this unfairness, because we each come into this world burdened with the histories of our foremothers and forefathers. We build our lives on their triumphs as well as on their most humiliating errors. We learn our deepest emotional skills and our self-images in the context of families where we have little power as babies and young children.

The puritanical, or racist, or sexist, or violent cultural backgrounds of our families may have affected us deeply. And that's naming only a few of the many troubles that beset our families. It's not fair, but it is very human. And it is not optional. Our mothers and fathers had the same experience in their turn.

Furthermore, it's usually quite complex. The puritanical home may have taught self-respect and hard work. The sexist home may have created unbreakable loyalties and love between sisters. The violent home may have created an adult whose psychic powers are incredibly well trained by childhood vigilance and who can now easily tell what other people are thinking and feeling.

When we dig into our personal process by asking hard questions and being attentive to our intuition, we may discover painful or challenging truths about ourselves and our histories, and we may blame others. In some cases, our troubles may truly be someone else's fault, as Rose's were. But if we want to be like Rose, we have to go beyond blaming. We have to walk away from that old castle into the promise of the wild. We cannot afford to tie ourselves to old injustice, which will only keep us stuck inside the lonely, rigid walls of our castles.

Walking out the Doorway: Shame

We cannot get out of the difficult journey by blaming the old queen, but how about blaming ourselves? This has been one of the great pitfalls in my own magical healing process. The image from my dream that showed my father shooting me from the sky also included me defeated and falling helplessly.

It's tempting to define ourselves by our past experience with its inevitable challenges and injustices. Few of us in this culture, with its burden of racism, sexism, and classism, have been treated entirely fairly or valued as highly as we hoped. In fact, some of us have been treated very badly and seriously harmed emotionally and/or physically.

Sometimes we can feel so victimized, so fearful of conflict, so abused, that we cannot possibly do anything to help ourselves. It's important to honestly admit how crippling injustices can be. But it's equally important to refuse to accept being defined, either by ourselves or others, as helpless.

Rose could have responded by feeling helpless and stayed in the castle nursing her wounds: "I've been lied to all my life. My own mother and father never even told me about my brothers. Now I'm a miserable, lonely person." Instead, she sets a definite intention: "I'm going to find my brothers and break the spell that binds them." She walks through her own reactions to her family history to do what she has to do. She walks out the door of the castle, into the wild.

Finding Courage to Walk out the Doorway

How does she find the courage to walk out the door? Rose didn't have to do it all by herself. When the time was right, she questioned her old nurse and got the information she needed. She emerged from that conversation ready to act.

We also have questions—or rather, our Younger Self has questions—in the form of disturbing images and sensations that we discovered in the exercises earlier in this chapter. We have taken a moment to ask ourselves whether we are stuck in blame or shame as a reaction to these discoveries. Now we are ready to take our questions to the old nurse. She will be able to guide us.

Meditation: Asking the Old Nurse

Arrange for some undisturbed time, and either alone or with friends, create sacred space. Prepare yourself to take a trance journey to the old nurse to ask questions and get guidance. Use whatever trance induction works best for you, or use the "Rainbow Induction" trance from the Elements Path in chapter 4.

Find your way to the Castle of Family Secrets. Walk down its halls; peek into its doorways. Lean your head against the walls and listen. The walls are whispering secrets. What can you hear? Take your time. There are doors leading into the many different rooms of the Castle of Family Secrets. Do you want to explore any of them?

Find a doorway with a staircase leading downward. Know that this stairway leads to the chamber of the old nurse. Go deeper, on a deep breath, down each of seven steps.

> She was always there to care for you when you were little.
> She was always there to care for you when you were ill.
> She knows all the secrets of your family history.
> She will only tell you things that you are ready to handle.
> She is wise and kind.
> She is very, very old.
> She herself honors the old gods and the Goddess.

Now you are at her chamber door. Open it and enter. Take a moment to open all your senses to the old nurse and this room, knowing that she is different for each of us. Show her, and tell her, the mysterious image or sensation that you discovered in the previous exercises. She has guidance for you. (Allow some quiet time while each trancer interacts with the old nurse.)

She has known you all your life; she knows that you have a spark, that you have what it takes to pursue this mystery. Find the spark of will and courage inside, and feed the flame. When you feel your will and courage burning brightly, thank her and say good-bye, knowing that she is always here for you, and you can return at will. Return up the seven steps and out of the Castle of Family Secrets. Reverse the induction, and allow yourself to return to normal consciousness. Take your time, making sure you and your friends are all the way back. Share some food, and take time to discuss your experience and write about it in your Book of Shadows. Only when you are completely ready, open the circle.

Exercise: Walking Away from the Old Castle

Now you have discovered a mysterious question about your own inner life. With the help of the old nurse, you have found the courage to pursue it. It's time to make a break with the past and begin a new cycle in your own life story. Since a Witch's altar reflects her own inner landscape, it's time to do a bit of altar magic.

Set aside some undisturbed time for yourself, and create sacred space at your altar. If you are working in circle, your circle may already be keeping an altar together. If not, now is an opportunity to build an altar together as you work through the story of the Twelve Wild Swans.

If your altar is at all like mine, it is likely to be full of bits of old magic: the candle holder with traces of wax from a candle I burned for a friend's healing, a moving bit of poetry I copied, a dry, faded flower from a meditative walk, a once-beautiful piece of fruit I offered to the Goddess.

Take the time to clean your altar thoroughly. Wash the altar cloths, clean the candleholders with hot water and salt, dispose properly of old spells, wash your magical tools, and create some fresh space for yourself. Dress some new candles, of a color that pleases you, to burn for your new project of self-healing. Place your notes, drawings, and objects from the exercises in this chapter on your fresh, clean altar, light your candles, and sit quietly. Breathe in the circle of your own living warmth, your courage. Breathe in your commitment to yourself—and to your circle sisters, if you are working in a group. Breathe in your openness to your own mysteries. When you are ready, open the circle.

Searching for What Was Lost

Now Rose knows her task: she must find her brothers and break the spell. They have flown into the wild, and she must pull them back into human form. She has gained the courage to take the first step, which is always the hardest one. She walks away from her old life.

Just like Rose, we have also found our task. Using Rose's story to guide us, we will search for what we have lost. Something of ourselves has flown into the wild, through no fault of our own. We must search for it and pull it back into our human lives. It is hiding behind our own veils, but it still calls out to us in the disturbing dream or divination image, or the mysterious gesture or sensation we have chosen to investigate. And as we search for what we have lost, we will learn some magical practices that will serve us well if we choose to lead a Witch's life and seek to know and love ourselves. We choose to commit ourselves to our own healing, to our own wholeness, because a healthy priestess makes all things whole and because this is part of the Goddess's charge to us: "If that which you seek, you find not in yourself, you will never find it without. For behold! I have been with you from the beginning, and I am that which is attained at the end of desire." (Charge of the Goddess, *Spiral Dance*, p. 90)

The Outer Path

In our fairy tale, Rose sets off on a quest to redeem her brothers. Something is very wrong in her world, and she decides to change it. In doing so, she becomes a priestess, one who takes on responsibility not just for her own spiritual well-being, but for the well-being of others.

The Outer Path takes Rose's story as a framework for offering the tools and skills we need to foster community, to create public ritual, and to teach ritual skills. The lessons we learn in our magical growth infuse our activism, so that when we write a letter to an elected official, or serve food to the homeless, or facilitate a meeting, or plant the garden, or sit down and link arms at a blockade, we are consciously and intentionally doing magic, with all our allies in all the worlds acting with us.

While the Inner Path is about self-transformation, the Outer Path is about world transformation. In the Reclaiming Principles of Unity, we say that "everyone can do the life-changing, world-renewing work of magic." As we become empowered to change our own lives, we become conduits of the great healing powers that will be needed to restore the living diversity of the earth. Our awakened creativity can renew the vitality of our communities; our sheer hard work can make our visions real.

Our story offers a deep challenge for those of us following the Outer Path. How do we take on appropriate responsibility for healing ills we did not create? How do we come to terms with the mixed inheritance from our families and our ancestors? In the Inner Path, we worked with these questions from a personal and individual perspective. Now we must look at them from the perspective of a community leader, of an activist.

The Dalai Lama, in his 1999 address to the World Conference of Religions, said, "It's not enough to pray and meditate; you must act if you want to see results." Rose doesn't just pray about the fate of her brothers; she sets out to free them. Like Rose, we are called to offer real service to others, to the Goddess. That service may take many forms: mopping the floor after the party, priestessing rituals, healing, planning, teaching, carrying the heavy cauldron from the car, sitting with a dying friend, writing up the minutes for a neighborhood meeting, organizing a protest to protect a sacred place from development, writing letters to Congress, training others in nonviolent civil disobedience, growing food, or changing the baby's diapers. All of these can be life-changing, world-renewing acts of magic.

Years ago, I spoke on a panel with a Native American woman named Inez Talamantes. She said something I've never forgotten: "In our tradition, if you have a vision of a Goddess, if you dream of her, it means you have to work for her for the rest of your life." A dream, a vision, an insight, has power because we take it into action and do the work that is needed to serve the cycles of growth, decay, and renewal. Aligned with those cycles, our own lives become filled with rich experiences and deep meaning. It was said of the Goddess Isis in ancient times: "Her service is perfect freedom." *Freedom* may not be the word that leaps to mind when you're pushing the broom at 1 A.M. after the ritual or trying to stay calm at the demonstration while the riot cops prepare to drag you away. The Goddess's service is not free from discomfort, inconvenience, even sacrifice. But we are sustained by a deeper sense of freedom: the joy of acting in accordance with our deepest ideals.

The service we offer to others emerges out of our own growth and empowerment. In the Elements Path, we are introduced to the world of magic. We learn to tap the rich creative sources we each carry within. As we move deeper into the practice of magic, the world we inhabit becomes infused by great life-sustaining powers. We become creatures of air and fire, water and earth, attuned to the wild, alive to our own erotic connection to all of life. Our ears begin to open to the great conversation around us, through which all of life communicates with itself.

As we work the Inner Path, the healing path, we begin to close the wounds that have kept us less than fully alive. Our sense of personal power and efficacy grows stronger. We no longer believe that we deserve pain or humiliation. And as our sense of interconnectedness deepens, we no longer believe that anyone deserves pain or humiliation.

The practice of magic may make us less comfortable. When we come alive to the mythic dimensions of our lives, we may find it intolerable to go to work every day at a job where our boss regularly humiliates us. When we know, with the deepest fiber of our being, that all of us are interconnected, we cannot pass by the homeless beggar undisturbed. When our blood is alive and singing with the sound of the wind in the forests, we can't be complacent about the clear-cutting of the trees. And when we've tasted the communion of the circle, the ecstasy of raising power together as a group and feeling love and support and appreciation surrounding us, we cannot settle for isolation and alienation as our daily fare.

Why, you might ask, would we want to do this to ourselves? Why make ourselves uncomfortable, dissatisfied with what is? Magic is our birthright: to know nature unsubjugated, to live fully from our depths, to be enfolded in the embrace of a nurturing community. We can't just settle for what is; like Rose, we claim our right to determine what will be.

Changing the world is a big job—too big for any of us to tackle alone. The big issues of injustice, inequality, and the destruction of life around us are collectively created, and it is only collectively that they can effectively be addressed. To become world shapers, earth healers, we need the support of a community. The tools, exercises, and rituals of the Outer Path focus on creating, developing, and nurturing magical community.

A guiding value of Witchcraft is that each of us carries the responsibility for guiding and shaping our communities. Traditionally, every Witch is a priestess or priest, an empowered leader, an active cocreator of our spiritual lives. In the Outer Path, we take on the responsibility of becoming leaders, priestesses, and healers in our communities.

We call this the Outer Path because this work requires putting your attention and focus outside yourself for a time, as we must when leading rituals, teaching, facilitating meetings, or taking on any of the roles that indicate leadership in a community. You don't have to be a Great High Priestess to do Outer Path work; you simply need the desire to make it happen, a sense of integrity and honesty, and a good dosage of basic human kindness and compassion.

In hierarchical groups, leadership roles are often the occasion for someone to be the boss or the star. The group may focus on the personality, desires, and vision of the leader. In contrast, our vision of leadership is service.

Being a priestess of the Goddess, we often say, is a lot like being a waitress of the Goddess. When you work as a waitress, you serve up the meal for the diners, setting the stage with china and cutlery, bringing on each course in turn, paying attention to whether or not they're enjoying the fare and to when they've finished the appetizer and are ready for the entree. At the end, you take away each dish you set out. As a priestess, you also set the stage for the ritual with altars and tools, "serve up" each phase of the ceremony, paying attention to the timing of each part, the attention level of the participants, and their readiness for the next movement. To end the ritual, you must clear away the energies you've brought in, and many a priestess has finished a night of ritual by packing away the altar tools and sweeping the floor with her Witch's broom.

A good waitress can make a meal smooth and enjoyable—but the experience of the meal is not about the waitress. The focus of ritual is on the spiritual food: the work, the magic, the Goddess—not the server. Of course, the server needs to get fed, and in Reclaiming rituals when we are priestessing we may also help choose the menus, cook a dish or two, present the courses, and sit down and eat along with everybody else. But still the focus remains on the work, not the priestess.

We need to have done some of our own healing before we take on the work of serving others. If we're so wounded we're bleeding all over the tablecloth, the meal may be not only unpleasant but even dangerous to the diners. The work of personal healing may be a lifelong task. We don't need to be completely done with it; if we did, none of us would be teaching. As Hilary says in the introduction to the Inner Path, part of our gift to our students is our willingness, as teachers, to go through a healing process together. But we do need to be far enough along so that we can comfortably set our focus outside ourselves and our own needs. If our healing becomes the major issue in a class, or if we are teaching to satisfy our own needs for approval, admiration, or support, something is wrong. Yes, praise and support feel good, and we need to be able to take them in, but we also need to have other ongoing sources of esteem in our lives beyond our students.

As our personal power grows and we direct our efforts at the world around us, we become agents of change. The good we do is amplified, but the mistakes we make will reverberate far beyond us.

In fact, our story begins with the consequences of a magical mistake: the ill wish of the queen. The world we live in today is also full of the results of ill wishes, unbalanced desires, and thoughtless programs. To heal that world, we must be capable of seeing far-reaching consequences, of setting aside our whims of the moment and looking at the needs of the whole. Yet none of us are all-seeing wise elders or selfless saints. We each have our full human share of blind spots, illusions, arrogance, and self-interest. How do we presume to become teachers and leaders of others?

We can walk with integrity upon the Outer Path only if we are willing to deepen our inner work. Before we can delve into the material our story presents, we need something that can serve as an anchor to our true worth. We must deepen the daily practices we have already developed and strengthen our sources of energy and nourishment. But we also need some specific tools to keep us sane and grounded as we take our magic out into the world.

The following practice is the one with which I begin any program of advanced magical training. I use it myself on a daily and sometimes hourly basis, and it is a key exercise that we will refer back to many times in this book.

Anchoring to Core Worth

When we begin our magical training, we are often exhilarated to discover that the range of human consciousness is far broader than our culture has led us to believe. As our skills advance, we must first learn to recognize the psychic/emotional states we tend to fall into, and then learn how to make choices about them.

Anchoring is one of the key "magic tricks" we use for moving in and out of particular states at will. We first use a meditation or physical exercise to evoke a particular state of consciousness, and then create a visual image, a word or phrase we can say, and a gesture or place on our body we can touch to associate with that state. Anchoring is a concept used in hypnosis, but it is a far older technique. In fact, it is key to the effectiveness of much ritual, particularly of those parts of ritual that are repeated. If we always use the same words to end a ritual, they become an anchor to the shift in consciousness we make when we leave sacred space and return to ordinary space and time. If we use the same grounding meditation again and again, in time just a breath and a memory of the image will ground us.

Bringing in three different sensory modes means we are speaking three different dialects that Younger Self understands. Some of us respond more powerfully to visual images; others are more kinesthetic or more auditory in the way we take in the world. When we lead an anchoring exercise for a group, we incorporate all three modes so that everyone, regardless of their sensory orientation, will find the exercise effective. Often an anchor works most powerfully through a sense that is not our primary mode of experiencing the world. A highly verbal person may find that touch shifts consciousness better than words; a visual person may find that a magic word or rhyme works best.

The other key concept in this practice is the idea of our core worth. In the Goddess tradition, each one of us is valued simply for being who we are. Core value is not something we have to acquire, achieve, or prove. It cannot be ranked, and no one has more of it than anyone else. We may make mistakes or commit wrong acts, but we still are creatures of worth, part of a larger whole. This recognition of the inherent value of every being is the foundation of our nonhierarchical tradition. We try to teach, work, and plan in ways that honor the core worth of every person involved.

When we are in touch with our core worth, we are firmly grounded in our own inherent value as human beings who are part of the living Goddess. We are in "neutral"—relaxed, at ease, comfortably ourselves, not trying to impress anybody or project any image of who we are.

In our larger society, we often expect leaders, teachers, or celebrities to come from a place of self-inflation, to project a strong image that may or may not reflect a core reality. Our politicians spend millions of dollars on image creation: our entire advertising industry is based on "selling the sizzle, not the steak."

Think of inflation as "false glory," the consolation prize we are offered in systems of domination when our true worth has been taken from us. The flip side of inflation is deflation and self-hate.

The more we grow in personal power, the more strongly our state of being impacts those around us. Just as the queen's ill wish affected her universe, our own energetic state sets a tone that creates a resonance in each person we encounter. If we are inflated, other people respond unconsciously by puffing up, contracting down, or simply resisting our control. If we are deflated, others may shield themselves to protect their energies from being drained, or respond with boredom or with irritation. And so, in teaching, leading, and priestessing, we try to avoid inflation or deflation and remain connected to our core worth.

Whenever we step out on the Outer Path, whether as a writer of books or a teacher of small classes in our living rooms, we open ourselves to the force of others' projections. A strong anchor and a deep sense of our core worth can help us stay grounded and centered regardless of how others perceive us.

In this exercise, we will create an anchor to our core worth and then explore our own images of inflation and deflation, using our anchor to bring us back.

In sacred space, sit, stand, or lie in a relaxed position. Breathe deeply, and let yourself think of the times and places in which you feel most relaxed, most yourself, when you are in touch with your inner power but don't need to use it, when you can truly let your hair down and just be who you are. Pick one situation, one place, and slowly let it fill your awareness. How does the air feel on your skin here? What do you smell and taste? What do you hear? What do you see around you? How do you feel in your body? How are you holding your body, and where is your breath coming from? Make this situation, this state of being, as real as you can.

Is there a place in your body you can identify as holding this state—or a posture you can take, or a gesture you can make? Touch that place and breathe into it.

Pick one image, one thing you can visualize from this place. Hold it in your mind's eye as you touch that special place on your body.

Find a word or phrase you can say that reminds you of this state. Say the word, touch the place on your body, and hold your image in your mind.

When you do these three things together, you have created your anchor. You can use your anchor anytime to bring you into this core state of being. Breathe into your anchor; tell yourself that the more you use it, the stronger it will become.

Now let go of your anchor and come back, or go on to the following:

Inflated/Deflated Self

In sacred space, use your anchor to your core worth. Take a moment to notice how your body feels, how you're breathing. Open your eyes and notice how you perceive the people or scene around you.

Now drop your anchor. Shake out your hands, close your eyes, and let yourself begin to spin the most inflated, puffed-up vision you can invent about yourself as a leader, teacher, healer. Really let your ego run wild here, and don't censor yourself.

What are you wearing in this fantasy? How does your body look? How do you feel inside it?

What situation are you in? What are you doing or saying? Who is around you, and how are they responding to you?

What thoughts go through your head? What is your inner dialogue?

What energies do you sense around you? Directed at you? Coming from you?

What emotions are you feeling?

What are the benefits you receive from this state of being?

Is there a price you pay for being in this state?

In this state, what choices do you perceive that you have?

Are there people or situations in your daily life that pull you into or toward this state of being?

Open your eyes for a moment. Look around you. How do you perceive others from this state?

Now close your eyes, shake out your hands, and drop this state. Use your anchor, breathe deeply, and bring yourself back to your core worth.

What has changed? What do you notice that is different?

When you've firmly reestablished your core worth, close your eyes and let your anchor drop. Shake out your hands, breathe deeply, and now let yourself move into your most deflated state. You know—that state you're in when you look in the mirror and gasp, when you can't do anything right. We've all been there; just take a moment and find it. Breathe into it and let it fill you.

What are you wearing in this deflated state? How does your body look? How do you feel inside it?

What situation are you in? What are you doing or saying? Who is around you, and how are they responding to you?

What thoughts go through your head? What is your inner dialogue?

What energies do you sense around you? Directed at you? Coming from you?

What emotions are you feeling?

What are the benefits you receive from this state of being?

Is there a price you pay for being in this state?

In this state, what choices do you perceive that you have?

Are there people or situations in your daily life that pull you into or toward this state of being?

Open your eyes for a moment. Look around you. How do you perceive others from this state?

Now close your eyes, shake out your hands, and drop this state. Use your anchor, breathe deeply, and bring yourself back into your core state of being.

What has changed? What do you notice that is different?

Now relax, and come back into your ordinary consciousness. Take some time to talk over this exercise with your partner and then with the group. If you are alone, get out your journal and write out what you remember and what insights you may have received.

When we first did this exercise in the Vancouver Witchcamp many years ago, I had a truly life-changing experience. My inflated self was a fiery, spiritual/political revolutionary: slim, gorgeous, dressed in torn jeans, and making a speech to a large crowd that was inspiring them to action. All eyes were on me: I was the center of attention and yet essentially alone, all my personal needs subsumed to my total dedication to the cause.

To my surprise, I found that my deflated self was very similar. I was physically puffier, more sluggish, and not nearly so gorgeous, still dressed in ragged clothes and this time making a speech that no one was listening to. I was still utterly alone, isolated and lonely, marked by a tragic sense of grief.

But anchored to my core sense of worth, I was a friendly, gregarious, social person who had lots of friends. Not a noble or tragic figure, just an ordinary human being who was actually more interested in the people around her than concerned about how they saw her. My anchoring phrase was *I can love and be loved.*

The exercise shook my self-perception. My life had been colored by the sorrow of my father's death when I was five years old and by my mother's ongoing grief and depression. In fact, I had always secretly felt that underlying grief was my true core.

The exercise revealed to me that the opposite was true. Grief was something that had happened to me—but it was not me. My mother's life had been lonely—but mine, in reality, wasn't. At my deepest level, I had strong needs for real, vitalizing connections with others, and great abilities for making those connections. Not only that: I tended to be happy, cheerful, and optimistic. What a blow to the ego!

It was, however, a lifesaving blow, part of the work that allows me to keep some semblance of sanity while leading a life as a public Witch. Many people find that their inflated and deflated selves are mirror images of each other. And they both are often characterized by disconnection and isolation, while the core worth state allows us to bond with others.

The key to inflation/deflation is the inner state, not the outer circumstances. Some people find that their inflated fantasy is an indication of some valid, real-life dream or goal. In the years since we first invented this exercise, I have lived out both my inflated and my deflated fantasies: that is, I've given fiery speeches that moved people, and other talks that fell flat. I'm not always aware of when I'm being pulled into inflation or deflation, but I use my anchor constantly, and I work on it.

The more you use your anchor, the easier it becomes to move into your state of core worth. A strong, well-developed anchor is also a necessary safety line when practicing other advanced techniques we will explore on this path.

As Pagans practicing an earth-based spirituality in North America, we inherit a deeply painful contradiction. The very core of our spiritual life is our bond with the land, yet the land we live on was stolen from its original people. Their bonds were too often forcibly ruptured; their sacred places continue to be desecrated. Most of us come from ancestors that originated elsewhere. Yet this is where we were born; this is the land we know and love. How do we even begin healing this wound?

Like Rose, we must begin by facing the reality of our situation, unearthing the hidden histories. But Rose does not wallow in guilt, nor does she remain fixed on the past. She sets out on a quest. We must do the same. We can resolve the pain of the past only by looking toward the future, asking, "What work do we need to do to make our communities ones that can foster diversity and resilience? How can we learn to know and begin to heal the land we live on? How do we become indigenous again?"

In the Goddess tradition, the community we serve is not limited to those who are alive today. We serve the unborn, those generations who will come after us, and we are constantly called to think of their interests, to create and preserve a world that can offer them a vibrant and healthy life. Our community also includes our beloved dead, our ancestors, those who have gone before us, who may be a source of both wisdom and challenges. The world we come into is full of the consequences of ill wishes, greed, and shortsighted decisions. We inherit the resulting injustices and imbalances. Yet we also inherit a world of skills, knowledge, and material goods that are also gifts of the ancestors.

In the Craft, the traditional time for working with the beloved dead is around Samhain or Halloween—when, we say, "the veil is thin that divides the worlds." In many other indigenous traditions, however, the ancestors are honored on a daily basis.

"In West African tradition, we address the ancestors every day, as well as at specific times of the year," says Luisah Teish, author of *Jambalaya* and *Carnival of the Spirit*. Because she comes out of an unbroken tradition that has preserved knowledge long lost to the Craft, her insights and perspectives have been a strong influence on the development of the Reclaiming tradition.

Teish is a big woman in every way—tall, charismatic, bighearted, with a loud, deep voice and a striking presence. When she enters a room, every eye turns toward her. A trained dancer, she moves with sensual grace and contained power. She wears bright clothes and head wraps that reflect her African heritage and the Yoruba religious traditions in which she is an initiated priestess of Oshun, the *orisha* or spirit power that rules love and sexuality.

Teish describes how, in West Africa, the largest yam is saved back after the harvest to become the ancestral yam. Honor is paid and ceremonies are performed, and then it is broken into pieces to provide the seed for the next year's crop. "We are like the pieces of that ancestral yam," she says. "We each contain all the knowledge that was coded into the original, and we can draw on that knowledge when we need it."

For many of us, calling on our ancestors is not easy. Our ancestors are inevitably entwined with our families, and for many of us our families have been a source of wounding as well as strength. And most of us have come to the Goddess tradition from some other religious background. Our immediate ancestors may have been Catholics, Jews, Protestants, Muslims, Hindus, Buddhists, or staunch secular humanists, but few of them were Witches. They may have been people whose values we have rejected. How then, can we call on them as allies and helpers?

The work of coming to terms with our heritage can begin, very simply, by naming our ancestors.

Naming Our Ancestors

Many years ago, at a feminist conference in Barcelona, I was invited to be part of a panel entitled "Reclaiming Our Ancestors." We were an eclectic group: besides me, there was a Frenchwoman discussing forgotten women authors, a Spanish woman historian, an Australian aboriginal woman, and a Maori. The Maori woman began, with a smile, by saying that the title of the panel didn't apply to her. She had no need to reclaim her ancestors; she had never lost them, and indeed could recite their names for twenty-five generations back. The aboriginal woman chimed in to agree. She, too, knew the names of her ancestors back to the dawn of time.

Few of us can say the same. The simple challenge of naming our ancestors may make us aware of just how limited our knowledge is. As a nation of immigrants, we tend to cut off the past.

If you are adopted, you may wish to name both the lineage of your adoptive family and that of your biological family, if you know it.

If you are working alone, you can write these names out in your Book of Shadows. If you are working in a group, ground, create sacred space, and go in a circle clockwise, naming yourself and your lineage as far back as you know names—first your mother's side, and then your father's. You might also use this exercise as a way to cast a circle.

"I am Starhawk, daughter of Bertha, daughter of Hannah Rivkeh, daughter of Fanny. And I am Starhawk, daughter of Jack, daughter of Mordechai and Fanny."

Name your biological ancestry: "I am Starhawk, daughter of Ukrainian Jews."

As simple as this sounds, in a group it can become profoundly uncomfortable and therefore illuminating. In one recent ritual, it must have taken at least forty-five minutes for a group of forty people to simply name themselves in this way. As we went around the circle, people hemmed, hawed, and resisted. Our instructions had been clear—to name one's biological ancestors—but many people instead named those whom they considered their spiritual ancestors, as if sticking with their biological heritage was simply too uncomfortable. While our circle appeared to be almost all "white," naming our ancestors brought out the hidden heritages in our group. A third or more of the people there, for example, claimed some Native American ancestry. This exercise is probably most valuable when time is set aside for discussing the emotions it evokes.

Name those you claim as your spiritual ancestors.

"I am Starhawk, daughter of Enheduanna and the priestess/poets of ancient Sumer, daughter of the Witches, daughter of Emma Goldman, daughter of the redwoods."

In Teish's tradition, every ritual includes the naming and honoring of the ancestors. She has created a simple chant: "Mojuba O" (moh-yoo-BAH-oh), "love and respect to you."

"When we address the ancestors, *Mojuba* is the first word that is spoken. In Africa, the chanting and naming can go on for hours, or even days," Teish says.

In Yoruba ritual, each villager would have an ancestor stick, tied with strips of cloth from the garb of those who had died. The stick is pounded on the earth in rhythm to the chant. When Teish and I work together, she often has people imagine the stick, and we stomp our feet as we do a simple dance around the room. The chant and the pounding of our feet create a base rhythm, above which we call the names of our ancestors, and then Teish begins calling the unknown ancestors by the ways they have died:

"Those who died on the slave ships, those who died in the concentration camps, those who died in the Witch burnings, those who died in war . . ."

She also calls the ancestors in by the qualities of their lives:

"Those who were fighters for justice, those who were dancers, those who were poets, those who were midwives . . ."

We can name the ancestors we don't know by naming their gifts and legacies as well as their sufferings. In so doing, we acknowledge those "pieces of the yam" that still exist within us.

"I call those who spoke up for the rights of women."

"I call those who struggled to feed their families."

"I call those who made people laugh."

Besides naming your ancestors, you may want to create an altar, a special place where you can work with them and honor them regularly.

Ancestor Altar

Create an altar for your ancestors, where you can place their pictures and set out offerings of food, drink, or flowers. Include some of their favorite objects or symbols of your relationship to them. Traditionally, we do this seasonally, around Samhain or Halloween. But if you are doing serious ancestor work, you might want to create a permanent altar—or even a picture wall with a small shelf for a vase and candle.

When we take on roles of leadership in our community, we also take on the responsibility of shaping our vision of what that community can be. If we truly open ourselves to learning from the elements, we will realize that, in nature, an ecological system that is highly diverse is more resilient than one that is not. A prairie, with hundreds of different plants in every square yard, can resist disease, pests, or climate change far better than a monoculture field of hybrid corn. In human communities, too, diversity can be our strength. Reclaiming has a strong commitment to openness and inclusiveness, and we recognize the gifts that people of varied backgrounds, heritages, and perspectives can bring.

But too often in our larger culture, our differences divide us. The work we do to foster diversity can be exhilarating, but it can also be awkward and even deeply painful. To embrace diversity, we must first come to terms with our own identity, with the heritage we carry of gifts and burdens. And that heritage always includes pain. For some of us, it may be the pain of our people's history of oppression, of enslavement or poverty or massacre. Just as Rose cannot enjoy the castle when she learns the price her brothers paid for her birth, others among us carry the pain of descent from the oppressors and the guilty knowledge that we inherit privileges and wealth gained through others' suffering.

If we could know the full truth of our ancestry, all of us carry both gifts and pain. No heritage is free of oppressors; and no heritage is devoid of those who resisted oppression, who stood up for freedom, tolerance, and compassion as best they could.

Reclaiming communities are full of many sorts of diversity: age, gender, class background, religious and geographic background, sexual orientation. But often we are not nearly as diverse in terms of ancestry and race as we would like to be. Over the years, we have explored many approaches to the challenges that arise when we attempt to broaden our diversity. One of the most powerful bridges we have found is to simply tell our stories.

Telling Ancestor Stories

For many years in the early 1990s, Reclaiming sponsored a Multicultural Ritual Group that planned an annual ritual honoring the ancestors of many cultures. The group was a rich and fruitful gathering of amazing people, and the issues that came up in the course of our ritual planning sparked intense discussions, sometimes exhilarating, sometimes painful. One of the most important things we did was to take time in the group to tell our own stories and the stories of our families and ancestors.

Each of us is a rich and complex being. Our gender, our ancestry, all the ways in which we can be described and labeled make up aspects of who we are—but they do not fully describe us. I am a woman, a Jew, a Witch, a bisexual married woman with a hearing loss—but neither the terms themselves nor any list of them really conveys who I am. If I'm seen in a community as The Jew or The Witch, I feel diminished, unseen in my fullness.

Hearing each other's stories allows us to more truly know each other in our full complexity. Remaining grounded in our roots, we can each express something of our multiple dimensions. We can identify and honor our differences and also see the common threads that weave through our tales.

A group might want to set aside several sessions for this process, so that each person can have half an hour or more to tell their story without being interrupted. The storytellers of the night can bring pictures of their ancestors, important symbols or objects, and appropriate food to share. Create sacred space. Set up an altar or altars with the offerings brought by the storytellers. Let the first person begin, speaking without being interrupted or questioned until she or he is done. When each storyteller is finished, seat her in the center of the circle, chant her name to affirm her story, or sing an ancestor chant.

In sacred space, tell the story of one of your ancestors or family members in the first person. "I am Hannah Rivkeh. I live in a small shtetl outside Kiev, and I'm five years old. My father has just died . . ." This exercise can bring us to a deep place of understanding and empathy for our ancestors, but be aware that it can bring up very powerful emotions. We may become overwhelmed by the pain and grief of the past. Be sure to have some help and support available. Use your anchor to your core worth to bring you back, and consciously release the spirit of your ancestor. Make a libation or put food or flowers on your ancestor altar.

If you are working alone, you can write out your ancestor story in your Book of Shadows. Be sure you have someone you can go to for support, however, for the insights and emotions that may surface.

Heritage Ritual

This can be a powerful ritual for a small group, or it could be done as part of a larger ritual.

In sacred space, four special altars are set up in the four directions. In the east is a small bowl of essential oil, provided no one in the group is allergic. (If someone is, substitute a bowl of strong-smelling herbs such as bay leaves that can be crushed and sniffed. But be careful with bay leaves: sniff lightly, or your sinuses will burn for a long time afterward.)

In the south, place a lit candle.

In the west, place a bowl of water and a bowl of salt.

In the north, place a bowl of fruit.

In a small group (ten or less), each participant in turn can make the circle of the altars after a time of meditation.

In the east, I anoint myself with the essential oil (or sniff the herbs) and name what I'm proud of in my heritage: "I take pride in the Jewish tradition of struggle for social justice."

In the south, I pluck a hair from my head and burn it in the candle flame. As it shrivels, I name what I want to release from my heritage: "I release my anger and frustration, and my mother's anger, about the preference given to men in our heritage."

In the west, I take a pinch of salt and drop it into the water and name what I grieve for in my heritage: "I grieve for all the victims of the Holocaust."

In the north, I take a piece of fruit and name what nurtures and sustains me: "I am fed by the warmth, the music, the lively arguments and intellectual stimulation of my heritage."

In a larger group ritual, priestesses can stand at the elemental altars and ask participants individually, "What is your pride in your heritage?"; "What do you need to release from your heritage?"; and so forth. Participants can be given time to wander among the altars at random or to meditate on a central fire or cauldron. The stations can also be set up in sequence as an entrance transition into sacred space. At one multicultural ritual, where people came and went throughout a long day of storytelling, we used altars much like these, positioned within a maze of curtains, to help people enter and leave our sacred space.

_____

Racism is one of the worst "ill wishes" that plague our society. It goes hand in hand with the other "'ism' brothers," as Teish calls them: sexism, heterosexism, classism, ageism, and all other forms of discrimination. In our story, Rose was not the cause of her brothers' transformation, yet she benefited from it, and through no desire of her own. So many of us benefit from the privileges conferred by the "ism" brothers even when the deepest desire of our hearts is to eradicate all of them. And the "ism" brothers live inside us: none of us has been raised free of prejudice. As Rose must first learn of her brothers' existence before she can set out to free them, so we must be able to see those "isms" within if we are to free ourselves and make our communities truly open and inclusive.

Center Invocation and Exercise

The center of the circle can be a powerful place for confronting issues of centrality and exclusion. Flame is a transgendered Reclaiming teacher who knows only too well what it feels like to be the outsider. Her heritage is Latina, and she is a living challenge to our concept of a world divided into clearly defined realms of "male" and "female." Flame is both, neither, and something else entirely: uniquely herself. Her own struggles with recovery from addiction and with disease have given her a deep sense of compassion and a strong commitment to justice. She wrote the following invocation: "Our society and dominant culture tells us that to be in the center is to be white, heterosexual. We know this is an illusion and call forth the vision of our future into the center, the future that recognizes diversity as the true, unifying centering force. We call Huey Newton, Oshun, La Diosa Del Mar, Drag Sky Father . . . [elements of diversity that mostly go unnamed in the dominant culture—names of Gods and Goddesses of indigenous cultures of color, queer powers, names of slain civil rights activists, and so forth]."

Flame suggests: "Look around at your next ritual and see who is present, and also see who is _not_ present. This invocation can begin to raise this awareness."

Working with our ancestors and with issues of diversity was one of the central themes of our Texas Witchcamp when Flame and I both taught there in 1999.

One of the other teachers was Brook, who has been a friend and fellow activist since we met at the Diablo Canyon blockade in 1981. A devoted father, skilled group facilitator, and software designer, he bridges many worlds. After talking with Flame about her center invocation, we created the following exercise for the path on power that we were co-teaching:

In sacred space, ground and center. Imagine for a moment that you are the center of the universe. (Don't we all often secretly think so!) Now imagine that the center of power and status in your culture is peopled with those of your gender, who look like you, come from similar backgrounds, think and talk like you. How do you feel? Mentally run through a typical day—your home, your work, your relationships. Imagine people like yourself depicted on billboards, in magazines, and on TV as models of attractiveness and success. Imagine them writing the most prestigious books, staffing the universities, peopling Congress, the Supreme Court, the White House, the highest ranks of government and power. What changes? In what way are those like you truly at center? In what ways are they not?

Now for a moment imagine someone you think is exactly opposite to you. Don't think too much; just go with whoever comes to mind. In what ways is this person different? Gender? Race? Class? Values? Now imagine a society in which this person and others like her or him are at center. Envision them depicted on billboards, in magazines, and on TV as models of attractiveness and success. Imagine them writing the most prestigious books, staffing the universities, peopling Congress, the Supreme Court, the White House, the highest ranks of government and power. What would change? Imagine looking at the world through this person's eyes. How do you see yourself? Others like you?

Now let go of your opposite. Reflect for a moment on the qualities you chose as opposite to yourself. Most likely there were different choices you could have made in some areas. For example, you might have chosen someone much poorer—but you could also have chosen someone much richer. Quickly think of another opposite, with different qualities, and run through the questions above again.

Now come back, and let go of your opposites. Imagine the center as growing bigger and bigger, with room for you and your opposites and a wide range of diversity. How do you feel in that center? What do you give up, and what do you gain?

In discussion or journaling afterward, reflect again on the choices you made. Do they represent certain stereotypes about groups of people? We all have them, and acknowledging them consciously can make it easier to go beyond them. And what do your choices reveal about how you see yourself?

In the group Brook and I led, a high proportion of people saw their opposite as "a corporate executive." This struck us as odd, since most of the group were in many ways much closer to the demographics of corporate executives than to 90 percent of the people in the world. I also felt compelled to point out that long-haired, bearded, groovy Brook was himself, in his day job, a corporate executive—albeit in the somewhat more tolerant world of high tech.

This exercise can reveal a lot about our own sense of relative power in the world. Ask yourself, "Are my stereotypes limiting my vision? Are they empowering or disempowering to me?"

The Treasure Cave of the Ancestors: A Trance

(This trance evolved from many of the journeys led by poet Rafael Jesus Gonzalez and me for the Multicultural Ritual Group.)

In sacred space, use your favorite trance induction to lead the group into a deep place of awareness.

Breathe deeply. . . .

Look around you. You have come into the landscape of your ancestry. Breathe deeply, and feel the air on your skin, notice its temperature, how it smells and feels as you breathe it in. Look to the east, and notice what you see and hear and feel and sense . . . Look to the south, and notice what you see and hear and feel and sense . . . Look to the west, and notice what you see and hear and feel and sense . . . Look to the north, and notice what you see and hear and feel and sense . . . Look to the center, and notice what you see and hear and feel and sense . . .

And now as you look around you, you'll notice that somewhere in this place there is an opening, an opening to a cave, a cave that is the treasure-house of the ancestors. And you take a deep breath, and you stand for a moment at the entrance to this cave. Notice how it looks to you, how it feels, what you can touch and sense at the threshold. Know that across this threshold lie the treasures and also the burdens of the ancestors. Ask yourself if you truly wish to enter. Are you called to enter? Is it right for you to enter at this moment?

And if it is right for you, what is the offering you leave at the threshold? What offering do the ancestors ask of you? Feel its weight as you place it at the threshold; know where you place it.

And now you step across the threshold into the cave. Feel the air; feel how it changes, what changes around you as you enter. And you begin to walk through the cave, feeling the weight of your body shift from foot to foot, feeling the air on your skin, and noticing what you can see and hear and feel and sense around you.

This cave has many branches, many twists and turnings, but you know your way. Something is calling you, and you follow, noticing what you see and feel and hear and sense as you go.

And now you come to the chamber that has been calling you. Take a deep breath, and enter. You can see here, and you look around, for this is the treasure chamber of your ancestors.

Take your time now; examine what is here. The ancestors have left many things for you. Among them you will find gifts, great treasures, things that you need.

And among them you will find things that were useful to your ancestors but are not useful to you.

And among them you will find things that were hurtful to your ancestors and to others.

And among them you will find things that have rotted away in time.

And among them you will find things buried deep in dust.

And among them you will find things your ancestors did not value but that are treasures to you.

And among them you will find things that need repair and healing.

Take your time; take all the time you need. Pick and sort, cleanse and choose. Remember all your magical tools and the great powers you can draw on, and decide what to do in this treasure cave.

What will you bury? What will you burn?

What are the gifts of the ancestors you will take?

What will you work to heal? What unfinished tasks are you willing to take on?

Pick and sort, cleanse and choose. Take your time; take all the time that you need . . .

And when you are done, look around this treasure cave. What do you carry with you, and how do you carry it? Take a few more moments to complete anything you need to finish.

And thank your ancestors for what they have given you. And say good-bye to the treasure cave. Take one last look around.

And now begin to make your way back through the cave, feeling the air on your skin, and the weight of your body shifting from foot to foot, noticing what you see and hear and feel and sense as you go.

And now you pause for a moment at the threshold. Say good-bye to the cave, and give thanks for all you have learned. Is there another offering you need to make?

Now step across the threshold. Look back at the cave, at the offering you've left, and know you can return here again if you need to or want to.

And now you stand once again in the landscape of your ancestors. Feel the gifts that you carry, think about the work you've done, and know that you will carry their memory and these changes with you as you say good-bye. Look to the center, and notice what you see and hear and feel and sense, and say good-bye ... Look to the north, and notice what you see and hear and feel and sense, and say good-bye ... Look to the west, and notice what you see and hear and feel and sense, and say good-bye ... Look to the south, and notice what you see and hear and feel and sense, and say good-bye ... Look to the east, and notice what you see and hear and feel and sense, and say good-bye ...

Reverse your induction to bring the group back, and allow time for discussion.

When the ancestors are close to us, they may come to us in unexpected ways even when our beliefs and practices differ greatly from theirs. My Orthodox Jewish grandmother is with me when I bake bread on Solstice night. My father, a radical and activist, marches with me to demonstrations. My mother occasionally insists that I clean out my files.

We can also call on the ancestors we don't know to help us, to infuse us with forgotten knowledge, to inspire us and protect us whenever we take up the tasks that can make the world a more welcoming place for the children and the unborn.

Before she could take up her task of healing, Rose needed to know the truth about her brothers and the unfair bargain that brought her into the world. When we have acknowledged and integrated our own heritage and found those ancestors who can truly be our allies, we can begin to envision communities in which we are free to grow beyond the constraints of the past. We can welcome the diversity that gives our communities the resilience of a prairie or a pristine forest.

We have begun our journey upon the Outer Path. We have each found an anchor to our core worth. Willing to heal the ills we did not create, we have begun the work of gathering our allies, of acknowledging the complexity of our heritages and honoring our ancestors. Now we can step outside the castle, into the wilderness that awaits us.

T W O

Wandering in the Wilderness

Comments on the Story

Rose leaves the castle and sets out to find her brothers. Not knowing where she is going, she wanders in the wilderness. She meets an Old Woman, and to her Rose gives half of her meager store of bread. "Follow the river to its end," the Old Woman advises, "and there you may meet your brothers."

Rose has undertaken responsibility. She has left the castle and set out to save her brothers. Of course, she has no idea how to find her brothers, let alone save them. So she simply wanders.

On an initiatory journey, we're not given a map. There are no instruction books for how to find our personal power. To set off without a destination is a kind of madness, but it is just that type of courage we need in order to create and heal: the courage to enter unknown territory.

Rose knows she has undertaken the right task, and she trusts that if she begins, the way will become clear. An initiatory journey is also a creative process, and every work of creation requires a period of wandering in the wilderness: juggling ideas and possibilities, doodling on the blank page, scribbling draft after draft only to discard them. Life often works the same way. While some people manage to go smoothly from high school to college to graduate school to a successful career, with marriage and children interspersed at exactly the right time, many of us spend time traipsing up and down, following deer trails that peter out, and occasionally slipping into the bog. Our friends and family shake their heads or nag, and often it is not clear for years at a time whether we've embarked on a journey of empowerment or are simply quite lost. In fact, many people do get lost and never find their way to the river.

Rose finds help. More important, when help appears, she meets it with generosity. She shares her food with the Old Woman. This is the classic test of worthiness in fairy tales. Guides and helpers often appear as beggars. The willingness to share even with those who appear lowly is what marks a hera or hero as worthy of guidance.

Help is always around us, but to make use of it, we must first recognize it and respond with an open hand and heart. We cannot be misled by marks of status or outward appearance. We cannot wait for the experts to appear when we wander in the unknown. And when help does come, we cannot hold back the resources we have. We must give in exchange for what we receive. Thus we can meet our guides as equals, not dependents.

Rose's generosity sets her on the path. The river appears, and she must follow it to its end. To make use of guidance, to emerge empowered from our wanderings, we must be willing to follow the path that eventually comes clear to us, and to follow it as far as it goes. In magic, in art, in writing, in ritual, it is easy to give up too soon. The first draft of almost anything is usually pretty poor. Success or failure often depends on our willingness to rewrite, to listen to criticism and revise, over and over, until we get it just right.

Following the river to its end requires all the qualities we've developed so far in this journey. We must continue to have the courage to follow our path. We must recognize guidance when it comes and meet it with generosity, as we must be generous with the work we undertake, willing to go all the way and not hold back. Creativity, generosity, and guidance form the basis of our work with this second section of the story.

The Elements Path

Rose walks away from her parents' castle and from the old life where her privilege was based on her brothers' misfortune. She is determined to restore justice in her world but does not know where to begin. She finds herself in the wild and unknown green world of the forest. There she meets the magical old woman. Rose offers the Old Woman food and accepts her guidance.

Like Rose, when we first learn to work with the art of magic in our own lives, we are choosing to leave a known world for an unknown one. We are choosing to leave behind a familiar, orderly form of consciousness and seek experience with our own secret depths, which may not be very orderly or predictable! This is an act of courage as great as Rose's. Her story can inspire us to make the attempt. In the Elements Path for this part of the story, we will wander like Rose in the green world of nature and then find guidance.

Wandering

When Rose steps out of her old world, she finds herself at once in the forest, the fresh and wild body of Mother Nature herself. For those of us trying to establish a spiritual practice based on Mother Nature, we must follow Rose's example. We do not have a book or sacred text or commandments to obey. We must "follow our noses." In the growth habit of every plant, in the wheeling stars, in the life patterns of every bird and animal we can find insights and lessons about the nature of our green world and of our green selves. Careful and open attention to the living world is nothing other than careful and open attention to our living deity, the Goddess who is the "soul of nature."

Like our ancestors, we must experience the life around us in its simplicity and its interconnectedness. The answer to the most intractable spiritual problem might be found in the quality of water to run under or around any obstacle as it searches for the sea, or in the insistent peeping of baby birds in a nest, or in the mystery of a snake shedding its skin. Each and every natural event is part of the sacred text of the Goddess. So, like Rose, we need to open our doors and walk through them into the fresh, green world of the Goddess. But first we need to learn how to pay attention.

Wandering Exercise: Taking a Witch's Walk

Set aside some special time for yourself. It's great if you can take this walk without a watch on. If you need to be back home at a certain time, maybe you can let the movement of the sun in the sky alert you to the time passing, just this once. If you watch the sun over the course of several days, you will begin to get the feel of where it stands in the sky at different times of day. This varies a lot with the season and the latitude, so count on your own observations.

Now get ready to take your walk. You may wish to do a grounding and purification before you go: after all, this walk is a ritual. You can cast a circle around yourself, if you like, and bring it along with you as you go. It's very interesting to observe how different it feels to walk around while in circle. Don't forget to let the circle go when you are finished.

During this walk, we will use a meditation practice we call "dropped and open attention." The practice of focusing attention, and then dropping it deep into our bodies so that it can open up again from the deepest part of our nonverbal knowing, comes into Reclaiming tradition through the work of Reclaiming teacher and Witch Cybele. She developed it and taught it to us based on her work with aikido teacher Wendy Palmer. "Dropped and open attention" is described in detail in Wendy Palmer's book *The Intuitive Body*. It is one of the basic tools in our magical tool kit, and we use it frequently as we learn to "change consciousness at will."

Once you have made sacred space, take a moment to focus your attention into a compact, glowing ball in the center of your head. Now, on easy breaths, allow the ball to drop deep into your center. Open your attention again, but this time from your deep body wisdom. During your walk, whenever you find that your attention has moved back up into your head, simply gather it up and drop it again on your easy breath. During this walk, you are practicing "dropped and open attention."

Now, out the front door. With no particular destination in mind, allow your feet, your nose, your impulse and intuition to guide you. Open your eyes and ears! Even in a very urban neighborhood, with houses built shoulder to shoulder and concrete everywhere, there are sparrows chattering in the street trees or sneaking a sip from the gutter. Pigeons perform their ancient courtship dances on a spring day, or hurry to feed their babies, or struggle to overwinter. The wind and weather perform great dramas in the sky, and the native herbs struggle up through sidewalk cracks. There are spots where the sound of running water can be heard even under concrete, or where seeps and springs miraculously run through the city after rain. If you are lucky enough to live where there is more green and less concrete, so much the better.

When and if your thoughts and feelings begin to distract you, when and if you begin worrying, or planning, or remembering, or imagining, simply drop your attention again, and direct it gently outward, to what you can hear and feel and smell. Just for a little while, it's time to give your undivided attention to a great Teacher. She's always teaching there, by day and by night, but we too rarely attend the class.

Now, try asking for guidance from Mother Nature on a question that has been troubling you. She answers any question, if you have the patience and the open, waiting mind of a hunter. Be still in her, or walk through her, and wait. She will answer, perhaps in an unexpected way.

I remember a time when I was asking for guidance about restoring a feeling of balance in my life. My daughter was a teenager and an amateur party animal, my husband was having a midlife crisis, and I was experiencing a change of identity as my children grew and became more independent of me. I returned to the same spot under an oak tree for several days, asking my question and simply looking around me with open attention. Finally, on the fourth or fifth day, I *saw*, really saw, what had been there the whole time. Not a single plant on the hillside was in what I would think of as balance. Each one, from the tiniest blade of grass to the massive oak herself, was straining and stretching south, toward the sunlight, hopelessly overbalanced. The angle of each leaf, of each branch, was held out to its utmost limit in order to capture as much of the sun as it could get. My answer was to stop worrying about balance and to fully commit myself to what I loved. I had to take the risk of imbalance and fall forward into my life with all the longing, desire, and commitment of those leaves stretching themselves toward their limit. This would be the source of wholeness and health for my next forty years, not some artificial balance of being equally passionate and reserved about my life.

"Thank you, Mother Nature." If you receive guidance, or insight, or even just a moment of peace, remember to give thanks to Mother Nature.

Wandering: Finding a Special Outdoors Spot

As you practice taking a Witch's walk, you may find your feet returning frequently to some spot that is becoming special to you. Many women and men have found support and comfort in their spiritual practice by adopting a special outdoor spot, a familiar tree to sit under (or up in), a hilltop where the sea breeze and the blue distance inspire perspective, a bridge under which a tiny creek dances in summer and roars in early spring. Choose a special spot outdoors for yourself, and begin using it as frequently as possible. Learn its moods and seasons, its little or big dramas. Allow it to become your teacher.

Generosity: Giving Back

When you do find a special spot and begin to rely on its elemental powers and natural wisdom as a support for your spiritual practice, it is important to give something back. Just as Rose shared her food with the old woman, we must give back when we receive. Taking from nature irresponsibly, with no thought for return, has been the root of great evils in our time, and we must not mimic this attitude in our spiritual practice.

Many Witches begin the project of giving back with whatever might be in their pockets or handy at the time: a coin, a bead, a pretty ribbon, a ticket stub from a pleasant evening. Making such an offering may please Younger Self and show a sincere generosity. But if this practice grows on you, you will need to use your intuition and also your intelligence to find an appropriate way to return energy to your power spot.

I've spoken with Witches who wanted to cast a circle with salt to protect a sacred spot. The impulse behind this plan was generous, but luckily it didn't happen that way because the salt would have killed any plants that grew there. Almost everyone who has wanted to thank a dry California hillside in summer has an impulse to bring water, but that is the very worst thing for live oaks, which are liable to develop oak root fungus if their feet get wet in the summertime.

So learning about your spot—the names of the plants there and the natural history and seasonal cycles of your hill, or your creek, or your meadow—is very important. If you approach this part of the Witch's walk with open-mindedness and determination, you will find that Mother Nature is indeed guiding and changing you. Your whole attitude about the part of the world you live in and your sense of place and belonging will grow green. And you may end up joining the Audubon Society or the Sierra Club and meeting other nature lovers and activists.

If you are ready, it is also a good idea to learn what you can about the peoples who lived on and cared for this land before the Europeans came. These ancestors and their way of life are an important part of the magic of any power spot. It is impossible to work deeply with the plants and animals and weather and land without acknowledging and seeking peace with those who cared for the land before. Although it may be painful or frightening to face the truth about what happened to the first people who lived on the land where you live now, this is a part of the earth's story.

Guidance: Finding the Old Woman

Although Rose struggled in the forest at first, eventually she found the stream that helped her with her thirst, and that would later guide her to her brothers. Like Rose, we have begun to find out how to take care of ourselves here in the green world, but we still don't actually have any idea where we are going. Rose found an "Old Woman" to help her, someone who actually knew where to go, and we need to do the same.

It may seem like a big jump to go from relying on nature to relying on a human being, even a magical "Old Woman." But actually it is not so very different. Our modern culture assumes that people are separate from and superior to nature and that it is our job to dominate nature for our own benefit. But the insightful words of Chief Seattle reflect an older wisdom: "The earth does not belong to us; we belong to the earth."

Human nature is just another part of nature, and we can learn as much from open attention to human nature as we can from open attention to non-human nature. Just as we can learn much from relying on the power of a tree to channel energy from earth and sky when we practice grounding, so we can learn much by relying on an "Old Woman." We can imagine the very best qualities we have observed in older women wrapped up into one wonderful personal mentor: humor, frankness, inner peace, feisty crankiness—whatever those qualities may be, it can do us good to imagine what she would say to us. By practicing reliance on her advice in meditation, we can create a path to a deep knowing and intuition that may become a reliable source of help in our lives. We can begin to hear the voice of our own intuitive wisdom.

The next time you feel confused or doubtful, take a deep breath. Ask the "Old Woman" for guidance, and drop your attention deep in your center. Listen. Breathe and keep listening. Perhaps you can learn to "hear" the voice of your own ancestral wisdom—the simple, quiet voice of the many generations of survivors whose lives bore you as their fruit.

In addition to learning to ask the "Old Woman" for help, it can also be of great benefit to choose one or several deities to begin working closely with. The wonderful Goddesses and Gods from every ancient culture carry with them deep truths about human and nonhuman nature. These truths can be discovered if we begin to develop a personal relationship with deity. These relationships will be different for each person; each person has their own gifts to give and receive from deity. Much can also be learned by studying the traditional teaching about these deities if one is lucky enough to come across a traditional teacher. Otherwise, an excellent place for beginners to start this process is the home altar.

Guidance: Creating a Home Altar

Just as the great outdoors offers us an opportunity to practice the craft of the wise, so it is possible to seek the wisdom of Mother Nature in the wildness of inner space. Many Witches set aside a special spot or corner of their living space for meditation, and set up a personal altar there. These altars are as beautiful, expressive, and varied as the people who build them. They tend to be ever-changing, as the spiritual practices of the maker change. They range from incredibly skilled art installations to a simple white cloth with a candle and a Goddess image.

The simplest one I ever saw was built by a woman who was experiencing a deep spiritual crisis after a frightening personal loss. She didn't believe in anything right then, not even a candle. Her altar space, which had been overflowing with beautiful and unusual Goddess sculptures, weird little natural objects, and personal mementos, was swept clean and bare. In the center was the only thing she could bear to start over with: a mirror, which showed her own ever-changing face.

Another woman had her altar on top of the refrigerator for years, to keep it safe while her toddlers and puppies grew up. Years later she was finally able to bring it down, but for a long time she practiced that part of her craft standing on a kitchen chair!

Guidance: Working at the Home Altar

A home altar is a personal power spot, just like the special power spot outdoors, where we can continue to develop our relationships with the Goddess and with ourselves and seek guidance. Just as we need to make time and space in our lives for lovers, children, or special friends, our altars can help us remember to make time and space for our relationships with the divine and with our own souls. Our altars remind us that our inner lives need attention. Our altars need to be kept clean, and their flowers, or candles, or food offerings need to be renewed. But that is just the beginning. The purpose of keeping an altar is to provide a center for personal magic.

You can leave a trouble or concern at your altar by writing it on a slip of paper or by breathing it into a pebble or shell. You can ask for insight and intuitive guidance by scrying in a candle flame or a bowl of water or by using your tarot cards. You can pray for yourself or for others, sending off blessings and good wishes like birds from your open hands. You can bless a candle for your own good luck or a friend's and burn it as a lovely, fragrant, three-dimensional prayer. Or you can meditate, dropping deep into your own Otherworld to enlarge your self-knowledge and open yourself to visions. You can seek inspiration, strength, or perspective by meditating on the images and stories of the Goddess, on any of her names in every human language, and on her myriad multicultural adventures.

Or you can just sit there and weep, if it's one of those days. The Goddess doesn't ask for anything from us in our devotions but what we have to give. Sometimes I feel like I'm just walking up to my altar and turning myself in: "Help your daughter, Goddess. I'm a mess today."

When I was newly interested in Witchcraft, I sat at my altar and worked through many of the exercises in The Spiral Dance, long before I dared to actually find a class or public ritual with "real" Witches. Some of these exercises never grow old and help on any day—for example, "The Tree of Life" and "Saltwater Purification." Then other times come when I want to make up or try something new.

Learning to keep an altar is a good opportunity to seek advice from a human spiritual teacher, if you are lucky enough to find one. A teacher may be able to offer exercises and meditations that she thinks will be helpful for you, but a skillful teacher will also encourage you to search for your own inner authority.

While it is important to seek advice and feedback from others and to accept teaching from them, in Reclaiming tradition we are each our own authority. We are each the creatrix of our relationships with our Creatrix. When it comes to what we incorporate into our own ongoing practices, we each have the final say as to what works for us and what appeals to our own Younger Self. The practices that enrich and support one person's life may seem uninspiring to someone else. We each need to look long and deep inside and find our guidance there. At times we may need challenges from others, but we need to find our own solutions to them.

Giving Back: Generosity

When Rose meets the old woman in the wood, she offers her half of her meager meal. When we begin to create a relationship with the divine powers at our own altars, we must also be careful to give back when we have received. Witches traditionally offer food and drink at their altars. I always offer money there as well and also anything that particularly pleases me and makes me proud. I like to take these things to my altar in the same way a first-grader would take her painting or her aced spelling test to her mom. Mom likes it!

Giving Back: Getting Active

In addition to making sure we give back to the powers at our altars, Witches of all skill levels need to keep a sharp weather eye on the balance between personal, devotional practice on one hand, and physical work and social activity on the other. Physical and social activity is especially healthy when it puts us in service to life, whether it be walking the dog, watering the garden, or working at a soup kitchen. Ecstatic, mystical practices in circle or at our altars can produce strong insight and altered emotional and psychic states. Good! We need to alter our state, as individuals, as a society, and as a species.

But these strong experiences can also be difficult to integrate into our "normal" psyche. The best preventive medicines we know are regular, healthy physical activity and regular, healthy service to life, human and nonhuman. Intimate and honest relations with others are especially important, as our friends can tell if we get off base.

Guidance: Invoking Deity

By now, we have found some new ways to rely on the power of the Goddess in our lives. We have sought Her guidance by open attention to nature, by finding a special outdoor spot, by questioning the "Old Woman," and by spending time at our home altars. We have remembered to give back whenever we have received guidance or inspiration.

Now we are ready to complete the creation of sacred space with the invocation of deity. We already learned how to ground, purify, cast a circle, and invoke the Elements of Life. After these steps are complete, we invoke the Goddess and the God.

Prepare yourself by learning about and meditating on at least one Goddess whose stories and powers particularly appeal to you. Some Goddess stories and myth cycles include a God, who is the Goddess's lover and/or child: such as the stories of Isis and Osiris, Freya and Odin, Morgan and Arthur, Inanna and Demuzi. Other Goddess stories, like that of Diana, the virgin huntress, do not involve a God. You and you alone are the authority on your personal relationship with deity, and if you are a beginner in the craft of the wise, you yourself may just be beginning to have a hint or clue as to where your devotion lies. So feel free to experiment; be curious, open-minded, gentle, and persistent. You can learn to feel the presence of deity at your altar and in your life.

You may wish to begin investigating deities who were important to your ancestors, whose tales were told in the land of your great-grandmothers. Or you may be called to learn about a Goddess whose qualities or powers resonate with your own character and challenges. A woman struggling with infertility might invoke Hestia, Goddess of the hearth, of sanctuary, and of infertile women. A woman facing big decisions might call on Hecate, who stands where three roads meet. A woman facing overwhelming odds might want help from Ganesh, the elephant God who assists the Goddess, overcoming all obstacles with his strength. Or she might need to call on a trickster spirit, Anansi or Coyote, to help her against seemingly impossible opposition. Sometimes, you may need help from a deity whose powers are opposite to what appears to be your challenge. A woman overwhelmed by caring for small children might need help not from a mother Goddess, but from Artemis, inviolable virgin, forever free. When you know whose help and inspiration and wisdom you need, you are ready to invoke deity. It is our own raw need, more than any fancy poetry, that brings the deities when we call them.

Ground and purify. Cast the Circle and call the powers of the elements and center. Take a moment to still and open your heart, your ears, and your vision. Listen. Where is she? Call her name. Can you feel her coming? Praise her and tell her story. Now she's nearer. If you feel her prompting you, do what you feel would please her. Move, sing, make up poetry, offer gifts and food. Now she's here, inside you, inside your circle, throughout and about. Say, "She is here. Welcome." If you're working with friends, pass a kiss around the circle: "Thou art Goddess." If you're working alone, look in your mirror: "Thou art Goddess."

In Reclaiming circles we usually call the Goddess and the God, sometimes more than one God or Goddess if someone present wants or needs the influence of another deity. You can repeat the process above to call in the God, or you can call him along with her. Try both ways, and see what works best for you. Sometimes in women's circles we call only the Goddess if we're feeling private.

Now we have learned to complete the creation of sacred space with the invocation of deity. We have walked out of our castles into the green and begun to rely on guidance from Mother Nature and from the Old Woman within. We are practicing the devotional arts, building a personal relationship with deity at our own altars. Now we are ready to take the next step on our journeys. Following Rose, we will seek the salt shore, and there we will find the voice of our siblings, the voice of bitterness over past injustices.

The Inner Path

Rose has found the courage to walk away from everything she has ever known. She simply cannot continue to live a life based on a lie and an injustice. She has committed herself to a clear purpose: to find her brothers and free them. But she becomes lost at once, in the wild green life of nature. She has no map, only her clear intent and her determination. Finally, she finds a little stream and the Old Woman. They can guide her to the next step of her journey.

We who walk the Inner Path follow Rose. We have left behind the familiar castle, our old patterns of thinking and feeling. When we listened to our intuition, from dreams, divination, and sensation, we found a doorway out of the castle. Now we must wander, and our wandering will take us deep into the undergrowth of our own inner lives, giving ourselves our own undivided attention and care. As we bend over the little stream and see our reflections, we are drawn into the mystery of our own wild selves. When we have wandered long enough, we must find guidance.

Rose finds a little stream, the first sign of help or comfort she has come across in the unfamiliar wilderness outside the castle. We can imagine her relief. She allows herself to sit down, to rest, to bathe her hands and face, to wash the fear and confusion away, to drink. As she leans over the stream, like Narcissus and many other figures in myth and story, she sees, as she must, her own reflection.

This moment of insight, the sudden view of the self in the luminous surface of the water, marks a beginning for Rose. It is the beginning of the journey that leads first to the ocean, and then to the Otherworld, and thence to the fulfillment of her life's purpose. But now, like Rose, we have just discovered the beginning of our path, the first hint or sign of what it might be—a journey that begins with the self. Those of us who walk the Inner Path must take the time to linger by the stream.

For ancient peoples, who had little metal and no mirrors as we know them, the surface of water would have been the most common way to catch a glimpse of one's own face. And so in Western mystery tradition, the meaning of water includes self-knowledge and the dissolving, healing power of love and self-love. The story tells us that when we have found a source of water, we have found a thread that we can follow to the ultimate power of the sea.

Just as Rose wanders in the wood and follows the wanderings of the stream, we learned in the Elements Path to wander outdoors, observing Mother Nature with open attention. Now in the Inner Path, we will take the time to wander in the mystery of our own reflections, with open attention to our sweet selves. We are each a beautiful act of Mother Nature, as much as any mountain meadow or river mouth, flight of starlings or summer storm.

Finding Time for Wandering Within

So, like Rose, we must stop and rest our selves. We must allow the water to heal and soothe and mirror us. Here is a challenge that for modern people may be among the most profound of the whole story. Never have people been so hurried, so frantic, so overstimulated, so dissatisfied, so out of touch with themselves as we find ourselves at the turn of the millennium. We are lost in a concrete jungle, with a million things pulling and pricking us like the thorns and branches in Rose's woods. Our cancer doctors, our heart doctors, our psychiatrists, and our spiritual teachers tell us to relax and meditate, but we look at them in confusion and disbelief. Where will we find the time? How can we stop the barrage of ringing phones, advertising jingles, billboards? After all, we've got mail!

When I find myself unwilling or unable to set time aside for my soul-life, I sometimes ask myself the following question: If I had a lively and sensitive little daughter—say, four or five years of age—who loved me dearly and longed for my attention, how much of my time would I make sure to give her every day? Five minutes of undivided attention? Twenty? Wouldn't I want to plan my whole day and my whole life around her?

But how much of my attention do I give to my own soul-life? Why is it so hard to give myself the love and attention I would willingly give others? It's a little sad, isn't it? This is a question I have asked many women over years of mentoring, and it is amazing how frequently we are determined to love, protect, and care for an imaginary daughter and yet are unwilling or unable to take the time to care for our own dear souls. It's surprisingly difficult to give ourselves undivided attention for even a few minutes a day of meditation, self-care, and devotion. It helps a lot to give ourselves a regular time to meet with friends and attend to our soul-life in circle. Many Witches work on their personal healing with others, in circle, precisely because it is so hard to be regular and consistent about spiritual practices on one's own. There are also things to be learned from other people and our interactions with them that are very hard to learn alone.

The rewards of developing a spiritual practice are enormous. We can find the little stream that leads to an enormous sea of love. In the Charge of the Goddess, she says, "My law is love unto all beings, . . . for behold, I am the mother of all things, and my love is poured out upon the earth." When the Goddess says this, she means that love is the law for all the endangered species, for the poor polluted streams and bays, for the smoky air, for the hungry and hopeless, and also for me, one sometimes confused woman living a seemingly trivial life. Her love is poured out upon me. It's sometimes hard to believe that unconditional love is already mine, should I choose to accept it. If I stop my frantic efforts and listen to the voice of nature, I can hear her on the wind, through the trees, or over the rooftops: "*Shhhhhhh*. All will be well."

This kind of love, although we may long for it, may seem very distant and unlikely. But it is no more distant than the sea is from Rose, as she kneels by the little stream, not far yet from her ancestral home. If she follows the stream, it will inevitably lead her to the ocean. The same is true for us. If we follow that first glimpse of the self, if we begin to give our souls a little love and attention, if we stop and rest in view of the self, if we don't get discouraged or give up or become distracted, our efforts will inevitably lead us to an immensely powerful salty sea full of love.

Now, if you are ready to commit yourself to a little bit of self-care and self-love, you can try the following series of exercises, which will help bind your own soul journey with that of Rose. Since we are Witches, this commitment to self-love and care is nothing abstract. Just as we would try to express our love for children with good meals, silly games, clean T-shirts, and open-hearted listening, so we practice our love for ourselves with concrete practices, which appeal to Younger Self. These are some ideas to help you get started on your own path of self-love. As always, take what you like, and leave the rest.

The following exercises are meditations on self-knowledge and self-love. They are dreamy and interior. If you are working in circle, you may wish to use one of these meditations and follow it with some singing, dancing, games, and drumming to raise energy, raising a cone of power to bless and empower your healing work. Then your circle will need to relax, eat, and cool off.

Wandering Within Exercise: A Rose

You will need a rose, a little water, scissors, and a bud vase. If you are working in circle, everyone may bring a rose, and you'll need a bigger vase. Create sacred space at your altar, and light your candles. Bless the water and the vase, and pour the water in.

Now prepare the roses. Trim the stems and lower leaves, and place the roses in the vase.

Take time to meditate on the roses, as though you were looking in a mirror. Can you sense your own softness, freshness, fragrance, complexity, your beauty, your colors, dark or pale, which are so perfect for you and no one else? Can you see how the roses have secret depths as well as welcoming openness? Can you see how your colors compliment one another, how your different styles of elegant tightness and lush openness work together for beauty?

Know that just as your soul needs your attention, so your roses will need regular attention. The water must be changed, the stems trimmed; from time to time the roses must be composted and replaced, or soon your home altar, or your circle's altar, will be strewn with dead petals and a dank smell of old water and dying foliage. It is a law of magic that changes on your altar can create changes in your soul. Placing the roses on your altar is a commitment to your own soul-life. Keep a bouquet of roses on your altar while you work through the story of the Twelve Wild Swans, since each of you is Rose.

Wandering Within Exercise: In-drinking

For this exercise, you will need special cups. If you have a cup that you've charged as one of your magical tools, use it. If not, use any cup that appeals to you. You will also need some liquid that you like drinking. This exercise works best with a dark liquid; grape or cranberry juice works well.

Create sacred space—alone or with your circle. Now, fill the cup partway, and find your reflection in the surface of the liquid. This may take a few tries, as you may have to adjust your vision to see yourself. When you begin to catch glimpses of yourself in the cup, allow your responses to yourself to surface. If some of the responses are harsh ("God, I look old"; "She really needs to lose some weight"), simply take note of them and then release them on a breath. It may take some patience to get through the layer of comparing, judging responses, but it will be worth it. Soon you may catch a real glimpse of your self, although it may be just for a split second. Even the briefest true impression of our selves—a single fresh, wild image—is worth working for. When you see something that seems true, say it out loud: "I see a woman who . . ." Now drink it in (drink the juice, OK?). Let it become part of your self forever. If you don't see something fresh on the first try, drink that in, too, with compassion for yourself: "I see a woman who has had trouble seeing herself fairly. I see a woman who is committed to helping herself in this area."

Try this exercise with various kinds of light. Try to find your true reflection by candlelight, by moonlight, by sunlight, by starlight. In circle, you may wish to discuss what you've seen; if working alone, make some notes in your Book of Shadows. When you begin to be expert at in-drinking, go on to the next two exercises.

Wandering Within Exercise: Self-Blessing

When you have begun to feel comfortable with your reflection, try giving yourself a blessing. Use your cup, as in the last exercise, or use a mirror. A hand mirror is one of my most important magical tools. I try to use it frequently with the formula "I see a woman who . . ." as a tool for self-knowledge and self-love. It may seem odd to say anything out loud to yourself in a mirror. If it feels too strange, start by just saying "Hi." Then try saying your name out loud to yourself, and try your nicknames too. It's amazing how much raw emotion can surface from hearing a nickname that was important in some past time. When you're ready, try saying a simple blessing to yourself in the mirror: "Blessed be." Remember, love for *you* is part of the Goddess's only law; her love is poured out upon *you*. One of my most powerful experiences with this exercise was when I tried singing a love song, which had been a favorite of mine when I was a young teenager, to myself in the mirror. Try it sometime.

Wandering Within Exercise: Asymmetry

As you get used to looking at yourself, you may notice that the left and right sides of your face are not exactly the same. In fact, it's worth taking a piece of cloth and veiling first one side of your face and then the other. Take the time to get to know both sides of yourself. Right-handed people may find that the expression on the left side of their face shows an unexpected emotion. A very upbeat person may show sadness on the left side of the face, while a timid person may show fierceness. Or the opposite. One of my students did self-portraits of both sides of her face, and the pictures expressed completely different feelings. When you are working with this exercise, be sure to bless both sides of yourself. You don't have a "bad" side and a "good" side; you have two beautifully human sides.

Wandering Within Spell: A Valentine

Since I take my magical name from the folk tradition of the valentine, you can guess that this exercise is a very important one for me. It's deep, and it's simple.

Create sacred space, alone or with your circle, and break out the art supplies. The only rule is that you have to use the materials that appeal most to Younger Self. Using glitter, stickers, pictures cut out of magazines, colorful paper, doilies, and glue, make a valentine for yourself. Sing love songs to yourself and to the Goddess while you work.

Write your vows to yourself somewhere on the valentine: "I will never forsake you, I will always be with you . . ." When you are done, charge and bind the spell, and keep the valentine on your altar, or keep the valentines on your circle's altar, for as long as it pleases you. Never throw a spell like this in the garbage can when you are done with it. Bury it in your compost to keep feeding your garden and your family; leave it at a crossroads and walk away without looking back to feed the heart of whoever needs it most; tie it on the wicker man on Midsummer Day and burn it as a sacrifice to the gods. Do something with it that works magically for you.

Wandering Within Exercise: Sensation and Self-Comforting

For this exercise, you will need to get yourself warm and comfortable. A special blanket or teddy bear are the magical tools of choice. Create sacred space, alone or with your circle. Close your eyes and relax completely. Turn your attention inward, and let it draw together into a glowing sphere behind and between your eyes, in the center of your head. Allow your attention to drop on each easy breath until it reaches a resting place deep in your belly that feels like your center.

If the space of your lower belly or lower back is difficult for you, remember that you are trying to cultivate a place you *like* to return to, so be gentle and persistent, and encourage yourself. If you sense part of your attention observing or directing from up in your head, gently use your exhalation to drop the observing self down into sensation in the belly, bit by bit.

This state, when your attention is focused and dropped deep into your center, is "home base," and if you get distracted during this exercise, simply retrace these steps and return to "home base" on a few easy breaths. We call this state *dropped attention*.

Now allow a sensation somewhere in your body to draw your attention. Open your attention toward this sensation, and explore it with your inner senses. Note the texture, temperature, pressure, motion of the sensation. Does it feel like a huge frozen sponge? An explosion of orange prickling? Do images and associations arise? Does it feel like you're underwater? Do you hear words or sounds? Do you smell Christmas cookies? Notice each sensation, image, and emotion as it arises, and tell yourself that you will be able to remember them. It's amazing how quickly they can vanish when you open your eyes, just like the details of a dream. So far, we're just noticing sensation, not trying to change anything.

Next allow yourself to make a slight, subtle adjustment in your physical body, to make yourself a little more comfortable. Maybe you can open your hand just a little bit more; maybe your neck, which is usually tilted subtly to one side, might like to be a bit straighter. Maybe you can uncross your ankles or yawn.

Sometimes it helps to direct a deep breath toward a tense or painful area. Sometimes it helps to work with an image, such as that of wrapping a sore, tired knee in warm red flannel, or dipping a hot face in a cool tide pool. Sometimes it helps to send a strong mental image of a color that feels soothing or energizing to a trouble spot in the inner landscape. Try making a humming sound or long vowel tone (*aaaah*, or *ooooh*) and sending it into the area you are working with. Try allowing a sound to come out of that area.

The purpose of this exercise is to find whatever helps comfort, soothe, and energize your body, no matter how silly it might sound. After all, you don't have to tell anyone if you don't want to. Take note of what was helpful, and tell yourself that you will be able to remember.

Now pull your attention back into the center of your body, and return to "home base." Let yourself rest in your center for a few breaths, and then slowly begin to allow your attention to rise on each breath until it is gathered again in a glowing sphere behind your eyes. Open your eyes, stretch thoroughly, and then grab your Book of Shadows and make some notes, before the detail and intensity of the experience fade. In circle, you may wish to discuss what you experienced. With practice you can get to know your own inner landscape well and gain tools and skills that allow you to care for and comfort yourself.

If you have been lucky enough or patient enough to get specific suggestions from Younger Self, by all means take them literally and use them. If the color blue helped, sleep in blue sheets, wear your lapis earrings and a blue T-shirt, burn blue candles, eat blueberries. Just like anyone else, Younger Self is more likely to speak up if you show that you are listening carefully and willing to help. If you keep practicing and paying attention, you will also know when it's time to stop or change. You don't have to eat blueberries forever!

Wandering Within Exercise: A Mirror

The ancient texts say that above the entrance to the Delphic oracle were written the words *Know Yourself* (in Greek, of course). Place a mirror on your altar or on your circle's altar, behind the roses, to "reflect" your commitment to self-knowledge. Now when you work at your altar you can see yourselves and the roses reflected together. Now your altar, which holds the mysterious images or objects that brought you to the inner path, together with the roses and the mirror, is beginning to reflect your commitment to your own process of self-discovery, self-healing, and self-love.

Wandering Within Exercise: The Mystery

Now that you have begun to be an adept in the art and craft of self-love, what happens if you use one of these exercises to go to a place of powerful self-love, and *from that perspective* look at the disturbing or mysterious images, dreams, or sensations that opened the door of the Inner Path for you. What if you bring your dream symbol, your cards, your posture or gesture into the mirror of self-love with you? Can you find the same deep acceptance of your difficulties, your challenges, and your mystery that you have learned to have for yourself? If so, you have found the little stream that will lead you to the powerful sea of love, the love that turns the stars, the love that says, "For I am the mother of all things, and my love is poured out upon the earth."

Seeking Guidance

As Rose rests by the stream, lost in the wood, the Old Woman appears. Rose shares what she has with the Old Woman. Although she has little, her heart is generous. In turn, the Old Woman gives her exactly the information that is most needed. The Old Woman knows how to find Rose's brothers. Like Rose, we must learn to ask for guidance. In the Elements Path, we learned to ask for guidance from nature and from our wisdom voice, deep within. We learned to keep an altar and rely on our relationship with deity. In the Inner Path, we are going to ask for guidance from real people and in trance.

With any magical practice, it's good to check your efforts from time to time with other people. This is especially important if you are doing most of your magical work alone. We all need attention and insight from others as well as from ourselves, or we can lose our perspective. Everyone, even the most experienced priestess, has blind spots, and they are often about ourselves. As we pursue a self-healing process, we need guidance and advice from outside ourselves. This may be the advice of friends, of our circle sisters, or of casual acquaintances, or it may be the guidance we seek from finding a formal relationship with a spiritual teacher, bodyworker, or counselor.

Guidance from a Circle or Coven

In Reclaiming tradition, we often form intimate, committed circles and covens, which meet regularly to celebrate the full and new moons, to do magic together, and to support and challenge each other as we each move toward our personal fulfillment and our life's purpose. These bonds are often as strong as or even stronger than family ties. How many people really know that you felt like leaving your husband every fall for the last six years, but you loved him again by Christmas? How many people remember a really important dream you had last year and can remind you of it? How many people know that you always get a stomachache when you start a new project? When circle sisters know each other well, they can be the "Old Woman" for each other, using their wisdom and humor to help one another.

Guidance from Teachers

We can also find the Old Woman disguised as teachers offering public classes in the Goddess traditions. These teachers aren't all old, and they aren't all women, but I have gained tremendous personal growth and healing for myself when I have sought out teachers in my tradition. None of them have been the perfect mentor; all of them have been human, with their own personal stories and growth unfolding along with mine. One moment they might offer the perfect encouragement or challenge; the next moment they might say something really dumb and thoughtless. But if they had been perfect, or tried to be, I wouldn't have felt at home in the classes. I wouldn't have felt I belonged, because I know perfectly well that I'm far from perfect. So why would I want a perfect teacher? She wouldn't be able to help with my real dilemma, with my humanness. Almost every metropolitan area now has teachers offering classes in the Goddess traditions. Consider the possibility of taking a class to support your work or your circle's work on the story of the Twelve Wild Swans. Here are two stories to encourage you, about how a teacher can be the "Old Woman" for one magic moment.

Guidance: A Story

I met Cybele as the teacher in a Reclaiming class during the years I was first studying Witchcraft. A small, lithe woman with the movements of a dancer, Cybele had a face that was both mysterious and oddly open. I felt I had known her for years.

The circle was cast, and Cybele began the invocation of the Goddess as She Who Listens, Shhhhhh. I felt the familiar prickling sensation as the tiny hairs on my arms stood up, and shivers ran down my spine—the physical sensation of present power. I somehow knew that Cybele was calling in a deity as familiar as the back of her own hand.

As I came to know Cybele over the years, this first impression deepened. Cybele has dedicated her life to therapeutic bodywork and healing with women and men who have survived childhood trauma and abuse. She has literally heard it all. When Cybele listens, a quiet, reflective acceptance spreads out from her center like the stillest alpine lake, reflecting, accepting the tiniest detail of the trees and sky. Calm, still, reflecting, accepting—absolutely. Then suddenly her crooked grin breaks through, half the worldly cynicism of someone who has heard the worst of human nature, half the wicked resilience of the survivor.

One day, one of Cybele's students had come to a particularly difficult moment in trance. She was releasing her memories of a frightening childhood experience, and suddenly she felt that she couldn't breathe. From her experience as a bodyworker, Cybele knew what to do. "Don't try to breathe in," Cybele said quietly. "Just breathe out." As the woman breathed all the way out, her body's wisdom took over and the next in-breath came quite naturally.

Guidance: Another Story

Another wonderful Reclaiming teacher story involved Egret. A big, strong woman with a lush Texan accent, Egret is a slow talker and a deep listener. She's not a bandwagon kind of gal; her independent thinking and personal courage to speak unpopular truths have enriched every circle she's been part of. The slow silences and deep devotion of her practice lit up her classes when I was a student.

The circle was cast that night at class, and we tranced deep and far into the Otherworld. When we returned, my friend Bessie had a strange tale to tell. She had been joined over yonder by a spirit like a little flame, and it had wanted to come back with her. All the women in the class, including myself, started giving our different bits of advice and warnings about birth control and getting rid of unwanted spirit visitors. Meanwhile, Bessie was getting quieter and quieter. Finally the chatter and well-meaning advice slowed down. As the silence drew out and Bessie still didn't say anything, Egret finally spoke up: "Maybe this is a good thing."

This "good thing" is in second grade now, with hair like flames and little feet that fly like sparks in the Irish jig competitions.

In these stories, Cybele's student and Bessie were able to hear the perfect, helpful advice from the "Old Woman" of the moment. These special moments, highly valued by both teacher and student, are powerful magic when they occur. But the same quality that makes a teacher the perfect "Old Woman" in one situation may make her irritatingly human a moment later. We all are ultimately teachers and guides for one another, students in one situation and teachers in another.

Guidance Exercise: Recognizing the Teacher in the Beggar Woman

We can also receive guidance in completely unexpected ways, from strangers or casual acquaintances or from our everyday companions. Here is another exercise that reminds us to pay attention, so that we can recognize guidance when it comes our way. It can help us practice generosity and recognize the wisdom of the Goddess in unexpected places. Set aside a day for it, or weave it into your life as an ongoing practice.

In Aldous Huxley's utopian novel *Island*, mynah birds were trained to fly around the village crying out, "Attention! Attention!" as a constant reminder to people to put their attention on the here and now. The teachers at the Wilderness Awareness School, who train students in nature awareness and the development of the relaxed alertness we need for literally wandering in the wild, suggest that we choose our own version of the mynah bird, something that occurs periodically in our lives as a constant reminder to notice the life and detail around us.

For this meditation, choose your own wake-up bell—perhaps the ringing of the phone, or the cry of a blue jay, or seeing a blue car on the road. Whenever your "wake-up bell" appears, imagine it is telling you that the very next person you meet may be the Old Woman who will set you on your path.

Make an offering to the next person you meet. This might mean literally giving spare change to a street person, or giving your child a spontaneous hug, or offering to make a cup of tea for a tired friend. Then listen to whatever that person says as if it were a piece of true wisdom or a clue for your journey. You may ask a question if it is appropriate to your interaction. Act on the advice you receive (within the bounds of your own ethics and common sense).

Guidance: Giving Back

Can you think of someone, or maybe a few people, in whom you could trust and confide, from whom you could seek counsel? Are you willing to commit yourself to doing so? If so, try this simple exercise. By making a food offering at our altars, we will ask to be sent the guidance that we need.

Take a moment to think about the loaf of bread in the story. For the Northern European people who told this tale, the loaf of bread would be the staple food, eaten daily, and carried on journeys—the staff of life. But this may not be the staple food you rely on for life, or the staff of life of your ancestors. If yams, or rice, or bean cakes, or salt fish, or some other food works for you and your ancestors instead of the bread in the story, by all means use that instead.

Exercise: A Food Offering

You, or you and your circle, will need some food, prepared so that it is especially delicious. Create sacred space at your altar, and light your candles. Bless the food. Place part of the food on your altar as an offering. Make prayers for yourselves with words, drawings, silence, gestures, songs—whatever works for you and your circle sisters. Ask for the willingness and the courage and the luck to meet the guides who are just right for you at this moment in your lives. Ask for what you know you want and need. Ask to be surprised, too, by wonderful assistance that you cannot anticipate. Commit yourselves to *paying attention* to what happens between you and other people over the next few days or weeks. Eat the rest of the food. It is done. Thank the powers and open the circle.

Trance for Guidance: Asking the Old Woman

Let's take this opportunity to get the advice and guidance of the "Old Woman." Return for a moment to the disturbing sensation, or dream, or image that provided you with your door into the Inner Path. Let's take this to the "Old Woman" and ask for her help.

Create sacred space alone or with your circle, and use your favorite induction to enter trance and go to your place of power. Greet the directions in your place of power; find your path and begin to walk it.

There is a glow of light in front of you on the path. As you approach and can see more clearly, you find the Old Wise One. Offer to share with her whatever you have. Show her the mysterious dream or divination image, or the mysterious sensation or posture, that opened the door of the Inner Path for you. She can counsel you and answer your questions. She will point you in the right direction. Notice where she points and the features of the path: the landscape and the weather that she is directing you toward. She may have something unexpected to add. When you are finished, thank her and say farewell. Know that you will be able to remember what has taken place and that you can return here whenever you wish.

Return to your place of power on your path. Does your path seem different now?

Thank the four directions, and return, using the exact opposite of your induction. Stretch, say your name three times, and discuss what happened with your circle sisters. Make some notes in your Book of Shadows, eat a little something, and, only when you are ready, open the circle.

―――――――――

We have followed Rose into the wild. We have lingered by the little stream and begun to practice the art of wandering deep into the wilds of self-knowledge and self-love. We have shared our food and accepted guidance. Now we must follow the little stream to the seashore, where we will face the next challenge of our journey.

The Outer Path

Nobody knows how to remake the world. There are no sets of instructions for rebuilding a healthy society, no manual for healing our social wounds. Like Rose, we know that we are called to set the world to rights, but we often don't know how to do it.

This section of the story teaches that the great creative powers we need can be awakened only when we give ourselves over to the unknown. Not knowing what to do is no excuse for doing nothing. The wildwoods are calling us to explore their depths and find unexpected allies and guidance. When we allow ourselves time to wander, we discover new trails and hear the songs of unfamiliar birds. Our experience is enriched, and that broadening of understanding will inform all our actions and creations.

Wandering requires courage and confidence. We live in a society that expects us to have clear goals and efficient plans for reaching them, to follow set timetables and know where we're going and what we're doing. But creativity is not efficient. Efficiency belongs to the realm of Talking Self, but art, poetry, music, dance, and visionary organizing arise from Younger Self, who loves to skip through the woods freely without being constrained to follow a trail.

When we allow Younger Self freedom, when we let the form emerge from the block of marble, the characters tell the story of a novel, the song sings itself, and we open the way for Deep Self to speak through our art and our work.

When we take on roles of leadership in a group, we must be comfortable not only with our own unknowing but with allowing the group its chance to wander. If we're planning a ritual, a political action, or a creative project as a group, we need to allow time for open discussion of all the possibilities. Our conventional image of a leader is of someone who knows what to do, who sets the direction of a group and moves it toward her or his personal vision. But empowering leadership is very different. Instead of pushing the group ahead, our role might be to say, "Slow down." Instead of offering a clear solution to a problem, our role may be to make time for a broad discussion of all the issues and let the solution emerge from the group.

For me, this is a lesson I learn over and over again. My natural tendency is to leap ahead, see a vision far down the road, and then attempt to drag the group there along the path I see as most direct. I want to move faster, faster, *faster!* and have been known to literally writhe on the ground with frustration when someone slows the group down.

But I've learned the hard way about the value of that slower pace. A few years ago, the Reclaiming Witchcamps had grown to be eight or nine in number. Each was autonomous, and while several teachers had worked at more than one camp, most had never met. We had planned a first-ever gathering of teachers and organizers in Portland, Oregon, that March. Meanwhile, sentiment began to grow for creating some sort of structure that would link the camps, and a meeting was scheduled during the Portland gathering.

Paul, a longtime Witchcamp teacher who has an extensive background in management training, and I had come up with what we thought was a fine proposed structure, all neatly diagrammed. But Brook, whom we'd asked to facilitate the meeting, stopped us.

He wisely recognized that the group had not yet done its wandering, that I was laying a path that was clear to me when others had not yet even scouted the territory. At that time, I was the only person who had taught at every camp and who knew every person involved in that meeting of sixty teachers and organizers. The need for a larger structure was clear to me, but not to everybody else. They didn't know each other; they were meeting for the first time and had not yet established a basis of trust. They had no way to know if a formal structure would empower them or simply create a new bureaucracy that would take away their autonomy. Trust needed to be built, and there was no way to shortcut that process. We had to wander in the wilderness and struggle together through the briars in order to get to know each other. I couldn't impose a structure on the group from above; it had to emerge slowly, from within.

Wandering requires patience, the willingness to let patterns and pathways emerge into awareness from what seems like chaos. It calls for a shift in consciousness, from a narrow focus to a broad awareness of all that surrounds us. The following exercise is adapted from the Wilderness Awareness School, which teaches tracking and wilderness skills.

Wide Vision

Go to your special spot or to a place where you can be outside in nature and wander (without the risk of getting seriously lost). Stand for a moment and fix your eyes on a spot directly in front of you. Open your arms wide, pressing them back so that you can't see your hands. Now, wiggling your thumbs, bring your arms slowly forward until you can see the movement with your peripheral vision. Notice how wide that vision can be. Imagine that you can send a pulse of energy that circles around the edge of your peripheral vision, to keep it active at its farthest extent.

Now take a walk, and wander. If you need to, stop periodically and repeat this exercise to reawaken your wide vision. How does your experience change with this mode of awareness?

Dropped and Open Attention

Cybele brought this awareness technique into the broader Reclaiming community. She learned it from aikido teacher Wendy Palmer, but in our community it has taken on a slightly different form and many new uses.

When we set out with a purpose, but no road map or clear destination, we need to pay attention to all the cues from our environment and all the promptings of intuition. Dropped and open attention is another way of shifting our usual focus and opening up a new center of awareness.

Get into a relaxed position, and take some deep breaths. Ground and center yourself.

Imagine that your awareness is a point of light in the center of your head, directly behind your third eye. Take a moment and feel your consciousness centered here.

Now, breathing deeply, let your awareness begin to sink down. Imagine that point of light slowly moving down your spine, a little farther with each breath.

When it reaches your heart, pause for a moment. Take a few deep breaths and feel your awareness centered in your heart.

Now continue breathing, and let that point of light sink down again, until it rests in that energy center just below your navel. Breathe deeply, and let yourself experience dropped attention.

Now as you breathe, imagine that your awareness can expand. That point of light becomes a disc, or a plane of attention. Let it expand out until it reaches the edges of your physical body. Breathe deeply, and feel your awareness encompass your physical body, while still remaining connected to your center.

Now let your awareness expand until it reaches the edge of your aura, your energy body. Breathe deeply, and feel your awareness encompass your energy body, while still remaining connected to your center.

Now as you breathe, let your awareness expand until it encompasses this circle. Notice how as we all do this, our consciousness merges until we create one plane of attention. Notice what it feels like to let your awareness include each person in this circle, while still remaining connected to your center. You may find that your attention moves around the circle like a radar sweep, or you may be able to hold the circle as one seamless whole.

Now as you breathe, draw your attention inward again. Thank the circle, and bring your awareness back to the edges of your energy body. Feel how we separate as we do this.

Now breathe deeply again, and bring your attention back to the edges of your physical body. And now as you breathe, draw it back into a point of light in the center of your belly.

Breathe deeply again, and slowly let that point of light rise. Pause again for a moment at your heart, and then let it continue upward to your head or wherever you feel comfortable.

Open your eyes and come back into your usual awareness.

When you have practiced dropped and open attention enough so that you feel comfortable and can easily move in and out, go back to your special spot or out to some natural area where you can safely wander a bit. Sit still or take a walk in dropped and open attention, and notice how your experience changes. How is it different from wandering in wide attention? In your normal state of consciousness?

Spontaneous Ritual Sequence

For us as ritual makers, the equivalent of wandering in the wilderness without a map is to attempt a spontaneous ritual without a plan. We recommend you try these exercises in a circle of close friends committed to this work—not in a public ritual and not as a way of introducing the concept of magic to your Aunt Freda who never heard of it before. Sometimes spontaneous rituals can be incredibly alive, exciting, and empowering; at other times the value will lie not so much in the ritual itself as in what you learn from the process.

Spontaneous Ritual 1

Alert the group ahead of time that the meeting that is to follow will be a spontaneous ritual. Encourage people to bring drums, instruments—whatever ritual objects suggest themselves. When the circle gathers, the usual leaders or

teachers should refrain from speaking or offering guidance. Eventually, someone will remember that a spontaneous ritual is planned, and things will begin
to happen. Let the energy develop and complete itself; but attempt to bring
closure at least forty-five minutes before the end of the meeting time. Then
discuss some of the following questions:

What happened? Who took leadership? Who initiated actions? Which
ideas were adopted by the group? Which fell flat? Why? Who mirrored and
amplified ideas and impulses suggested by others? What unspoken rules did the
group adopt? (For example, many times the group interprets this exercise to
mean wordless ritual, even though no such instructions have been given.)
How much power did each participant feel she or he had to affect the group?
Did the group come together as a coherent whole? What transformation
occurred in the ritual?

Did you think to use your anchor to your core worth in this process? Did
you get pulled into inflation or deflation?

For those who are working alone, experiment with creating a spontaneous ritual for yourself, using whatever tools come to hand, flowing with
your own energy. Note what seems to encourage your flow and what seems to
block it.

Identifying/Clarifying Ritual Intention

Create sacred space. In the center of the circle, place something to focus on: a
bowl of salt water, a cauldron, a candle flame, a symbol of the group. Use your
anchor, and bring yourselves into your anchored connection to your core
worth. Ask, "What do we need?"; "What does our community need?"; "What
does the Goddess need?"; "What transformation might a ritual bring?" Go into
dropped and open attention, focus on your central object, and consider the
questions. As answers emerge, individuals are free to speak them out. One person might volunteer to record the ideas. Allow time for everyone to speak at
least once. You might hear such words as *bonding, celebrating, resolving old conflicts, marking our transitions.*

Come back from dropped and open attention, turn on the lights, break out
the food, and discuss what came up. Identify a clear intention for the ritual,
one that you can formulate in one sentence. For example: "The intention of
this ritual is to release our old conflicts and celebrate the growth we've made
as a group." Make sure everyone feels heard and can support the intention of
the ritual.

If you are working alone, give yourself time to drop, open, and focus, considering your needs and what a ritual might provide. Clarify your own intention.

Spontaneous Ritual 2

At the next group meeting, begin by reminding the circle of the intention they've agreed upon and that this session will also involve spontaneous ritual. Use your anchor to your core worth, and then go into dropped and open attention. Let a spontaneous ritual emerge. Again, be sure to leave enough time to process. Discuss the questions suggested earlier for the first spontaneous ritual. Ask also: "How was this ritual different from our first spontaneous ritual?"

If you are working alone, notice how your own ritual is different when your intention is clear.

In our story, after Rose wanders long enough in the wilderness, she finds help. The old woman comes to her and offers guidance. As teachers, leaders, activists, and ritual makers, we also need to learn to recognize help and guidance, and to meet it with generosity. And we need to learn how to offer guidance that can be truly empowering to others.

Rose is not misled by appearances or marks of status; her guide may look like an old beggar woman, but still Rose listens to her words. So, too, we may receive the teachings we need from someone who has none of the outer trappings of success or the marks of status we expect. Our guide may even be caught in her or his own inflation or deflation. Few teachers, even spiritual teachers, are exempt from ordinary human failings. Yet the message may be valid even if the messenger is flawed.

Few of us have had the gift of true mentoring. Most of us have experienced teaching in situations of power-over. In resistance to hierarchy, we often have trouble allowing ourselves to admit that someone else might have something to teach us. When we are not grounded in our own power, we may respond to help with hostility or resentment instead of generosity. We cannot differentiate between true guidance and control. If we are caught in an inflated image of ourselves or stuck in a place of deflation and low self-esteem, someone else's greater experience or knowledge may seem threatening rather than enlightening. We may long for the perfect teacher yet find ourselves unable to accept the help that actually comes to us in imperfect human forms.

When we take on roles of leadership, we become guides for each other. In Reclaiming, we know that every person—whether teacher, student, elder, or newcomer—can potentially be the wise woman. But offering advice and guidance is a delicate matter. How do we offer help without disempowering the recipient? How does guidance differ from control?

The work that follows is designed to help us explore these issues.

Guidance Meditation

In sacred space, ground, center, and sit or lie in a relaxed position. Think of someone who has given you true help or guidance, who has taught you something or opened a new opportunity for you. Did you ask for their help, or did they offer it? What made it an empowering experience for you? Was there anything they said or did that made it easy for you to receive?

What mistakes did they make? What imperfections do they have? Do they get in the way of your learning, or can you take what they offer and leave what doesn't fit?

What offering did you give in return? Have you expressed your gratitude?

Breathe in, and consciously take in the help you've been offered. Breathe out, and consciously offer gratitude back to your guide. Take your time. With each breath, allow your lungs to open more fully and open yourself more deeply to the help that is around us.

When you are done, take time in your circle to share your insights. Or, if you are alone, write in your journal about what you experienced.

Offering Guidance/Anchor Exercise

This exercise can be done in pairs or in a group. Begin by reviewing the "Anchoring to Core Worth" and "Inflated/Deflated Self" exercises in the Outer Path in chapter 1.

One partner, or one person in the group, will be the Guide. The other or others will be the Witness/es.

The task of the Witness/es is simply to listen and to notice how your feelings change throughout this exercise.

You, as the Guide, should think of some subject about which you have knowledge—ideally something fairly nonemotional, such as how to clean the kitchen floor or how to change the oil in your car.

Use your anchor, and bring yourself into your core worth state. Then drop your anchor, and allow yourself to move into inflation. When you are confidently there, begin to advise your Witness/es on the subject you have chosen.

Witnesses, listen to the Guide. Notice how you feel, how your body is positioned, and how you are breathing. What state of consciousness are you pulled into? Are you interested? Engaged? Bored? Annoyed? Is it easy or difficult to take in information from the Guide in this state?

Now, Guide, let go of your inflated state. Take a moment to reground, and then let yourself go into deflation. Again, give guidance from this state. Witnesses, again notice how you feel and respond.

Now, Guide, let go of your deflated state. Breathe deeply, shake out your hands, and use your anchor to bring yourself back into your core worth. Give guidance to your Witness/es from this state. Witness/es, again notice and observe what happens to you, considering all the questions raised earlier.

In partners, you can now repeat this exercise, reversing roles. In a group, you might want to stop and discuss what you've observed. Witness/es, how did you respond to the changing state of the Guide? When was it easiest or most difficult to take in information? What other subtle messages were conveyed along with the overt information? Repeat this exercise with Witnesses exploring different states of consciousness: wide awareness, dropped and open attention. What insights do these bring?

Now, Guide, tell or teach something you feel passionate about, attempting to stay anchored to your core worth. Is that easy or difficult to do? Are there other states besides inflation or deflation you get pulled into? For example, when trying this exercise around an important political issue, one group noticed the Guide getting pulled into urgency and fear. What other emotional states arise?

After exploring this exercise, notice your response to guidance, advice, information, or instructions offered in your daily life. What state of being are your teachers speaking from? Your boss? The politicians in the debates?

Use this exercise to become aware of the state of being you are in when you offer help or advice. Are you connected to your core worth when you help your first-grader with her homework or tell your teenager about the dangers of unprotected sex? When you fire off that irate e-mail at 2 A.M. or tell your lover just how to improve her job situation and general character? When you facilitate the meeting or present your plan for a new project?

When you catch yourself getting inflated or deflated, whether as a giver or as a receiver of help, make it a conscious practice to use your anchor and bring yourself back to your core worth. How does that change the situation? Sometimes simply speaking from your anchored state can shift the consciousness around you.

Rose receives guidance because of her generosity. She offers the old woman bread. She makes her offering before she receives anything in return, acting with true generosity, which is always what opens the door to great gifts. In our lives, too, when guidance comes we must offer something in return. We are not spoiled children, expecting everything to come to us with no expenditure of effort on our part; we are empowered people who have something to give, embarking on an initiatory journey. We can be empowered by help only when we give something back.

Those offerings may take many forms. We may give service to our communities or pass on help or offerings to someone else. We may find something we can do for our teacher directly. We may offer our time or our labor or something less tangible—our enthusiasm, our appreciation, our beginner's mind for a subject.

In mainstream society, every exchange of value is mediated by money, and money may be the offering of choice in exchange for teaching or counseling. No matter how ethereal the teaching, teachers cannot live on air. Money, like oxygen, permeates the very air we breathe in this society, and we cannot live in this time period without it. But our attitudes toward money are often much more highly charged than our attitudes toward air. Oxygen, after all, is fairly evenly distributed at any given altitude, and we all have access to it simply by breathing in. Money could perhaps be more realistically compared to water: it flows through society in tiny streams and broad rivers. Some people capture huge amounts of it behind dams; others wander desperately in search of a few spare drops to sustain life another day. Most of us live from springs that sometimes flow abundantly and at other times may run nearly dry. And to make money more problematic, our society equates it with value. When our water tank is empty and the spring is slow, we may find it hard to maintain our sense of personal pride and esteem. Not only is money identified with power; it often conveys power, both power over the lives of others and power in the sense of our ability to do something.

Because money is equated with value, we fear that if we do something for pay we will value only the money, that the money somehow diminishes the intrinsic value of the work. And because money is equated with power, we fear that those who have more money will wield more power. These fears arise whenever money comes up as a subject of discussion in our groups. While in many areas of our larger culture money confers status and those who have it want other people to know they have it, in alternative circles, money is often a source of embarrassment. We often avoid talking about it or dealing with it. We are far more comfortable disclosing the most intimate details of our sex lives than we are talking about money.

Money in relation to the community work we do becomes problematic because of all the attitudes discussed above. But more, as soon as we begin to discuss money for services rendered in the name of spirituality, we find ourselves wrestling with two basic deeply felt and often antithetical positions.

The first is that spiritual teaching and organizing should be an act of love and service. We shouldn't need or want monetary rewards for doing what the Goddess calls us to do, and money should never be the determining factor in what we offer.

The second is that work, if it is to be sustainable, needs to be rewarded. In a world where we all must have money to live, if an endeavor is to be sustainable over the long run, people need to get paid for their work.

The difficulty in resolving these positions is that both are morally right. Good arguments can be made for each.

Some of the arguments for the first position are that charging money may lead to teaching from greed and will make the material less accessible to those who need it most. Teaching and ritual making should be their own reward. The Goddess tradition is supposed to be a "religion of clergy": we should all be leaders, teachers; we should not professionalize the work of the Goddess. The mysteries are priceless. How can we assign them a monetary value without accepting the larger society's view of money as the determiner of all value?

Arguments for charging money might be that teaching and organizing in service to the community are "right livelihood." We all offer much unpaid service to the Goddess, but we all have to live as well. We may be able to do something occasionally on a volunteer basis, but if we are to do something consistently over time, we need it to contribute to our livelihood. Many religions hold out ideals of selfless service or ask for vows of poverty from those who join their religious orders, but in practice they also provide lifelong security for those people, be they nuns, monks, or priests. Our community does not. In order to devote a major portion of our time and energy to Goddess work, we need to be compensated. Our ideal is balance. To oppress ourselves in the name of serving others doesn't make sense.

For centuries, women have been kept dependent by the dominant society's definition of work in the home as something that should be done for love, not money. In practice, such work becomes devalued and is often not perceived as "real work." If we don't ask for compensation for our Goddess work, are we not falling into the same trap?

Many of us also believe that, just as Rose gave half her bread to the old woman, students need to give back something in order to retain their own self-esteem and sense of power in a learning situation. Eliminating money does not eliminate greed. A teacher who charges nothing may be getting payment in the form of adulation or dependence from her students. Money may actually make a transaction clearer and cleaner.

In reality, the structure of the broader Pagan community has changed greatly over the past thirty years. Once, it was true, only those truly dedicated and committed were willing to call themselves Witches, and the only public teaching that went on took the form of quiet meetings in someone's living room for the purpose of instructing new candidates for the coven. Today, the broader Pagan community has grown enormously and includes people of widely varying levels of knowledge and experience as well as differing levels of interest and commitment. We have the Pagan equivalent of "Christmas and Easter" Christians in those people who turn out for rituals only on Halloween. We have people who plan and organize seasonal rituals and others who only want to attend them. And we have public classes, camp-outs, festivals, workshops, magazines, Web pages, and intensives that cost money to put on and must generate a certain amount of money to be sustained over time.

In Reclaiming, money issues are often difficult to resolve because we do believe strongly in the validity of both positions described above. In reality, we achieve a rough and often inconsistent balance between the two. Following are some of the general guidelines we use. Most are not formal agreements reached through consensus; rather, they are simply what I've observed us do in practice:

- When we offer a class or workshop or ongoing program, setting aside specific times and places and preparing material, we charge money for it just as we would for teaching the violin or teaching at a university.
- We do not charge money for initiations or for any of the direct preparation that leads to an initiation. An initiation involves a close, personal commitment, a karmic bond comparable to marriage. We don't want initiation to depend on a candidate's ability to pay. And we want potential initiators to take on the task for love, not money—to be motivated only by a deep inner sense that they are the right mentors for this person.
- Organizational and administrative work deserves to be paid. This is our ideal, but in practice organizers often donate their time and skills in order to make an event happen.
- Teachers need to develop a certain level of skill and experience before they are paid for their work. Generally they apprentice by student teaching at least twice in the company of a more experienced person before they are paid for their work.
- Money should not be a barrier to learning or practicing the Craft. Events should be made accessible by providing scholarships, sliding scales, and work exchanges, and communities need to provide a variety of events so that there is always something available to those with low incomes. When we offer outdoor community rituals for the seasonal holidays, they are generally free, although we do pass a hat for donations. When we rent an indoor space, we generally need to charge money to cover our costs. Any extra is often donated to the community or to a specific cause.
- People generally do not get paid for creating, planning, or taking roles in community rituals. If a ritual becomes a major event that demands a

huge time commitment to organize, someone may be paid to coordinate the organizing.

- People do get paid for creating events—and for giving talks, workshops, or rituals—that require travel or time commitments beyond their home communities. So, for example, if I help to organize and create a Fire Protection Ritual with my neighbors for our area, we charge no money. We're doing work for ourselves, our homes, our friends and families. But if you want me to fly to Missoula and teach a weekend workshop titled "Fire: Energetic, Elemental, and Practical Aspects" that culminates in a Fire Protection Ritual, I would need to get paid.

- When people make money from work that is supported by community resources, they should give back to the community. If I teach classes advertised in Reclaiming's magazine, on its Web site and events line, and using material I learned myself in Reclaiming classes, I need to give back something, whether it is a formal tithe of money or a percentage of my time and energy, to support the larger organization. Because this book draws so heavily on the experience of an entire community, we are also giving back a percentage of our advance to Reclaiming programs.

None of these issues are simple, and our guidelines may not fit for you. Each group and organization needs to hold open and honest discussions about money. Ideally, you do this before it becomes a major issue or crisis.

Our attitudes to money are often tied to that difficult concept we call *class*—the constellation of resources, expectations, and assumptions we grew up in. Class, like Rose's missing brothers, is often not named or discussed, and when it does arise it is often in the context of judgment: "Your attitude is so middle-class!"

Issues of class are complex and subtle. Our unseen class assumptions may profoundly influence all our interactions around giving, receiving, and asking. Class, like ancestry, is another aspect of our heritage that needs to be made visible so that we may expand the range of our choices and know where healing is needed.

Again, one of the most powerful and nonjudgmental ways to approach issues of class and money is through telling our personal stories.

Telling Our Money Stories

In sacred space, give each person a protected time to talk. Tell your life story in terms of money. How much money did your family of origin have? What class did you consider yourselves?

What expectations did you have about money? About education and success? Have you met, exceeded, or betrayed those expectations?

What role has money played in your adult life? How do you earn it? What do you spend it on? What percentage do you give away to support causes and organizations you believe in? To those who have less than you do? Are you in debt? Do you feel that you have abundance? And, if this exercise is difficult, can you identify what makes it so hard to do? What state of being do you get pulled into by these questions? If you use your anchor and come back to your core worth, does anything shift?

If you are working alone, take time to discuss these questions in your journal, ideally writing on your money story two or three times a week for a moon cycle.

Money/Breath Exercise

Lie down in a comfortable position. Take a deep breath in, holding it as long as you can. When you are as full as you can possibly be, take in more air. Now, without letting the breath go, try to make a sound.

Relax; breathe normally for a few minutes. Now push all of the air out of your lungs. When they are as empty as they can be, push out some more air. Without inhaling, try to make a sound.

Relax; breathe normally again. Now, taking in as much air as you can, allow your breath to flow from inbreath to outbreath without stopping. Push out as much air as you can, and again, without stopping, let yourself take air in. Focus on flow and balance, and try to make a sound.

Now, in the group, take time to discuss how the exercise felt. (Or journal about it, if you are working alone.) Where in your life do you feel like you did during the first breath? Is there anywhere you are taking in too much—money, energy, stimulation, criticism, responsibility—without an outlet? How effective can you be in that state?

Is there anywhere in your life you are continually giving out without being replenished? How effective can you be in that state?

Where in your life is there a balance, a flow of giving and receiving? How deep do you let yourself take in? How far do you let yourself give out? How effective can you be in that state?

When you've looked at your own energy balance, consider that of your circle or community, and answer the same questions.

This exercise was suggested by John, who consults with major corporations. "I think of money as being like breath for a business," he told me once. "You need to take in enough to keep the business alive. Beyond that, you don't need to focus on it; you can focus on other things. Applying this principle to our lives and our enterprises, we need to receive enough to maintain ourselves and our projects so that we can honestly focus on our activities, with our whole hearts, without resentment and without sabotage of ourselves or others."

When we receive guidance and find that river, that right impulse, that true inspiration, we need to follow it to its end, to ride it to completion. In the context of ritual, this means letting the energy itself be our guide: letting a chant, a song, a moment of silence, or a roar of power go as far as it can go; following our inspiration; not backing off from intensity. Riding the river of energy, we create an *energy base*: a high, sustained base-level energy in the circle that allows healing, transformation, and ecstasy to arise.

Beverly is a dancer, yoga teacher, and gymnast who has brought her understanding of the power of movement into her teaching with Reclaiming. Following are two of her exercises:

Moving with Energy

You can do this exercise alone or in a group. In sacred space, put on some music you have chosen to help you re-create an emotional state you want to express. Or just begin by sounding together. Allow the music to move you. Take some time; then go deeper: stomp or wave your arms, or do whatever your body wants to do. Then go deeper still. Let go of the idea that anyone is watching you, and allow your movements to get larger and stronger.

An image or intense feeling may occur as you're moving or sounding. Don't stop, but continue to move and sound and explore, whether it's an image or a sensation or a releasing feeling that comes. Take it where you need to go, until you feel complete or exhausted.

This work usually comes to its own closure. In a group, people will finish in their own time. They may find a quiet spot to lie down and rest while waiting for others to complete their work. When all are done, take some time to rest. Then talk about what you experienced. How hard was it to get started? Did the sounds and movements of others help you or hold you back? What transformed?

"It's important at the end of any nonverbal exercise to leave time to bring it back into the verbal," Beverly says. "Otherwise, like a dream, the memory and insights tend to float away."

Symphony of Sounds: Building an Energy Base

Beverly uses this exercise in a group to deepen people's connection and ability to listen so they can work together as an ensemble. It's also a powerful way of building an *energy base* in a ritual—a level of sustained power from which healing and transformation can happen in many ways.

One person begins by repeating a simple sound again and again. It's important that the first person be rhythmically consistent. She or he doesn't have to be a great drummer or singer, just able to keep a strong, steady beat.

As people are moved, they begin to add their voices. The first person or perhaps a pair hold the pulse. Others can improvise and change their sounds as the energy develops.

The sounding may peak and resolve itself, or it may become a base energy for a more elaborate ritual.

This exercise can also be done with drums instead of or along with voices.

Beverly sometimes precedes this exercise with a period of time in which people are asked to go out and observe nature. "The last time I structured it that way," she says, "we got a symphony of sighs."

Following an Energy

Jeffrey Alphonsus is a gifted drummer, musician, and performance artist, an activist and Witchcamp teacher. He offers the following exercise for building and following an energy as a group.

In sacred space, start in silence, standing still, breathing normally. Slowly, each person begins a movement that is at first very internal. As the stillness deepens, open to a fuller breath, and begin slowly letting the movement become more external. Continue letting the breath grow more full and the movement bigger. Begin letting out sound, and let the sound and movement build. Take time to just sound and sing, hearing the song that emerges. Then begin saying simply, "I am," letting that be enough as it becomes a chant. (Alternatively, you might use "I see" or "I want.") After a time, encourage people to say something that they are, something affirming: "I am this"; "I am that"; or "I see this"; or "I want that." The group affirms each statement, saying, "Oh yeah!" It's the good old gospel idea. Then add hand clapping, so that "I am this" becomes a call and response with a chorus of "Oh yeah!" When everyone has had the experience of affirming themselves, raise the energy, hold the tone together until it becomes a cone of power, and then bring it back down and ground it.

Finding the Song of the Moment

Suzanne is a dancer, singer, and musician who has a special gift for helping people find their voice. This exercise helps us learn to follow an impulse through sound and voice:

In sacred space, have paper and pens available. Create an energy base. Move, sing, dance, or drum until the group is in a light trance state. Then stop and simply write whatever comes through, without censoring or stopping, just letting your hand and words flow in "automatic" writing.

Gather the circle together, and give each person a chance to read her or his writing to the group.

Now each person picks one sentence to sing. All sing simultaneously, and at first the sound may be chaotic. Sing each sentence over and over, improvise, echo and sing each others' pieces as well as your own. Eventually, one or two major pieces will emerge and weave together to form the song of the moment.

"It takes a lot of repetition and exploration to get to the song," Suzanne says. "The process is very much like songwriting, in that ideas set to music become distilled and focused."

Sacred Voice

When we lead or guide a ritual or trance, our own voice serves as the river. Participants may flow along with us, being guided toward the intention and purpose of the ritual. When we are conscious of which voice we choose, we can create a ritual that has rich texture and variety. It's helpful to think about both invocations and the central section—the "meat" or, in deference to vegetarians, the "tofu"—of the ritual as encompassing a variety of voices.

Donald, one of our Witchcamp teachers from the Midwest, has many years of experience leading rituals in a variety of settings, from gay men's circles to art installations. He has helped identify some of what he calls "the Sacred Voices":

SILENCE: Movement, moments of silence, simple presence can sometimes be far more powerful than words.

WHISPERING: Want to know a secret? When a ritual priestess whispers in your ear, you know you are hearing a mystery.

TRANCE VOICE: Just a little more rhythmic, a little more resonant, a little less variable in tone, this voice moves people into trance. Trance voice is also useful for linking elements in ritual. If you need to give instructions in the midst of a ritual, try speaking in trance voice. They will seem much more like part of the magic.

NORMAL TALKING: Normal speech in ritual creates a great sense of intimacy and immediacy. Shifting from trance voice to normal talking in the midst of a guided meditation helps keep people awake and focused and can deepen the emotional tone of the work.

LOUD TALKING: Sometimes we just need to be heard. Vocal work and practice can help you be loud without simply shouting at people. Breathe deep from your belly, open your throat, and visualize your voice reaching the farthest point of the circle.

POETIC CHANT: Something between trance voice and a bad imitation of Allen Ginsberg reading *Howl*. Rhythmic; often useful for the parts of a trance that are repeated.

CALL AND RESPONSE/REVIVAL: Southern Baptist preachers are the masters at this kind of energy-raising, rhythmic speech.

SONG: Not just chants and songs, but invocations and parts of meditations, can be sung.

There are also voices we like to avoid in ritual: the Voice of Authority, the Nursery School Teacher, Whining, Mumbling, and so forth.

Voice Practice

1. Volunteers invoke the directions, each choosing a different voice.
2. Choose a text: "The Charge of the Goddess," "The Reclaiming Principles of Unity," or something from this book. As the leader calls out different voices, each person reads two or three lines in that voice.
3. Repeat the exercise above, but this time each person reads four or five lines, first matching the tone of the person before and gradually shifting into a new voice.

Leading Trance/Trance Induction

The image of the river is a helpful one to hold in our minds when we lead a meditation, a guided visualization, or a trance. In some sense, these terms are nearly interchangeable: a trance is simply an intensified guided visualization, a more clearly directed meditation.

While we include scripts for trances in this book, we don't recommend that you read them aloud, rather that you use them as a loose structure around which to improvise your own journey, so that the work stays alive. When guiding a trance, let your voice flow, soft and rhythmic. Begin with an induction, an image that moves people into a deep, internal state and shifts their focus away from the external world. One very simple one I might use is:

Take a deep breath now, and let your breath flow in and out of your lungs. And as you breathe, you become aware of your body, aware of that place between breaths where your breath begins and ends. And you feel yourself sinking down there, as you breathe, down and down, into a deep place, an inner place of power where you can be in touch with the deepest parts of yourself. And your breath is carrying you, down and down. Let's take three deep breaths together, in and out, linking our breath, flowing down, in and out, deeper and deeper, in and out, until you reach that deep place within which is the beginning of breath.

And you feel what lies beneath your feet in this place, what you stand on. Breathe in and smell the air of this place. Hear what sounds surround you. Open your inner eyes, and turn to the east, and notice what you see and hear and feel and sense.

[Pause.]

And you turn to the south, and notice what you see and hear and feel and sense.

[Pause.]

And you turn to the west, and notice what you see and hear and feel and sense.

[Pause.]

And you turn to the north, and notice what you see and hear and feel and sense.

[Pause.]

And you turn to the center, and notice what you see and hear and feel and sense.

[Pause.]

And now you've arrived, in your own inner place of power.

In the induction above, we use many linking words such as *and* to connect our sentences. We use rhythm and repetition to help move us into trance. Many of our directions are phrased as statements rather than commands: "And you turn . . ." rather than "Turn . . ."

Part of the art of trance is to create just enough structure—but not too much—to guide participants through a landscape, leaving them free to experience it as it appears to them. So we may ask them to turn to the four directions, but not describe in detail what they might see. We might suggest that their feet will find a path and ask them how that path feels underfoot, but not tell them that it is smooth, rocky, or slippery unless that is an important element of the work. Remember, the trance belongs to the person experiencing it, not to the guide.

We should also avoid the temptation to interpret the images or stories for people as we guide them or to tell people what meaning they should take from the symbols we offer. "And as you flow downstream, you become aware of a block, and you feel what that is for you"; not "You become aware of all your childhood pain blocking your flow." William Carlos Williams said poetry should contain "no ideas, but in things." The same holds true for a trance: embody your intention in concrete images, lead people through the landscape of those images, but leave them free to draw their own interpretations.

Beware of inflation and deflation when guiding trance. A deflated mono- tone becomes simply boring. Trance voice spoken in a state of inflation becomes the Thunderous Voice of the Authority Echoing in the Cathedral. Use your anchor to your core worth.

In the body of the trance, an experienced leader may shift voices, dropping into normal speech for intimacy, rising into poetic chant, raising energy with call and response, letting speech flow into song. Just as a river may sometimes meander and sometimes rush headlong over rapids, a trance flows best when we vary pace and tone but keep a strong, underlying rhythmic pulse.

When we are done with trance, we reverse the induction:

Now take a deep breath, and look around in your place of power. As you say good-bye, notice if there's an image you can remember to help you come back here again. And remember you can return here whenever you need to or want to.

And you turn to the center, and notice what you hear and sense and see and feel, and you notice if anything has changed. And you say good-bye.

[Pause.]

And you turn to the north, and notice what you hear and sense and see and feel, and you notice if anything has changed. And you say good-bye.

[Pause.]

And you turn to the west, and notice what you hear and sense and see and feel, and you notice if anything has changed. And you say good-bye.

[Pause.]

And you turn to the south, and notice what you hear and sense and see and feel, and you notice if anything has changed. And you say good-bye.

[Pause.]

And you turn to the east, and notice what you hear and sense and see and feel, and you notice if anything has changed. And you say good-bye.

[Pause.]

And now we're going to take three deep breaths together, breathing in and out, coming back slowly, up and up, in and out, and remembering what you've learned on this journey, in and out, and returning to this circle, this place and time. And now open your eyes, and pat the edges of your body. Clap your hands three times, and say your own name out loud. And that's the end of the story.

Spontaneous Ritual: Following the River

After completing the energy exercises and the other work of this chapter, again clarify an intention and perform a ritual in your anchored, core state and in dropped and open attention. This time, commit yourselves to be conscious both of initiating actions and of supporting the ideas of others. Be aware of which voices you use, and how they affect the energy. Follow each energy impulse to its end. Notice what changes.

We have wandered in the wilderness and followed the river to its end. There, if we are lucky, we will hear the beat of wings in the air, just at sunset, and meet our brothers on the shore.

THREE

The Wicked Vow

Comments on the Story

Rose reaches the river's mouth, and there she finds her brothers. They are swans by day, but at night reassume the form of men. When the brothers realize who she is, they weep and wail, because they have made a vow to kill the first young girl they meet as a revenge for their misfortune. But the Old Woman appears again, to say, "Break that wicked vow, which you never should have made!" Relieved and happy, the brothers agree.

The brothers are undergoing their own initiatory journey. Swans by day and men by night, they live on the boundary between the human and the wild. They are shamans, who mediate between the human and nonhuman realms.

In one sense, the brothers are entrapped in a divine possession. The Bird Goddess is one of the most ancient forms of the Goddess. Birds fly between earth and sky, linking vision to grounding. Water birds such as swans also link the life-giving waters to sky and land. Their long necks remind us of snakes, another ancient symbol of the Goddess of rebirth and regeneration. The brothers have become incarnations of the Bird Goddess's transformative power. But they are stuck halfway, neither divine nor mortal. The knowledge and power they acquire as swans is not yet useful to them. Until they regain their true form and return to the human community, they cannot integrate the wisdom of the wild.

Their vow is "wicked," a word that comes from the Anglo-Saxon root *wic-* or *weg-*, related to *Witch*. *Wic-* means to bend or twist. Willow branches are pliable and can be twisted into "wicker" baskets. Just as we can bend and change reality to create healing, so we can, through ignorance or fear, twist fate in the other direction, away from healing and balance.

As swans, the brothers have attempted to redress the imbalance and injustice of their transformation. Since it was for the sake of a girl that they were transformed, they will kill the first girl they meet. A brutal sort of fairness is at work here, and when they do meet Rose, they feel deep remorse. Their commitment to revenge will cause them not only to murder their beloved sister, but to destroy the one being that can potentially restore their humanity.

Revenge is not true power. To become empowered, we must acknowledge and relinquish that part of each of us that wants to get even. We cannot truly restore balance by equalizing the pain; we must undertake the longer and more difficult journey of healing.

Rose must simply stand her ground. She has persevered; she has succeeded in the first stage of her task by finding her brothers. Now she must withstand their rage at the fact that her life was chosen over theirs.

In general in our society, men are preferred over women. In this story that pattern is reversed. Rose, the daughter, is preferred over her brothers. She is the most loved and privileged one. Her task is what women ask of men, what all oppressed groups from time to time demand of those who have been their oppressors: to hear the rage and the pain, to witness without personalizing or defending, without needing to affirm that men have been oppressed too, or that rich people also have their problems. She is not asked to let herself be killed, but simply to hear that her brothers long to kill her.

At this moment, the old woman appears. In a triumph of common sense she tells the brothers to simply break their vow. We're not caught here in a Greek tragedy, where vows and prophecies work their destruction in spite of human will and intention. We're in a different realm, where freedom is a possibility, where the power we've already gathered on our magical journey allows us, if we choose, to break the negative patterns of the past.

The old woman holds the authority to release the brothers' vow, presumably because they have made it to her, the Old One, the Crone. Blood sacrifice is not what the Goddess wants. She is presiding over an initiation, not a slaughter. The brothers cannot be redeemed by Rose's death or martyrdom, only by her life and willing assumption of the task of healing.

The work of this section of the story is to learn to handle fire, to understand energy in its intense forms, to withstand and transform anger and rage, relinquish revenge, and hold our ground.

The Elements Path

Rose has learned to live in the wild and to find and follow guidance. Now the stream leads her to her brothers. She vowed to find and free them, little thinking that they would have their own reaction to the injustice of their plight. They've vowed, in revenge, to kill the first young girl they meet. In order to let themselves be helped, the swan brothers will have to give up their vow of revenge. The Elements Path work for this section of the story requires us to look into our own spiritual pasts for any resentment and bitterness we may feel. Where we find anger, we will have an opportunity to express it, release it, and channel it into creativity. Then we will be introduced to the element fire and the magical tools that correspond with fire.

Women and men who choose to explore the path of the Goddess make a conscious choice to step away from mainstream culture and many of its values. Each of us has her reasons for making this challenging choice. Like Rose's brothers, we may have suffered because our gender, our ancestry, our class position may not have been the preferred one. Many of us may be appalled by a culture that sacrifices the delicate webs of nature and of human community again and again in favor of profit for a few. Many of us may be deeply disturbed by a culture that allows, assumes, and creates imprisonment, addiction, poverty, madness, and violence at the rates our society does. We long for a culture that values each and every member; we long for justice; we long for a nurturing guardianship of nature and for one another. We long for art, for love, for devotion, for play, for community, for healing. We long to create a culture where these are the most highly valued.

Like Rose's brothers, we may be angry. In fact, we may be very angry at previous spiritual teachings we have received or values we may have been exposed to. In order to step onto the path of the Goddess tradition, we must take a good look at ourselves. Because if we want to truly embrace a spiritual practice where the only law is love and respect for all life and all natural processes, we must find a way to take our anger and channel it away from revenge, bitterness, and hopelessness, and toward creativity. If our anger ties us to the past and stands in the way of a fresh, effective, loving engagement with our world, we, like the swan brothers, have to find a way to break our wicked vows.

Honoring Our Anger

Anger is like a forest fire that scours the landscape clean of the old and creates the hot temperatures needed to crack open seeds and pinecones. The ashes of the old, unhealthy forest create intense fertility to bring a whole new ecosystem to life. But before new growth can begin, the soil must be cooled and moistened by the rain and must lie resting under the snow. Spring and the wild and luxuriant growth that follows can come only with time.

The heat of anger and resistance are nature's way of raising energy for needed change, and so they are blessed and welcome. But they are only part of the foundation for a spiritual way of life that will help us through a whole lifetime, with the subtle and complex changes of all our seasons. We will have times when anger powers us to struggle and create change, but we will also have our times of recovering from illness and injury, our times of absorbed creativity and fun, and our times of barely keeping up with rapid and demanding transition. We will have our times of grief and our times of reflection.

The aged, overgrown forest, the wildness of the fire, and the springing of the new green all depend on the mountain, and the mountain is unmoved. So in order to cleanse and open our deepest selves to a Goddess who will give us a strong foundation for a whole life, it is best to cleanse ourselves of anger and bitterness, which may only bind us to past injustices. For health, we need to base our spiritual practice on all the moods and faces of our emotional lives, not only on our anger, no matter how justified it may be. Here is a ritual that will allow our anger to speak and that will allow us to reshape its energy, if we choose to do so.

Anger Ritual

When honestly facing our feelings about our past experiences with spirituality, we have to start by allowing the feelings themselves to arise. We may be angry over injustices we have experienced, or ways we've been misunderstood, or things we've been told or taught that we believe are wrong. If we've been angry, we've often had to numb ourselves to those feelings of anger in order to survive in a culture hostile or indifferent to our soul-lives.

This ritual raises and releases feelings of anger and the hurt and grief that may underlie them. It is intended to be done in a group, but it can be adapted for solitary work. This ritual works best outdoors, around a fire. Before the ritual begins, go over the plan so that everyone understands what is going to happen and why. Then ask the question, What feelings do you need to release about your own spiritual past? Give each participant time to wander in the area and find a stick to represent what she or he wants to release.

Gather; create sacred space. Take time to focus on the stick, breathing in the pain, the rage, or the hurt you want to release. Gradually let your breath become a sound, and build a base of energy from the chorus of sounds that arise. Some people may want to use words. Let the energy move you into a dance, counterclockwise around the fire. The sounds may coalesce into a chant or remain wordless. One by one, as you are ready, throw your sticks into the fire. You might scream or shout out what you want to release.

When everyone has had a chance to toss their sticks, allow the sounds to peak. Visualize the fire transforming rage into creative energy. When the energy quiets, allow a time of silence, to gaze into the fire and reflect on the passion and creativity that can arise when rage is transformed. Breathe in that power from the flames. Each of you may speak of something you want to bring into your life, moving clockwise around the circle.

When each person has spoken, food and drink may be blessed and passed around. Allow some time for informal visiting, and when everyone is ready, open the circle.

Ritual: Breaking the Wicked Vow, Affirming the Wonderful Ones

Here is another ritual we can use to release whatever burdens from the past we do not wish to keep carrying. Again, this purification is not meant to sugar-coat, or excuse, or allow, or even forget past injustices, but rather to free us from any bitterness or hopelessness we may feel because of them. Like Rose's brothers, we must break the wicked vow that binds us to our past. We are stepping out onto the path of a new spiritual practice, and we need to make peace with our past spiritual experiences.

Take your time, and think back on your own spiritual background. Were you raised in a mainstream religion? How about the values in your home, in your schools, and in the media? What were your experiences and feelings? Try to remember both the disturbing and the comforting parts, if you experienced both. Were you taught, directly or indirectly, ideas that valued some people over others? That valued people over nature? If you were raised outside mainstream religions, what values were you taught directly or indirectly? What was disturbing, what affirming? As an adult, what experiences and feelings have you had about religions and spiritual practices? How have you developed your values? Why have you chosen to explore the Goddess traditions?

Take the time to write down your insights, memories, and feelings as they come up. As you work, begin to sort through these treasures of self-knowledge. There may be some thoughts and feelings that you know you would like to be free of. There may be some that you are uncomfortable with, or unsure about. And there may be some that you value highly and want to keep forever.

Once you have found out what you think and feel, and have sorted through it, it's time to do something about it. At your altar, solitary, or in circle with friends, create sacred space. Make salt water, and do a saltwater purification to release the thoughts, feelings, and values that you know you don't want to keep carrying. We all have some of these. They may have remained unexamined for decades, and they may sound childish or stupid when you say them out loud. But it's important to state them, or shout them, or weep them, as clearly as you can, into the salt water, and release them with sounds, gestures, emotion, as fully as you are able.

Now take the thoughts and feelings and values that you aren't sure about, and whisper them into a pebble or shell, or write them on a slip of paper, and put them in a special box or bowl or basket that you can cover, and place it on your altar for now. Ask the Goddess to work on them for you and clarify them for you. Plan to check your box or basket in a month or so, knowing that your feelings about the contents will have changed. For now, resolve to let them rest in capable hands and not to worry yourself about them.

Now break out the art supplies, and make something beautiful and pleasing for yourself, a spell to celebrate the wonderful values you found within yourself. If you are working in circle, it's fun to sing or hum a chant together while you do art projects and spells. You could make a collage, a diorama in a shoe box, a self-portrait, or a fancy diploma from the School of Hard Knocks. Use your imagination and please Younger Self. Include through images, and colors, and prayers, and writing, the thoughts, feelings, and values you found that you are proud of and that you want to keep forever. You may find yourself feeling unexpected gratitude toward long-forgotten teachers and elders or toward the treasures of mystic awareness and love hidden in the doctrines of a religion or tradition you have walked away from for other reasons.

Thank the powers, and open the circle. Now dispose of the salt water mindfully, knowing that as the salt water makes its journey toward the sea, so you will feel the old, restricting thoughts and feelings waning in you. (Incidentally, salt water can kill plants and sterilize soil, so it's usually best not to dump salt water into soil.) Place the box or basket of questions, and the artwork you have made to honor your values, on your altar or on your circle's altar.

The Element Fire

The image of Rose, confronted by her hurt, angry brothers, bearing the heat of their frustration and rage, brings us to the study of the element fire. Magical techniques traditionally associated with fire include sensing, projecting, and shielding energy, and healing. The tool of fire is the wand. The power of the wise in the south is "to will."

Witches (and modern physicists and mystics of all religious backgrounds) regard the physical world we know as a complex illusion, one that our minds create because we cannot directly perceive the incredible detail of the truth.

Our human brains are organized to perceive the world as an assortment of separate and static objects, when it is actually more like a continuous web of energies in constant motion and harmony. We ourselves appear to be physical objects, bodies, but we are in fact a swirl or standing wave in an energy pattern that is connected to all creation.

Our bodies, which may appear to be still, are surrounded and interpenetrated by an energy "body" somewhat larger than our physical body, one that is never still. Witches refer to this energy body as the *aura*. The Reclaiming tradition (drawing on the Feri tradition of magic) describes our energy body as cohabited by three souls: Talking Self, Younger Self, and Deep Self. The three souls are bound together for a lifetime with each other and with the physical body of the individual. The foundation of the health and the energy of an individual is the harmony of these three souls with each other and with the individual's energy and physical bodies. A basic principle of magic is that changes in the energy body can create changes in the physical body, and vice versa.

The idea that we have energy bodies, or that our bodies create energy fields larger than our physical bodies, is really common sense and widely understood. It's expressed in ordinary language by phrases like "I need some space" or "You're getting in my space." Often these phrases are used when no one is really touching, to describe the physical discomfort of having someone else standing or moving into the area occupied by one's energy body. Just remember the last time you were on a crowded bus or train with someone's elbow almost touching your armpit and someone else almost snuggled up against your back.

If you've ever seen a magnet in a field of iron filings, you've also "seen" an aura. As the iron filings respond to the force of the magnet, they create shapes and swirls following the lines of the electromagnetic force field created by the magnet. Our bodies, and the bodies of plants, animals, and minerals, are also generating mild electromagnetic force fields. These force fields aren't going to move iron filings, but they are very real, and they can be perceived.

Fire: Working "As If"

Some people perceive energy visually, some kinetically, and some as sensory or even auditory impressions. When we pick up psychic or intuitive information from our environment, it tends to translate itself as though it were information being picked up by one of the physical senses. So some people hear voices or words in their heads, others "see" color or movement, others receive strong dreamlike images or story fragments or strong sensory impressions such as heat or cold or vibration. There is also a "bleed-through" of senses, where we seem to "see" with our fingertips, "hear" with our eyes, and so on.

A very important part of learning how to open up to intuition and psychic information is to suspend the critical voice that discounts these impressions as silly. "Purple ants aren't having a picnic in your lower belly. That's ridiculous," says the critical voice. But Rose May Dance, a Reclaiming Witch and teacher who has taught many students to perceive energy, says, "You have to be willing to work 'as if.'" In other words, if we can learn to hold the possibility of many different forms of perception, maybe purple ants both are, and aren't, having a picnic inside our bellies. On one level, of course, it's not "real." On another level, Younger Self is trying her hardest to talk to us in a sensory language that we only dimly understand. Why not try these exercises "as if" you could read auras and effect change on an energetic level?

If you are willing to try practicing "as if," the following exercises can help you begin to perceive your own and other people's energy bodies. We will use several different perceptive modes—visual, sensory, kinetic—to try to open the "doors of perception."

Fire Exercise: The Candle

At your altar, create sacred space. Light a candle and gaze at the flame. Imagine that as the flame surrounds the wick, so a living, dancing energy body surrounds your physical body. Dance with the candle flame, echo its movements, feel how alive you are. Say, "By the fire of her bright spirit." Thank the powers, and open the circle.

Fire Exercise: The Hairbrush

This exercise works best if you can do it with a friend and alternate roles. In circle, you can take turns pairing with each other. It can also be done by yourself.

You will need a hairbrush. Create sacred space. First just ease your fingers into your friend's hair, and feel her scalp. Relax; slow yourself down until you can sense the life pulsing beneath your fingers. Begin to groom her hair and massage her scalp with your fingers, making sure it feels good to her, too. When you're ready, begin using the hairbrush. Notice that you can still feel her life pulsing, even though you are no longer touching her directly. If it's difficult to feel, simply relax and breathe more deeply. Reground if necessary. Chanting something simple together may help.

When you can feel her energy clearly while brushing her hair, put the brush aside, and simply use your hands, open as if you were warming them at a fire, in the area around her head and neck and shoulders where you have been brushing. Can you still feel her energy body pulsing under your hands? Can you feel it changing and moving subtly like the candle flame? Can you feel hot spots and cool spots, tight zingy spots, and dead spots? Everyone experiences these sensations slightly differently. What matters right now is how *you* experience them. It's OK if the sensations are very subtle. With practice you will notice them much more easily.

Fire Exercise: Seeing Auras

Every so often, I'll meet someone who has always seen auras. Some people apparently see them quite easily, even involuntarily. Others have to work at it, but it is possible to learn to see auras by practicing. Here are some suggestions from Rose May Dance on how to learn to see auras.

The ideal way to practice is in half-light or candlelight, with a friend. Very bright light can sometimes work also. Ask your friend to stand against a plain, white or light-colored wall, or if that's not available, you can drape a plain, light-colored sheet behind her.

Try several different eye tricks to open your perception. First, rub up a little energy in your hands, and then cup your hands over your eyes, so that you have a completely dark, compressed interior vision. Squeeze your eyes tightly a few times. Most people will begin to see shapes and dots of etheric color floating and dancing in their inner vision. Now open your eyes and look at your friend standing against the white wall. Do you see a shape around her and somewhat larger than her physical body, transparent but visually dense and full of movement and etheric colors, similar to what you saw with your eyes closed?

A second eye trick is to look at your friend and either blink very rapidly or stare without blinking at all. In either case you may begin to get a visual impression of her aura as if it were arising out of her skin. Or, without moving your head, look up at your friend, then quickly away, then up again, repeating several times. Her aura will spring into place.

I had to work "as if" and practice seeing energy for years before it first clicked in and worked effortlessly. As a matter of fact, I had my first experience seeing auras involuntarily when I was ill with a high fever. Traditional shamanic training in some cultures opens "the doors of perception" with the use of hallucinogenic plant medicines. Reclaiming tradition recommends psychic exercise and practice to achieve the same results.

Fire Exercise: The Brushdown

Brushing down a friend's aura is a fun and helpful exercise for beginners learning how to work with energy. There's nothing like getting your hair done, or your nails done, or your aura done, by a friend! Here is how Starhawk teaches a brushdown, a basic energy-body grooming.

The brushdown is a basic psychic cleansing technique, useful whenever you've done deep work with someone. It can help us separate when we've merged too deeply, clear out anything we might have picked up, and release anything that might have been directed toward us in a tense situation. And it's quick and simple: just chop, comb, and fluff! Have your friend stand in front of you. Using both hands, chop up her aura with quick motions. Be sure to get the area above her head, and don't forget her back and her feet.

Now comb out your friend's aura, using your fingers as the teeth of the comb. Imagine pulling out any negative, slimy, sick energies, and flick them off either into the earth, into compost, or into a fire or running water.

Finally, shake off your hands, and then fluff your friend's aura with a motion somewhat like back-combing a beehive hairdo. When you're done, shake out your hands and notice how shiny clean her energy looks.

You can do a brushdown for yourself, too. I often do one in the shower at the end of the day to cleanse psychically as well as physically, or I do it quickly in the bathroom in the midst of a tense meeting.

Fire Exercise: Aura Car Wash

In a group, form two lines. The first two or three pairs will chop, the next will comb, and the last will fluff. One by one, each person walks down the center to be cleansed, and then joins a line. As the lines move up, change tasks as needed.

Starhawk tells this story about the "aura car wash" in jail.

"My favorite aura car wash took place in jail. I was in a cell block with twenty women who had all been arrested after protesting the World Trade Organization meeting in Seattle in 1999. We'd been held for five days and were finally waiting to be released—exhausted, tired, and impatient as the process was taking long hours. One woman had begun leading us all in massage when we heard the guard's voice over the loudspeaker: 'Ladies! We are in jail!' she admonished us. We had, in fact, noticed this already. 'In jail, we keep our hands to ourselves. We don't touch each other!'

"As we'd been exchanging massages for five days, we were somewhat surprised to hear this information. A few of the women were starting to argue, so I suggested an aura car wash. When we were about halfway through, we heard the same authoritarian voice crackling over the loudspeaker: 'Ladies!' it announced. 'Aura cleansing is all right! Just no touching!'"

Fire Exercise: Healing

Healing is another important part of energy work. For beginners, the best place to start experimenting with healing work is on oneself. The energy that we use for healing is not our personal energy; it does not come out of our own bodies. We connect with the great energy of the natural world and allow it to move through us; in this way we can use tremendous energy in healing without depleting ourselves personally. So the beginning of any healing work is a thorough grounding.

In sacred space, use the "Tree of Life" meditation to establish a strong connection to the energies of the earth and the sky. When you feel them moving through you, hold your hands out comfortably in front of you, palms up. Feel how the earth and sky energy that is pouring through you fills up your hands, pooling, spiraling, and overflowing. Now clap your hands together, and rub them as if you were trying to get warmer. Can you feel a little ball of energy beginning to glow between your hands? It may take a few tries. When you can feel it, blow on it, as you would on a bed of coals to start a fire, and keep rubbing until you feel a nice, warm ball of earth and sky energy glowing between your hands.

Now take what you've made and put it into your own body, into some part of you that could use a little extra healing energy. Feel it moving into your physical body and glowing there, doing what is needed for that part of your body, softening or strengthening, warming or cooling, cleansing or toning.

Fire Exercise: Healing with a Partner

When we do healing work on someone else, or receive healing, we are also working with the energy of the natural world, not our own personal energy. With a partner, begin by deciding which of you will first be the receiver and which the healer. We will do this exercise twice, switching roles.

In healing, we can simplify the work into two stages: first we take something out; then we put something in. It's very important that the two partners explore the receiver's images about her body and her health, and work together to develop one or two strong images to work with. For example, "I feel as though there is a cold fog in my chest and lungs. I want to move the cold fog out and put a tiny glowing yellow sun in my chest to dry up my cold."

Begin by doing a "Tree of Life" meditation. Follow this with an aura-sensing exercise, so that both partners have a chance to explore and sense one another's auras, awakening their intuition. Now the healer can begin to "comb," pulling handfuls of cold fog out of your partner's aura. Let your hands do the work, "playing" at pulling out stuck energies and shaking out your hands, shaking off the unhealthy energies. Shake these off into a bowl of salt water, or into a candle flame. Or you create a strong image for yourself of running water draining into a hole in the floor, or a very hot fire, or the transforming, consuming darkness of earth. Literally throw the handfuls of fog into one of these, and shake off your hands as if you were shaking water off them. See the unhealthy energy disappearing into the power of the element.

When you and your partner feel that you have created some movement in the fog and some free space in her chest, you may be ready to put the tiny yellow sun energy into her chest. Whenever you create space, or an opening, in healing work, be sure to fill it with something the receiver wants. Otherwise the next strong influence the person runs into may fill the empty space.

The healer can begin sending energy into the receiver through the agreed-upon image—in this case, the tiny sun. If you want to move to touching the receiver's body, be sure to ask her permission, and keep checking to make sure your touch is welcome and feels good. No one should attempt physical manipulations or more than light massage unless they are trained in those areas. But you might, in this example, want to lay your hands on her chest, one in front and one in back, and strongly visualize the energy flowing through your hands and into the tiny sun in her chest. Keep communicating about the image, the sensations, and the timing. In this kind of healing work, the receiver needs to be in charge; she is the authority on herself.

The session does not need to be lengthy. A short time of truly focused energy exchange is more helpful than a long time with the concentration of the partners wavering. When you feel ready, bring the session to a close, and do an aura brushdown on each other to fully separate your two energy bodies. Switch, and let the other person become the healer.

Please be very alert to power dynamics between the two of you. We are handicapped by a culture that gives all the power in a healing interaction to the healer. We need to be alert to our own grandiosity when we are in the role of healer, and our own helplessness when we are in the role of receiver.

If you wish to do healing work on a person who is not present, get her permission and discuss with her the images she is working with for her own healing. Then you can work with a strong visualization of the person, or you can put the energies that she wants to receive into an object and send it to her.

Shielding

Now that we have some sense of our energy bodies and what they can do, we need to look at the skill of protecting or shielding our energy bodies. In our story, Rose must withstand the blame and anger her brothers direct at her until the Old Woman can arrive to save the day. We are no different. Just as we sometimes need to protect our physical body, we sometimes need to protect our energy bodies. The pointing finger of an angry adversary, their dirty looks, their tone of speech can actually hurt even if we haven't been touched. We deserve protection from this kind of attack.

Each of us feels intuitively that we take up a certain amount of space, a space larger than our physical bodies. With a little exploration, we can feel how big that space is and where its boundaries are. Let's use the image from biology of a living cell, the smallest unit of life. The structures of the cell are suspended in a living field that is bounded by a cell wall, just as my physical body exists in an energy field that has its own natural boundaries. A cell's wall can both protect the contents of the cell and also allow nutrients to cross into the cell. In high school biology we were told that this was a "semi-permeable membrane," which means some things can penetrate it and others can't.

This is an ideal image for the shielding that I want to be able to create on the boundaries of my energy body. I want to be able to take in, for example, information, inspiration, beauty, and love without taking in hostility, unfair criticism, hopelessness, and so forth. So I might imagine my "cell wall" as made out of a rubbery, resilient material that protects my energy body, with selective, star-shaped openings in it, so that the good things I want and need from my environment can get in quite easily. In an emergency, faced with hot aggression or shredding criticism, I might change my image to one of a mirrored surface that sends incoming energy back where it came from. With someone I love, I might choose a surface similar to a flower petal—soft, receptive, and organic. If images aren't working that day, I can simply tell my boundaries what I want them to do: "Please filter out any jealous or vengeful energy coming my way today" or "Please alert me if I meet a person who might become a truly sympathetic friend."

Fire Exercise: Shielding

With a partner, in sacred space choose a criticism or attack that you know for sure is inaccurate. Pick something goofy and irrelevant to start with, like "You're always wasting our money on your sled-dog team" (apologies to anyone who keeps sled dogs) or "I hate it when you dress like Scarlett O'Hara" (apologies to anyone who does so). Use the candle-flame meditation described earlier to awaken your sense of your energy body; then find your boundaries, and shield them with a strong protective image. Now ask your partner to attack you in the agreed-upon way. Depending on the image you are using, see if you can actually feel the attack bounce or reflect or bead up and run off your shield. Try several different images for your protective surface, and see which works best for you. Now switch, and let the other person try it.

Fire: Giving Back

It's important for us to consider giving something back to the element of fire, just as we have with the element air. Do you know where the power in your home comes from? Are these renewable energy sources? Do they pollute? How about the power for your transportation?

How about the energy in your own body? Do you renew your own energy sources with nutritious food, rest, and exercise? Do you get enough fun to keep the twinkle in your eye and the spring in your step? How about great sex? That's an excellent renewable energy source. Decide on one concrete way in which you can make change for the better in the energy flow of your life; and when you use energy, which is always, make sure you give something back.

Like Rose and her brothers, we have traveled to the salty, desolate shore where we faced our anger. Where we found that we had made wicked vows, binding us to past injustice, creating bitterness and revenge, we found the courage to break them. We learned to become aware of, and care for, and protect our energy bodies. We have begun a right relation with the element of fire. Now we are ready to take the next step in our journey.

The Inner Path

Rose follows the stream and finds her brothers. But instead of being greeted like the heroic rescuer, she finds that in their bitterness her brothers have resolved to kill the first young girl they meet as revenge for their plight. They, too, are trying to restore balance in their world. Although we may be horrified by their resolve, it rings true. It is a familiar human impulse to want to get back at someone who has caused harm. When we experience grave injuries and losses, it's only human to try to regain control of the situation, even through negative or destructive decisions.

The Inner Path offers us each an opportunity to scrutinize our own life stories, to take a long look back and find "the wicked vows that we never should have made." The wonder and magic of the story are that the brothers are not bound by their vow. When, with the Old Woman's help, they see how wrong it was, they simply let it go and take up the threads of their lives again. The story offers us an opportunity to do the same, should we choose to do so.

Like the swan brothers, each of us has thoughts and feelings, even vows and resolves, based on our past experiences. The past is full of valuable information for us; it is a great resource that teaches us about ourselves and about others. It is the earth our wisdom grows in. But when our reactions to past experiences dominate our present in ways we are not fully aware of, we are not free. These wicked vows continue to affect our lives, making us do and say things that don't really help us at all. We've got to break those wicked vows we never should have made.

It's the most natural thing in the world for someone who has suffered from a painful or unfair experience to vow to never let it happen again. The swan brothers are not bad people; they are responding quite naturally to their rage and helplessness about the betrayal they have experienced. It's the *vow* that is wicked, not the perfectly understandable feelings of the person who makes it. The vow is wicked because it binds us, not allowing us a fresh, powerful, effective engagement with the present. Rose's brothers don't actually want to harm her when they meet her; it is the old vow that is causing the trouble.

Most of us have made vows or decisions about ourselves based on our past experiences: "I'll never love anyone as much as I love poor old Mom"; "I'm the kind and generous one, she's the pretty one"; "I'm the kind of person other people pick on"; "I'll never betray my financially struggling parents by having enough money"; "If I work hard enough in school, I'll never get in trouble." But years later we may find ourselves working eighteen-hour days, or broke again for no observable reason, or compulsively drawn into relationships with people who are mean to us, or repeatedly walking out on perfectly good love relationships. It's clear that our wicked vows come with a high price. The vows often end up hurting us far more than the original injury did. This is the case with Rose's brothers, who have vowed to kill the one creature who can help them, heal them, and weave their lives back into the design.

We are often not even aware that we have made these decisions. They may be well hidden under painful layers of anger and grief and shame. But no matter how well our vows and decisions about ourselves are hidden, Younger Self knows where to find them. If we ask gently and persistently, if we respect Younger Self's language of sensation and image, trance and dream, we will be able to uncover our wicked vows and release them.

This is a moment of very delicate negotiation in the art and craft of self-love and self-care. Anger, grief, and shame often defend the most tender, the most raw parts of the self, those that are the least willing to see the light of day. When we search deep within, looking for the wicked vows we never should have made, we must keep the perspective of getting acquainted with ourselves in a gentle, friendly way. We must keep the perspective of the Goddess tradition, which honors all things in nature—the bee sting and the honey, the thorn and the rose. Our reactions to past events, no matter how much we may want to change them, are part of our natures and not to be judged harshly or disrespected.

We may find thoughts and feelings we judge as monstrous, like the swan brothers' feeling that they'd like to kill the first young girl they meet. But we are not monsters. We are creatures of the Goddess, responding as we are meant to respond, and with our instinct and our intuition we have done our best. Everything in this world casts a shadow, and we are no exception. Our experiences, painful and joyful, all create reactions in the self, and some of them become imbedded and fossilized in our imaginations, our body wisdom, our emotional ecology, in ways that are not healthy. It is part of ongoing inner work to continuously seek out and release these forms of bondage. This work is part of the price of freedom and power. Now we seek healing; we seek to be whole and to be drawn back into the whole. Gently and persistently exploring our old scars and injuries, seeking ways to open where we are blocked, seeking release and relief—all are part of our task.

Breaking the Wicked Vow: Francie's Story

Francie's story is the one I always return to when I think about the wicked vow. The youngest child of an Irish family, she was the one still at home as her parents grew older. Her father drank too much, and when he would stumble home, it was Francie's job to help him undress, get his shoes off, and get him to bed. She would have to get close to him, although he was sometimes violent and always maudlin. "Big Frank," he would say to her, as though she were a son, "you're the last of the Madisons; you're our only hope." Flooded with love and repulsion, pity and fear, the little girl resolved to herself that she'd make him proud someday.

I met Francie years later in Reclaiming circles. Her dad had died; she hadn't saved him or made him proud. She still had a "deer in the headlights" look about her. She felt self-conscious and ashamed of her appearance. She'd had unsatisfying love relationships with men who weren't very nice to her. She longed to write fiction but couldn't get started. She was still bound by the "wicked vow that never should have been made."

It took several years of trance work, dream work, and persistent, gentle self-care for Francie to uncover the raw, powerful memory that illuminated her childhood vow. Her voice was trembling when, safe in a powerfully cast and intimate circle of women, she finally described the exact feelings of trying to get her drunk father's shoes off.

Francie was able, over the course of the next month, to do some private work at her own altar, releasing both herself and her father from the mutual bond of their pact. "The last of the Madisons" then proceeded to meet a lover and to start work on the first chapter of a detective novel. Francie had needed years of patient questioning to find out what was wrong. But once she knew, her "wicked vow" could be released at once, like that of the swan brothers.

Now, of course, Francie's vow wasn't wicked in exactly the same way as that of Rose's swan brothers. Francie was binding herself to something that seemed kind and helpful, committing herself to somehow making sense out of the tragedy of her dad's life by being Big Frank, the Last of the Madisons. But this was a wicked vow nonetheless, because no one can make sense out of another person's life, no matter how hard they try. And another life may well be wasted in the process.

Do you have a guess already about your own wicked vows? What would it be like to look for a wicked vow of your own that underlies the disturbing sensation, or dream, or image that opened the door of the Inner Path for you? Maybe it's just a matter of admitting to yourself something you already know. Did something pop into your head when you read that last sentence? Take a moment to close the book, close your eyes, and take a deep breath. If you allow yourself a moment of slow, deep honesty, do you have an idea of what your "wicked vow" might be? You can also try the following meditation.

Finding the Wicked Vow: Trance to the Salt Shore

For this meditation, you will need a bit of salt. When your circle meets, or alone at your altar, create sacred space, use your favorite trance induction, and go to your place of power. Greet the directions in your place of power. There is a path leading to the west. Follow it toward the place where the sun sets, into your own past, the land of memory.

Find the shore of the sea. Open all your senses to the sea, smell and taste the salt (please actually taste the salt), feel the salt air. There is a little dwelling here, on the seashore. Here are your brothers and sisters, and your own child self, and the other children your parents never had. Here you can talk with them or just be with them. You can ask their names and exchange tokens or gifts. You can ask, "What is the wicked vow that I never should have made?" They may be able to tell you, or at least offer some clues and signs. If you need help, allow the Old Woman to appear and help you.

When you are ready, thank everyone, and say good-bye. Know that you can return here at will, that this place is reached through your own place of power. This doesn't have to be your only visit; you don't have to do everything this time. Return the same way you came. Say good-bye to the directions in your place of power, and reverse the induction. Take your time returning to normal consciousness; stretch and say your name. Leave some time for discussion; let people talk about what they found on the salt shore. If you are working alone, write down what you discovered in your Book of Shadows.

Breaking the Wicked Vow: Another Story

Here's another story about how I discovered one of my own wicked vows, with some help from Rose May Dance. Rose is one of the founding members of

Reclaiming. A founder of the Prevention Point needle-exchange program, Rose has played an important part in making sure clean, safe needles were available to drug users and street people who would otherwise be at risk for AIDS and hepatitis C—even when providing clean needles was illegal. One night when I was first teaching in Reclaiming classes, Rose gave me a Witch's greatest gift: she saw me more clearly than I could see myself, and she challenged me.

Rose and I were teaching a class together, and the women had paired off to do trance work. All the students were successfully absorbed in the work, and suddenly I, the inexperienced teacher, didn't have anything to do. I went and stood awkwardly in the center of the room, arms crossed, certain that I should be doing something incredibly magical, but unsure what it was. Suddenly I noticed Rose beckoning to me silently. I went over quietly and sat down next to her.

As she pointed to my back, Rose said, "You're pregnant. It's on your back." Her eyes were half blank, with the incredible depth of one who was seeing the unseen world. A moment later she was back to herself, and she said with a grin and a gleam in her eye, "At least you could try to get it around to the front!"

Although what she was saying seemed bizarre and maybe even offensive to Talking Self, Younger Self leaped at the suggestion. Part of me knew that the awkward posture in which I had been standing expressed a feeling of carrying a great weight of responsibility on my shoulders and back, a part of my body that was often tense and sore. Rose had "seen" this unhealthy knot in my energy body.

Throughout that class, I worked magically with Rose's vision of me, which I experienced as being like my carrying a backpack full of rocks. I actually did fill a backpack with rocks, which I carried at class, feeling in the physical world what my energy body felt and looked like to Rose. Over the weeks of the class, my Younger Self, Talking Self, and Deep Self slowly came into agreement that this was no way to live and that something should be done about it. Talking Self was able to understand that I had made childish "wicked vows" that put me at risk of seeing myself as the savior and protector of others. These vows gave me the burden of making what I imagined to be superhuman efforts for other people, efforts that they might in fact experience as interference, condescension, or simply showing off.

Now, I wasn't wicked for making these vows, any more than Francie was. In fact, my feelings are quite common for the oldest child of a troubled family. Nevertheless, the vows were wicked, and they were holding me back from the fullest possible passionate engagement with my life, from becoming the woman the Goddess meant for me to be. So it was up to me to do something about them.

Finally I was ready to go to the beach and do a ritual to release the sensation of overresponsibility, weight, and pressure on my back. I took along a friend to help me, and we cast a circle. Inside it I ran around as long as I could with the backpack of rocks. Let me tell you, it's hard to run in the sand with a heavy backpack! When I was utterly exhausted, I sat (or rather fell) down in the sand. I brought the backpack around to the front. What a relief! Taking out the rocks one by one, I named them with the false ideas I had about myself that gave me the feeling of overresponsibility for others. As I named each rock, I threw it as far as I could into the surf. Since I was still playing softball at the time, my arm was pretty good, and it was incredibly satisfying to see the rocks flying out beyond the breaking waves and sinking, literally like a stone. I gave my troubles to Mama Ocean, opened the circle, and walked away a free woman.

It would be inaccurate to say that I never again felt overly responsible for a child or a student or a friend. But that day marked a definite turning point in my relationship with myself and the beginning of a long-term, always improving release in that area of my life.

The following meditation is widely used in the Reclaiming tradition. We use it to find the wicked vows hidden in knots in our energy bodies. You're welcome to give it a try if you'd like to find more clues to your own "wicked vows." Remember, it's the vows that are wicked, not the perfectly understandable feelings of the hurt or angry person who made the vows.

Finding the Wicked Vow in Your Energy Body

In the following exercise, we will move through our bodies' energy centers, one by one. We will seek help from sensation, from images and visions that arise, and from our inner voices. We will listen to the language of Younger Self as we ask for clues and signs that can show us how our bodies hold on to strong patterning from our reactions to past events.

For this exercise we use the seven energy centers in our bodies called *chakras*. Although most Westerners have heard the word *chakra* only in association with Hinduism, the idea that our energy bodies have seven centers that correspond to the colors of the rainbow, the notes of the octave, and the energies of the sun, the moon, and the five visible planets has been part of the Western mystery traditions since pre-Christian times. These ideas are found in our oldest systems of symbols, such as the tarot deck. One route by which some of these ideas came into the Western mystery traditions long ago was through the Rosicrucians.

Rose May Dance brought these psychic practices into Reclaiming. Rose reminds us: "This exercise is only a guideline. These are only some of the

images associated with the chakras. Only you know all that is contained anywhere in your body and aura." Here is one way we might do a chakra cleansing
in the Reclaiming tradition.

Exercise: Chakra Cleansing

With your circle, create sacred space. You may wish to take turns leading this
meditation, with one person beginning by running energy, and then trading
off so each person leads the meditation for one chakra.

Using the "Tree of Life" meditation, begin running energy. As you breathe
in, draw in the earth and sky energy, and let them mix and dance inside you;
on the outbreath, feel the energy flowing back to the earth. When your energy
body is fully awakened, allow your attention to settle into your first chakra:
your legs, butt, colon, anus, and perineum. Feel the earth beneath your feet,
feel the bowl of your pelvic bones, and find the center of your energy in this
part of your body. Let the color red light up this part of your body. Some of the
gifts and challenges you may find here involve physical security, physical
health, home, work and money, survival, and fear.

Open your inner senses to find out if you are bound here to past or current
relationships with other people, to images, to emotions, to memories that are
not truly part of your self. If so, simply allow them to move out of your energy
body, beyond your boundaries, allowing these attachments to melt into the
past, into the earth. If they hang on stubbornly, try using the powers of the elements on them, imagine them composting, washing away, burning away, or
blowing away. Ask for help from deity, remembering that the Goddess wants
and needs you free, powerful, whole, joyful, moving toward your life purpose
and fulfillment. She will surely help you. Be open to help from your spirit, animal, and plant helpers and from your tools. Use sound and movement to help
yourself: cry, hum, roar, shake, tremble, dance.

Whenever we create space inside ourselves with a purification, we need to
fill it up again with something we consciously choose. Otherwise, the next
strong influence we run into may fill the empty space for us. So when you
move energy forms out of your energy body, be sure to replace them. You may
have a strong image of the energy you would like to feel in this part of your
body: a warm hearth, a still lake, a flourishing tree. But if you don't have something specific in mind, please fill the open space with the color associated with
that chakra. Take a specific, concrete example of the color from nature; otherwise even a color can be too abstract. For red, choose the color of garnets, or
the red rock of the desert, or the red of a poppy or rose you've seen, or the
color of the planet Mars if you're a stargazer. Choose something that has
meaning for you personally and that you can strongly imagine. When your first

chakra is glowing clean and red, move on to your second chakra, and repeat the exercise.

When you investigate your second chakra, you will focus your attention on your lower belly and back, kidneys, bladder, lower intestines, and reproductive organs. As you explore this part of your body, freeing yourself from any bondage there, light up your second chakra with the color orange. Some of the gifts and challenges in the second chakra may involve creativity, sexuality, and fertility of all kinds.

As you move your attention to your third chakra, you will give attention to your upper belly, between the solar plexus and the navel, digestive organs, stomach, liver, upper intestines, spleen and gallbladder, and your spine. Some of the gifts and challenges you may find here may include power and will. As you work through this area of your body, opening up space and freeing yourself, light it up with the color yellow.

Moving on to the fourth chakra, we will attend to our rib cage, heart and lungs, back and shoulders, breasts, lymph glands, arms, and hands. Some of the gifts and challenges in this part of your body may include love, hurt, breath, and working with the hands. As you work through the sensations and associations in this part of your body, freeing yourself, fill it up with the color green.

For the fifth chakra, we will work with the neck and throat, mouth and nose, jaw and ears, voice, and sinuses. Some of the gifts and challenges we find here may include communication and the expression of emotion. As we free ourselves in this part of the body, we light ourselves up with the color blue.

Moving on to the sixth chakra, we investigate our thoughts, eyes, and mind, as well as our third eye—the spot between and right above the eyes. Gifts and challenges we may find here include memory, psychic abilities, intuition, and the inner senses. As we work through this part of our bodies, finding release from old bondage, we light it up with the color indigo, a dark blue-black like the summer midnight sky between the stars.

Now we complete the work by moving to the seventh chakra, the crown, the top of the head. Here we may find gifts and challenges involving yearning for spirit and divinity. As we work through this part of our bodies, we light ourselves up with the color violet.

Now that you have worked through each of your chakras once, take a moment to check in with yourself. Are there people or situations that are important in your life that did not show up as you worked through the chakras? If so, you may take another moment to ask yourself where in your energy body you are still affected by those people or situations. You may need to go back and redo part of the work if someone important like your mother didn't show up your first time through.

A thorough chakra cleansing is a big working, especially the first time you try it. Please make sure that you have allowed yourself plenty of time for cooldown and for discussion in your circle or for journaling if you are working alone. Be sure to eat something substantial, including protein. After you've opened your circle, you may wish to bathe or shower, cleaning yourself with salts. Please don't rush straight from this meditation to driving the carpool or going to work or falling asleep. Allow yourself a period of self-care first.

This is a meditation that many Reclaiming Witches use on a regular basis to keep themselves free of bondage to the past. We use it to make sure we are progressing toward our own life's meaning and purpose and to free ourselves from our "wicked vows."

Getting Acquainted with Anger

Did you notice that in the story about the backpack full of rocks, my first reaction to Rose's insight was to be slightly offended? That is actually a very important detail of the story, which parallels the swan brothers' anger at their sister and their desire to kill her. When we find places in ourselves where we are bound to the past in unhealthy ways, whether through our trance work or through energy work, or in any other way, we may feel angry or ashamed or repelled by what we find.

We all have secrets that we keep from ourselves, and often those secrets are the powerful dynamos behind our most difficult, intractable personal suffering. Francie didn't want to know that her problems with men stemmed from her childhood failure to live up to the role her father had assigned her—that of "Big Frank, Last of the Madisons." I didn't want to know that I was walking around awkward and stiff from the weight of false heroics. In fact, if someone had simply told me, I would probably have been very angry. When Rose told me her intuition of the pregnancy on my back, the strong, primitive imagery and the context of the circle work allowed Younger Self to hear what Talking Self could never have endured.

For the swan brothers, their sister is not only the cause of their suffering, but is also their only hope of escape. When they meet her and want to kill her in their blindness of anger and desire for revenge, they risk killing the one creature that can help them, transform them, and heal them. In the same way, it is often the most-needed insight about ourselves that we resist most heavily. This irony is so painfully human, and so strangely familiar, that we dare not ignore it. Perhaps we can even use that knee-jerk overreaction of anger as a clue or sign to help us find our wicked vows where they lie hidden.

Anger Exercise: An Anger Observatory

Is there some situation or person in your life who brings up an extreme, irrational annoyance or even rage in you? Perhaps you already know exactly what you need to work with, but if not, try this little trick. Just think about traffic.

Whether you're driving, walking, or on the bus, isn't there something that drives you crazy? Is it the double-parked beer trucks outside the market? Is it the oblivious teenager who doesn't get up and give his seat on the bus to the pregnant lady with the toddler and grocery bags? The lost tourist driving three miles an hour down a congested street? The little red sports car that zooms from lane to lane, passing everyone?

If I can catch myself in a moment of annoyance like this, I can observe a very interesting fact. There are probably several other people behaving just as badly who aren't bothering me at all. Perhaps behind the oblivious teenager on the bus is a self-centered elder detailing her illnesses to a neighbor who is obviously trying to read his paper and ignore her. But neither of them is driving me crazy. It's the oblivious teen who draws my enraged attention again and again. I can hardly stop glaring at him.

Here is an opportunity to learn something about myself. If the teenager's bad behavior is getting such a strong reaction from me, while other people's bad behavior seems normal or understandable or excusable, then my reaction tells me something about *myself*, not something about the teenager. In most cases, if I'm honest with myself, my process goes something like this: "*I* would never act like that. *I* am a caring person. *I* would get up and give my seat to the pregnant lady." And immediately under that, if I apply a deep, slow honesty, I often find some situation in my own life in which I am similar to the person I am angry with. Perhaps I am being oblivious of and not acknowledging a friend who really needs help.

This is another form of my wicked vow. I decided long ago that I am a caring person, and I have a right to be mad at people who aren't. If I find myself in a situation where a friend needs help and I'm not offering it, *I have to keep this secret from myself*. While I may have a very good reason for not offering to help my friend, I can't make a conscious or flexible choice about the situation.

Just as the swan brothers are stuck on the idea that they hate girls, so I am stuck on the idea that I am a helpful person. I am skewered on my own rigid, fragile self-definition, my "wicked vow," and I simply cannot allow conflicting observations and insights into my awareness. Meanwhile my friend is not getting the help she may need, and I can't tell her why because I'm busy glaring at people on the bus.

Why not try this observation on yourself? Give yourself some time, and find several situations where your irritation or anger seems disproportionate to the cause. Simply write these down for several days in your Book of Shadows. In each case, note any strong absolute statements you may be making about yourself or others. The words *never* and *always* are key clues that cry out for more self-examination: "I never would say something that mean"; or "I always hang up my towel." In each case, ask yourself in what ways could you be similar to the offending person or incident, perhaps in some completely different area of life.

You may wish to discuss some of these situations and observations with your circle. Your circle sisters may point out at once that the cautious lost tourist driving three miles an hour is just like you: you've been waiting a year to ask for a well-deserved raise. They may know right away that the speedster in the red sports car is just like the sixteen new classes and projects you started this year but were unable to finish. The more accurate they are, the more likely you are to be annoyed, so be prepared!

Releasing Your Wicked Vow

Now, perhaps, you are beginning to have a pretty good idea about your own "wicked vows." You may have found them in the trance to the salt shore or in the sensory inner world of your own body, in your chakras. You've also observed the patterns of your own anger and acknowledged how the things that make you angry on the outside may also be reflected inside you.

For many of us, the anger we feel is something we have kept closely under wraps, never fully admitting it to ourselves or to others, never expressing it fully. But sometimes allowing emotion to express itself and peak can lead to liberation. Anger that threatens to overwhelm or numb or swamp us in its first flood can become a powerful river, even a focused laser beam, for change. Here is a story told by a Reclaiming Witch I'll call Hermine, who was able to give full rein to her anger in the safe, sacred space of her circle. See what happened next.

Breaking the Wicked Vow: Twelve Pounds of Purple Jell-O

I was recently having a hard time with the residue of my relationship with my mother and the way I had been brought up. An important issue for me was the issue of boundaries. My mother had no sense of boundaries with me, still was invading my boundaries, and I was letting myself get overrun by people, was too wide open, and in turn habitually climbed all over other people's "space." I also was suffering from a pretty bad self-image even though I knew what my strong points were. I was in a bad depression, was ill with bronchial trouble, and was stressed out about money.

I asked my therapist for suggestions on what to do, how to stop being a victim, how to grow up. He sent me into a trance state to find the answers to these questions.

As soon as I arrived in my special trance place, I saw a large purple monster coming for me. I recognized it immediately. It was the same monster that had frightened me badly in a fever dream when I was a child, sick with bronchial trouble. The monster, which was blobby and changed form rapidly, sat on me to smother me. I began to call for my mother, as I had the first time I saw the monster. But when Mother appeared, I realized it was foolish to ask her for help, since she seemed just as harmful to me as the monster; in fact, she seemed to be part of the monster. I began to beat the monster back with fists and knives, and sometimes I seemed to be fighting my mother, too.

My therapist brought me up out of the trance before I got any resolution. I saw that the trance had to do with my mother's and my boundary problem, and I congratulated myself for not wanting to make myself helpless to someone who was harming me. But I wanted a "how": I wanted to know what to *do* to stop being a victim, a helpless baby. I felt that the "how" must have something to do with my ritual knife, my *athalme*. The therapist suggested I make a monster out of Jell-O—nice and blobby and purple—and play with it and my knife.

So I asked my coven, Sea Hags, to give me time at our next meeting, and I prepared a Jell-O monster, using red and blue food coloring and sixteen packets of Knox gelatin in a big kettle. I slid the Jell-O out of the kettle and onto a tray, and it began to undulate, which looked very promising to me. My coven cast a circle and asked for the powers to help us in our work, and I took a baby doll, blessed it, named it with my name—"Blessed be thou, creature of art, thou art no longer a poppet but a living child, and I name thee Hermine"—and blessed my sacred knife. I lay down next to these tools and the Jell-O blob, and my coveners put me in a very deep trance.

I had asked them to remind me that I could move and talk during this trance, that I had asked them to participate in the trance by saying things to me, goading me, doing whatever they saw fit. I arrived at a place of power and observed the four directions. Then my coveners told me I was in the center in a big bed and far off I saw something coming toward me.

I saw that it was the monster, and I began to scream and shake, calling and calling for my mother. She did not come. I felt that the monster was on top of me, and I began to choke and cough. I got up and leaned over into the Jell-O and put my face into it. Then I rose up and began to pound and smash it with my fists, crying and shouting. I grabbed my *athalme* and stabbed at the monster, but this was unsatisfactory because the knife hit the metal tray under the Jell-O and there was no feeling that I had penetrated or hurt the monster. So I returned to pounding it, and it broke apart and scattered all over. Then I took my knife and carefully put the Jell-O back onto the tray.

The Sea Hags reached over and messed up the Jell-O, scattering it on the floor and throwing it at me, taunting me: "Hermine, you've made a mess!"; "Hermine, you're always such a mess"; "Hermine, clean it up!" The Sea Hags, who were being my mother, would not leave me alone. They started to physically attack me, pushing and pinching me. I threatened them with my *athalme* and demanded that all my coveners—my mother—leave the room. Still they would not shut up.

Suddenly I lay on the floor and took my *athalme* and drew around the outlines of my body. I heard the Sea Hags go "Ah!" and I breathed easy. I asked, "If there are any of my coveners, my real friends, in the room, could they please come brush up my energy?"

My covener Spider took my feet and said, "Whose feet are these?" "Mine, Hermine's," I replied. "Whose legs are these?" "Mine." And so on up the body. I took hold of the baby doll and placed her inside my shirt and comforted her. I heard my coveners make baby complaints: "Who will take care of me?"; "I'm afraid I'll never be happy"; "I'm afraid you won't give me enough." And I soothed the baby. I told her, "Well, I'm sorry you feel that way. You just have a good cry. You'll be all right; everybody feels that way sometimes," being careful to not make myself any promises I couldn't keep.

Finally I asked the Sea Hags to bring me up out of trance. I showered, and we feasted.

Since that time, I have had some amazing breakthroughs about my love life, about my mother—understanding and forgiving her, sending her healing—about my money trip, and I am not running myself down very much. I am doing better about discharging my responsibilities and have not posed as a victim once! I use the mental image of cutting a boundary around myself with my knife when I am in an intense situation that would usually make me lose it. I am a Witch because I get to work with tools.

Hermine was able to find her rage, tracing it all the way back to her childhood. By allowing her anger to come to the surface and be fully expressed, she was able to work directly with it and gain some tools and self-confidence for protecting her boundaries. Only then was she able to embark on the journey of forgiveness, breaking her "wicked vows."

Fire Ritual: Breaking the Wicked Vow

Here is a ritual that can help you tie your story to Rose's and give you another opportunity to break your "wicked vows." Arrange for some private undisturbed time if you are working alone, or do this ritual with your circle sisters.

You will need a safe place to build a fire, and fire-building materials. You will also need paper and writing materials.

Create sacred space together. Build a good strong fire, and let it burn until there are hot coals and some good-sized pieces of wood burning well. Each person should try to write down her "wicked vows" that never should have been made, as clearly and simply as possible, on a piece of paper that she is willing to part with. When you are all ready, prepare to burn the papers. Sing over them, chanting songs of fire, of purification, and of freedom. Allow yourselves to enter a light trance.

When the time is right, burn the papers. Watch how they burn, how fragile the paper and the vows were. Watch, too, how the fire keeps right on burning. Meditate on your own lives. What are the deeper sources, the deeper motivations that remain when the wicked vows are gone? What are the burning logs, the hot coals in your life? What powers you, at your core? There may be some healthy anger left burning there—anger at injustice, at unnecessary suffering, the anger that arises when the innocent, or the very web of life itself, is threatened. Not all anger is wicked. Anger can be healthy fuel, raising energy for change, when it is channeled not toward blame or shame, revenge or self-destruction, but toward transformation. You may wish to speak of your values and passions. Try to use single words, not losing focus with lengthy discussion.

When you are finished, put out the fire safely, and open the circle. Take a bit of the ashes of this fire and place them on your Rose altar, to remind you that you have the power to release your "wicked vows" as you continue to discover more about yourself and that you have deep sources of energy for your life that go far beyond your "wicked vows."

Exercise: Creating a Personal Anger Ritual

Now that we have done a purification by fire and thought over the stories of Big Frank, of the backpack of rocks, and of the purple Jell-O, do you feel called to craft a "wicked vow" spell of your own? Is there something specific that you need to do between the worlds to bring up and to release your own wicked vows? In the fire purification ritual, we released our anger into a bonfire. In the story of the backpack full of rocks, I released my troubles into the ocean. In Hermine's story, she released her anger into a physical object, the purple Jell-O. What element could help you with your release?

Find a way to translate your own personal story, with its colors, images, and sensations, into a spell of your very own. Assemble your tools and toys—whatever Younger Self wants and needs. If you are lucky enough to have a circle of sympathetic friends, let your friends help you act it out in sacred space. If you do your magic alone, create sacred space at your Rose altar, and complete the spell by working there. But even if you do magic alone, remember to get help and support from friends and teachers when you allow your hurt and anger over past injustice to arise. When doing challenging magic, we each need the perspective and care that can come only from other people.

You have faced bitterness on the salt seashore. You have acknowledged and released your own "wicked vows." You have left behind the burdens that kept you earthbound. You are lit up from within with a beautiful rainbow of healthy energy. Now you are ready to ally with your own "dear sister" and fly free. Now you have the passion and the power you will need for that flight.

The Outer Path

When, like Rose, we have listened to our own intuition telling us that something is out of balance, when we have sought the truth and left our protective shelters, when we have followed the river to its end, then we are brought face-to-face with great injustices that we can no longer ignore. Our world abounds in inequality. Daily the media bombard us with images of wealth and success, yet beggars crowd our streets. We are building prisons faster than schools, and whole groups among us see their opportunities limited, their dreams blighted, their jobs threatened, their communities under siege. In spite of all the liberation movements of the last century, society still too often discriminates against people because of their gender, color, sexual preference, age, or class.

Injustice brings forth rage. Rose's brothers are filled with rage at the loss of their human lives because of their mother's preference for a girl. We empathize with their hurt and anger, for at some point in our lives we have all seen someone else preferred above us, and we know how it feels to envy the favored one.

Rage is a powerful and dangerous emotion. Anger is life-force energy that can mobilize strength we didn't know we had. Channeled and directed, rage can be a gift, a great creative force. Undirected, it can destroy the very things that might have healed us, as Rose's brothers might have killed her because of the vow their anger and jealousy led them to make.

To change the world, to be true healers and shapers, we must be able both to withstand the rage of others and to channel and contain our own anger. As leaders, we must take up Rose's challenge: to hold her ground, not to slip into being a victim. She must neither allow herself to be killed nor respond with her own rage and disappointment; rather, she must trust that the powers and allies she has already gathered will speak for her now. Rose may seem passive, but that is only because she has already acted to set in motion the forces that will protect her. Her willing assumption of the task of healing, her generosity toward the old beggar woman, have won her the protection of the Crone. We too must find and know our allies, and the work of this chapter begins with identifying our sources of strength and support.

We need strong support to acknowledge and transform our own rage and jealousy—not the personal anger we explored in the Inner Path but the collective anger, the deep and ancient rage, associated with all the ways in which our differences have marked us as targets of oppression. The pain of discrimination goes back centuries, millennia, and when it surfaces it can be overwhelming. When we have been hurt or oppressed, we can easily become the swan brothers, wanting to kill the first person we meet. If we bring that rage into a position of leadership, we can become destructive and even abusive to others.

When we take a stand for what we believe is right, when we challenge systems of injustice, we often face powerful opposition. As Martin Luther King Jr. said in his "Letter from the Birmingham Jail," "The privileged seldom give up their privileges voluntarily." We must channel our rage into focused action that can undermine unfair privilege and bring about true justice. We cannot afford to squander our rage on our brothers or sisters. We need allies as powerful as the old woman, and we need to learn to be allies to ourselves and to each other as well.

What is an ally? In the magical realm, an ally is an aspect of the Goddess or God, an Old Woman, an ancestor, a spirit, a constellation of forces we deeply identify with and feel a special connection with. Those spirit forces also have their own tasks and works and may come to us with aid and blessings when we take up challenges that augment theirs.

In our daily relationships, an ally is someone who offers us support, who stands beside us in our struggles, who watches our back. "An ally is someone who, although not the target of an oppression, is outraged by its existence and is willing to act on that outrage," says Katrina, a Witchcamp teacher who as a lifelong activist and an African-American woman knows the power of a strong ally in confronting injustice. "We are all potentially allies in the struggle against oppression."

Remembering Our Allies

The power of our outer work in the world depends on the depth of our connection to the springs of life that feed us. To make our work effective, and to stay sane while doing it, we need a strong, daily personal practice. The tools we've developed to deepen our connection to the Goddess—grounding, calling on the elements, working with our anchor, and bringing ourselves back to our core worth—are all important aspects of inner healing, but they are more important than ever on the Outer Path. We very easily crowd our lives with work for others and forget to leave time for our own work. We may be teaching so many classes on meditation that we don't have time to meditate, or facilitating so many rituals that we never do ritual for ourselves.

Many of the rituals and exercises in this book are designed to deepen our relationship with the Goddess and our connection to the mysteries. Now is a good time to review them and to ask yourself the following questions:

Who are my allies between the worlds? Which aspects of the Goddess, of the Gods, which ancestors, do I feel most deeply connected to?

What can I do to deepen my daily, ongoing connection with them? Are there offerings I can make? Specific meditations, prayers, or exercises? How do I express my gratitude?

Before beginning a project, a class, a campaign, ask:

Who are my allies in this work? How can I invoke them? What offerings should I make? How will I work with them? Thank them?

Who are my human allies? What are the issues and struggles that I must ally with in order to do this work?

Love Bathing

Sage is a Reclaiming teacher from British Columbia who has a strong daily practice and a powerful connection with a very personal Goddess. She suggests the following simple daily practice:

In sacred space, ground, center, and breathe deeply. Imagine your awareness dropping down into the center of your belly. Let yourself be still in that place, and just open to a vision of the Goddess sitting opposite you. Experience her opening her heart and pouring out her love for you. Remember, you don't need to do anything to earn her love. She's going to love you no matter who you are or what you've done or failed to do. Breathe in her love, fill yourself with it, and know that you are her beloved child. When you are ready, return and open your circle.

To move in the world as a person grounded in our true, creative, wild power is to walk with a sense of honor. *Honor* is an old-fashioned word we tend to asso-

ciate with a testosterone-driven urge to leap into sword fights over every imagined insult. True honor, however, is grounded in the deep knowledge that we
deserve to be treated with respect and compassion and is made manifest in the
way we treat others. Honor is balanced with humility in the Witches' liturgy
"The Charge of the Goddess," in which we are told: "May there be beauty and
strength, power and compassion, honor and humility, mirth and reverence
within you." *Humility* comes from the same root as *humus*, earth. It means to
remain close to the earth, grounded in the deep willingness to offer others the
respect we would receive. To walk with honor is to acknowledge our gifts,
experience, and skills, to be able to offer without imposing, advise without
believing ourselves infallible, share our experience while admitting we might
not know what is best for someone else.

As honorable people, we keep commitments and act in a way consistent
with our own ideals—not out of fear of punishment or of divine judgment, but
out of a deep sense of self-respect, a sense that to do less would be unworthy of
us. And so to walk with honor, we must also learn a lesson from Rose's brothers. We must not mistake honor for the blind following of unwise promises and
vows or the seeking of revenge. To be fearless shamans linking the realms of
earth and sky, walkers between the worlds of magic and manifestation, we
must relinquish our desire for retaliation.

None of us like to think of ourselves as jealous or revengeful people. But we
are all also subject to the temptations of revenge. They arise daily in the most
ordinary of situations, and the vengeful urge often disguises itself as a righteous
sense of justice.

Once a Reclaiming teacher who shall remain nameless sent out an e-mail
commenting on a task I and some others had taken on. Her post sent me off
fuming, feeling that our work was unappreciated and that we were being
patronized as well. I composed a stunning response. It was calm, thoughtful,
full of forbearance and the wisdom only an elder can muster up. But before
pushing the Send button, I decided to get a second opinion. I asked my friend
Rose May Dance to read the post. She did, and then she asked me, "Why do
you want to send this?"

I thought for a moment and then had to answer honestly, "I want to make
so-and-so look *really bad*."

I didn't send the post.

Like Rose's brothers, we must overcome the desire for vengeance if we are
to nurture the powers that can truly heal us. Our revenge may be expressed so
subtly it is hard to recognize. Daggers and poisons are easily identified as
weapons and challenged; hostile remarks, unfair criticisms, and toxic atmos-
pheres are harder to confront. The more power we have—whether it be
power-over, the formal power to allocate resources or make decisions; or

power-with, the influence we wield—the more potentially destructive our revenge can be.

We relinquish revenge because of our sense of pride and honor, as an act of self-respect. We let go of vengeance out of love and concern for our larger community. To be a true leader, we must be able to look at each of our acts and say, "How will this affect the community? Is it worth dividing the community for me to be proved right? Would I not be destroying the very source of support and healing I most need?"

And we relinquish revenge because we hold a vision of healing, for ourselves and for the world. Magic teaches us that the ends do not justify the means. Instead, the means themselves shape the ends that follow. We cannot achieve healing through vengeance. We cannot serve a broad vision by being petty and spiteful.

Revenge and Impact Meditation

This is a meditation to help us let go of anger and hurt and consider the impact of our actions. It's a good one to do in the midst of conflict or before answering your e-mail.

At your altar, place a bowl of salt water in front of you. Breathing deeply, think about the conflict you're involved in. Let yourself feel your anger and fantasize about your revenge.

Now, stop and ask yourself, "If I did this act, if I sent this message, how would it affect my community? What is the truest good of the whole community in this matter? What true allies would it bring me? What is my vision, and would this really serve it?"

Allow your desires for revenge to swirl and flow into the water. Breathe up power from the earth to charge and transform those energies. Remember your allies, and bathe in their care for you, and in the love of the Goddess. When you are ready, drink a sip of the water. Take back your energy as creativity, compassion, and love.

Subtle Forms of Revenge

Following are some examples of the kind of subtle revenge an empowering leader must relinquish in order to act with honor:

- The urge to make someone else look bad to the group or feel bad about their behavior;
- The urge to punish someone who has criticized you or not supported your program;
- The urge to get rid of someone who causes you problems.

We cannot afford to exclude people simply because they do not agree with us or because they once slept with our lover or have an annoying personality. Over the years, I've found that every single person I might have at some point wanted to eliminate from our groups has gone on to undertake important work that I didn't have the time, skills, or energy to do myself.

And often that person I most want to get rid of is merely a shadow of myself, the mirrored image of qualities I can't acknowledge in myself. Rose is the swan brothers' sister: she is deeply akin to them. Were they to kill her, they would be killing a part of themselves. So, too, we often lash out at just those qualities that are our own mirrored shadows. Part of our magical training is in learning to see, know, and work with the energies locked in our shadows.

Meeting Your Shadow Self

In a safe, relaxed space, consider the previous discussion. When have you acted as the swan brothers? When have you fallen prey to your own urge for revenge? For control? In what ways does it manifest itself uniquely for you?

Think about one situation in which you've behaved in a way that is out of balance. Just for a moment, let that energy and emotion take you over. Who are you when you're caught up in it? Imagine that you literally become a new character, a vengeful swan brother, a different self. Let yourself create that character as if it were a character in a book or play. What is its name? What does it look like? What is a typical thing it might say? A gesture or posture it might take?

When your character has taken form, introduce yourself to the group, along with your typical statement: "I am Attila—stay out of my way!" "I am Pathetica—and, oh, never mind, I can't do this sort of thing."

While you might expect this process to be painful and embarrassing, in reality it usually becomes bonding and funny. It's a wonderful thing to do in a group that has experienced conflict, perhaps before a long meeting or a mediation. People's faults are much easier to accept when you know that they recognize them and can even laugh at them. And we feel much more relaxed in a group when we know that our worser selves have been seen and are not unique.

One summer at Vermont Witchcamp, I led this exercise together with Baruch, who is a therapist in his day job. My negative self was Ilsa, the Fascist Healer: "You must do what I say, or you will not get the full benefit of the program!" One thing that struck both of us was how quickly, in the group of forty people, we learned everybody's name. Each person became distinctive once we knew their shadow character, and most of the characters were actually quite endearing.

Throughout the rest of the week, every time I issued an instruction, someone would inevitably ask, "Do we have to do that?" "You don't have to," I'd begin to reply, "but . . ." A chorus of voices would gleefully interrupt: "If you don't, you will not get the full benefit of the program!" My control issues were dealt a gentle but effective blow.

After a time of working with your shadow self (which will vary according to the setting), go back into sacred space. Remember that Rose does love her brothers, and her love allows them to give up their revenge and to change. Call up your shadow self, and take some time to examine it and meditate on its positive qualities. Ilsa, for example, really cares about people. Give each person in the circle a chance to reintroduce their character and claim its positive qualities. This is often a good way to end a class or workshop.

There are many levels of shadow work. For Rose, her brothers' desire to kill her is, in a sense, the shadow of her desire to save them. To truly integrate our shadows, we must also examine our assumptions and beliefs. Katrina is a woman of many facets: a strong psychic, powerful priestess, activist, and engineer. She trains groups in diversity work, which inevitably involves confronting our shadows. She suggests the following approach to identifying some of our shadow beliefs and desires:

Meditation on Opposites

At your altar, write down some of the things you think, want, need, intend, or desire. Pick the top five.

Now, say out loud the opposite of each one. If you believe that people are basically good, you might say, "I believe that people are by nature evil and sinful." If you deeply desire a committed relationship, you might say, "I don't need or want love."

Notice the things that are most intense for you, that carry the most charge. They are clues to where your shadow lies. What happens when you meet people or groups who espouse those beliefs?

Sometimes identifying our shadow can tell us something surprising about our true beliefs. Katrina describes what happened when she was working with this exercise: "I thought, What's the opposite of something I believe? And what popped out of my mouth was, 'I'm beautiful.' So I had to stop and go, 'Whoa, I don't believe I'm beautiful? I really need to work with that!' And that means the beautiful sister is my shadow."

Shadow Beliefs

Following is an exercise I suggest for those of us with strong political convictions. It's especially helpful when we are trying to build coalitions with those whose beliefs differ from our own.

1. Write out a list of five to a dozen of the principles and ideas you most deeply believe in.
2. Now, over a moon cycle, devote a day to each. Walk through your day asking yourself how you would look at the world and at each choice you make if you held the opposite belief.
3. Keep a journal of your insights.

When we are familiar with our own shadows, when we know and acknowledge our worser selves, we are ready to work toward a new level of community healing. We can embrace diversity without projecting onto others our own unintegrated selves.

Rose has run forward to embrace her brothers. Her deepest desire is to connect with them. But first she must hear their anger, their vengeful vow. So, too, when we attempt to connect across the barriers of our differences, we may encounter hostility or anger instead of gratitude. And we may make mistakes. Try as we might to be sensitive, we may say things that offend others or may be heard in ways we didn't intend. We have different triggers that set off our pain; we cause hurt when we mean to bring comfort.

A man walks up to a woman, gives her a warm, affectionate hug—and restimulates all her memories of sexual abuse. A woman walks up to one of the few African-American women in a group and tells her, "I'm so glad one of your people is here," instantly making her feel set apart, isolated, and seen only as a category, not as a person. We can put out lists of things not to do or say, but we can never anticipate all the things we might do wrong or say wrong.

What we can do is learn to listen well when we've made a mistake. When we are the targets of rage, like Rose we must learn to stand our ground without ourselves becoming either vengeful or victims. Sometimes our part in healing centuries of oppression may simply be to hear the pain, to bear the rage, without retaliating and without becoming guilty or defensive. When we can simply listen, trusting in who we truly are, magic can happen. Energies can shift, old promises can be broken, patterns can change.

The co-counseling community has a useful descriptive phrase, *target groups*, to delineate the groups that have historically been on the receiving end of oppression: women, people of color, lesbians, gays, transgender folk, the disabled, the young, the old, and so forth. Oppression is more than just prejudice. Prejudice consists of the prejudgments we make about people because of their gender, color, age, nationality, or other characteristic. Prejudice can be hurtful, limiting, and shortsighted. But, as Katrina puts it, "when your personal prejudices are backed up by the military, the legislative and judicial branches of government, as well as industry, academia, and religion, it becomes more than just being impolite or ignorant or rude or displaying poor taste. It is oppression." Oppression is structural, embedded in all the institutions of society. Your Aunt Lucy's discomfort with your homosexual relationship is prejudice. The fact that you cannot marry your partner is oppression.

As Witches, we experience prejudice almost every time we name our religion. We experience oppression when our Pagan identity is used as an excuse to deny us jobs, custody of our children, or the respect and privileges given to members of other religions. We daily see our beliefs trivialized or falsified by the media or sensationalized to promote horror movies or right-wing political agendas. We know what it is to be a target group, and our experience can help us learn to be allies of all people fighting oppression.

When we're in the target group and somebody says or does something hurtful, how do we say, "You've just victimized me!" without taking the stance of a victim? How can we empower ourselves in such a situation?

Silence, in Rose's story, becomes a magical tool by which she gathers power. But silence in the face of oppression is not empowering. Instead, we must speak.

"I" Statements

Gail is a Reclaiming teacher from a Jewish background who facilitates empowerment workshops for at-risk populations of diverse racial, cultural, and economic backgrounds. She works with the homeless, with battered women, with women in transitional facilities and prerelease programs, and with recovering addicts.

"It's a real self-esteem issue to stand in our power and speak out when we feel attacked," she says.

Witches have tools for mobilizing that power: breathing, grounding, and anchoring to our core worth. In Gail's workshops, she teaches a formula for using "I" statements: "I feel [state the emotion] when you [name the behavior] because [say why]. I prefer [state what you want] and then [name the change that would follow]."

She cautions that the emotion named must truly be a feeling, not a judgment: "I feel hurt [or scared, angry, humiliated, etc.]," not "I feel that you are an insensitive jerk."

"I feel angry when you interrupt me because, in my experience, men often interrupt women as a way of not listening to us. I want you to wait until I finish speaking, and then I will feel respected."

"I feel hurt when you look directly at me every time you mention race or racism, because I feel you are seeing me only as an African American, not as a person. I prefer you to address your remarks to everybody, and then it will be more clear that we all have a stake in fighting racism."

Formulas such as these can be restrictive, but also helpful. "When we respond in a reactive way, that's a learned behavior, something we learned way back," Gail says. "We have to learn a new behavior, and you can do that only by practicing it and really believing it. Once you practice it, it sinks in to an unconscious level, and then when you're in a more charged situation, the new, more desirable communication skill will automatically come out."

To undermine the "ism" brothers, we must speak out when we feel oppressed or when we notice behavior that is oppressing others. We all must be responsible for changing the communication patterns and power structures in our group.

Four Steps in Fighting Oppression

Katrina suggests four steps for those who want to be allies in fighting oppression: see it, believe it, say it, act on it.

SEE IT: Racism, sexism, and homophobia are often subtle. We don't put Whites Only signs up in our meeting rooms or ritual spaces. But we may unconsciously ignore the contribution of a person of color while listening attentively to a white person who makes the same point. We may not notice that while only a third of the people in the room are men, most of those asking questions or speaking are male.

BELIEVE IT: We are all experts on our own oppression. When oppression is named by members of target groups or allies, believe that their perceptions are real. Understand that what you might see as an isolated incident is part of a larger pattern, a structure of unequal power that may be operating in ways you aren't conscious of.

SAY IT: When someone around us behaves in an oppressive way, it is our responsibility to name it. As allies, we must challenge the racist remark, the sexist joke. Countering prejudice and educating people on all the complex issues around diversity are burdens that should not be placed on the target groups alone.

ACT ON IT: White people ran the stations on the Underground Railroad during slavery times. Germans hid Jews from the Nazis. Men have been allies of women's liberation; straight people have marched, petitioned, and gone to jail for gay liberation. Rose does more than deplore the state of her brothers: she determines to free them from their enspelled state. In acting to free ourselves and all people from oppression, we, too, will gather power.

When we have hurt someone, deliberately or inadvertently, we must learn, like Rose, to hear their anger without denying our actions or responding with our own rage. Sometimes the anger directed at us may be out of all proportion to our actions. It may carry with it the residue of thousands of years of pain. If we can stand firm under the onslaught, listening without personalizing what does not belong to us while being willing to own and change what does, we open an opportunity for healing.

Such skills do not come easily or automatically. Gail suggests the following exercise for working on deepening our ability to listen.

She Who Listens

In sacred space, invoke the Goddess as She Who Listens, the old woman. We might call her Stone Woman, for she can be silent as the mountains. Each person chooses a partner. One in each pair imagines herself as the old woman of our story, wise, silent, and deep. The second partner tells her story, while the old woman listens in total silence and acceptance. Then reverse roles.

How did it feel to be listened to without judgment? How did it feel to simply sit in silence and listen?

The group might also experiment with variations. You might invoke Echo and reflect back to your partner what you have heard. Or call in She Who Feels, and affirm your partner's emotions. Discussion might take place in sacred space or after you have opened your circle.

If you are working alone, go to your sacred spot. Find a special tree or a boulder or something else that can represent the old woman. Invoke her into your object, and tell her your story. Remember the energy, the feeling of being held in silence and attention, so you can call it back the next time you are asked to deeply listen.

Diversity Walk

Gail suggests another exercise that can help open up and focus discussion around difference.

The group stands in a line against a wall. The leaders call out a category: "Anyone who identifies as African-American, take the walk."

Those who take the walk go to the opposite side of the room and turn and face the group. The leaders ask the following three questions, reminding everyone to breathe, ground, and speak and listen from their core:

What do you want the others to know about you?
What do you never want to hear again?
What can those who didn't walk do to support you?

Creating a Welcoming Space

Katrina, in a leadership retreat for the National Organization for Women, found herself constantly being asked, "How can we bring in more women of color?"

She led the following meditation for the mostly white group:

Close your eyes, take a deep breath, and imagine yourself walking into a room full of men. What would they have to do for you to feel included?

When the women reported back their answers, she told them, "Now you know what you need to do to make women of color feel included."

The meditation can be varied to reflect different issues.

Identify a group that has more structural power than you do. Imagine walking into a room full of executives, senators, tenured professors—whatever. What could they do to make you feel included? How can you build that process into your group to include others?

"It's not about superficial diversity—what the group looks like," Katrina says. "We need to nurture the root structure to support a greater diversity. It's about being accessible, so everyone who wants to can come and can understand what the hell we're doing. And making sure we have an inclusive process, so that when people do come, they have a chance to contribute and feel that they were heard. "

Wherever injustice exists, rage is born. Whenever one group is sacrificed for the interests of another, anger and the desire for revenge arise. In the story, Rose's brothers resent the favoritism shown to a woman. In real life, most often the favor goes to men. In our communities, when we work with gender issues or with other forms of diversity, we encounter the depth of rage and pain that arise from the past.

In the Inner Path, we worked with our personal anger. But when we move out into the world and confront entrenched systems of power, we often encounter within ourselves a rage that is all the more intense for being impersonal.

Rage is a powerful, life-giving energy. Anger motivates us to change, to fight injustice, to right wrongs. But rage and anger can literally burn us out if they remain in their raw forms. To hold them, to mobilize their power, we need to transmute them into creativity and passion.

Rage Ritual

Donald is a warmhearted, funny, flamboyantly queer man and artist in middle age, who usually sports some outrageous hairstyle and a few earrings in each ear. He is called the Widow Engstrom, for he has seen two beloved husbands and many friends and lovers die of AIDS. He lives with AIDS himself, and his intimate knowledge of death has deepened both his rage and his compassion.

"My life has been full of rage," Donald says. "It started with Vietnam, and it just kept going. When AIDS began killing people in the gay community, I was surrounded by a sea of people dying a preventable death. I'd go into uncontrollable rage, striking out against anything.

"I had to figure out a way to work with that rage. When I first got really serious about studying this form of magic, I could never go visit the south, the direction of fire. It was the hardest place for me to go. I felt like I was swimming down a river of fire. Then I thought, That's a good transition for me from being in a whole ocean of fire!"

Donald created the following meditation:

In sacred space, imagine that your rage and anger are a sea of fire. Breathing deeply, slowly begin to breathe in that sea, to focus and narrow it down into a flow, a river. Say, "This is a gift, this rage is a gift," and bring it in tighter and tighter.

When the sea of rage has become a river, keep breathing. Imagine it growing tighter and more focused still until it becomes a laser beam. Where in your body does that beam originate? Your belly? Your solar plexus? Tell yourself that it will give you the courage and focus to do what you need to do. How will you direct it? How can you call it up when you need it?

Working with Gender Issues

When we have acknowledged our pain and rage, we can begin to consider how to work together. In Reclaiming, we commonly hold rituals in which women and men celebrate the Goddess together. While many of us prefer covens that are all women or all men, our large seasonal rituals and most of our Witchcamps are mixed.

In many communities, however, the growth of the Goddess tradition has centered around women who have desired a space free from men in which to develop our magic and our power without having to contend with the residues of patriarchal structures. In time, some of those women may wish to work with men and yet find it hard to imagine how to create a mixed sacred space that continues to empower women. Many men have also explored the power of men's circles and drumming groups, yet they may feel unsure of how to bring their bonding and insights back to a mixed group. Other groups may work happily with both genders, yet unless the underlying issues of power are addressed in some way, we risk replicating the subtle hierarchies of the larger society.

My partner, David Miller, and I have for many years led groups and workshops together specifically focused on consciously bringing women and men together in sacred space, with awareness of the energies and issues that arise. Over the years we've developed a structure that works and some guiding disciplines.

David is a big man in his late fifties, gray bearded, bald, round bellied, quiet, and warm. A radical Catholic in his youth, he was the first draft-card burner to be prosecuted during the Vietnam War and spent two years in federal prison for his commitment to peace. Since then he has worked as a social worker, a cabdriver, an attorney, and a writer, and raised four wonderful daughters. When we work together, he is able to both support me and hold his own, allowing us to model a shared flow of power.

"The work has changed a lot over the past decade," David says. "Ten years ago, men were often much more reluctant to meet as a group of men. Women aren't afraid of other women the way men are afraid of men. But what's most important is for the leaders to model safety and respect. You set a tone for the group, by being confident, relaxed, content in yourself, and secure in your power as a man or as a woman."

From our work together, we've also learned the following guidelines:

1. Allow enough time. The group needs time to bond, to experience being in sacred space together, to build trust. Ideally, we like to work for at least five sessions. Over a weekend, this would typically mean a Friday night session, sessions on Saturday morning, afternoon, and evening, and at least one session on Sunday morning.

2. The energetic experience, not intellectual analysis, creates transformation. Insight emerges from experience. We don't present feminist theory, nor do we discourse on differences between women and men. Instead, we let the group experience sacred space, together and also in separate women's and men's groups. Discussion and insight come toward the end, out of our reflections on the work we've done.

3. The simplest forms and processes often evoke the most profound transformation. A simple chance to speak from the heart and be heard can be more
transformative than the flashiest drum trance.

On the first night of a workshop, we do introductions, explanations, and
movement, using a combination of seriousness and humor to set a tone of safety.
The following day, energy work makes interrelationships visible. We have at least
one session where men and women meet separately. I might lead the women in a
trance or healing work, drawing from many of the exercises in this book.

"The trick in men's space," David says, "is to do the centering and breathing that really relaxes people. We always do a long check-in. I would start first,
to model how long and how intimate each person's story can be. We're not all
schooled in good communication skills. Sometimes I have to tell people not to
talk across the circle or remind them to speak from their own experience. The
check-ins can take a long time, up to an hour and a half or two hours of a
three-hour session. But by the time they're done, there's a higher level of trust.
Then we share energy with hands-on healing. Each man is given the opportunity to step into the center of the circle and ask for the kind of energy he
wants. I always go first, to model how to relax, and I say, 'You can sing my
name, touch me anywhere, sing and hum, give me energy.'"

In the evening, we gather back together, to feel what it's like to reconnect
after we have grounded ourselves in our power as women or as men. Often we
ask the women to invoke the Goddess and the men to invoke the God. This
simple task may bring up deep feelings. At times it becomes deeply moving to
see men and women express their power together in calling deity. At other
times it brings up fear, anger, or resentment. We welcome whatever happens,
as all of it becomes important material we can later work with. The evening
might culminate in a drum trance and/or a spiral dance and cone of power.

In the morning, we create sacred space and then open the group to discussion. Now the real insights and issues arise and transformation occurs. This is
always a risky moment for us. What happens if nobody brings anything up?
And what happens if issues arise that we can't resolve or at least move forward
in some constructive way? We can't plan this session ahead of time; we are
forced to "wander in the wilderness" and respond spontaneously.

We do, however, have our Witches' bag of tricks ready—a set of processes
and exercises to facilitate communication and transformation.

Council with Witnesses and/or Questions

One group is called into the center and asked to ground and center and
anchor to their core worth. For example, the women may be called into the

center to speak while the men witness. They are asked to say what they have always truly wished to say to men, while the men hold their own anchors and simply listen without responding.

When the women have spoken, the men can be given time to ask questions. The questions are often deeply meaningful and touching, but some groups will use this opportunity to become defensive or subtly accusatory. If that begins to happen, stop the process and move on.

Now switch places, and give the men a chance to speak while the women listen, and then let the women ask questions.

This is a form that can be used for gender work and for other sorts of work around diversity: people of color and European Americans; old, middle-aged, and young people; people who have been in the group for years and newcomers. It creates a formal, ritualized structure that can allow people to express truths they might otherwise be reluctant to. But it works effectively only when a group has had time to build trust—or, at least, relationships. Sprung cold on a group that doesn't know each other, it is likely to evoke superficialities.

A variation might be to build on the Old Woman exercise given earlier and ask the listeners to imagine themselves as She Who Listens (or He Who Listens).

Many Genders

Donald has also explored the issue of gender. Like many queer men and women, he finds the two genders recognized by the dominant culture inadequate to describe his reality.

"Gender is a construct," he says. "It's the way we build our lives around the core gifts we receive at birth or as young children, the way we choose to be, how we act in the world, how we physically respond. It's not just about who you have sex with. Most of us go through life with our concepts around gender totally unexamined."

Historically, many cultures recognized more than two genders. When Donald teaches a class in magic, he has his students write a poem, song, or statement or create a dance or performance that describes their true gender without using the words man or woman, masculine or feminine.

"The idea is that a Witch's power is in her word," he says. "If you don't know the word for the gender you have, you lose power. And if the culture does not provide you with a word, you may have to invent one."

Transmuting our rage, healing ourselves, and learning to give and receive feedback and communicate honestly within our communities are important and political tasks. But they are not enough. Ultimately, we must change the conditions that have caused the pain.

Reclaiming has strong roots in the political tradition of nonviolent direct action. We are committed to nonviolence because we believe that each of us is the Goddess. Nonviolence as a philosophy recognizes that within each person is a spark of the sacred. We may disagree with our opponents' actions or beliefs, but we must honor that they, too, are part of the Goddess. We respect our opponents and communicate with them. Our goal is not to destroy them, but to change a situation.

"I burned my draft card and went to prison," David says, "because I wanted my hands to do the works of mercy and not the works of war. That was the Catholic worker formulation. Today I'd say that the law of Witchcraft is that everything that you put out returns to you threefold, and the law of Witchcraft is that I am the beloved son of Mother Earth and the cosmos and it is she and her partner who give me my life and my sustenance. So I won't harm my sisters and brothers and myself, or the air, the fire, the water, or the earth. As a Witch, I honor the sacredness of all life, and I see injustice not as evil that has to be destroyed, but as imbalance."

Of course, there is much diversity within our community in our understanding of nonviolence. David, on one end of the spectrum, is a lifelong pacifist. Others in our community are war veterans, and a few are actively in the military. Some see activism as a "warrior" path, in the sense that being a warrior means being present, aware, and willing to put oneself physically on the line. Others dislike the term *warrior*.

Nonviolence is a constant experiment, a challenge to think beyond the confines of domination and envision creative possibilities. It draws on our deepest imagination and demands all the powers and skills we have learned through our magical practice.

Magic has been called "the art of changing consciousness at will." The same definition works for political activism. When we take action as Witches, we're not working merely to change who has power within an unjust system; we are enacting a spell that challenges the structure of power itself and the consciousness that sustains it.

When the Old Woman in our story tells the brothers to break their wicked vow, she changes their consciousness. She opens a new choice for them—a choice that was always there but that their preconceived ideas did not let them see. Political action can serve in the same way. When Rosa Parks refused to move to the back of the bus, the segregated area reserved for blacks in the pre–civil rights South, she opened up a whole range of choices that faced every person in the community, black or white: to continue to accept an unjust situation or to refuse to comply with it.

The world today is still far from just, free, and healed. When we look around us, we may see our society caught in many unfortunate promises and wicked vows that never should have been made: the vow to protect property and profits at the expense of people and the environment; the vow to suppress those whose color, gender, speech, or sexual preference offends us; the vow to use force against those who threaten the powers that be.

When the early suffragists marched, picketed the White House, and went to jail, they were acting as the Old Woman, saying, "Break your vow to keep women from equality and public power!" When Martin Luther King Jr. led civil rights marches, he was saying, "Break your vow to keep my people oppressed!" When many Reclaiming folks joined the blockade of the meeting of the World Trade Organization in Seattle, we were saying, "Take apart your unjust system that overrides our laws in the name of profit and benefits the rich at the expense of the poor!"

The systems that support those vows may seem invulnerable, but they are not. When we become the Old Woman who appears out of some other dimension, we refuse to accept the terms and definitions of the systems in power. We come at them sideways, with a perspective they don't expect, and bring to light what has been unspoken and unseen.

Nonviolence does not mean *nonconfrontational*. "Nonviolence isn't passive, it's active," Katrina says. "You need strong support to stand with your anger and not strike out."

All the work we've done on finding and being allies and honoring diversity comes together when we step forward and put our bodies on the line for something we believe in. Katrina describes a tense situation when she was defending a women's health clinic from anti-abortionists.

"We had a diverse coalition and a lot of disagreement about nonviolence. Not all of the groups were willing to renounce violence, but I defended their right to be with us as long as they would agree not to use violence in this action. In fact, I said that I had not renounced violence, either, but that for this action I would hold to nonviolence. When it came time for the worst part of the defense, at a clinic in suburban Maryland, anti-choice folks in army fatigues were coming up to us yelling and screaming. At one point there was this black woman screaming in my face that I was a traitor to my race because I was there, and I was so angry I was losing it. And guess who were the ones who helped me? It was the radical folks I'd defended who stood beside me and said, 'No, she's not a traitor to her race,' and helped me keep from lashing out. Because they understood what I was feeling, and they had made an active commitment to nonviolence. They weren't like some of the more conservative folks who would never be violent anyway; they had to work hard at it, as I did. It takes an active effort."

Nonviolent direct action may bring us into situations of enormous tension and danger. We may face the attacks of those threatened by our stand, or the violence of police gone out of control. And any type of political action, whether we're blockading a bulldozer or running for a local office, can bring us into situations of conflict and stress. When our system is flooded with adrenaline, we can become filled with anger or fear. "Fight or flight" is the body's response.

Don't Panic

Effective nonviolence depends on our ability to remain calm under tension, to continue to choose to communicate even when we are being threatened. "Don't Panic!"—the helpful words engraved on the cover of *The Hitchhiker's Guide to the Galaxy*—are also good advice for activists—or priestesses, for that matter. Magic can teach us how to not panic, in three words: breathe, ground, and anchor.

BREATHE: The deep belly breath we use in grounding will help keep you calm in an emergency. Again, practice regularly until you find yourself automatically shifting to your belly breath under stress.

GROUND: Again, the more regularly we practice the grounding techniques described in this book, the more reliably we can quickly ground in a tense situation.

ANCHOR: Speak and act from your core, anchored state. Whether you're testifying at a public hearing, resolving a difference of viewpoints in a meeting, or attempting to calm a riot cop gone out of control, you are most effective if you can ground and speak from your core worth. Use the anchoring exercises in the Outer Path in chapter 1. Practice them regularly, in safe and calm situations, and you will be able to quickly anchor in a crisis.

All the work of this chapter—calling in our allies, relinquishing revenge, learning to listen, channeling our rage, and understanding the views and visions of those different from us—is preparation for nonviolent action. The same skills and qualities that allow us to serve our communities as priestesses, teachers, and organizers allow us to serve the world as the Old Woman who will stand forth and demand that a wicked pattern be broken.

We have reached the sea and found our brothers. We've learned to stand our ground in the face of rage, to call our allies to help us, and to become allies ourselves of all who are willing to break the wicked vows that keep others chained. We've looked at our own shadows and relinquished our desires for revenge.

Now we're ready to be carried away into a deeper realm of magic.

FOUR

Carried Away

Comments on the Story

The brothers weave a basket to carry Rose with them in their journey across the sea, a journey that can be made only on the two longest days of the year—those that flank Midsummer Night. Resting one night on a tiny island in the sea, they fly to the magic land ruled by the dark fairy, the Fata Morgana.

The brothers, who are time incarnate, are bound by time. Only at the hinge point of the year, the summer solstice, can they pass between the worlds and travel the great distance from the magical realm to the land of their birth. To learn magic is to learn the art of timing. The power of a ritual, or of any creative work, lies in giving just enough and not too much. We must catch the energy, the impulse, and follow it all the way to its end, but not beat it to death. We must also know how to edit, what to cut, when to let go.

The brothers are shamans, Witches. Not only can they fly to the realm of magic; they can carry Rose there. To create a ritual is to weave a basket, a container, in which we can be carried away to realms of magic and ecstasy. The container must be strong enough to hold us. The higher we hope to fly, the more tightly woven it must be.

Up until now, Rose has followed her call, her intuition, her river. Now she must simply let go and allow herself to be carried away. In any initiation, there comes a moment when the initiate must give over control. In any creative process, there comes a moment when the work takes over, the characters come alive and take on a will of their own. In ritual, the true moments of ecstasy occur when we let the power move us. But for those moments to happen, the basket needs to be woven, the container needs to be strong.

The work of this section of the story is to dance the balance between risks and boundaries, between containing our power and letting it loose, between holding to a strong intention and letting ourselves be carried away.

The Elements Path

Rose's brothers weave a basket of willow wands to carry her over the sea to the magical land of the Fata Morgana. The journey can be made only on the longest day of the year, Midsummer Day. Only then do they have enough winged daylight hours to reach a tiny rock in the middle of the ocean where they can huddle in human form until the short night is over. They will be able to complete the journey on the next day, which is almost as long.

Like Rose, we must be willing to be carried to strange and wonderful lands in order to learn how to create a satisfying spiritual practice based on Mother Nature. Like Rose, we must be willing to take a "long journey over water."

In Western mystery tradition, the "long journey over water" refers to using meditation techniques that give us access to other forms of consciousness besides that of Talking Self. Stilling our bodies and conscious minds with deep breathing and relaxation, we can reach a state that we call *trance* in the Reclaiming tradition. In this super-relaxed but alert state, we find that our spirits can "travel" while our bodies rest, and we can directly experience the world of Younger Self, with its powerful sensation and dreamlike imagery. We can go to the land east of the sun and west of the moon where time shifts so that past and future become accessible and where intuitive guidance from Deep Self is close at hand. Here our demons walk the earth where we can find and face them and sometimes even befriend them. The work of the Elements Path for this section of the story is to learn basic trance techniques and practice some beginner's trances.

Trance: The Story of Jaybird's Dream

Jaybird was a woman who was feeling stuck in her troubled relationships with her mother and sister. One night she dreamed that she was back in the house where she grew up, with all her mother's precious and unusual art objects collected from around the world. Her sister was there, too, and the young women were supposed to take care of the house.

Jaybird's sister told her to go ahead and take a rest, assuring Jaybird that she would watch the special items. But when Jaybird woke up, everything was gone. "We sold them," said her sister.

This dream was very disturbing, and Jaybird brought it to a Reclaiming class to work on. The other women in the circle helped her lie down comfortably, with pillows and blankets, and then asked her to relax.

Trance: The Rainbow Induction

Breathe deeply, and imagine that you're floating in a red sea, buoyed up by the water, which is the perfect temperature. Breathe in red, flood yourself with red, a red woman floating in a red sea, sinking gently, finding you can breathe easily, creature of water.

Breathe deeply and sink into the orange sea that lies beneath the red sea, breathing orange, smelling and tasting orange, an orange woman in an orange sea, sinking, breathing, into . . .

A yellow sea, breathing yellow, tasting yellow, held by yellow, filled with yellow sensation, a yellow woman floating, sinking, breathing easily into . . .

A green sea, deeper now, drifting, smelling green, breathing in green, flooding inside and outside, a green woman drifting deeper into . . .

A blue sea, breathing deeply, resting, held by the blue waters, a blue woman, smelling and tasting blue, full of blue sensation, sinking, breathing, deep into . . .

An indigo sea, the darkest blue of the sky between the midwinter stars, deep, dark, breathing indigo, smelling, tasting, flooding indigo, the color darkness would be if darkness could shine, an indigo woman, lit up by the dark light of the Otherworld, sinking, breathing, deeper into . . .

An ultraviolet sea, lit by the inner light no mortal eye can see, drifting, deep, breathing deep, a violet woman breathing violet, smelling, tasting violet, touching bottom now, standing in the center of her place of power, a woman of power, prepared to travel her own Otherworld.

We suggested to Jaybird that she could find her way back into the landscape of her dream—in this case, the house she had grown up in. There we suggested that she could find a wise old woman who would help her. Jaybird's breathing became very, very slow, and her body stilled completely, as she entered a very deep but alert state. She was closely tended by another woman, who would occasionally ask her a question to make sure she was doing OK.

"Where are you?"

"I'm in the living room. The lights are off."

"Is anyone there?"

"Yes, it's the Baba Yaga [a wise but fierce old crone of Russian fairy stories]."

(Long pause) "What's happening now?"

"She's given me a powder I can throw on people to see if they're trustworthy."

Soon the energy in the room began to change. The women were talking in lighter tones, and there was a little giggling. It was time to come back from the long journey over water.

Trance: Returning the Way You Came

Take a moment to finish anything you may be doing, and prepare to say good-bye. Remember to thank any beings you have met here. Remember, this is your personal place of power; you can return here at will if you wish, if you have more to do. Find your way back to the center of your place of power, where your journey began.

Say good-bye . . . breathing deeply violet, resting now in violet, flooding yourself inside and outside with violet, rising slowly through a violet sea, smelling and tasting violet, a violet woman rising, breathing into . . .

An indigo sea, rising, breathing, flooding yourself with indigo, a body of indigo sensation, comfortable, smelling, tasting indigo, an indigo woman rising into . . .

A blue sea, knowing that you will be able to remember what happened in your Otherworld, breathing blue, smelling blue, tasting, flooding, rising into . . .

A green sea, the perfect temperature, breathing green, smelling green, flooding inside and outside green, a body of green sensation, rising slowly into . . .

A yellow sea, breathing yellow, smelling and tasting yellow, rising, breathing, yellow inside and outside, a yellow woman rising into . . .

An orange sea, orange within and without, floating gently, breathing, smelling and tasting orange, a body of orange sensation, rising gently, feeling rested and alert, into . . .

A red sea, a red woman floating, drifting in a red sea, breathing normally now, beginning to stretch her red body, smelling and tasting red, coming back now, feeling the floor, opening her eyes, sitting up and stretching . . . all the way back now.

It's very important to stretch thoroughly and make sure that you and your friends are completely "back" after an experience like this one. We often stretch, and tap or pat ourselves lightly all over, say our names out loud, and say each other's names. We turn the lights up a little brighter, giving everyone time to adjust thoroughly. It's important to share some food and drink and a little relaxed social time before opening the circle and sending each other off into the "real" world. Just as airplane travelers need time to adjust to jet lag, travelers to the Otherworld need time to adjust to "normal" time and space. It's respectful to ourselves, and to the Otherworld, not to take shortcuts either with the trance induction or with the resurfacing process.

Trance: Changing All the Worlds

Jaybird's story doesn't stop with her Otherworld experience. During the months that followed, her relationships with her mother and sister, but also with her close women friends, changed. She was better able to challenge others and protect herself when necessary, and she made changes in several relationships where she had felt subtly victimized.

Here is another important rule of magic: change in the Otherworld of trance can create change in the "real" world.

How many times have I thought, "I just can't seem to stand up to my mother when she's angry," or "I know that my husband loves me, but every morning when he reads the paper and doesn't want to talk, I feel ignored and unloved." These are the times when more thinking and more analyzing of the situation may not work. It is Younger Self who is having the problem, and solving it with Talking Self sometimes just won't help. This is the kind of situation where trance and dream work can directly address long-standing difficulties, often with good results. It's time for a "long journey over water."

Trance: Visiting the World of Younger Self

Every person holds inside themselves a bottomless, salty sea of old memories, vivid sensory impression, unprocessed emotion from yesterday's run-in with a rude driver or a run-in thirty years ago with a kindergarten teacher. This is the territory of Younger Self, and when the contents of this sea swim up to the surface from time to time, they appear in the language of Younger Self, as vivid, primitive images and impulses, as they did for Jaybird in her dream. Swimming in this sea are unresolved conflicts that are too painful to deal with, and facts about ourselves that we don't wish to admit, even to ourselves. This is the shadow land, where our fears and envies, our vivid, primitive feelings, walk. Here we can eat our mother for lunch, and knock our father's block off. Here, too, the monsters from under our childhood bed can eat us up. In the Otherworld, we are all truly wild things.

Since Freud, it has been popular to refer to this part of the self as "the unconscious." While Younger Self is certainly not conscious in the same way as Talking Self, in some ways Younger Self is much craftier, wiser, and more adapted for survival. When I hear a loud, unexpected noise, I hunch my shoulders and throw up my hands to protect my head *before* Talking Self realizes what has happened. My miracle body takes care of itself; my miracle soul follows its true purpose, like a coyote on a scent. Younger Self is even willing to take on and defeat Talking Self if necessary. Younger Self has its own will, makes its own plans, has its own intelligence.

Witches rarely refer to Younger Self as "unconscious." It is Younger Self who holds the animal health and energy of our being, who can chop wood or weave for hours, who can run marathons. It is Younger Self who holds our intuition and psychic abilities. Since it is Younger Self, and not Talking Self, who has the ability to bring the power of Deep Self to bear, it is wise to be respectful in all dealings between the selves.

Experienced Witches also know that beneath and beyond the personal shadow land of Younger Self lie the doorways to the shadow lands of our ancestors, our species, and our planet. By braving and traveling through our own personal shadows, we can find the shadows of our people, and work magic that goes beyond the personal issues of our private lives. Why do we humans cut down trees, anyway? Why are men and women engaged in gender wars in so many kitchens and bedrooms? Why do we keep making art, even in concentration camps? Why do we try to turn wild animals, and humans from other tribes, into our domestic slaves? Why do the wonderful gods and tales of so many peoples echo the same themes? Why do we find ourselves turning away from our friends when they are sick or dying? Why do we react so protectively to children? What is so right, and so wrong, with us, anyway? What do we have to face to make change here—at the ugly, gorgeous depths of our common soul?

Trance: Why We Need Border Patrol

Of course, it would be impossible to make lunches, drop off the kids, run to the grocery store, get to work, pick up the dry cleaning, make dinner, and catch a video if all these glories and monsters were swimming about in our heads all day long. The internal economy of our souls includes healthy boundaries that (usually) prevent our childhood conflict with our kindergarten teacher from causing us to snarl at the very nice lady who looks like her at the grocery checkout counter. Maintaining and policing these boundaries is an effort that ties up some of the energy of our spirits.

And from time to time we may experience border wars, in which urgent and nonnegotiable information from our own depths comes spilling over, disrupting our ordinary lives. If I can no longer stand living with my partner of twenty years, if I absolutely must quit a high-paying job or die of stress, my internal economy may be thrown off. If an endless round of consumerism is leaving my life meaningless, and I must a find a purpose for my life or jump off the bridge, Younger Self may create a crisis.

Younger Self may begin sending guerrilla bands and spies over my boundaries in the form of disturbing dreams, accidents, reveries that keep recurring. I may find myself constantly humming a pop song about leaving my lover or learning how to fly. I may experience some disorientation, moodiness, inability to sleep, while my soul energy is bound up with the ever more difficult task of preventing entry of the unbearable insight.

People often call these times *breakdowns*, but they are equally *breakthroughs*. Younger Self may finally break through and insist on a hearing. And if Talking Self is able, perhaps a new balance can be reached. A solution may be found that admits the information Younger Self has been holding, which brings much-needed change and which liberates the soul energy that was formerly used up by the conflict.

Trance: Crossing the Border at the Checkpoint

But there is an easier way to improve communication between our inner worlds, between our selves, without waiting for a crisis. When we have cast our circle, called on the powers of the elements and the divine power of the Goddess and God to aid and protect us in our search, then we can cross those boundaries intentionally *when we want to* and make adjustments and bring healing between the worlds, returning finally to our everyday mind, with gleaming treasures from the deep in our nets.

This is the old definition of magic again, the art of changing consciousness *at will*. With years of practice, the wills and intelligences of Younger Self and Talking Self can become aligned, so that the power of Deep Self can be brought to bear on the central meaning and purpose of our lives. This alignment allows us to become women and men of deep compassion, energy, humor, and purpose, fully capable of accomplishing the tasks of our life stories, fully able to fulfill our fates.

If you are ready, you can try taking a look around in your own Otherworld. You may want to do this with a trusted friend, and the two of you can take turns trancing. Or you may want to do this with a small group of friends. In either case, the love and trust between you is the willow basket that carries you over the ocean to the Otherworld.

A Beginner's Trance: To a Place of Personal Power

Use the rainbow induction given earlier, if you like. When you are standing in the center of your own place of power, take a moment to honor the directions. Look to the east, and open all your senses to the east. What do you smell and hear on the east wind? What emotions come up for you? Do the same for the other directions. Honor each in turn, casting a circle about yourself in the Otherworld.

Now take a moment to investigate your own surroundings. What's under your feet? What's above your head? What (if anything) are you wearing? Do you have anything with you, any tools or power objects? How are you carrying them? Check out your landscape. What grows here? What's the weather? The time of day and year? The time of moon? Are there any birds or animals about?

Notice that paths lead out from this place, going in many directions. Each leads to a different adventure, a different opportunity. This is your place of power, and you can return to it at will. You can explore every one of those paths, if you want to.

Thank your place of power, and leave a gift or offering there. You may find that you receive one in return. Return, using the reverse rainbow induction given earlier.

Trance to the Well of Healing

Use the beginner's trance just described. When you are in the center of your place of power and you have greeted all the directions, notice the path leading to the west. This path leads to the Well of Healing. Begin to walk this path, opening all your senses to the experience. Up ahead, you notice that there is an obstacle blocking your path. Use all your senses and your magical tools to investigate the obstacle, and learn as much as you can about it. Seek allies in the surrounding lands, weather, plants, animals. Pray for assistance, and notice what happens. Next, use your tools and allies to find your way over, around, or through the obstacle. Or get rid of it completely.

Now the path begins to slope downward. You reach the Well of Healing. Take a moment to use all your senses to explore the well and its surroundings. Notice the time of sun and moon, the landscape, the plants and animals. The well may have a caretaker you can meet. If you find the caretaker, greet them, ask their name and offer yours, and ask permission to touch the water. There is a gift for you in the surface of the water. There is a gift for you in the middle of the water. There is a gift for you in the depths. You also have an offering to leave at the well. Make your thank-yous and good-byes, and return the way you came. Notice if there are any changes on your path as you return from the well. When you reach the center of your place of power, thank the directions, bid them farewell, and reverse the induction.

Trance into a Mysterious Dream

A common psychic practice we use when learning these skills is the trance back into a disturbing or mysterious dream. This can be done in stages: first, just find your way back to the dream landscape, and look around from a safe distance; second, reenter the dream landscape and gather allies, seeking guidance and assistance from the weather, plants and animals, magical tools, a wise old guide, or directly from deity; finally, once these stages are complete, it is possible to reenter the dream and take action there on your own behalf.

Trance Tending

Here are some basic techniques for helping a friend trance. First, create sacred space together. Next, agree on what the basic intent of the work will be. The beginner's trances given earlier in this chapter, or any other trances in this book, can also be used.

After creating sacred space and agreeing on an intent, settle your friend in a comfortable position and make sure she is warm, since when people trance deeply their body temperature often drops. Double-check your candle safety, since you will both be absorbed for a while.

Now make sure your friend's body is relaxed and that her arms and legs are uncrossed. A useful relaxation trick is to name the body parts one by one and ask your friend to tighten them up as much as possible, and then release the tension on a breath. Once she is fully relaxed, use a trance induction, such as the rainbow induction described earlier. We also use a staircase, spiraling downward with different-colored steps, or imagine finding a cave in a hillside and entering. We can walk through seven gardens, each planted with a rainbow color. Or we can simply count out breaths together, stating clearly that on each breath the trancer is going deeper. Singing "Row, row, row your boat, gently down the stream . . ." or some other watery, dreamy, underworld chant can also be used to induce trance, if the chant is allowed to slow and then drift away into silence.

When the tracer has "landed" in the center of her own place of power, she can find her path and begin the work you have agreed on. The most important job of the trance tender is to stay grounded. When in doubt, take a deep breath and reground yourself. Only then can you be helpful to your friend. Be aware of her nonverbal cues. Remind her to breathe and relax, if necessary. Remember, she is not alone in her trance world. You can remind her to call on the powers of the elements, plants and animals, her magical tools, the Goddess and the old Gods. But you cannot direct or interpret her trance. You can't do someone else's inner work, no matter how much you might want to help. So, for example, please don't say, "You look down and find a sword," but rather "You look around. . . . Is there anything you can find that can help you?"

You may notice her gathering tension in some part of her body. Ask her permission, and then, only if it's OK with her, touch her where it might be helpful. You can ask her to direct her breath or a sound toward a part of her body where tension is gathering. Allow her time to do her work, but stay alert for a shift of energy when she becomes tired or loses focus. It's not necessary to do everything in one session. Remind her that she can return here anytime she wishes, that this is *her* place of power.

If she has been able to complete only part of her work, you may wish to suggest that she "bind" the scene until she can return. This might involve ropes or nets or marking the scene with her name or a personal symbol. Many modern Witches also get good results by visualizing a video remote control pointed at the scene and hitting Pause.

Remind her to thank any helpful beings she may have encountered and to say good-bye. Encourage her to return on her path the same way she came, back to the center of her place of power. Ask her to thank and say good-bye to the directions in her place of power, and then reverse the induction. Both partners need to stretch, pat the surfaces of their bodies, and say their names to themselves, to make sure they are completely "back" from the Otherworld.

After doing pairs trance, use the aura "brushdown" described in chapter 3 to completely cleanse and separate the energies of the people who have worked together. Share food and drink and some informal time before opening the circle.

The Element Water

Traditionally, the powers of water include trance and techniques that connect us to our psychic and intuitive abilities. As well as practicing trance journeying, many Witches learn some form of divination, whether it be palm reading, card reading, astrology, psychic reading, pendulum divination, or scrying in fire or water or crystal.

The tool of water is the cup or chalice. When filled with liquid, the cup becomes a mirror when we gaze into it, a tool of self-knowledge, self-acceptance, and self-love. We can literally drink these in from our cups. The power of the wise in the west is "to dare." If you tried the beginner's trance described earlier, then you have put it to the test already. You dared!

Take some time for yourself, and spend it with living water—the ocean, a lake, or a little creek. Make your next bath or shower a ritual for cleansing and healing. Dance in the rain; walk through the deep snow. Say, "By the waters of her living womb."

Remember, whenever we receive blessings from Mother Nature, we must give back. To give back to water, first find out where the water you drink comes from. What protects the quality of your personal drinking water? Where is your watershed? Is that land protected from logging, from skimobiles and motorboats leaking oil and gas in their exhaust? From runoff of pesticides and fertilizers? Make and keep a commitment to do one thing in your life to help and protect the water. You need to drink it every day, so it's only fair!

Like Rose and her brothers, we have woven a willow basket for ourselves and dared to take a long journey over water to another land. We have soared over the gray sea and begun a right relationship with the element water. Now our journey calls us onward, to the land of the Fata Morgana and her challenge.

The Inner Path

Rose has overcome the first obstacles on her voyage. She has broken the rule of silence and exposed the injustice of her family history by her questioning. She has chosen the wild, and she has accepted guidance. She has endured the anger that comes from past injustice and allowed its release. Now she must overcome her fear and step into the basket, to be carried away on a wild flight few mortals will ever experience.

> *Old Mother Goose, when she wanted to wander,*
> *would ride through the air on a very fine gander.*

Can you imagine our ancestors, standing in a harvested fall field, leaning on their rakes and pitchforks, watching the great migration overhead, and listening to the wild cries of the birds heading south, the powerful song of the beating wings? Imagine how they must have felt, as the coldness and dark closed in on their villages, knowing that somewhere it was summer? Or in the spring, hearing the cries of the sky-darkening flocks and knowing they traveled to the glittering ice country, at the back of the north wind? Can you imagine their longing to lay down the round of chores and familiarity to follow? Can you imagine their fear, when, even in the next valley, people wore different clothes and spoke with a barely understandable accent?

Our world has no secrets anymore; we can get on a plane and follow the geese or the swans and beat them there. We could hardly find a country in the world that did not seem familiar, with the same newspapers and fast food as on any street corner at home. We can only imagine what our ancestors meant when they told this tale of a journey across the dark and deadly sea, when the swans could fly a brave girl to the strange and distant land of the Fata Morgana. And yet we, too, can know the desire to fly away on powerful wings from the endless round of everyday things. The work of the Inner Path for this section of the story is to create our baskets, woven from strong and flexible trust and love in our circles, strong enough to carry us into the sky. Once we have woven our baskets, we can fly high, experiencing the ecstatic practice that is at the heart of Witchcraft.

Seeking Ecstasy

Witches share with mystics from every religious and cultural background a common insight into the nature of reality. The day-to-day world of apparently separate things—its tasks and worries, its striving, lonely, consciousness—is an illusion. Like a veil, it covers an infinitely complex, unified, and joyful dance of ever-becoming, ensouled creation. The god Shiva, dancing in the circle of flames, holds his hand up in a gesture that means "Fear not!" And this is excellent advice. With trancing and chanting, dancing and drumming, in lightly or deeply altered states of awareness, we can experience directly the wondrous, ecstatic dance of creation, the galaxy-creating explosion of passion that even now moves through our human bodies, our living bodies, which at every moment gleam with spirit light and move and flow with the dance of the universe. This passionate melting of our individual consciousness into the great dance, this direct experience of the joyful oneness of all things, is part of the personal and community practice of Witchcraft. Our developing ability to experience ecstatic states "at will" builds our self-confidence and personal power and reinforces our right place in a joyous world that is immanent deity. These experiences reinspire and reenergize us to return to the world, where we then can continue to love and work and, when necessary, fight to protect the web of life, the ones we love, and all the living.

Weaving a Willow Basket

But Rose is not a swan; she is a human girl. And we Witches are human also, regardless of how ecstatic we may become while trancing, chanting, and dancing. Rose can survive this journey across the sea only because she and her brothers weave a basket of willow wands, strong enough to safely carry a person who has no wings. We, too, must weave a basket to ride in. But instead of weaving it out of willow, we must weave it out of another plant that grows by water, out of our love and trust for the other people in our circles, and out of love and trust for ourselves and the Goddess.

It is often said in our oral tradition that coveners are closer than family. In circles and covens, women and men share on the deepest levels their devotions and fears, their longings and visions, their dreams and intuitions.

Witches who have tranced together for years sometimes reach a level of attunement with one another that is amazing to see. They literally know what the other is thinking, and sometimes even seem to an outsider to talk in their own language, jumping from thought to thought like twins or close siblings who can send each other off into gales of laughter with a word, or know just the right thing to say or do without any discussion. It is the truly lucky woman or man who can achieve this kind of intimacy in circle with a few close friends. It doesn't always happen, and never without conflict along the way.

But most of our rituals and classes don't require this level of intimacy. There are many ways to deepen trust and affection in a group that may be together for only one ritual or may only occasionally work together. The most important of these, and one we generally use at the beginning of every Reclaiming class, is the round. This is the simplest and most basic stitch we use to weave our basket.

Weaving the Basket Exercise: The Round

The rules for a round are simple, but learning how to apply them is the study of a lifetime. Here are the rules for a round:

1. One person talks at a time. We often pass a rock, a stick, or some other special object, and only the person holding it may speak.
2. Everyone else listens without interrupting.
3. Each person gets one turn to talk.
4. Each person has the right to pass.
5. Everything said in the circle is held in confidentiality by those present. There will be no gossip or speculation by people who were not present.

Sometimes the round is focused by a question, which everyone agrees on ahead of time. Sometimes it is a chance for us to share generally what is going on in our lives outside the circle and gain a little insight into one another's process. In my circle for many years we would begin with a round and listen deeply to one another. When the round was over, we would begin to pull out common themes and threads from what we each had shared. From those common threads we wove a vision of what to do for our ritual that night.

Opening up and sharing from the heart is a skill that requires practice. Each of us has our favorite ways to present ourselves, our masks, which we use without even being aware of them. A good exercise that we use to illuminate this for ourselves is to actually make masks. These can be as simple as paper plates on a stick, or as complex as plaster casts.

Weaving the Basket Exercise: A Masked Tea Party

You will need art supplies and good friends or a good mirror. Create sacred space, and light your candles. Allow yourself a few moments of meditation. Close your eyes and reflect back on several difficult or disturbing interactions you've had recently. How do you present yourself when you are under pressure or when you feel threatened? Can you see any patterns? Victim? Martyr? Genius? Saint? Tough guy? Baby? Mother? Pope? Villain?

When you feel that you are sniffing on your own tracks, like a hound that can follow a tricky fox, then it's time to open your eyes and grab those art supplies. Make yourself a mask that represents one of your favorite defensive postures. As you hum and work, try out some one-liners that your mask character might say: "I'm only saying this for your own good"; "But you don't understand how hurt I am . . ."; "After all I've done for you . . ."; "When you've lived as long as I have . . ."

If you are working with friends, put on the masks and use the one-liners to have a little tea party. It's a strangely familiar feeling to talk with people who simply repeat the same thing over and over and never change their facial expression. It's even more eerie to *be* one. If you are working alone, try it in the mirror. When you've had enough, take the mask off.

Take a moment to really feel the sensation of being free of the mask. What would it be like to live this way, both free and vulnerable? If you enjoyed working with this exercise, you will find more like it in Starhawk's book *Truth or Dare*.

Weaving the Basket Exercise: The Mystery

Each and every one of us is mystery. We will never know each other or our own selves at our deepest: whole, powerful, shape-shifting, divine. We can come closer and closer to complete knowledge and love of ourselves and others, but it will always remain a goal and a source of human longing, never completely attained in this life. One of the best ways to experience and acknowledge this mystery in ritual is by using veils.

You will need a thin scarf or long veil and good friends or a good mirror. Create sacred space, and light your candles. Choose one person to go first, and veil her in the center of the circle; or if you are working alone with a mirror, veil yourself. Now make a statement about this person—for example, "You are a wife and mother" or "You are shy" or "You are an incredible artist." Allow a moment of listening silence, or ring a bell and wait while the echoes die down. Now let the veiled person answer: "Perhaps, and I am so much more. . . ." Keep making statements as long as you can think of more true things to say about this person. No statement can capture her whole nature. Allow your sense of wonder and awe to awaken toward your friends and toward yourself. Who will ever know any soul to the deep source of her beauty and strength?

Weaving the Basket Exercise: She Who Listens

Learning to reveal oneself fully in circle is the work of a lifetime, and so is learning to listen fully. It is impossible to go through life always listening to each person as though she were the Goddess herself, speaking from the deep source we can never fully know. But with practice we can learn to direct this kind of listening to people we really care about in sacred space. We each will have to unlearn our normal habits as listeners, which we use to distance ourselves from the person speaking and to protect ourselves. Some of the most common habits include thinking up what you're going to say when it's your turn, judging the person speaking, arguing with her in your mind, or spacing out and thinking about something else. Learning to listen well and to stay fully present is as difficult an art as any known to womankind.

Weaving the Basket Exercise: Listening Exercise

With a circle of friends, create sacred space and light your candles. Choose one person to lead a brief meditation, bringing everyone to dropped and open attention. Now begin a check-in round, where each person takes a turn. Focus on the experience of listening to your friends, with dropped and open attention. It's normal for the listener to begin to lose focus and drift into reverie, judgment, reaction—a million forms of distraction.

When you notice that you have lost your attention, you will usually find that you are experiencing your awareness up in your head again. Simply breathe deeply, and drop and open your attention again, gently returning it outward toward the person speaking. Try to listen deeply—to what is unsaid, to body language, and to emotion. If your circle is close, and everyone agrees on it beforehand, it can be very enlightening to share your reactions with each other, and especially the difference between your reactions from a dropped state of deep listening and your normal reactions.

Weaving the Basket: Circle Safety

These exercises are just the beginning of a lifetime of practice. It is difficult but well worth the effort to learn to fully open one's heart to others and to listen deeply to friends. Because, although we may make rules of various kinds (confidentiality, right to pass, no put-downs, nonjudgmental listening, and so forth) to try to create safety in circles, the bottom line is that one size never fits all. The same rule that creates safety in one situation may make another situation impossible or unbearable. Particularly after the honeymoon is over, after the time for politeness has passed, when the core issues and deep attraction and repulsion between people begin to operate, it may simply be unrealistic to expect no negative attacks or to expect someone not to share part of what is going on with a partner or therapist or some other special person outside the circle.

At the core, the safety of a circle comes from the creativity, compassion, intelligence, and sense of humor of the women and men in it. The safety of the circle comes from each member's commitment to express herself fully and to listen to others deeply. We must rely on our own and each other's deepening ability to respect all life, and each person, as part of an immanent deity. We must rely on each other's intentions, skills, and efforts as we learn to love and understand ourselves and others.

And of course, at times mistakes will be made, hard words will be spoken, feelings will be hurt. Just as in any love relationship, the safety of the circle relies on its members' abilities to get angry and fight at times, passionately, honestly, flexibly, fairly. Not every circle will survive every fight. Just as in love, some people just don't work well together, or sometimes they do for a year or twenty years, and then they change and it's time to move on. This is never an easy or painless process, and it may not feel "safe" at all, but this is how we weave the basket of willow. We know from experience that this basket, homemade and imperfect though it may be, can safely carry a wingless creature on a breathtaking flight beyond the realm of night and day, beyond the gates of now and then.

Weaving a Basket: A Spellworking

Now it's time to take a walk outside—alone or with your circle sisters. If you live in a city, find a park, hilltop, or other slightly wild area. If you can get into the wild, bless your lucky stars. As you walk, meditate on your relationships with others. Whom could you learn to trust, or do you already trust, enough to carry you over the sea? When in doubt, allow the wisdom of nature to guide you or offer insight. If you dream of creating collaborative magic with others, what is the next step you can take to make your own dreams come true? If you already are working in circle, what can you do to weave your basket stronger? As you walk, gather bits and pieces of wild growing things. (Never take all of a wild plant, or the only one growing in a certain area.) Weave yourself a bit of basket out of natural, gathered plant material, and place it on your Rose altar as a magical commitment to "take flight."

Ecstasy: Dance, Trance, and Chants

In the Elements Path, we learned the basic skill of trance journeying. In the trance state we sought there, the induction brought us to a super-relaxed, still, and dreamlike state while we were awake, in which the vivid sensory world of Younger Self could communicate with Talking Self. But we can also induce trance states through music and movement.

In San Francisco at Winter Solstice, after we have jumped into the freezing ocean naked, we dance and drum together around a bonfire, singing songs for the laboring earth and to bring the new sun to birth. As the drums repeat their insistent heartbeat message, and the flames reveal the beautiful rhythms of our naked animal bodies, time shifts and blurs, and a deep sensory certainty opens that we are animal, divine, and human at once, powerful, connected, and that a passionate and a loving life is possible, one that goes far beyond the alienated culture that binds us. Rhythm, dancing, and chanting can connect us to a deep sensory and kinetic certainty of our soul-life.

Beverly Frederick is a Reclaiming Witch and teacher who has worked for years to help bring the body wisdom of dance and rhythm into Reclaiming's practice of ritual magic. Beverly has taught dance, acrobatics, and yoga for years, and she moves with the powerful, sinuous grace of her profession. An accomplished vocalist and musician, she knows how to help a circle of Witches start improvising and building beautiful rhythmic, wordless power through chanting. Here are some tips Beverly offers for Witches who want to start using chanting and movement in their circle work.

Ecstasy: The Weave

The first step is to create a weave of sound that a group can keep up for a long time. Beverly suggests that groups build this skill up in stages. "Some people think they can't sing or can't keep rhythm," she says. "But everyone can make sound." Beverly emphasizes that the weave of sound is what's important; she stresses that listening is actually much more important in creating the weave than the skill of the sound you make. When people really listen to each other, even nonmusicians can create beautiful, or eerie, or passionate sounding together.

In sacred space with your friends, start by simply sending a sound into the center of the circle together. This may begin tentatively, but if you keep listening to each other, you can allow the tone to build and change. When you hear something you like, you can pick it up or repeat it. A group whose members have struggled in traffic, or traveled long distances to be together, or had to juggle dinner, homework, and bedtimes to free up a few hours for circle may find their tone building at first into shrieks or howls, moans or groans. This is simply more purification, which the group needs in order to get all the way into sacred space. And it feels good to let loose! Finally, the toning will begin to come together, graceful or passionate, expressive or eerie, depending on the energy of the group. The first time this happens, it is a truly magic moment.

Ecstasy: Group Chanting

In the very first Reclaiming class I ever took, our teacher, Raven Moonshadow, started the group singing with a very simple chant: "Born of water, cleansing, powerful, healing, changing, we are . . ." We were a fairly large group, and we were passing a bowl of salt water around the circle as each person did their own private purification, releasing the tension from their day and any nervousness about the class into the bowl. As the first few people had their turn, I remember thinking how long it was going to take, and whether I could possibly put up with this. But as I relaxed into the chant, closed my eyes, and really listened, I got swept up in the beauty and variations of those voices and the simple nine-word chant. By the time we actually stopped, I didn't want to. Fortunately, there is now quite a bit of pagan ritual music recorded, so that people everywhere can learn simple and beautiful music to help their ritual work. (See the Resources section at the back of this book for sources.)

Beverly recommends choosing a chant that has two simple parts, or a simple round. Simple chants are important because they allow us to bypass our intellectual roadblocks to ecstasy. Begin singing and really listening to each other. Hold the image of the "weave," remembering that the pattern is more important than any one sound and that variation of rhythm and tone add energy. When you are ready, begin to introduce a variation. A person who needs to sing higher or lower than the group might find a harmonizing tone above or below the chant and just hold it or make it rhythmic. Someone might introduce a finger snap or hand clap or a "bop, bop, shu-wop." When you take the plunge and introduce a variation, stick with it for at least six repetitions. It's easy to get embarrassed and give up on your variation too quickly, but your group's chant will soon die away if it turns into a drone, so the variations are important. It's also important for at least one singer/listener to keep the basic chant going so that the variation people have a base to return to. You can take turns with this role. If your group is small or if you are just starting out, it may help to use recorded music under your own voices to sustain you at first. Before you know it, your group will be carried away on a magic carpet of sound, voice, and breath.

Ecstasy: Adding Movement

Once you have learned to create a weave of sound and rhythm for yourselves, try adding movement. A very simple place to start is dancing in a circle.

Although there are many fun and beautiful circle dances where the dancers hold hands, for this improvisation it's better if each dancer has the full use of her own body, so people who easily make big movements, or people whose movement style is smaller, don't impact each other. To begin, simply put something in the center of the circle. It can be a complex altar that you have built together, or it can just be a candle or saltwater bowl. Begin building a weave of sound and rhythm with a chant, and start moving clockwise around the bowl, letting your sounds and your bodies guide you. Allow the energy to build, peak, and die down. This exercise is so simple it's hard to believe that it holds the heart of much ritual magic.

Here's another piece of circle work from Beverly's tool kit that can help groups begin moving together. In circle, choose an energy to work with—an element, a deity, an emotion, whatever fits your needs that night—and choose one person to go first. She closes her eyes and allows the energy of, say, fire to come through her and create a movement. Fire may also make sound through her. Everyone else is watching her, and as she begins to move, everyone mirrors her movement and sound, until the whole group is moving fire together. Now the first person can open her eyes and see what has been created, and when she is ready she can pass leadership to someone else as the energy moves through the circle.

Ecstasy: Moving Through

Here is another Beverly exercise, one that allows a group to focus on one member and help her express and work through an emotion. Decide together what your group member is going to be working with, and either put on recorded music or create music that reflects that emotional state. Give her space to create movements and sounds that express her feeling. Support her, if necessary, to let go of any inner voices that tell her she doesn't have the right to this movement, or that it's not proper, or that she should consider what people will think. She can let her movement become whatever it needs to be. For some people it may get very big and loud; for others it may change or intensify or even get very small and compressed. When she's ready, she can begin to release her movement into the earth. It's very important to remember to release into the earth, and not onto each other.

These exercises are a wonderful starting place for circles that want to bring rhythm and movement into their ritual work. And they are just the beginning, because Reclaiming Witches have used many resources to learn to let rhythm and movement bring them into an altered state where time runs differently. We know that the ecstatic, integrated sensation of our own living, moving bodies can open a deep sensory certainty of being one with the Goddess. Morris dancing, belly dancing, martial arts, tai chi, yoga, sitting meditation practices, backpacking, chanting in groups—are all possibilities, so let your imagination and intuition be your guide!

Ecstasy: Committing to a Practice

Choose one of these ways to bring rhythm, movement, and a heightened sensory awareness into your own altar work or circle work, and try it at least once. Try to commit yourself to practicing regularly in a class or circle or, if you are working alone, to a regular practice on your own. Bring your drums, or dance music, or yoga mats, or meditation cushions into your circle's altar space, which is now beginning to fill up with a Witch's paraphernalia of self-care, of soul care. Mirrors, roses, bread, ashes, basketry—we are continuing to build ourselves a multilayered spell for self-healing, following Rose's story.

Trance: Going Deeper

In the Elements Path, we learned the basics of trance journeying and practiced a few beginner's trances, including trancing to a place of power, trancing back into a mysterious dream, and trancing to the Well of Healing. If you have practiced these trances and made them your own, it is possible to go further in exploring your own Otherworld. Here are some additional trance workings you can try.

Trance into a Tarot Card

Choose one tarot card out of your deck that has a powerful and mysterious effect on you. You can let magic choose the card for you, either by simply praying for guidance and then cutting the deck, or by taking a card that "accidentally" falls out of your deck. Or you can choose a card that comes up repeatedly in your readings.

Meditate on the card. I also like to either trace the card and color the tracing with crayons, or trace the card and needlepoint it. In this way I get every detail of the image deeply into my awareness.

Create sacred space, and prepare yourself for a trance journey. Arrange yourself so that you can see the card when your eyes are open and so that as you begin your induction and your eyes close, you can still see the card image, glowing in your inner senses. Allow the outlines of the card to become a doorway, and step through it into the world of the card. Now you can explore this landscape at will. The features of the landscape can come alive, and the characters can talk with you. You can return at any time simply by retracing your steps. Remember to thank this world for letting you visit, and also thank any helpful creatures or spirits you met. Step back out of the card, and see it again as though through a doorway. Reverse the induction, and return to normal consciousness.

Trance into a Natural Process

It is also possible to trance into any natural process or occurrence. Imagine trancing into a summer rainstorm, or into a snowy evergreen forest deep in dormancy and cold, or into the secret lives of plants and animals. Nature is a great teacher, and she has written an exciting, fanciful, humorous, powerful tale for us, should we care to read it.

First it's important to do a little actual research, either in books or, even better, with fingertips, eyes, ears, and nose. Remember, the meditations of our tradition are based on simple natural processes that we can easily observe for ourselves, such as the way salt dissolves in water or the way trees reach and open to earth and to sky. While it would be wonderful to trance into the lives of eagles, if you live in a city it may be more productive to trance into the lives of pigeons, because it's possible to actually observe them closely over time and to get a receptive, sensory understanding of their lives. Much can be learned from a humble bird: patience and perseverance for nest building, care of the egg, ruffling up the chest feathers and spreading the tail feathers for courting, soaring.

Once you have gathered your own sensory information and impressions of the natural process you've chosen, create sacred space, and prepare yourself for trance. Go to your place of power, and at the center of your place of power allow the Tree of Life to grow and appear. You can find any natural process or event either among the roots or branches or in the trunk of the Tree of Life. Once you find what you are looking for, you can enter its world. You can learn from the inside out both about the natural world and about yourself. You will find that every natural process gives you images and insights and powers that can become tools for your own growth. Wouldn't you like to have bark, so that the next mean comment doesn't hurt you? Wouldn't you like to be able to make pearls around the little things that annoy you? Wouldn't you like to get an owl's-eye perspective, looking down on your life from a soaring height while everyone is asleep and the moon sails high in the sky, lighting up every detail with an unearthly glow?

Trance into a Fairy Story

Get to know a fairy story well enough so that you can tell the whole tale without forgetting important details. Your circle can choose a tale that illuminates some difficult issue in one person's life or an issue that concerns everyone. In sacred space, take turns telling the tale with the lights low, while creating a soft rhythm behind the words. When you reach the part of the tale you choose to work with, go into trance together. You can explore the landscape of the tale together or interact with the characters. You can explore details of the story that are particularly powerful or moving. Each fairy story opens up into a world of ancestral wisdom. When you are ready, return to normal consciousness by retracing your steps out of the fairy-tale world. Finish telling the tale to the end. Once the tale is complete, come all the way out of trance, patting yourselves all over, stretching, saying your names and the names of your circle sisters. Share food and drink, and open the circle when you are ready.

Flying

Just as Rose steps into the basket and flies over the sea to the Otherworld, so do we—stepping into the basket woven by our love and trust of each other, creating ritual that takes us to ecstatic states through drum and dance, through chanting and trance. As we learn that we can change our consciousness at will, that ecstatic states are available to us for the taking, that we can reinvigorate our visions and our lives by "taking a long journey over water," we build our self-confidence and our Goddess confidence. Like Rose, we are ready for the next stage of our initiatory journey.

The Outer Path

Dion Fortune called magic "the art of changing consciousness at will." We could rephrase that slightly and term magic "the art of letting ourselves get carried away—and of arriving safely on the other shore."

In this section of the story, Rose is literally carried away by her brothers to the magic realm across the far seas. Her safe arrival on the other shore depends on the strength of the basket they weave for her.

The brothers create a vessel, a container, in which to carry Rose. We can think of ritual as the container we weave in which we can be carried away by magic and ecstasy. To land safely on the other shore, that container must be strong enough to withstand the journey. A ritual must have a strong structure if it is to allow us to move into deep and powerful states of consciousness. We weave our vessel from the withes of clear boundaries in time and space, a clear and open intention, a commitment to ground the energy we raise and to reground ourselves after reaching deep states of consciousness. The symbols we choose, the actions we decide upon, the chants and meditations and the patterns of the drumbeats we use—all become aspects of the container we weave.

In many versions of the story, the basket the brothers weave is made from willow. Willow is an ancient, sacred tree, long associated with Witches. Willow is flexible: it can be bent, twisted, and shaped into many forms. To be a Witch meant to be a person who could bend or twist fate, who could reweave reality.

Our basket must be strong, but it must also be flexible, open enough for us to feel the wind and see the lands we pass over. Our ritual structure must leave room for openness and spontaneity. If it is too tightly controlled, if we are focused on following a plan instead of flowing with the energy, the basket will be too heavy, and we will not get carried away.

In looking for structure, we might think about organic order, the structure that arises from the needs and energies of the work. Just as our muscles are formed and shaped by the work we do, so too the particular form a ritual takes is determined by our intention, by the work of transformation we hope to accomplish.

Ritual has the potential to move us into altered states of consciousness, to move us into the deep places of our psyches where we are most vulnerable. To lead ritual with integrity, we must be aware of others' boundaries and conscious of which acts or symbols might transgress them. We need to learn a deep respect for our own and others' limits on sharing. We must never force intimacy, but rather learn to create the conditions in which deep connection may emerge.

So too in any group endeavor, whenever we try to evoke creativity and healing in community with others, we must always weave a vessel that is both strong and open. We must always dance between earth and fire, between boundaries and exuberance. The Outer Path work for this chapter focuses on the dynamic tension between these poles, on learning to weave the vessel of ritual, and on some of the specific patterns of ritual we in Reclaiming have developed.

When I first moved to San Francisco twenty-five years ago, I formed a circle of people interested in Wiccan ritual. None of us had much formal training, and all of us were interested in experimenting and creating rather than following directions. We would gather, begin chanting, drumming, and playing music, and let the ritual evolve. Those early rituals had an excitement and spontaneity about them, but after a while we noticed that a pattern had formed. Somebody led most of the beginning parts, casting a circle and calling the directions. Our spontaneous energy building tended to rise to a peak and then fall, leaving us in a quiet, meditative state. The same people tended to take leadership over and over again. Quieter, more shy people were hesitant to jump in. They didn't know what was supposed to be happening, and when.

Eventually we realized that, rather than liberating us, complete lack of structure was actually preventing full participation. Only those of us who were either more confident in speaking out or perhaps simply more uncomfortable with silence were taking roles in the ritual. A structure that we all could agree upon would allow each person to make clearer choices about how they might contribute.

Reclaiming rituals do have a basic, agreed-upon structure. Knowing the underlying pattern allows us to work together in planned ways and spontaneously. We have similar ideas and expectations about how the energy should flow.

Basic Ritual Structure

We begin Reclaiming rituals by grounding, casting a circle, and calling in the elements, deities, and other allies into sacred space. There are many creative ways we might do all of these.

Within the circle, we do the work of the ritual, which varies according to our intention. In its simplest form, we raise energy and direct it through a magical image that embodies our purpose.

We end every ritual by grounding the energy we've raised and by offering gratitude to the allies we've worked with. We say good-bye and thanks to everything we've invoked and then open the circle, releasing our sacred space.

Within that basic structure is infinite room for creativity, improvisation, and spontaneity. But the structure serves as the ribs of the basket, giving it form and cohesion.

Ritual Creation

How do we create a ritual so that it becomes a basket to carry us to the land of magic? How do we set a structure that invites ecstasy, yet links us firmly to the ground? How do we make it possible to open up to altered states of consciousness safely?

If we literally set out to weave a basket, we would need to know what that basket is supposed to do. Should it be wide and flat for collecting cut roses, or shaped to hold bread? Tightly woven to hold grain, or made with a loose weave to allow air to circulate?

When we set out to plan a ritual, we first need to know what the ritual is meant to do. What is our intention?

Beginning with our intention seems so logical that it should be unnecessary to mention it. However, I can't tell you how many hundreds of times I've sat down with a group to plan a ritual, and only after hours of batting around ideas does it occur to us to ask, "Yes, but what are we actually doing this ritual for?"

When the intention of the ritual is clear, the symbols, the actions, and the chants and invocations all have clear meaning and carry power. When the intention is unclear, the elements of the ritual may individually be beautiful and heartful, but unless they are linked to a central meaning, the power will not build, and participants will leave feeling the ritual as a whole is lacking.

Review the meditation in the Outer Path in chapter 2 on finding a ritual intention. *Intention* is a noun, but a ritual intention is a verb, something the ritual is meant to do, a transformation that is meant to take place. A clear intention can be stated in one sentence, albeit with many clauses:

"Our intention is to give Maureen healing."

"Our intention is to use the energies of the Samhain season, when the veil between the worlds is thin, to support each other in honoring our ancestors and mourning our beloved dead, and to plant the seeds of new things to be born."

"Our intention is to explore the blocks that disempower us, release them, connect to our sources of inner power, and celebrate."

"Our intention is to honor Marnie's passage into Cronehood."

Once our intention is clear, we need to find the central imagery and symbols that can embody our purpose. We might use our magical tools to scry, candle gaze, meditate, or trance to find the right images. We might brainstorm, throwing forth every wild and crazy idea that comes to us, without judgment or criticism, and later synthesize our ideas or choose one image to work with. Allowing people to express ideas without judgment helps set an atmosphere in which creativity can flourish:

"I see a circle of women all lined up in order of age."

"I see a labyrinth."

"I see Marnie sitting on a golden throne."

When we know what images we want to work with, the next question I find useful is, What's the story? What is the transformation we want to enact? Who is the protagonist, and what challenges does she or he face? Who are we in the story? Knowing the story is like having a strong ball of twine that ties the ribs of the basket together.

In Marnie's Croning, for example, she is the protagonist, and the story, were we to tell it, might go something like this: "Marnie is making the passage into Cronehood and wisdom. She enters the labyrinth, to walk its winding way from youth to age. In the center, she receives power and blessings. When she emerges, she is enthroned and asked to speak her wisdom."

In our Winter Solstice ritual, the protagonist is the Goddess herself. We, the participants, are the support team for her labor. The story might go something like this:

"Throughout the longest night of the year, Mother Night is in labor to bring forth the Sun Child. We cleanse and purify ourselves, letting go of all we need to release from the year before. Then we gather in our homes to feast and entertain her throughout her labor. We bake bread, which rises and swells like her pregnant belly, and knead into it our hopes and dreams to be brought to birth with the Sun Child. All night we keep vigil, and at dawn we climb a hill to watch the moment of birth as the new sun rises."

The story of a healing ritual might be as simple as: "We all gather in sacred space to draw healing power from the earth for Ron."

Or it might be more complex: "We, Susan's friends and sisters, gather to support her as she goes deep within to search out the root of her illness, listen to its messages, release the blocks to her healing, and gather the power to kick the virus out of her system."

It's helpful to keep the intention and the story clear and simple. If we're taken on a trance journey and given a gift in each of the four directions, we'll have forgotten the first one by the time we get the last. If we raise a cone of power to heal Ron, the clear-cut redwoods, and the greed in the hearts of CEOs of global corporations, we'll end up with diffused energy that cannot focus power. Our rule of thumb is: one gift per trance; one intention per cone of power.

The Tofu of Ritual

The story will guide us in planning the heart of the ritual. We always begin by planning the central section—the "meat" or, if you prefer, the "tofu." The work of the core section will then tell us what we need to invoke, what kind of circle we need to cast, and so on.

To plan the tofu, I find it helpful to ask, "What is the simplest and most powerful way we can enact this story? What form of ritual is called for?" In Ron's ritual, for example, the core might be placing him in the center of the circle, chanting his name, and visualizing golden light bathing him. For Susan, we might ask one person to lead her on a trance journey into her own body and let the images that arise direct what happens. For both rituals, we'd need a solid grounding that prepares us for channeling energy, a clear, strong circle, and we might want to invoke the elements in their healing aspects as well as a Goddess and possibly a God of healing. Before we devoke, we'd want food to share to help us ground, and we might want to plan a cleansing or brushdown for the healers to be sure we don't pick up any negative energies.

Making Sacred Space

Once we have an idea about what the heart of the ritual work will be, we can plan the creation of sacred space, the grounding, casting, and invocations. In most of our public rituals, we ask volunteers either beforehand or on the spot to take these roles, so that the ritual reflects many voices and so that many people have an opportunity to be priestesses. Volunteers need to know the intention of the ritual and something of the flow, and coordination is important.

The invocations create the texture of the ritual and set the pace and tone. There are an infinite number of ways to invoke. At times you might simply stand in the center of the circle, take a deep breath, feel that hollow feeling in the pit of your stomach, that fear of making a fool of yourself, let it go, open your mouth, and let something come out.

At other times you might carefully craft a poem, song, or dance. A spoken invocation sometimes comes as close as we get in our tradition to a sermon: a reflection on the deeper meaning of the element, a call to participants to change. At our big Spiral Dance, which draws close to two thousand people, we've had directions invoked by trapeze artists, rope dancers, stilt walkers, and fire jugglers.

If the tofu of the ritual involves a lot of movement and wild dance, the invocations might be thoughtful and reflective. But if the heart of the ritual body centers on quiet talk or stillness, the invocations can provide a chance for movement. One of our favorite ways of incorporating movement into an invocation was pioneered by Beverly and Suzanne:

Drumming and Dancing in the Directions

Drummers are chosen before the ritual begins. They may agree on different rhythms for each direction or may choose one person for each direction to lead off with a beat.

Dancers may also be chosen to stand in the center and lead a simple movement. Participants may follow or improvise freely. The central dancers open each invocation with a few words—for example, "Let's turn to the east, and call the air."

The drummers begin their beat, everyone dances, and when the energy begins to wane, dancers cue the drummers by raising their hands high and then dropping to the ground. Drums may roll to a peak or fade out. The lead dancer for that direction says a simple phrase—in this case, "Welcome, East! Welcome, Air!" And we move on, around the circle.

A ritual that works is an orchestration of energy. It may move from moments of profound stillness to wild ecstatic dancing, from quiet meditation to howling around a fire, but the underlying pattern and flow of energy must support the intention of the ritual. All the skills we've learned in other paths around identifying and channeling our own energies now come into play on a larger scale.

Energy Observation

To priestess a ritual, we must first become aware of the energies in a group. When you are in a ritual, or in a meeting at work, a concert, a performance, or a demonstration, ground and anchor yourself. From your core state, observe what is happening as a flow of energy. When is the energy moving? When is it stuck? If it were a river, would it be clear and free running or muddy and full of sludge?

What happens to shift the energy? What do the priestesses, the facilitators, the performers do that creates a change in the flow? Are they conscious or unconscious of their impact? How does their state of being impact the energy?

In a ritual, consciously move to different parts of the circle. How does the energy feel in the center? On the edges? Does it have different qualities in different quarters?

After the event is over, draw or diagram the energy flow. If you are working with a group of observers, compare notes. Did you experience the same shifts and variations? What have you learned from this experience?

Energy Tending

When you have practiced observing the energy, explore the ways you can affect it. To move energy, we use our bodies, our breath, our voices, and our ability to visualize.

TEND THE EDGES: In a ritual, position yourself around the outer edge. Use your energy-moving skills to help keep the edges coherent and focused and to keep the energy moving strongly, not dribbling away.

WORK THE CENTER: Move into the center, and use your voice, body, and vision to help the energy rise to a cone in a smooth and focused way. Hold the central image clearly in your mind, and focus your will on the intention of the magic.

When you've explored tending individually, make an agreement with two or three others to consciously tend and focus together, and see what power a group can have.

In Reclaiming, all of us who have some level of experience in ritual naturally co-priestess: we work the energy together. We take responsibility for tending the edges, holding the intention, and raising the cone in the center. We consult during the ritual, whispering to each other, "This chant has gone on long enough—let's change it." We often keep eye contact with others in the center and stay in subtle communication.

Moving Energy

Priestessing a ritual is like surfing: you can move with the water, changing direction and steering with art and skill, but you can't fight the waves. In a ritual, you must sense, reflect, and guide the energy, but you cannot control it. As priestesses, we always want to hold our intention for the ritual clearly, but we must often let go of our picture of just how that intention is supposed to be realized.

We might imagine a slow, quiet meditation and find that the group is raucously laughing. We might start a chant and find that it builds into power long before we imagined it would. Or we might plan for ecstatic dancing and find the group simply bobbing in place, bored.

When the energy of a ritual refuses to go according to your plan, take a moment to reground and anchor. With a breath, consciously let go of your expectations, of your ego investment in a particular outcome, of any voices that tell you that you, the great priestess, should be able to pull this off better. Ask, "How can I use the energy that's actually happening to move the group toward the work of this ritual?" If the energy simply won't rise, drop into it instead of fighting, letting the meditation be slow and thoughtful rather than wild. If the energy is high, let it run its course before trying to move it into a deeper, quiet place. If the energy hits a plateau and won't peak, and people around the edges are beginning to tire and drop out, try bringing the energy down to a quiet place from which to build it up again.

The most effective way to shift an energy is to first join with it. When you counter an energy from outside, you meet resistance. But if you entrain, you can gradually move it in a new direction.

Experiment. Know that the energy doesn't have to be perfect for the ritual to work. Afterward, compare experiences and reflect on what you've learned.

Even a few people working together can have a powerful impact on the energy of a much larger group. Many times in rallies and demonstrations, we've found that a few focused people can start a song, a chant, or even a spiral dance that moves the raw energy of a crowd into focused, directed power.

———————

Over the years, Reclaiming has created thousands of rituals, and several basic forms of large group ritual have evolved:

Drum Trance

Reclaiming's style of drum trance evolved in the mid-1980s out of guided meditations after one of our cranky students kept asking, "Why do we always have to lie down to go into trance?" "Stand up, then," we conceded, and a new form was born. When people were standing, they could move, dance, use their bodies to enact the images they saw in their mind's eye. They were active cocreators rather than passive recipients. Meditation could flow organically into chanting, dancing, and raising power.

At the same time, some of us were learning to drum. Eventually we learned the trick of drumming and talking at the same time. Now the drum could hold the base energy of the ritual, while the priestess's voice could weave images, chants, and stories around the beat.

At its best, a drum trance becomes an improvised prose poem where story, song, voice, and rhythm flow seamlessly into one another and transport participants into another world.

A drum trance is impossible to reproduce on paper. Throughout this book, however, we include "scores" that are at least approximations.

In creating a drum trance, we keep in mind that we are not writing a script to be memorized or read aloud. Reading and memorizing a trance is like weaving a basket out of rigid sticks that are dry and dead. Instead, we cocreate a landscape and decide on a flow of transformation. A drum trance begins with an induction that can be as simple as three breaths taken in common or as elaborate as any of the trance inductions suggested elsewhere. The leader sets a scene for us and usually takes us on a journey that may involve a challenge or opportunity. Chanting and singing can interweave with the spoken guidance.

A drum trance can be led by more than one person, each sharing sections of the story. Or priestesses may speak as characters or aspects of the Goddess. If you can't drum, or can't drum and talk at the same time, one person can drum while another leads the meditation. You can build your skills toward leading a drum trance by leading trances or meditations for yourself, for a partner, or for a small group.

In constructing a drum trance, it's helpful to ask the following questions:

What's the induction?
What's the setting, the landscape?
What work of transformation are we looking for?

Where is the peak of power, and what is its focus?
What is the resolution? How do we integrate the work?
How do we return?

The "One-Winged Brother" trance described in the Outer Path in chapter 7 is an example of a score for a drum trance.

Quest/Pilgrimage/Treasure Hunt

In this form of ritual, sacred space is created around a large area. Stations are set up that might represent different stops on a journey or different emotional or mythic states. Participants move through the space, literally making a physical journey that creates transformation. Priestesses may stay at the stations, holding the energy, asking questions, or offering something to those who come. Or they may wander as participants wander, offering their challenges in a mobile fashion.

There's a strong element of randomness and chance in this form of ritual, and a strong element of play and fun. (We sometimes call it the Spiritual Disneyland form.) The risks are that the energy can become scattered and that safety is harder to guarantee in a large space, especially in the dark. People who have mobility problems may need special help and consideration in order to participate. Timing is harder to control, and participants may finish at widely different times.

One of the most beautiful rituals I remember was a quest ritual at a Witchcamp in Missouri, at Diana's Grove, where priestesses Cynthia and Patricia Storm have created a truly magical space on their hundred acres of Ozark land. The big barn, where we eat and socialize, is separated from the ritual grove by a half-mile walk along the edge of a wood that skirts a hillside field where a huge labyrinth is mown, covering several acres. When you reach the edge of the grove, the path ducks into the trees and crosses a small stream on stepping-stones between altars. Inside the trees is a grassy clearing with a fire pit in the center and altars marking the directions, a wooded hill behind, and stars above.

That year, we were working with the Norse pantheon. For the ritual, we invited participants to go on a journey. The goal would be the fire pit at the big barn, where Thorn would create a warm hearth and offer meditations on compassion. The other nine of us on the team took on various roles: Norse Gods and Goddesses, demons, oracles. Most of us wandered among the journeyers, offering challenges and providing obstacles to be overcome.

I was the guardian of the gate of the labyrinth. I stood veiled at its entrance, and as participants came up to me, I challenged them to find the question that lay in their true hearts before they entered. The mist had come down over the hills, and between the fog and the veil, people literally disappeared as soon as they got a few feet away. As time went on, more and more people entered the labyrinth, but no one came back out. I began to feel as if I were truly ushering people into another dimension. It was an hour or two before anyone emerged, and when they did, they seemed transformed.

Much, much later, Idun and Loki walked up to the gate. Rationally I knew they were San and Paul, my fellow teachers, but in the mist they appeared shining and larger than life. They were following the last participants, and we decided to walk the labyrinth together. We could hear otherworldly voices floating over the hills as we wound our way in through the twists and turns. Finally, we reached the center, where Melusine at the heart of the labyrinth had all night long been offering a challenge to each person who came. We, too, faced our challenges, and as we wound our way out, we realized we were hearing the singing from the hearth fire.

A very different pilgrimage ritual form was created by Reclaiming's Multicultural Ritual Group in the early 1990s. Instead of working within a magic circle tightly bound in time, we were able to have rituals that lasted an entire day and evening. The transition into sacred space was made not by casting a circle, but by the entrance into ritual space, where black cloth was hung to make a winding maze. At the turning points, priestesses were stationed to challenge participants, perhaps asking, "What is your pride in your heritage?" or offering a pinch of salt to place in a bowl of water to symbolize the tears we shed for our ancestors' pain.

In one ritual, we had a huge altar to honor the ancestors of many cultures. As participants emerged from the entrance, they were welcomed and brought into an African singing game. Then they were free to visit the other altars, each of which included interactive processes: questions to answer, things to write or do, stories to listen to. We had an altar that was a shattered mirror with the simple legend "We have all been victims of violence." Another altar acknowledged the perpetrators of violence, with questions such as "What turns an innocent baby into a torturer?" We had an altar for those who resisted oppression and fought for justice, one that included pictures, collages, tapes of Union songs, and a large board where we could write our own family stories. In the center was a healing altar—a pool created with a huge wooden bowl and an overhanging leaning tree—that provided pillows, massage, and a chance to express our grief. Each altar offered participants a strip of cloth to take, to symbolize the stages of their journeys.

In the ritual, we later divided into small groups, where we told our own ancestor stories and braided our strips of cloth together. Each small group then tied their braids into a rope, and those ropes were then tied into one long, long strand. We had built a basket form that stood in the center of the circle. Singing and chanting, we literally wove an ancestor basket from that long rope and raised a cone of power to charge it with the energies of healing and transformation.

Portals

A transformed space can itself become an opening to another realm and a deeper level of experience. Pomegranate is an artist and painter as well as a priestess and teacher. "As an artist," she says, "I'm either painting a portal, where people are going to pass through into another realm, or painting an invocation, where something is going to come into this realm. That's my work as a priestess, too. Everything I do—decorating my house, working in the garden, talking to the plant spirits—it's all about portals and invocations. The house is a shrine; the garden is a shrine. That's the work of the shaman—to open a gateway and then to invoke and make offerings of healing and gratitude."

El Dia de los Muertos, November 2, is the traditional time in Latino communities for honoring the ancestors and the dead. In San Francisco, that night is marked by a candlelit procession through the streets that ends in a ritual in a small park, near housing projects, that has been the scene of violence and murders.

Many people in our Bay Area Reclaiming groups participate in the event and help with the planning. Juan Pablo Gutierrez and Rosa de Anda are two of the major organizers of the event. They have carefully considered the problems of orchestrating an outdoor ritual for thousands of people with no sound system. Artists, youth, old people, and neighborhood volunteers come together to create postmodern, multimedia art-installation altars based on the Latino tradition of building altars for the dead. The park is transformed. Shootings and gang fights are suspended for a night, while the whole neighborhood turns out to wander among the amazing altars, to sing, drum, and dance together. People light candles and pray, make offerings to their ancestors, or perform rituals from their tradition. One year, the ground was covered with puddles from a recent rain. A group of youth surrounded the largest puddle with greenery to protect people from slipping in it. They placed floating candles on the water, and it became a magic pool. Throughout the night, I saw people gather together in rapt meditation at the mud puddle. It had truly become a portal, a basket to carry us between the worlds.

Ritual Drama

A ritual can also enact a story. Ritual drama does not have to be wailing Greek choruses or highly costumed actors spouting memorized lines. In fact, unless the priestesses involved are truly connected to their intention behind the drama, the dramatic aspects will serve to distance the circle, warns Marnie, who teaches theater and mask work as well as magic. She is brilliant at combining some of the aspects of theater games, role-playing, and improvisational humor to create a transformational experience.

When we taught together on the Vermont team in 1999, our theme was the pentacle of life: birth, initiation, ripening, reflection, and death. Death, of course, leads back to birth. The team decided to start the ritual cycle with death, but because that ritual occurred very early in the week, we didn't want to overwhelm the group with grief and loss before they'd had a chance to bond. We knew that death was an important issue for that community. One beloved woman had died of liver cancer two years before. Another woman active in the local community had recently lost her husband. And others were struggling with serious and possibly terminal illnesses.

During the invocations, we honored those who had died by singing "Weaver, Weaver" (see The Pagan Book of Living and Dying), a beautiful and haunting lament. While people were still in a sad and quiet state, Kitty came forward.

Kitty, our first second-generation Witchcamp teacher, is a brilliant biologist who also looks stunning in gold lamé. Nobody can play the gracious hostess better than she. She informed us that because it was still so early in camp, the teachers wanted people to get to know each other. We were asked to circulate around the group, introducing ourselves and letting people know what we did back home.

Instantly the ritual circle became a cocktail party as people milled about. Although we had planned this section of the ritual purely as a setup for what was to follow, I found myself learning new things about people I'd known for years and enjoying it a great deal.

Our ritual space is a high, pristine meadow on a mountainside. Suddenly, we heard the roar of an engine, and a pickup truck careened up the grassy road, blaring loud music from the radio. It swung into the edge of our circle and stopped. Headlights pierced the fire circle. Everyone became silent, with just the music blaring. Some people were moving unobtrusively away from the "scene" as fast as possible, while others quickly moved forward to protect the circle.

The music stopped, and the doors were flung open. Out came a figure in a baseball cap, flannel shirt, and overalls, smoking a rolled cigarette (strictly prohibited!). The campers who had come forward approached with alarm and asked the driver of the truck what they could do for him. Even though they were looking directly into the interloper's face, it took them a few long seconds to register that this was Marnie, who truly has the ability to transform herself into another character.

"What the hell is going on here?" she demanded, swaggering up to the fire circle and putting her foot on a log, drawing on her cigarette in silence as she looked around the group. "Who told you you could have a party here? This is my land. My name is Mort."

After talking back and forth with several campers who challenged him, Mort proceeded to tell us that if we were going to have a party on his land, we had to play by his rules, which were these. We were to sing and dance. Mort would secretly tap a few of us and turn us into Morts. The rest of us wouldn't know who the Morts were, but if we were dancing with someone who squeezed our hands twice, we had to die—to go over to the "graveyard" by the fire and lie down. (We based this on the old party game Murder.) We began madly dancing and singing:

> Enjoy yourself, it's later than you think,
> Enjoy yourself, while you're still in the pink,
> The years go by, as quickly as a wink,
> So enjoy yourself, enjoy yourself,
> it's later than you think!

Beverly and I stood in the center and drummed. One by one, people began falling. Periodically, Mort would blow his whistle, everything would stop, and other teachers would make reassuring "official announcements": "This is just to inform you that the Committee on Public Safety has investigated this situation and ascertained that there is no immediate danger to the public!"

The dance would resume, and the deaths would continue. On the surface, the mood was lighthearted and hilarious. But as more and more people fell away, an uneasy undertone began to grow. The game slowly seemed more and more real.

Finally Raven, one of the camp organizers and a lifelong political activist, could stand it no longer. "What are we doing?" she cried out. "Why are we singing and dancing when our friends are dying?" We hadn't planned her intervention, but it was perfect. "Somebody kill that woman!" I called, and she was rapidly assassinated.

Another woman, Joan, ill with life-threatening cancer, kept dancing and singing and not getting killed. When Mort finally went up to her, she approached him and said, "Thank, God! Somebody finally killed me!" and went gratefully down to die.

After everyone had died and was lying still and cold on the ground, I moved into the center and began the drum trance.

The trance took us fairly quickly through death, but we spent a long time letting go of our bodies, step by step, letting them decay into the earth and feed the billion hungry mouths of the soil, the creatures that take us back into our original elements, which become food for roots and grasses and trees. As the dead lay looking up at the stars, I had them imagine the night sky as the womb/cauldron of the Goddess, the stars as all the new possibilities that could be born.

"It was a deep experience, to lie there and to let go of the body," Joan said later. "By the time Mort squeezed my hands, I was so grateful I said, "Thank God!" I was far outside of the fire circle. As I hit the cold ground I thought, 'How am I going to get through the rest of this ritual?' But as I lay there, something floated through my body, and I could feel the cold seep away into the ground. It came to me that the ritual was quite real to me because I really was facing my own death. The question arose: Was I going to be able to let go of my life essence? My partner? Again, something floated through my body, left me, and sank deep into the ground. I became the ground. The peace I felt was profound. When it was time to rise, I realized that my connection to life had changed."

Eventually, we rose again and danced ourselves back into life.

True humor is of depth, Marnie reminds us: "Just think of the times you've been in deep trauma, when humor has come ripping through and you laugh uproariously through your tears. We are, in reality, maybe laughing and alive one minute and maybe without warning we are dead the next. The priestess who makes the transition from a 'light' game to a deep trance must be strongly feeling the integration of life and death. If she can go to a truly deep place in the midst of laughter and chaos, she can then drop the group into a deep emotional and spiritual state. Experience and confidence are helpful in making this type of transition work, but most important is working from the heart."

Mummer's Plays

One way to gain experience or to experiment with ritual drama on a smaller scale is with mummer's plays. Mummer's plays were brought to Reclaiming by Pandora, who has a background both in theater and in medieval studies. Mummer's plays are miniplays on a sacred theme that are brought to an audience in a place where people gather. In medieval times, they might have been performed outside the church or in the market square. At a gathering, they might happen in the dining hall or on a path people take to go to a session. At a demonstration, they can take on a political theme and become street theater.

One year at the British Columbia Witchcamp, a group of students enacted the children's story of "Hortense Lays an Egg" in mime over a period of several days, appearing on the path to the dining hall or down by the lake at unexpected moments. In California, two women who had environmental sensitivities and were being made ill by other people's scents and bug sprays got tired of making plaintive announcements, dressed up as bandits complete with the masks they used to protect themselves, and raided the dining hall. A mummer's play might also enact a myth or even retell a nighttime story in a new way.

Mummer's plays and street theater are often effective ways to communicate a political message as well. Dancing sea turtles may be more effective than a hundred speeches at calling attention to the destructive impact on the environment of the World Trade Organization's rulings.

The Perfect Act

A ritual may also be built around a simple, perfect action that the group takes. Such a ritual is much less dependent on any individual's skill or brilliance. When we plunge into the ocean for cleansing at sunset on the Winter Solstice, that act alone will change our consciousness. When we each step up to Brigid's cauldron to make a pledge, we are individually responsible for the depth and intensity of our work. The priestesses and ritual structure can create a setting conducive to transformation: the invocations can draw in power, the chants can create an energy base, but no one person is responsible for guiding the transformative work.

Action can also intensify the work of a drum trance or a drama. In Missouri last year, our theme was weaving. In one ritual, we invited the group into the House of Spiders to weave. People were given rolled balls of pastel yarn and asked to toss them across the circle, back and forth, creating a web that glowed beautifully in the moonlight.

When the web was woven, we danced with it joyfully, until the drum trance leader began to spin a meditation that identified the web with all the structures of society that confine us. We were directed to drop the web on top of ourselves. Instantly we were all immobilized in the tangle. We were asked to think about the political, economic, and social structures that tie us down, to attempt to move and literally feel where we were held back and how firmly we were caught.

We let our voices raise energy. Slowly, priestesses began to move around the edges of the web, with scissors to help us get free. But we were not allowed to simply discard the strands of the web. Instead, we were asked to roll them up again, to take back the energy that had confined us and transform it into the creative power we could use to reweave our lives as we wished them to be.

At the California camp, we led a very similar ritual in the dark of the moon. There was no light to see by, and participants were at first utterly incredulous at the idea that they were expected to roll up all that yarn in the dark. We almost had an outright rebellion. But as they began to work, they got involved in the challenge. People who had flashlights helped those who didn't. Small teams developed, and groups cooperated to help each other. They searched the ground to find the last lost threads. They became the living model of the web of interconnectedness that could underlie a new vision.

Praising and Invoking

A ritual intention may also be simply to invoke the powers that sustain our lives and offer praise and thanksgiving. Its form may be simple, organic, and fluid.

One year at mid-Atlantic camp, our theme was "The Charge of the Goddess," the beautiful liturgy by Doreen Valiente that is widely used throughout the Craft. One section of the Charge says: "May there be beauty and strength, power and compassion, honor and humility, mirth and reverence within you."

We had used those pairs of qualities in many rituals throughout the week. On the night we worked with beauty and strength, we set up a simple ritual format. "We decided to do it simply," Pomegranate remembers, "just to offer praise and gratitude and thanks, and be present as fully as we could." In the center was an area where people could come and dance, express their own beauty, and be witnessed. Around the edge, others sang, danced, and kept the energy base high. The drummers stood together and kept the energy flowing. We sang a beauty chant and let people move in and out of the center. For about three hours, we sang and danced together, then let the energy peak and ground.

This ritual form has a tribal feel. Its power is not dependent on any one person's skill or brilliance, but on the willingness of the group to support and feed the energy of the whole.

Weaving the Basket: Safety in Ritual

As leaders, we are responsible for the safety of the circles we create. But the paradox we face is that transformative change requires risk. To gather power, we must be willing to face great challenges, to be brave, courageous, willing to take a stand. Of course, there are days when we feel like echoing three-year-old Kore, who, on being told she was a brave girl after having a piece of glass dug out of her heel, said, "I don't like brave! Brave is stupid!"

How do we be brave without being stupid? The risks that build our power come from the challenges of our internal healing and from the real situations we face in the outer world. The challenges that make us feel stupid are the ones that arise from badly conceived and ill-thought-out rituals.

We cannot make anyone heal. We cannot force or manipulate anyone into facing their challenges, nor can we bully anyone into empowerment. The challenges that empower are those that we freely choose to face. So when we create a ritual that offers a chance to deal with powerful material, we must always offer a choice. That choice might be built into a trance: "And breathe deeply, and ask your deep self if this is the right journey for you to make tonight. And if not, what is right for you might be just to remain here in your place of power, exploring, deepening your connections. And if it is . . ."

Pain is not always where we expect it to be. Over decades of taking people on inner journeys, I've found that most people will quite happily dive into the depths of hell, but many will fall apart when we go to places of ecstasy and celebration. If we feel isolated, if the erotic has been for us a place of abuse and humiliation, we may feel unimaginable pain at the expectation of dancing with others in love and connection. If we were to take people to an envisioned Temple of Love and Desire, we might create a "pavilion" just before the gates, where participants can stay for the duration of the trance if entering the temple itself is too painful. Sometimes we literally create a pavilion in one corner of the ritual space, with pillows, blankets, and somebody to tend.

Choice is also something to consider in the construction of our imagery, especially in leading trance. Part of our work is to face difficult and dangerous parts of ourselves, but the trance must be constructed with a kind of open-endedness. Not "You look down the road, and you see your worst fear," but "You look down the road, and if it's right for you, one of your fears appears. It may be just a small fear, or it may be a big fear, but it's the fear you are ready to look at right now . . ."

Another way we create safety in Reclaiming rituals is by not using drugs or allowing the use of drugs or alcohol in ritual space. Many people in our community are in recovery from addictions, and this agreement supports their growth and healing. But even those of us who like a glass of wine with dinner find that we enjoy the atmosphere of our public rituals more without the presence of alcohol or drugs. We can take people into deep and vulnerable places and feel confident about bringing them back only when we know no physical or chemical influences will prevent their return. People who attend a ritual advertised as drug and alcohol free are more likely to be those interested in serious magical work, not "party Pagans."

Support Roles

In a coven or close circle, we can do deep work because we have the support of the group. We know each other, and we have worked to build intimacy. In a Witchcamp, we can take people into deep places because we have a cast of thousands—or, at least, ten to a dozen—taking on different support roles. One person might be leading a trance; others might be deep witnessing, tending, gracing, wrangling.

Many of these support roles are useful in any large-scale or public ritual:

TENDERS: Tenders circulate through the group, keeping an eye open for someone who might be in trouble. Tending requires sensitivity, good boundaries, and a high level of comfort with strong emotions. We teach tenders not to automatically comfort someone who is weeping or wailing. The person who is sobbing is able to express her emotions and is moving energy. She may be having the breakthrough she'd been waiting years for, and smothering her in a hug might simply shut her down.

Instead, we look at more subtle cues to tell us if people are truly in need of help. Are they breathing? Where is their breath moving in their body? Are they stuck in one position? Do they appear shut down? How does their energy feel?

When I tend, I first move quietly into the aura of the person I suspect needs help. I might use my hands, or just my inner senses, to "taste" the quality of her energy. Do my hands itch to give her a brushdown? What do I start to feel in the pit of my stomach? Is she grounded?

Before I make direct contact, I ground myself and anchor to my core. Sometimes just standing next to a person and solidly grounding yourself will help her ground. Breathing deeply will help open her breath.

It's wise to ask permission before touching someone. Unexpected physical touch can restimulate old memories of abuse.

If someone does need help in the midst of a ritual, I work with him on an energetic level, getting him to breathe, ground, release what is blocking him, and move the energy through. I don't fish for personal details or information about the block; I am not this person's therapist. If he volunteers information, I am receptive, but I don't attempt to solve his problems or give advice. My goal in tending is to make sure the person is fully back in his body and not overwhelmed by energies or emotions. I might suggest he seek support in some way after the ritual or workshop is over.

DEEP WITNESSES: Deep witnessing is a role invented by Cybele, who perceived that we needed a role that would balance the intensity of the energies we were working with in some rituals. The deep witness is a useful role in a ritual where we expect deep work to be done, energies to be raised that may be difficult to contain or focus, or aspects of the Goddess or Gods to be called in to the priestesses. In a long ritual, deep witnesses may take shifts, and for a very large ritual we might have more than one.

The deep witness sits in a comfortable position in a protected corner of the ritual space, under a veil, and goes into dropped and open attention. She holds the ritual in her attention throughout the working, viewing it from "below." She may visualize the entire ritual taking place on her plane of attention, or, to use Cybele's image, she might let her attention sweep around the circle like a radar scope.

When a deep witness is present, the energy of the circle feels more coherent. The priestesses need to expend less of their own energy to keep the group focused. Deep witnesses sometimes receive information about the ritual or see visions. The meditative state has been described as "the next best thing to LSD."

Although deep witnesses appear to be doing nothing, the work of staying in meditation for a long period of time is intense. When David witnessed the Spiral Dance, he described the experience as "the hardest magical work I've ever done."

Deep witnessing is also one of those techniques that actually can be dangerous. The deep witness must be clear on the difference between observing the energy of the ritual and running the energy. Her job is *not* to ground the energy, channel it through her body, or attempt to affect it: doing any of those things from the deep witness state can be extremely draining and may even lead to illness. The deep witness simply observes. We affect what we observe: by holding the ritual as a whole in her attention, the deep witness makes it whole.

Before experimenting with deep witnessing, you should be able to ground easily and almost automatically. You should regularly work with an anchor and, again, be able to use it automatically to bring you back to your core worth state. And you should have a regular meditation practice that includes dropped and open attention. These are some of the safeguards that allow us to work in this state of consciousness.

A deep witness is a role that must be known and agreed upon by the priestessing team. Don't just decide, on a whim, to go into dropped and open attention in the middle of the ritual without alerting anyone else. A deep witness must also have a support person, a "wrangler."

WRANGLERS: *Wrangling* is the term we have adopted to describe the role of tending a deep witness or someone who goes into any deep trance state in a ritual. A wrangler is responsible for the physical safety and comfort of her charge. During the ritual, she watches out for dangers. Throughout the ritual, the wrangler checks on the deep witness periodically to make sure she is physically comfortable and to monitor her energy. When the ritual is over, she offers a brushdown and anything else that is needed, gets food and drink for her charge, and makes sure her charge gets safely home.

GRACES: Graces greet and welcome people at public rituals. They help move energy, people, and objects to enable the ritual to flow smoothly. With their aid, difficult transitions can be smoothly accomplished, whether it's moving fifteen hundred people from their seats into a spiral or whisking a cauldron into and out of the center of the circle.

DRAGONS: Dragons guard the boundaries. They are the security force of the ritual, available to handle crises, remove intruders nonviolently, talk to the police, or do whatever needs to be done.

CROWS: The crow keeps an overview of the ritual, remembers what's coming next, and prompts those who forget their parts. If needed, the crow stays aware of external time. We often perceive the crow role as "leader" but we do better to recognize this task as supportive to the whole.

Our basket may take many forms. But when it is woven to be strong and flexible, open yet safe, we can let go and allow ourselves to be carried away, over the sea to the land of magic. There we will find our true task and face new challenges.

F I V E

The Challenge

Comments on the Story

Rose receives her task from the Fata Morgana: she must gather stinging nettles, beat out the fibers, spin the thread, weave the cloth, and sew twelve shirts—all without speaking, laughing, or crying out loud. When the twelve shirts are complete, she must cast them over the brothers, who will then be restored to full humanness.

Rose has already faced many challenges, but in this section of the story she is given her true task. Her courage, generosity, perseverance, and willingness to surrender to ecstasy have proved her worthiness to undertake a great work of magic, and the task itself gives us a clue to the nature of the Goddess who is initiating her: the Weaver, ancestress of the Fates, who spin the thread of our lives, measure its length, and cut the cord at death.

In fairy tales, shirts are souls. Rose is asked to weave new souls for her brothers, souls that can restore them to the human world. This is a task that cannot be done in an ordinary state of consciousness. Rose must dedicate herself to the work and live as a priestess, keeping solemn silence until she is done.

From a feminist perspective, we might well question this part of the story. Rose is asked to suffer for the sake of others. Is this not what women are always called upon to do? Worse, she is told to suffer in silence. How can this possibly be empowering?

Great works of magic require great dedication. To be given such a task is a mark of respect, whether the challenge comes from the Goddess or from our inner self. We undertake a healing work because something in us believes that we can be healers, world shapers, active agents of change. We see ourselves as potentially powerful beings.

Creative work demands focus, concentration, and painstaking work as well as ecstasy. We may fly high, seeing visions of what the work may be, but we must still come back to earth and do it: write and rewrite every sentence, dig the garden, carefully thread the loom.

Nettles burn like fire, but the pain passes, leaving no damage behind. Rose is not asked to harm herself, but to bear pain. Soulweaving is a birth process, and birth is painful. But pain and silence can also be gateways into altered states of awareness.

As feminists, we have learned that silence can be oppression. Silence Equals Death is a slogan of the gay liberation movement. But what kind of silence is Rose asked to keep? She is not asked to keep silence about abuse, oppression, or hidden secrets. By discovering the truth about her brothers, she has already broken that silence. Nor is she asked to conceal her identity, to keep silent about who she is. She is asked not to complain about the task she has willingly taken on, not to whine or cry for pity. She is asked not to dissipate her energies or her attention, not to expend her creative force in talking about what she's going to do instead of doing it. She is asked to enter into that state of solitude and receptivity where the great powers of life can speak to us. Her silence is that of the shaman who must learn to listen to the realms of nature and spirit beyond human discourse, the silence of the healer, the counselor, the therapist, the journalist in whom we can safely confide. No one who cannot keep silence can truly receive our trust.

To know the elements, to hear voices in the wind, to understand the language of birds and frogs and follow the tracks of the deer, we must be able to listen in silence to nature. When we still our own voices, the crackling fire and the rushing water can speak to us. We begin to hear the deep communication that is always happening in the natural world.

The inner self must also be discovered in silence. When our outer voice is still, a space opens within us that can be filled with our truest passions, our deepest desires. Our real life task can reveal itself when we quiet the demands of the tasks of daily living and allow ourselves to dwell for a time in the hermit's cave.

When we are powerless or oppressed, our task is to find our voice, to learn to speak up for ourselves. But when we are in a position of power and trust, our task shifts. As victims, as underlings, we needed great forcefulness in order to be heard; but when we become authorities, that same vehemence can become abusive. Our words take on greater weight. A harsh criticism or an angry outburst can wound. In order for those we teach or lead to develop their own power, we may need to restrain ourselves, to hold back and not solve a problem, to let others make their own mistakes. To be a true healer or an empowering leader, we must know when to shut up as well as when to speak.

To know, to will, to dare, and to keep silent are the four powers of the mage in Western occult tradition. Rose's initiation journey encompasses all four. First she must know the truth about her brothers. She must dare to leave her home and wander in the wilderness. Now she must learn to work with will, with focused concentration and intention, and with silence to complete her task. The work of this section of the story is to know the elements and plants that are our allies, to discover our true tasks and life purpose, and to learn the power of silence.

The Elements Path

In the land across the sea, Rose dreams that she has entered the castle of the Fata Morgana. Here she is told what she must do to free her brothers from the spell. She must gather nettles, beat out the fiber, spin thread, weave cloth, and make a shirt for each of them. During the entire project she must not speak a single word. If she can do this, her brothers, when she throws the shirts over them, will be restored to their full humanness.

We who walk the Elements Path will take this opportunity to learn with Rose. We will look at how our ancestresses developed their close relationship with the earth and the plant world. We will learn about magical ethics to prepare ourselves to study spellcasting—a basic magical technique associated with the element earth. And we will do some basic meditations on the element earth.

For women in ancient, earth-based cultures all over the world, making fabric and basketry from natural fibers would have been the most familiar sort of daily work. Once again this reminds us of the root word of our religion, *wic*, like *wicker*, because we are the ones who can bend and weave new balance for the worlds. The work of weaving fabric from gathered and prepared plant material, along with the growing, gathering, preserving, and preparation of food from plants, was the bulk of the daily responsibility and also the skill and power of ancient women.

Our ancestresses had encyclopedic knowledge of the plants, both agricultural and wild, that grew around them, and they knew many ways to harvest and store plant material and prepare it for medicine, food, and fiber. This knowledge was the oral tradition and science of our foremothers. This was the inherited wisdom they taught their daughters, so that the young women would also be able to feed a family, tend the sick, and create what their families needed out of the materials at hand. No wonder there is so much detail in the ancient tales about weaving and spinning!

Modern people in industrialized countries rarely know the names of the plants around them, much less the particular skill and handling of specific plants and their uses. Often our closest contact with a plant comes with our arms deep in the prickly needles and our faces in the thick fragrance as we try to make the Christmas tree stand up in its base. Even the produce in the supermarket comes prewashed and cut up in packages now, so that the great cauliflower, still crowned with leaves, or the beets with roots and bits of soil hanging from them and their garland of fragrant leaves have become unfamiliar sights. But our senses, fine-tuned from ancient times to the delicate perception of the green world and its life, long for these sights, smells, and textures. For women and men trying to rediscover a spiritual practice that honors Mother Nature, reconnecting with our instinctive, ancestral knowledge of plants is a basic practice.

Meeting an Herbal Ally

Wilow Fire Zacubi is a Reclaiming Witch who has spent her life learning about and working with herbs. A mountain woman, big-boned and strong, Wilow is as comfortable chopping the wood for the night's bonfire as she is leading a meditation for a hundred people. Wilow has a favorite meditation she uses to teach her friends and students how to develop a personal relationship with an herbal ally. You are welcome to try it by yourself or with a group of friends.

For this meditation you will need a scarf and cuttings from a plant. Be sure you can identify poison oak, nettles, and any other toxic or stinging plants that grow locally before harvesting any wild plant. Remember not to take a whole plant from the wild, or any part of a plant, if it is the only one of its species growing in a certain location.

Next, create sacred space. With your scarf in your lap, remind yourself that the ability to understand plant life is your heritage from your grandmothers for hundreds of generations. Whether you are a woman or a man, your ancestresses closely observed and worked with plants for much of their waking life, and their knowledge is coiled tightly inside each of your cells and is your rightful inheritance. Breathe your reliance on the wisdom of the grandmothers into the scarf, and then pull it over your head. Take your plant, and begin to investigate it, using your curiosity and your wisdom. Look and touch; smell your plant and breathe in its green breath; listen to it. Taste it only if you have a positive ID on it and know it to be safe. Many useful and medicinal plants can also be poisonous.

After you have fully investigated your plant with all your senses, allow your attention to concentrate behind your third eye (a place between and slightly above your physical eyes, inside your head). When your attention is concentrated, ask the plant's permission to enter its energy body, and express gratitude for its lessons. Drawing on your inherited wisdom and your curiosity, allow your concentrated attention to turn green and stream out into the plant. Find entry through the roots, leaves, flower, stem, or some other door. Sense the energy of the plant from the inside—its color, rhythm, texture, temperature, rate of vibration, and so forth. Journey throughout the plant from stem to leaf to root, from bud to flower to seed. First, observe all your impressions without judging or interpreting. Second, ask the plant how it is used. What is its name? What is its story? Third, ask the plant if it has any message for you.

When you feel finished, thank the plant and express gratitude. Slowly pull your awareness out of the plant, leaving the same way you entered. Follow the green stream of awareness back into your own body, through your third eye. Allow the color of your attention to change from green back to whatever color is comfortable for you normally. Expand and open your attention, and return to your previous state of consciousness, feeling relaxed, awake, aware, and reenergized.

Thank your wisdom self and your ancestresses. Say good-bye, and take off your scarf. Devoke and open the circle only when you are completely ready.

It's amazing how often people who try this exercise, even if they normally know next to nothing about plants, will come up with qualities and powers and even names for plants that correspond closely with traditional plant lore.

A few years ago, Wilow and I had just finished teaching this meditation to a group of students. We had worked in the meager shade of a stand of live oaks on a blinding midsummer day on a dry California hillside. Under the oaks stood great granite boulders marked along their tops with the shallow mortar bowls where the ancestresses of the California first people had ground their acorns into meal. Around the boulders, caressing their bases, grew the soft streamers of poison oak.

Wilow turned to me with the dark eyes of a messenger from another world. "I did the trance myself," she said. "I tranced into the poison oak. They said they didn't used to be so poisonous before the Europeans came in the Gold Rush."

I was curious, and later I did some research about poison oak. Sure enough, it turns out that *Rhus* (poison oak) was used by the native Californian peoples for making baskets, for seasoning food, and for medicinal uses. Poison oak, which had been an ally of the native people, got a new job with the Gold Rush—defending the oaks from the new European people. And Wilow, after a lifetime of learning from and working with plants, could see and hear this from the plant itself.

Learning from Nettles

While it may be empowering to reconnect with our green allies, why does Rose have to work with nettles, with their terrible fiery sting? Is the Fata Morgana a horrible, sadistic Goddess? Why would she offer Rose such a painful challenge? What can possibly be empowering about this part of the story? The answer to this question can be found only if we are willing to give up our alienated modern relationship to nature and move in closely and carefully to the nettles, with our minds open and our hands fearless.

Most modern people, if they've ever had any contact with nettles, have had it by accident. I'll never forget blundering into a big patch of nettles with my daughter, then a toddler, when we were out hiking one day. I ended up running back down the trail with her screaming in my arms, my hands on fire. A very successful interaction, from the point of view of the nettle patch. It got our attention, and got rid of us, before we had disturbed it at all.

The hiking story is very different when we look at it from the point of view of the nettle patch, isn't it? It's a good day for our friend nettle when she successfully chases the humans away. There's a lesson for us here.

When we commit ourselves to a spiritual way of life based on Mother Nature, we must learn to honor and respect all parts of nature, not just those we find pleasant or appealing. Mother Nature predates humans by eons. She is not here for our comfort and convenience. Nature is both the honey and the bee sting, both the rose and the thorn.

By contrast, our familiar Western patriarchal cultures place humans above nature and thus justify our desire to dominate and control nature. So if we like the corn but not the worm, we invent a poisonous pesticide with our clever, tool-adept human brains. We spray the corn and kill all the worms. Now we have lovely, perfect ears of corn and happy humans.

But perhaps we've also killed all the predatory insects that used to feed on the corn worms and keep their numbers in balance. We've begun to build up toxins in the wild food chain, which is ultimately our own food chain. Next year, or in twenty years, we may have more corn worms than ever, but no wasps, or sparrows, or falcons. Our groundwater may test positive for carcinogens, and so may our corn, and so may our babies.

By contrast, the worldview of Witches sees both corn and worm, both hiker and nettle, as holy. Corn worms, nettles, bees, and roses are each living things, part of the immanent Goddess herself, part of the web of life. Each creature is on its own path through life; each has the right and responsibility to defend itself, including the right to defend itself from us humans. By careful observation, by living with and loving both corn and worm, we try to find an artful balance that provides for our needs, without tearing the web of life itself to shreds. Because our tradition teaches respect for this balance, many Witches are involved with organic gardening, sustainable agriculture, habitat restoration, and other earth works.

Practicing Magical Ethics

But honoring all of life does not mean that we Witches never kill plant pests or uproot nettles that are growing in our path. Our needs and desires are holy, too. It is the nature of the bee to sting me if I disturb its hive, and it is my nature to want to eat the honey. In each case we must find a skillful, mindful balance that respects all parts of a complex interaction. We must respect each wild and holy creature, including ourselves, knowing that each action we take has consequences that tremble through the whole fabric of nature for generations to come.

The Witch's law says, "Harm none, and do as you will." This is a simple saying, but incredibly difficult to apply. Do I do harm by smashing the snail eggs in my garden, or do I do harm by *not* smashing them? If I let them live, they will kill my seedlings. So which is the harm? The Witch's worldview comes with tremendous responsibility to weigh each action in the wisest possible view of the whole. There is no room here for simpleminded innocence: "I would never kill a living thing"; or "Don't cut down trees." If the trees are the weedy eucalyptuses that Europeans brought from Australia and that now threaten the few wild islands of California native plants and animals, maybe we need to work hard to cut them down. So now perhaps we can look over the nettle patch again with a Witch's eye. What is the Fata Morgana trying to teach Rose, trying to teach us?

Working in Balance with Nettles

For our ancestors who listened to and told this story, the task of making cloth out of nettles might have seemed laborious, but it would not have seemed punitive or sadistic. Nettles were widely used for fiber and homespun cloth before machine-made cloth and imported cotton became common. Most people wore homemade clothing and slept on homemade "linens" that had started out as flax or hemp or nettle or some other familiar plant. Creating cloth out of gathered plant material was the responsibility and one of the powers of adult women. Even in my mother's time, education for girls included needlework.

Nettles were also used medicinally and as wild food, and wise women and men continue to use them this way today. Wilow Fire, who harvests nettles, points out that if you avoid touching the underside of the leaves, you can avoid being stung. In Deb Soule's excellent herbal *The Roots of Healing*, she gives an account of modern women in Nepal making cloth from nettles. She reports that the plant is harvested in September: "Then the bark from the main stalk is stripped, cooked in wood ash water, pounded in running water, spun into a fiber, and woven into durable, non-itchy cloth." She adds, "Nettle was widely used for making cloth in many places throughout Europe until the beginning of the twentieth century."

While I have not worked with nettles, I can easily believe these accounts from my own experience. In the course of many years as a professional gardener, I have worked with roses and many other thorny and stinging plants. As I became more adept at handling roses, I discarded my gloves. Mindfulness and skill are much more helpful than gloves in staying safe among roses. The gloves actually hindered me and made me careless. My experience with blackberry brambles is that there are parts of the plant, especially the soft tips and the woody bases of each cane, that you can safely grasp without being hurt by the chemical weaponry in the thorns and in the tiny, stinging leaf and stem hairs.

So what the Fata Morgana is asking of Rose is not some sick, weird self-sacrifice. She is in fact asking Rose to act like an adult woman, to master (or mistress) the skill and labor, power and knowledge, that go with adult womanhood. She must learn to work in a skillful way with a plant that is a strict taskmistress. Loss of concentration, or careless hurry, would be immediately "stung" back into mindfulness.

Accepting the challenge of the nettles is like accepting the challenge to master any difficult spiritual practice. Many of these require tolerating a sometimes painful discipline. Becoming a martial artist or a Yoga or Zen meditator, or committing to a psychotherapy process or an abstinence program, requires tolerating some bumps, bruises, and stings. These are sought not as ends in themselves, but as part of a rigorous project of deepening self-knowledge and empowerment. The bruised ego, the stung self-image of the person committed to learning about herself, is as much a part of the final product as the sting is part of the honey and the thorn is part of the rose.

Spellcasting

Rose says yes to the challenge of the nettles. The shirts she must weave, however, are far more than just pieces of clothing. They are a powerful spell, born of her passionate desire for justice, woven in silence and solitude between the worlds, to bring her brothers back from their wild enchantment. The weaving of these shirts will restore justice and bring balance back into a family torn and wounded by her mother's wicked wish.

How does a spell like this work? How can we, as beginners in a spiritual practice based on Mother Nature, learn how to use spells?

Let's try following Rose's steps for spellcasting through the story. First, she became clear on her intention: to transform her brothers back into men. She followed guidance, gathered her allies, and took a "long journey over water." Here she found a translation of Talking Self's intention into the language of Younger Self. To turn swans into men, she must "make" each of them human arms, shoulders, chests, flanks, and necks. This she can do as she shapes each shirt. Her dream has revealed the concrete, sensual language to engage Younger Self in the project.

So, to cast her spell, Rose must work with her hands to align the intentions of Talking Self and Younger Self. This opens a door for the immense power of Deep Self to work between the worlds and create the longed-for change. When we cast spells, we cannot manipulate or force the divine powers that move the stars to do our will. But when we state our impassioned need in Younger Self's own sensual, concrete language, we invite whatever change is possible to rush in, and what is possible is usually much more than we could consciously imagine or hope for. So, lucky and curious and unexpected and funny help arrives. Spells never go unanswered, although the answers may not be what we consciously expected. Spells are the three-dimensional, sensual prayers of a Witch who has aligned the wills of her Talking Self and Younger Self and who now asks Deep Self's assistance.

When we create spells, we change ourselves first and foremost, and we are never the same again. If I work a spell of healing for a friend, I make myself a healer and draw healing to myself even before the spell has any effect on my friend. This is the basis of the Law of Threefold Return. It's like a simple and direct karma postal service: whatever energy a Witch sends out in a spell returns to her three times—or, as my first teacher, Raven Moonshadow, used to say, "once, but three times as hard." So, not just because of moral scruples, but out of concern for our own health and happiness, we never make spells with an intent to do harm, unless we are willing to be harmed three times as much.

Therefore, when creating a spell, it is very important to examine one's motives thoroughly. When trying to get rid of a noisy neighbor or annoying coworker, a Witch may try to justify her spell by stating it in a roundabout positive way: "May so-and-so be offered the opportunity of a lifetime, health, wealth, love, everything good, far away in some distant city." I've done this sort of thing myself. I've learned rarely to recommend it, and definitely not to beginners. There are too many ways for it to backfire.

Instead, try the following. Work for yourself only, especially when you are starting out. But if you are tempted to work magic on someone else, first try this simple test. Imagine how you would feel if you found out that someone was casting this spell on you. Would you feel manipulated? Your privacy violated? In that case, don't do it. Would you feel honored, well loved, and understood? Blessed? Lucky? Now you're on the right track. If in doubt, ask the person's permission. If you're reluctant to directly ask their permission to do this spell on them, it's probably not a good idea.

Just as in the difficult decision, introduced earlier in this chapter, of whether or not to smash the snail eggs, spellcasting ethics can become quite complex. If you are working between the worlds for the arrest of a serial rapist in your community, you are not going to ask his permission! One word of comfort: we all learn best from our own mistakes, and we all make them. In regular life we make our mistakes, apologize, and make amends where possible; it is no different between the worlds. This is how we learn to be more cautious and wiser the next time.

Basic Spellcasting

Every Witch would probably explain spellcasting just a little differently. Here is one way.

1. Develop a clear intention, strongly visualized. For example: "I want to be free of my bad habit of making unkind comments about people who are not present." Remember, we start by practicing on ourselves. Strongly imagine yourself sweet tongued, making appreciative and supportive comments and meaning them. Imagine this in as much concrete detail as possible.

2. Find a vigorous, sensory, concrete representation of the intent in the language of Younger Self. Use information from dreams, visions, and trance, and also advice from more experienced Witches. For example, to sweeten the tongue, bury a beef tongue from the butcher with bitter herbs under a large rock at midnight on a dark moon of winter. Do this somewhere where you are unlikely ever to return, and walk away without looking back. Then go home and put a drop of rose water on your own tongue.

3. Do your spellcasting with your real hands and real materials in the real world. At some crucial point during the actual doing of the spell, allow yourself to move into an altered consciousness through chanting, movement, deep concentrated breathing, or whatever works best for you. Allow your emotion and energy to peak, directing them into a strongly held image of the outcome you desire.

4. When you are finished, state loudly, in clear, simple, words, what you've done. The word *spell*, according to my dictionary, comes from the Middle

English word *spellen*, "to read letter by letter," which in turn is from an Indo-European root meaning "to speak loudly." "No more mean talk for me. I'm done, I'm free. So mote it be." If this rhymes, so much the better.

5. Go about your business, don't think about it too much, and don't talk about it. It will take care of itself.

The Element Earth

The tool of earth is the pentacle. Many Witches use a plate or shallow bowl with a pentacle inscribed inside it. I use my pentacle to make food offerings on my altar, as a receptacle for fun and beautiful things I want to show the Goddess, and for questions and prayers I want to bring to Her. The power of the wise in the north is "to be silent." The magical techniques that correspond to earth include spellcasting of all kinds and any workings for health, food, and money. Our physical bodies, our animal lives, and our mortality all belong in the north.

Choosing Your Own Herbal Ally

We already learned earlier in this chapter how to enter an herb in trance and explore its powers and properties. Now it is time for you to begin searching for your own herbal allies. This may involve some reading in books about herbs, but the most important way to research herbs is with your own senses. There may be an herb garden in your local park or botanical garden, where you can see the whole plant growing. You may find that many herbs, such as dandelion, burdock, and plantain, are the "weeds" you've been seeing in your lawn, garden, or sidewalk cracks. You may find that the low hedge you walk by every day is rosemary.

Choose an herb whose properties, smell, taste (taste only those plants that you can positively identify and that you know for sure are safe), and appearance appeal to Younger Self. Rose works with nettle because it has the power to break curses, to develop inner strength and will, and to nourish. Which herb will you choose? Whichever one is right for you, keep it with you daily. Drink its tea (if it's safe and wholesome), or carry it on your person. Wear its fragrance. Remember, each plant has its own spirit power, which you can use as guide, as inspiration, as healer, as guardian. There is an enormous well of power here, free for the taking.

Practical Food/Money Magic

Just as it is important to know where our air, power, and water come from, whether they are clean, safe, and renewable, so it is important to ask the same questions about the food we eat. Few of us can completely separate ourselves economically from destructive and shortsighted farming practices, but we can do our best to be mindful, within our personal and budgetary limitations, about where our food comes from.

For several years, I have set aside part of my food budget to buy a weekly basket of fresh-picked organic vegetables from a local organic farm. During the second year that I subscribed to this service, the farmer and his family bought an additional parcel of land, which had previously been conventionally farmed with pesticides and chemical fertilizers, and began the five-year project of converting that land to a certified organic farm. I like to think that the economic security the farmer got from the weekly subscribers helped make that land purchase possible.

These farms are located upstream from me, so having one more organic farm means my watershed is a little bit safer from pesticide and fertilizer runoff. Knowing that I can make choices with my food budget that affect the web of life, and my own personal life, for the better is empowering and exciting. My own personal eating habits and my health were also impacted for the better by making this one, fairly small commitment.

Earth Meditation

This is the simplest, and deepest, earth meditation I know. Arrange for some undisturbed time, go outside, and create sacred space. (If you are in a public place, like a park, please take normal precautions for your safety.) Lie down on the earth. Relax, breathe deeply, feel gravity pulling you down, cradling you, and open all your senses to the earth beneath you. Simply rest in the fact of being utterly supported. She's not going anywhere without you. Notice whatever images and emotions arise, and allow them to release on an easy breath. Say, "By the earth which is her body." When you are finished, open the circle and go home. For a slightly different insight into earth, try the same meditation sitting with your back against the trunk of a tree. For the wild and the bold, try the same meditation, but climb up into the tree and find a good spot with your back against the trunk. Now you are a creature of earth!

We have followed Rose into the nettle patch, learning a new way to relate to the earth and her green people. We have learned the ethical principles behind spellcasting and how to cast a spell. We have begun a right relationship with the element earth. Now the story sweeps us along with it, to the next stage of our study of the elements of magic.

The Inner Path

Now Rose receives from the Fata Morgana the challenge she has been seeking. This challenge, should she successfully complete it, will fulfill her vow and return her brothers to human form. But just as the transformation of swans to men seems impossible, so do the requirements of her task. Why must she take on such a prolonged and difficult challenge? Why weaving? Why must she work with a plant that can hurt her? Why must she remain silent?

Those of us who walk the Inner Path can use this part of Rose's story to make magic for our own life purposes and to gain the inner strength we need to meet the tasks we choose. We can look at how we each weave the fabric of human community when we speak and when we remain silent. We can ask why Rose must work with a plant that can sting her and what that might mean for us.

Finding Life Purpose

Rose learns from the Fata Morgana the details of her challenge. She gets specific instructions for how to cast a magic spell that can turn her swan brothers back into men. Rose already knew that her purpose was to break the spell that bound her brothers, restoring justice in her own life story and in her family line. Some of us may already be committed and purposeful, knowing just what we are meant to do with our lives. But others of us might be wondering what shirts we are supposed to be weaving. Those of us who are wondering may find some answers by trying Pomegranate Doyle's life-purpose meditation.

Pomegranate Doyle is a Reclaiming Witch, priestess, and artist. She's an ornery, funny Irish redhead who has found her life purpose in her art, her teaching, and her priestessing. Here is an exercise Pomegranate uses to help students find a sense of life purpose.

Pomegranate's Life-Purpose Exercise

Either alone or with your friends, create sacred space, and use your breath to drop deep into your center. In memory, sweep over your life journey, and pick the five times when you had the most joy in your body from actively doing something. Pom says, "We are all on the planet for a reason, and you know when you're engaged in it because of the joy you feel in your body. Your body will sing with it. You will have a sense of well-being. The joy is a signpost; it's saying, 'Yes! Go forward.' When we go toward goals that do not create this feeling of joy, we are going down the wrong path. This is a sign saying Wrong Way. Of course, you must also know that when you move toward your fulfillment, you will feel fear. It's a big adventure, and a little fear is what makes it an adventure."

Go back to the five joyful experiences, and ask yourself what it was about these experiences that made them good for you. Take five index cards. On the top of each one, write down a few words that describe one of the experiences. Try to create a declarative sentence for each one—for instance: "I am a worshiper of the earth"; "I am a dancer"; "I am a gardener"; "I am a mathematician"; "I am a pudding eater." Now you have five cards that represent five of your life's passions. Now on each card write the four directions, with space in between to write—like this:

I am a pudding eater
EAST

SOUTH

WEST

NORTH

In meditation, visualize yourself performing one of your life's passions, and as you do so, notice the quality of your thinking (east) while you are engaged in the activity. Is it fast and focused? Is it airy and open? How does it feel to you? Record your observations on the card under "East." Now notice your energy (south). Is it hot and intense? Is it slow and even? Is it big or small or another way? Record your observations under "South." Move your attention to your emotions (west). Are you soft, colorful, intense? Record under "West." In the north, notice how your physical body feels. Are you fully embodied, aware, excited, tired? Record.

It is important to remain open throughout this exercise. Do not be tempted to judge your experiences. You are getting to know yourself as you are, not as what others have told you to be.

Go through the four directions for each card. Thank the directions, and return to normal consciousness. Now find the common themes and threads that connect these five experiences. For instance, you may notice your thinking focused, emotions blank, body active on one card, while on another you may see your thinking scattered, emotions intense, and energy running like a house on fire. Does it give you passion to have a multidimensional approach, with many different ways of thinking and feeling, or are you very focused and find yourself doing most things the same way? Remember not to judge. This is the story of you; it tells you what makes you happy and fulfilled. Spend a moment to think about your daily life. Does it fit the you that is reflected in the cards?

Take your cards and order your life's passions in terms of how often you're doing them now. How does your life look? Are you doing what you want as often as would fulfill you? As a magical act, arrange your passions in the order you would like them to be in. What needs to change to make the second list more like the first? How do your priorities help you to reach your goals, and how do they block them? In a group, you may ask for support or challenges to help you move the things that give you joy and passion forward in your life.

Trance to the Fata Morgana to Receive a Challenge

Set aside some undisturbed time so that you, or you and your circle, can take a trance journey to the Fata Morgana to receive a challenge. Create sacred space, and prepare yourselves for trance. Using your favorite induction, go to your personal place of power. Greet each of the directions, opening all your senses to what is here for you today.

Find your way to a mountainside. There is a cave here, with sleeping places made of soft plants and branches. Lie down, and go to sleep. As you sleep, dream your way to the castle of the Fata Morgana. The castle looks different to each of us. How is it for you? What do you see, hear, taste, feel? Move through its halls and doorways until you find the Dark Fairy herself. Again, she appears differently to each of us. How is it for you? Open all your senses to her. She has a vision to show you of how to achieve your life purpose. (Leave time here for each trancer to do her work.) Now, it's time to complete anything that is still left undone. Say thank you and good-bye to the Dark Fairy. Return through the halls and doorways of her castle; begin to feel the call of your sleeping body in the mountainside cave. Allow yourself to return to it, to waken, and slowly, easily, rise up off the bed of soft plants and branches.

Make your way back to the center of your own place of power. Say thank you and good-bye to each of the directions, and reverse the induction. Take your time rousing yourself, pat your body all over, and say your name three times. In circle, you may wish to talk with your friends about your insights; if you are working alone, make some notes in your Book of Shadows. Eat, and share some informal time together, allowing yourself to come all the way back to your normal consciousness before opening the circle.

Compare the challenge you've received with the joyful activities you found in the previous exercise. Is there a connection?

Choosing to Do a Big Job

Rose knows what she has to do, but the task is awfully big. For Rose to harvest and prepare the nettles, work out the fibers, spin the thread, weave the cloth, and cut and sew the twelve shirts would take several years. Even for ancient women who were accustomed to this type of work and did it daily, this would sound like a big job.

Things that are worth doing are often very difficult. Having a child takes nine months, then it takes eighteen years, and then it takes the rest of your life. Perfecting an art form or learning to play an instrument may take years of work before the first really masterful experiences occur. Confronting intergenerational patterns of cruelty, shame, and pain in a family may take decades of patient and determined effort. Committing oneself to a struggle for social justice or to protecting the wild things may involve years of hard work that is sometimes difficult or frustrating. And even then the results may be hard to see. Planting an apple seedling means five or six years of watering, tending, and protecting the plant before the first ripe apple hangs on it, and then many more years of effort before the first full harvest.

So how is Rose going to manage? First of all, she has to be willing to say yes to the challenge. It takes great courage and inner strength to accept a challenge that will take years to fulfill. It takes tremendous self-confidence to commit to such a task, knowing that you may not succeed. And yet it is impossible to succeed without starting.

Rose is no longer an untried girl. She has already made tremendous progress on her own behalf. She has followed her intuition and asked the right questions. She has dared to leave the familiar castle. She has trusted herself to the wild and to guidance and followed the stream to the sea. She has endured her brothers' anger and allowed its release. She has woven a basket strong enough to fly in, and she has fearlessly taken that breathtaking flight. She has all this experience to draw on, and so do we.

Answering a Challenge

Arrange for some undisturbed time, alone or with your circle. Cast a circle at your altar, invoke the powers, and light your candles. By now your Rose altar is beginning to be full of magic and full of meaning. There are the mysterious dreams, images, or sensations that began your questioning. The beauty of the lovely, fragrant roses is reflected in your mirror, along with the dancing candlelight. There are food offerings to the ones who guide you (they might want a bite of your snack, too). There is a bit of ash from the fire where you released your "wicked vows" and touched the deep center of your own enduring fire.

There is a bit of homemade basket, and your drums or music, yoga mats or meditation cushions, your commitment to ecstatic practice. The spell of the Twelve Wild Swans is building.

Take a moment for meditation, here in sacred space you have created for yourselves, here amid the magic of your commitment to your inner work. Breath deeply, and let your awareness drop into your own centers. Be aware that you have already come a long way, that you have already shown courage, inner strength, creativity, willingness, and love. Know that you can count on yourselves. Give yourselves credit for the challenges you have already met; know yourselves to be profoundly capable. Take some time to raise energy, chanting, drumming, breathing, moving—whatever works for you. In circle, you may wish to take turns coming to the center of the circle. Each person may receive praise and blessings honoring her efforts so far. Each circle sister may give her a kiss: "Thou art Goddess."

Now return to the five joyful experiences you worked with in the life-purpose exercise described earlier. Remember the challenges that the Fata Morgana offered each of you. What would you have to do in order to bring your true life purposes forward in your life? What changes would you have to make, what would you have to let go of to make room for your true life purposes? Ask yourself if you want to take the challenge to make these changes. You can say yes, or no. Or you may also have another answer right now, one that is right for you, such as "After Megan starts kindergarten" or "After my hip surgery." You may wish to speak out loud the changes that you wish to make, so your circle sisters can be witnesses for you.

When everyone has had a turn to speak, eat and visit together, and open the circle only when you are ready. Know that challenges will come into your life. Sometimes the toughest challenge is actually doing the things you love to do, the things that bring you joy. When challenges come, you have what it takes to say yes, if you want to. You can also say no or "Not now." It's up to you.

Green Nettle Magic

So Rose is ready, and so are we. She says yes to the challenge of the nettle weaving. What are we to learn from her task? What is the Fata Morgana trying to teach us? First, let's take a look at some of the traditional magical and medicinal lore surrounding nettles. For Witches, all plants (as well as all animals, stones, stars, and so forth) have their own spirit powers and magical purposes, which can be discovered either by studying the traditional lore or just by studying and working with and caring for the plant. This is how the traditional sources developed their wisdom: by direct experience and observation.

Now, the herbalists' lore about nettles will tell us that although Rose may have plenty of difficulties as she completes her arduous task in the wild, she will not be weak or hungry. Nettles are an incredibly nourishing food, used by women for thousands of years because of their high mineral content and their ability to strengthen the adrenal system—seat of the will. The nettles, trying and painful as they may be, will also give Rose the strength she needs to meet the challenge they present. They will nourish her deeply, with a wild green strength, in a way we have almost forgotten that food can nourish us.

Nettles also have the traditional magical association of breaking curses and of sending negative magic back where it came from. This is no surprise, since nettles are extremely well defended. They definitely have the property of sending unwary intruders back wherever they came from. In this case, Rose's nettles will be part of a spell breaking the negative effects of her mother's ill wish that her twelve boys be exchanged for a girl.

And for the cautious and skillful harvester, nettles also offer the quality of inner strength, both because they are so nourishing and because their tough stems are held up by fibers that are considered to be among the strongest in the plant world. Once these shirts are made, they will definitely be sturdy.

Now, any woman who commits herself to attempting difficult challenges will need what the nettle has to offer. Perhaps you are already engaged in meaningful and challenging projects. Maybe you are considering taking some on, and the life-purpose exercise described earlier gave you some encouragement. Whether your projects are directed inward—at self-healing, self-knowledge, and self-love—or outward toward creative expression and responsible action, how will you nourish yourself? How can you gain the needed strength and energy, the strong fiber, the powerful self-defense to achieve your goals?

Nettle Magic: Nourishment

We have fed the powers that be, and now it is time to allow ourselves to be fed. You will need a favorite plate or bowl. Bring it with you to your altar, and alone or with your circle create sacred space, and light your candles. Place the bowls or plates on the altar, and ask the help of the powers; ask them to help you fill your bowl with the foods that will truly nourish you. Sing songs for them, dance for them, open your heart to them, and tell them your true need. Then let yourself sink into a light trance. Close your eyes, and let your inner vision open, knowing that the powers will fill your bowl with exactly what you need the most. What is that wondrous food in your bowl? Smell and taste, look and feel with your inner senses. When you have an impression or intuition, tell yourself that you will remember it, and allow yourself to return to normal consciousness.

You may have only a clue—an impression of color, or aroma, or texture. In this case, a trip to a good grocery store may prod your memory, and you may recognize the food from your trance. Or you may have received specific directions on exactly what to eat. In any case, it's a good idea to actually try the food, unless it's something that would be unhealthy for you, in which case further negotiations are needed.

But go ahead and take this insight a step further. What does this food mean to you? If it's chicken soup, does that mean you would be nourished by mothering energy from an older woman? If it's mushrooms, does that mean more walks in the greenwood? If it's kid food, is there a way for you to feed your heart and soul by being around the lovely, zesty energy of kids? Younger Self knows what we need to feed our deepest hungers: food and herbs, fun, love, and heartsease. If we ask for guidance and listen with an open mind, we will find all the clues we need to take excellent care of ourselves, to strengthen the fiber of our health and energy, so that we can do the difficult, long-term, committed, creative tasks that life asks of us and that we long to do.

Nettle Magic: Strong Fiber of Soul

Have you ever noticed how time flies when you are doing something you love? For me, it's gardening. I can start weeding, pruning, and reshaping a perennial border, and before I know it, it's getting dark. This still happens to me just as it did when I first started gardening professionally, fifteen years ago. I also lose my sense of time when I'm dancing to good drumming, or reading my tarot cards, or meditating. I hit a zone, and fifteen minutes or three hours later, when I rouse myself, my feet are all pins and needles from sitting cross-legged, or I'm breathless from dancing.

When the Fata Morgana asks Rose to spin, weave, and sew, she is asking her to spend long hours in the light trance state brought on by absorbing, repetitive work. Although the entire task might seem daunting, the actual doing of it on any one day may be quite healing and serenity inducing. Drummers, dancers, long-distance runners, artists, and craftswomen of all kinds can describe this kind of slightly altered state brought on by repetitive work. It's almost as if someone else has done the work.

Much of the daily work of our ancestors was of this sort: agricultural work, chopping wood, carrying water, weaving, and engaging in crafts of all kinds. No one needed a cell phone, an up-to-the-minute stock quote; no one "had mail." The constant interruptions, the multitasking, of the attention-deficit home and workplace had not been invented yet. We each have within ourselves the ability and the longing to spend this kind of creative, meditative time. It feeds one of our deep soul hungers.

So the stories our ancestors told are full of references to this kind of task. In "Rumpelstiltskin," the girl must spin huge chambers full of straw into gold. The shoemakers in "The Shoemakers and the Elves" must make many pairs of shoes, each with hundreds of tiny stitches, by morning. In "Vaselisa," the girl must sort a whole granary full of poppy seeds. In each case, someone else—a "little man," the elves, or Vaselisa's doll—does most of the work. In this way the stories reflect the universal experience of entering another world, peopled with strange beings, while doing otherwise overwhelming tasks.

We can each choose to "let the doll do most of the work," even if it is only for a small part of our day. Perhaps we can walk part way instead of driving or taking the bus. Perhaps we can put on some favorite music and chop vegetables instead of eating processed food. Perhaps we can embroider or play cards or whittle instead of watching TV. I find that I can "let the doll do most of the work" when I'm cleaning house, if I light a candle and put on some music. These are all ways of letting Younger Self come out and play, of feeding the ancestral part of ourselves that is capable of and longs to do trance-inducing, repetitive work. Younger Self will repay these efforts handsomely, with renewed energy, better appetite and sleep, and less worrying. Repetitive, trance-inducing work, whether it is embroidery or long-distance running, makes the nerve, fiber, and muscle tissue of our souls strong and flexible. Making sure we get this sort of activity and this sort of time woven into our lives is one of the ways we nourish ourselves energetically.

Cynthia's Sewing Meditation

Cynthia, of Diana's Grove, offers this meditation on repetitive, trance inducing work. She writes, "So many old stories are about women sewing, about the magic in daily tasks. It is easy to think that the story is about the shirts or the mantle or the cloth, the product and not the process. When our attention is on the product, it is really easy to forget about sewing and look for a good ready-made shirt, or mantle, or soul.

Find an activity you can use as a silent meditation. Sewing is one way to dedicate time for listening, but 'sewing' might take another form for you. What would you like to do? What project could be a companion in your reverie and a mentor as you practice the arts of silence, breath, visioning, and connecting? What can you do that will enable you to claim a time and commune with the world around you? You might make a basket or work with beads. Choose something that can become mindless and that will support rather than eclipse your process of deepening.

In sacred space, take up your task. Your fingers know what to do without any advice from your mind. Feel the sharpness of the needle, how, piercing and silver, it goes in and out, in and out, how its tip parts the weave as it comes and goes, comes and goes. The thread is strong and supple; it binds the edges together. It invokes silence.

Silence can be like a drop of water on a summer morning, when the whole world is captured in the convex lens of a drop of dew. Imagine entering a drop of silence and listening to the world around you with your eyes, body, and heart. Listen. The world is telling you stories about yourself and life. What do you hear when you don't hear your own words? In that space, listen deeply to a world that speaks without language. Can you imagine hearing a language without words? Your nose and body know how to listen to the wind. The temperature and direction of the wind will tell you stories about the weather.

Breathe. Sew. Listen. Let the act of sewing become an act of transformation."

Exercise: A Nettle Doll

Here is a simple exercise, which will give you a chance to do a little needlework and also to make a commitment to your own inner strength. When your circle meets, you can each make a doll stuffed with nettle, a spell for strong fiber and endurance to meet life goals. Or you can make one alone at your own altar, in sacred space. This doll can be as simple as an old, unmatched sock (everyone has at least one of these!) tied with thread for a neck and arms, or it can be as complex as you like. Fill your doll with the things you would like to have inside you. Start by putting in some dried nettle leaf. You can purchase this at your local health-food store or occult shop, or, if you know how, you can harvest the nettles yourself and dry them. You can also add many other things: herbs, stones, colorful threads, words written on scraps of paper, little precious objects, toys. You can use anything that represents qualities you wish for in your own inner life and in your own character.

Dress your doll, and give it eyes, hair, and other physical details to make it look like you and to please Younger Self. At some point in the process, let yourself do some repetitive, mindless stitching. Observe how your consciousness changes when you do simple, repetitive work. Place your doll on your circle's altar, or on your own home altar, which is now full of Rose magic, as a commitment to developing your own inner nettle-fiber strength and to "letting the doll do most of the work." Spells like this should never be disposed of carelessly when you are done with them.

Weaving with Words

As Rose sits in her green cave, sending the shuttle flying across the face of the loom, weaving human soul for her brothers and justice for her family line, she brings to mind the Goddess herself, the weaver of the web of life. As ancient women knew, individual threads are constantly being added to a piece of weaving, and old ones are coming to an end or being snipped off. Yet the whole pattern of the weaving continues.

Witches know that our individual human lives are like this. We enter a pattern that already exists, play our individual parts for a time, and then our lives come to an end. Our lives gain meaning in the context of the pattern of the whole web of life and the web of human community. These flow on unchanged.

And although we are not the Weaver, we are also weavers, each in our way. We weave together the threads of life when we choose to act responsibly and respectfully in our interactions with the natural world, whether by buying organic vegetables or by defending a redwood forest. We also weave the threads of human community together when we act responsibly and respectfully toward one another. Like Rose, we weave the fabric of soul for one another, and pull each other out of the wild and into human community, when we weave a pattern of love, trust, and respect in our families and communities.

Gossip is a wonderful old word that reflects the work that women have done since time began: weaving community by talking about one another and our family members. Although the word has come to have the connotation of frivolous or malicious talk, the original roots mean the "god sib," or extended family member. We women are famous for spending hours together, talking over the nuances of relationships, the development of children, the troubles of a friend and how to support her. We were originally called gossips to honor the fact that our talk with one another, our encouragement and insight and counsel, make up a powerful thread that weaves together family and community. We are each weavers of soul.

Many therapeutic and recovery programs now rely on this sort of honest talk about the personal details of life. There is nothing more healing and relieving than hearing someone who has already gone through a difficult experience detailing their exact feelings and reactions. My friend Seed, when she lost a pregnancy, felt bewildered and foolish for having a desperate need to know what the hospital had done with the tiny body. She was so relieved when she went to a recovery group for women with similar losses and found that the women there expected her to have these feelings and knew exactly how to help her find out what she needed to know. Many women and men recovering from addictions know the relief and even the humor of hearing others detailing the exact kind of odd thinking that the detoxing person experiences: "Well, if I had a beer with a tofu burger and salad, it would be good for my health, right?"

When we tell the truth about ourselves to one another, we find that we are each wounded healers weaving a tight, strong web, a safety net of human soul, which can hold each of our individual threads close to the design. It is only in the context of this high value we place on intimate, honest communication that the next part of the story makes sense.

Choosing Silence

There are also times when we must weave our communities and our human souls by silence. There are times when what we think or feel must not be spoken because the timing is wrong. And there are times when something must never be spoken, either because it is someone else's secret or because it would do harm. I wish I had a nickel for every time I was tempted to make some comparison between my two children but kept my mouth shut. I wish I had a dime for every time I felt an urge to criticize my husband and instead took a deep breath or a short walk or said a quick prayer. The worst part of having to keep quiet about something is that you never get any credit for it! But the worst part of speaking when silence would have been better is that it's impossible to take it back once "the cat's out of the bag."

The spoken word has great power in traditional magic. At the end of a spell (a word whose root actually means "to say out loud, to tell"), many Witches state clearly and firmly, in rhyme if possible, exactly what they have done. Because we know ourselves to be truth tellers, when we say it is so, it comes true: "So mote it be."

By the same token, sometimes to say something out loud prematurely takes all the power out of it. Old wives knew this when they said, "Don't count your chickens before they're hatched." Children everywhere agree that the wish that is made when the birthday candles are blown out must not be revealed. If it is told, it will not come true.

In our story, Rose must not speak until the shirts are finished, because all her intent and concentration is due this task, whose completion will bring justice into her own life story and into the story of her family line. Like all the wise, she must bend and weave her reality into a shape that will fit it back into the pattern of the Great Weaver. She must hold her power within, building her strength and focus. She must not boast, complain, or explain prematurely. What would sound sillier than explaining that her brothers have been turned into swans and that the Fata Morgana says she must weave nettle shirts for them? Really, she might find herself committed to a jail or hospital. Instead, she must do, complete, and show. The ability to stay silent is one of the powers of the wise, which some Witches (and mystics of many religious backgrounds) include as part of their spiritual practice.

Rose's silence is not the silence of a voiceless person who cannot speak up. We know Rose can speak up; she did so when she asked a million questions about the ominous silence and secrecy in her childhood castle. There she broke the rule of silence that hid the injustices of the past. But now her silence is chosen. It belongs to a Witch, deep in a meditative state while completing a spellworking.

Exercise: Practicing Silence

Choose to remain silent for a definite time period. A few hours may be good for practice, but many of the benefits of the exercise come when we allow ourselves longer periods of silence. We must not harm or confuse others with our spiritual practices, so it is important to negotiate with family members and friends before undertaking a period of silence. Sometimes because of outside responsibilities it can be done only by allowing a certain number of words that may be spoken during the day (thirteen is a popular number).

When you have completed a period of silence, make some notes about what you learned about yourself in your Book of Shadows. Were there times when your silence saved you from hasty or meaningless talk? Did silence speak more than words? Was it a relief? Were there times when you missed out on a chance for communication and intimacy? Were there frustrating moments when you needed words as a tool?

In circle, try creating a silent ritual. You will need to talk to plan it, but once it begins, use no words. Notice how the energy in the circle moves differently without language. Sometimes the people who are normally quieter in a circle really shine when language stops. Sometimes not speaking helps circle members open up other forms of sensitivity to one another.

These exercises, when practiced attentively over time, can help each of us make better choices about how we use our words. Like Rose, we all experience times when, instead of speaking, we must do, complete, and show.

Facing Pain

As Rose works among the nettles, no matter how careful she is there will be times when she feels the sting of the formic acid that makes up the nettles' early-warning system. For that matter, once the nettles are harvested and they no longer sting, the hard work of the fiber preparation, spinning, and weaving will sometimes hurt her hands. And so with us, when we live our lives as fully and passionately as possible, weaving our families and communities, stepping up to our life purposes, we will sometimes experience the "sting" of our imperfection, our humanness, and our mortality.

Initiatory practices everywhere, and the initiatory tales that reflect these practices, include some sort of ordeal. Not the pain itself, but rather the initiatory candidate's strength, resourcefulness, and ability to bear it, reflect an unavoidable piece of what human adulthood is all about.

Like the wise of all spiritual disciplines, Witches know that pain is part of the life of mortals just as winter is part of spring. The pain and struggle of labor are part of giving birth to a beautiful little baby. The disorientation and sickness of detox are part of breaking a pattern of addictive behavior and beginning a new life of freedom and wellness. Overcoming the frustration and hopelessness of creative blocks is part of courting the Muse in every artistic process.

Modern people, strongly influenced by a commodity-based, immediate-gratification culture, may sometimes feel that pain, whether physical or emotional, indicates a failure or a mistake of some sort. In extreme cases, even ill or recently bereaved people may find themselves being subtly blamed for their pain. When women and men approach huge life transitions, or when they experience personal or creative or healing breakthroughs, they may also experience pain, fear, physical symptoms—suffering in all its many forms.

Witches do not believe that the painful parts of life are a punishment, as in the biblical Garden of Eden story. So feeling guilty for being hurt or ill or troubled is not our way. Instead, we remember that the pattern of the whole web of life requires that each thread have a beginning and an end. As every moon waxes and wanes, every human life includes many different beginnings and endings, and lots of plateaus, diversions, and transitions in between. Each creature (even the vegetarian) lives by feeding off the deaths of others, and in the end we are all food for the future. Witches neither seek the pains of mortal life nor fear them. In fact, pain can at times be valuable information, enormously helpful in a healing process. And so Rose is tested, and she passes the test. She is willing to undertake the challenge of her own life purpose, even though it will inevitably involve some pain.

Pain and Silence: A Word of Caution

Suffering and silence are not good in themselves. We are not recommending them as a way of life or as a primary spiritual practice! If a person is sick, sad, silent, or hurting all the time, quite possibly there is something wrong, something that needs professional attention. There is no shame in consulting traditional and nontraditional doctors and healers for help when it is needed. We each deserve all the help we can get when we are going through periods of suffering.

Our idea of healthy human life is not all about suffering and silence, although these are mysteries that human life inevitably confronts us with. Instead, our recipe is as follows: a quart of health and happiness; a cup of ecstasy; a half gallon of committed, creative, collaborative work; a dash of pain; a handful of transition; and three tablespoons of yeast in warm water, so that we can rise. Adjust seasonings to taste!

Rose has accepted the Fata Morgana's challenge and undertaken a period of silent, focused work to fulfill her life purpose. But now the story sweeps her along, and we must go with her, toward the next set of challenges in our journey of healing.

The Outer Path

In the Elements Path and the Inner Path in this section of the story, we worked with will and with the power of silence. Now, in the Outer Path, we are asked to consider what qualities we need in order to take on a great task of healing and creation.

What is the task we are called to do? In the evolution of every project, there's a process of clarification. If I want to heal the earth, I might first wander in the wilderness, wondering how to go about it. Perhaps I'll find help and guidance, even get carried away by my enthusiasm for permaculture or biodynamic farming. I can fly high, ecstatically dreaming of what I'm going to plant and how I will meditate over every single seed for every healing herb. But eventually, to make the vision manifest, I have to undertake the healing of one piece of ground, the painful and sometimes tedious tasks of fertilization or erosion control, and I have to be prepared to sustain my efforts over the long term, until the job is done. The bigger and more important the task, the greater the effort that's called for.

In the Goddess tradition, pleasure is sacred. We don't romanticize pain. But we do know that a big working, a large change in consciousness, may require sacrifice. At the crossroads, if we take one path, we forgo the other. If I go to the hearing at the Board of Forestry, I won't be spending the day in my garden.

The word *sacrifice* literally means "to make sacred." The tasks worth doing, worth committing ourselves to with wholehearted passion, are the tasks that serve what is truly sacred to us, what is most vitally important. The following is a meditation I use over and over again, both personally and with groups.

The Sacred Task

In sacred space, go to your place of power. Ask yourself, "What is sacred to me? What is most important, so important that I don't want to see it harmed or compromised? What would I be willing to take a stand for, to risk myself for?" As the answers come to you, you might choose a symbol for each one. ("I see a redwood tree to stand for the trees and the earth, a beloved child's face to stand for the children, the homeless man on the street corner to stand for justice.") In a group, you can speak these out loud.

Breathe deeply, and go back into silence. Think for a moment about your work, your relationships, the way you spend your days. Ask yourself, "Are my best energies aligned with what is sacred to me?"

If the answer is no, ask yourself, "What do I need to make a change, to bring my best life energies into alignment with what is truly sacred to me? Is it support? Courage? Luck? Is there a sacrifice I would need to make, and am I willing to make it?" As the answers come, realize that this is your task.

If the answer is yes, if your best energies are being used in the service of what is truly sacred to you, then ask yourself, "What lies in front of me now?" Envision a road leading out from your place of power. What do you see immediately in front of you on that road? This is your task, the shirt that you must weave. What do you need in order to undertake this work? Support? Luck? Courage? Are there nettles you need to grasp? Is there a sacrifice you would need to make, and are you willing to make it?

Return from your place of power.

In a group, you might go around the circle, naming your task and asking for the support you need in order to undertake it. Alone, you might put symbols of what is sacred to you on your altar and consider whom you might ask for support.

Suppose your task is something you don't want to do or that requires a sacrifice you are unwilling to make. It is not always easy to tell if the images that arise for us are truly coming from the deepest source of all life or from some layer of guilt or illusion within us. If a task is truly in alignment with what is most sacred to you, it will feel joyous even when it requires hard work or sacrifice. It will present itself with a sense of calm knowing, not with anxiety or frantic urgency. The sacrifices it requires will be inherent in the nature of the task, not extraneous suffering for suffering's sake. And it will never require you to go against your conscience in any way.

One of the advantages of being in a polytheistic tradition is that, even if the Goddess herself tells you to do something, you have somewhere to go for a second opinion. You can say no to the Goddess. To gather power, we must freely choose to take up our challenge—and unless we are free to say no, we are not free to say yes.

Great tasks may present themselves in rituals, dreams, or visions. For me, they've often come in much more mundane circumstances—as a thought or an idea that might pop up while I'm driving down the freeway or having a conversation about something else. They carry a certain energetic quality I think of as a "feeling of doom." Clichéd as that phrase is, for me it is an anchor to a certain calm, neutral, almost emotionless state characterized by a heavy sense of inevitability. When I turned twenty-one, my mother gave me an electric typewriter as a birthday present. At that time I had no intention of becoming a writer, but the first morning I sat down to type, the feeling of doom overcame me. For fifteen years, Reclaiming had discussed the idea of writing a book to document our teaching material. I had firmly resisted involvement with the project, until one morning on the boat back from Gozo to Malta, I was talking with the friends who had gone with me to visit the Goddess temples there. The idea of this book came up, and sure enough, there was the old feeling of doom. At that point, I knew that the writing was, indeed, part of my task.

The Feeling of Doom

Reflect on the moments in your life when you have made a crucial choice or taken on an important task that was right for you. How did you know it was right? Are there particular qualities of energy or emotion you can identify that characterize that state? Is there a color, a phrase, an image, a bodily feeling that goes with it?

What has happened when you've listened to that feeling? What has happened when you've gone against it?

In a group, share your insights. Alone, you might wish to record them in your journal.

Be alert to the presence of that feeling. When it arises, know that you are being guided toward your true task.

Warning Signals

Just as a certain energy state characterizes our true tasks, we may find that particular energetic and emotional states are signs of danger, signals that we are about to turn down a wrong path. This may be a good moment to renew your anchor to your core state and review the exercise on identifying your inflated and deflated states. Often we make our worst choices when we are either puffed up with self-importance or sunk in self-hate.

Reflect on the moments in your life when you have made a wrong choice or taken on a task that is not truly yours. Can you remember what you were thinking? What energy characterized your state at that moment? What emotions or bodily feelings? Is there a color, a phrase, an image, or a place on your body you can anchor to this state as a warning bell? Are there different warning signals for different kinds of wrong turnings?

Again, share or write in your journal about your insights. And be alert for your warning bell when you are making choices.

Healers and activists are especially prone to the dangers of certain kinds of inflation. Reya is a Reclaiming teacher trained in shiatsu massage. She warns of what she calls "heroic thoughts or emotions." If as a healer I start thinking, 'I'm healing this person, I'm reducing their suffering, I'm taking their pain away"—uh-oh! Danger, danger! Western medicine has become a heroic act that actually has little to do with the person who is ill or the situation that needs resolution. All the light and glory shines on the healer, while the person who needs the healing is left out in the cold, energetically. I generally suggest people take a *big* step backward from whatever is making them feel heroic and let others take over some of the work."

Activists can easily get carried away by the heroic thrills of facing dangerous situations or doing dramatic acts. If we receive a lot of attention for our actions, and our sacrifices are carried out in front of TV cameras, our focus can gradually shift from the work itself to how we look doing it. And we may neglect the thousand and one unglamorous daily tasks that truly lay the groundwork for change.

The Person with the Pickup Truck

How do you know if a task is truly yours or can be delegated to someone else? Consider the metaphor of the pickup truck. In most city-based communities, there is often one person who for whatever reason owns a pickup truck. (In the country just about everyone owns a pickup.)

Owning a pickup truck is a mixed blessing. When something large and bulky needs to be moved, when the giant Goddess puppet needs to be transported to the ritual, when the garage is being cleaned out, the Person with the Pickup Truck is called upon to serve.

A wise Person with the Pickup Truck might ask some of the following questions:

Can this really be moved in a pickup truck, or is this a job for something
    larger—maybe even a dumpster or a garbage truck?
Is mine the only pickup truck available?
Is my truck available, or is it already full?

When we take on leadership in a group, some part of us may want to be the one to solve every problem, resolve every conflict, dry every tear. But to do so becomes disempowering to others and leads to exhaustion and burnout. When I'm teaching, when I'm leading a group or priestessing a ritual or a Witchcamp, I find it useful to ask myself, "Am I the Person with the Pickup Truck in this situation?"—that is, am I the person here who has the skills, experience, and knowledge to be helpful? Do I have the energy to take this on, or is the situation critical enough that I need to deal with it regardless? Am I the only person here who can be helpful, or is someone else already handling the situation?

One of the reasons we co-teach or teach in teams and collectively priestess rituals is so that no one person always has to be the Person with the Pickup Truck. In passing on our skills, in training others to take leadership, we assure that there will be many pickups in our communities, and trucks of various types and qualities. If someone has an emotional crisis in the midst of a ritual, I might be the Person with the Pickup Truck. If someone falls forward in a seizure during the grounding, I'm deeply grateful to let someone with medical training be the Person with the Pickup Truck. I can use my skills to support her by keeping the group calm, holding the energy of the circle, and channeling healing energy while we await the paramedics.

When we are the Person with the Pickup Truck, we have a responsibility to carry through our task until it is over. Hilary was once literally the person with the pickup truck who had brought the giant Goddess puppet to the ritual—in this case, the tenth-anniversary Spiral Dance a decade ago. At the end of a very long day and night, when the lighting crew was still high on ladders slinging heavy and breakable pieces of equipment over everyone's head and the more dedicated of us were pushing brooms, a bleary-eyed Hilary came to me and said, "I've got to take care of myself. I'm going home. Can you find someone else to take the giant Goddess puppet?"

"No!" I wailed in panic. "You can't! You can't leave me with the giant Goddess puppet! You are the only person with a pickup truck here!"

She did indeed take the puppet, and thus began our long friendship—the point being, if you take on a task, you can't drop it halfway unless there is someone in place to pick it up, or you may end up doing damage. It's better not to bring the giant Goddess puppet to the ritual at all than to bring it and abandon it. When we take on a task, we need to consider how to end it as well as how to begin it and how to harbor our energy so that we can carry it through.

Finding a Source of Strength

When we know that a task is ours, we need the strength to carry it out. Magic could be called "the art of finding unexpected sources of inner power." Our tools, our skills, and the ongoing relationship we have built with the elements and the Goddess can help us renew our energies and face our challenges.

———————

In sacred space, go to your place of power. Ask yourself, "Where can I find the support, the strength, the courage, or the luck I need to take up my task?"

Turn slowly and face the four directions. Notice which one draws you. Imagine a path into that direction. Breathing slowly, feel your feet on that path as you begin to walk. Feel the texture of the ground underfoot and the weight of your body as it shifts. Look around you; notice what you see and hear and feel and sense.

As you walk along this path, you begin to notice your helpers and allies. Who or what is there for you? Take time to explore, to speak and listen. Where can you look for luck? What do you find that can be a source of strength and courage? How can you hold and carry that source within you?

When you are ready, thank your allies. Walk slowly back to the center of your place of power. Turning counterclockwise, face and thank each of the four directions, and then return to the circle and your ordinary consciousness. In a group, you may share your visions and suggest ways in which you can help each other stay connected to your sources of strength. Alone, you might want to record your vision in your journal and place a symbol of your strength on your altar.

Resting in the Goddess

Sage reminds us that we are never without support. Even should we find no human sources of help and courage, the Goddess is still present, still offering her love.

"If you take time frequently to let yourself rest in the presence of the Goddess, then in a moment of crisis the pathway is open, and you can be very deep and present in the moment at the same time," Sage says. She suggests the following meditation:

In sacred space, sit before your altar with a cup filled with drinking water, juice, or milk. Invoke the Goddess, and picture her sitting opposite you. Take time to let your image of her develop clearly. How does she appear to you in this moment? The way you perceive her may give you information on what you need from her at this time.

Breathe deeply, and imagine that her heart is a cup, filled with love for you. As you breathe, see her cup begin to overflow. Let her love for you flow into your cup, charging your drink. If there is some special quality you need—

courage, or strength, or health—you can imagine her cup overflowing with that quality as well.

Take your time; just rest in the Goddess's presence. When your cup feels full, drink in her love. Thank her, and from your own, overflowing heart send back gratitude. Open your circle.

In the Outer Path we move beyond personal healing and self-transformation to take on the tasks that can heal others and that can potentially change the world. Rose's task is to weave twelve new souls, to reintegrate the wild and the human, to restore balance to a broken world. In the Reclaiming tradition, we are concerned, ultimately, with weaving a new soul for our culture, a garment of healing that can restore our balance and reintegrate us with the natural systems that sustain life. This work is neither simple nor easy, but deeply challenging. We are called not just to heal ourselves, but to offer service to our communities, to the Goddess, and to the earth. We aspire to become culture healers.

Every culture puts its shamans and healers through some sort of testing or ordeal, whether that takes the form of a Sun Dance for days without water, or of grueling years of medical school. Some challenges, of course, lead to deeper spiritual growth, while others may be more in the nature of a sadistic indoctrination into corporate workaholic culture. But the core of underlying wisdom is that healers must have fortitude, must be able to put aside their personal needs and give priority to the needs of others.

A healer must be able to bear pain. In Rose's case, she bears the pain of the nettles, which sting but do not damage. Therapists must be able to bear the pain their clients bring; doctors must be able to withstand the suffering of their patients without withdrawing or turning away. To be calm and confident in the face of suffering, we must have tasted some of it ourselves.

The Goddess tradition never asks for self-abnegation, nor do we promote asceticism. But to gather true power, fortitude is necessary. A midwife stays through the duration of a birth. She can't simply yawn halfway through and say, "I'm tired. I'm going to take care of myself and go home."

Taking care of ourselves has become something of a New Age watchword. Many of us have indeed learned that unless we take care of ourselves, we have nothing to offer anyone else, and that too much focus on fixing other people may be a way of maintaining their disease and avoiding looking at our own problems. But to learn magic, to gather power, is also to sometimes push ourselves, to test our limits, to go beyond our zone of comfort and ease.

Obviously, a balance is necessary. Part of the work of this section is to explore that balance. How do we know when we are being truly generous or simply codependent? When are extraordinary efforts really called for, and when are we simply in a workaholic pattern? What are the ordeals that expand and empower us, and when are we falling into the age-old women's pattern of putting everybody else's needs before our own?

Cynthia, together with her partner, Patricia Storm, together founded Diana's Grove, in Missouri. At any given time, they might be teaching workshops there, organizing Witchcamps or retreats, teaching their Mystery School program, and balancing a hundred demands for service that can range from healing an emotional crisis to clearing a blocked water line or removing a fallen tree. Cynthia has had many opportunities to contemplate questions of balance.

"The only way that self-care and service—'other care'—can be balanced is when I strive for integrity," Cynthia says. "Then what I do, I do from a wholeness that feeds me and serves my vision and the world I want to nurture into reality. I find that *integrity* is a misunderstood word. It isn't an invitation to do what I want, but a commitment to be true to myself and my vision or service. When I am in integrity, I choose my actions. I act for me, and I act to sustain the community and world that I value."

Melusine is another Witch who has taken on a big task. She was the first Witchcamp teacher we trained outside of our local San Francisco Bay area community. She lives in a small town in British Columbia, where she serves on the City Council.

"Where I live, the local council had done some incredibly stupid things," she told me. "They had clear-cut our park after some trees came down in a storm, and they had an official community plan that wiped out three neighborhoods. I had appeared in front of the council numerous times. I've always been a great rabble-rouser. But I thought, 'If I really want to make the world a better place, I have to put my money where my mouth is and run for office.' It took me a year to make that decision, because I knew it would be a very steep learning curve and a lot of things would fall by the wayside as far as teaching and workshops and my personal life. But as a city councilor, I use every skill I've ever learned at Witchcamp: moving energy, when to speak and when to keep silent, timing, and shielding. And I've learned a lot about being true to myself and about not being afraid to say that I don't know. It must have worked, because I increased my voter support by 25 percent in the second election and solidly defeated the woman who was my perpetual opposition."

Although there is a certain amount of glamour in being elected to public office, the work and responsibility outweigh the glory. "A lot of what I do is very mundane," Melusine admits. "It's committee meetings, it's showing up at Mrs. Swanson's house when she's having a little tea because the neighbor ladies are upset about the digging on their street. It's all the little things that will never get into the papers. Like crushing the nettles, it's doing the ongoing, painful, boring work."

That work, however, is sustained by a sense of joy. "I do also manage to have fun," she says, laughing. "There's not a week goes by that I don't get my picture in the paper for something. I said I was going to quit smoking, and I got in the paper. I hang out with the skateboarders as well as the tea ladies."

Before taking on the healing of the world, we might pause for a moment and consider what is necessary for healing individuals. "Healers are part of a continuum centered on whomever or whatever we're healing," Reya says. "All kinds of exercises that increase self-awareness, that help us center and ground, can help build the ability to endure and tolerate, and help us learn the rhythm of healing, which has everything to do with pacing, timing, and remembering to be 'right sized.' A daily meditation or sitting practice is crucial, especially the kind of practice that highlights connection with our own state of being. After sitting, you might realize, 'Oops, I'm feeling kind of fragile today,' or you might notice that your throat is kind of sore, and just that knowledge may help you pace yourself differently than you would if you were feeling perfect."

Reya has an exercise she uses to check for numbness and loss of feeling, both warning signs of overextension.

Checking for Numbness

To check for numbness, stop what you're doing and breathe. Run your attention around your body; simply doing that may allow you to identify numb areas.

Alone, you can hold one hand above an area of the body. Start with your back, shoulders, or arms, and work the whole body. If you're doing this with a partner, one will be the tester (the hand) and the other will be the receiver. The receiver sees if she can sense the heat from the hand. Slowly move the hand closer to the body until the receiver can feel either the heat or the hand itself.

Sometimes we're so numb we can't even sense when the hand makes contact with our skin. Move to another part of the body, testing for lifelessness everywhere, even your head, the soles of your feet, and so forth. Once you know which areas are numb and lifeless, ask yourself what you need in order to bring that part back. Are you thirsty? Hungry? Hot or cold? Do you need to get up and stretch or move around? Do you need some fresh air? Get someone to scratch or briskly rub your back. That really gets the circulation going again.

Over time, notice whether there are patterns to your numbness, particular places on your body that first lose feeling. Consider whether they correspond to emotional or energetic deadening or health problems.

After you complete this exercise, you might want to give your partner some energy in the numb area or some hands-on healing.

———————

While Rose completes her tasks, she must remain silent. Silence, for women and other target groups, has often been a component of our oppression, a way to keep us isolated and disempowered. But Rose's silence is of another order, the silence of the shaman engaged upon a magical task, the silence of the healer.

A healer must be able to keep silent. Otherwise, how can we trust her with our secrets and our pain? The silence, the confidentiality offered by our doctor or our therapist, is not the silence of disempowerment, but the containment of power. And some things can be learned only in silence. As long as I'm talking, I can't hear the intricate chorus of the birds and learn to know their language. If I move noisily through the woods, wildlife flees and I will never see the deer or the bobcat. If I cannot keep silence and listen, I will never truly hear another's pain or vulnerability or appreciate their gifts.

Silence, space, the quiet pause in which we can hear our true inner voice, become even more important when we undertake great tasks that move us out into the world. "To make the shirts of soul renewal, we must stop and take time for soul making," Cynthia says. "When we do, our own soul is the first one that is unraveled and remade."

"Entering into the Silence is not about being silent. It is about waiting. Listening. It is an acknowledgment that there may be something greater than the self worth listening to," says Gweneth Dwyn, who has studied at Cynthia and Patricia's Mystery School and who now teaches at Witchcamp. "Entering into the silence is a powerful tool of personal empowerment because it is a proactive act. It is within the act of being engaged with silence that discern- ment can begin to happen—discernment about what we are called to do apart from all that there is to do, about self-care as distinct from self-absorption, about when to discern and when to act."

Silence, for a healer, a leader, is also a question of power. As leaders, it is extremely important that we show respect for others in all that we do. The more power we have in a group, the greater the impact of our words and deci- sions. A thoughtless criticism can wound; a rebuke in a meeting can become a public humiliation.

Because our Reclaiming community has such a strong ethic of nonhierarchy and egalitarianism, we often have a hard time recognizing differences in power and status that do exist. In fact, to see clearly how we impact a group, we must recognize that there is more than one type of power operating in the world.

Power-over, or structural power, is the power we face every day, in our school systems, in our jobs, in the structure of our government, and in the police power of the state. It underlies hierarchical systems and might also be called domination or control. There are, however, times when power-over is necessary and benign, and it can be exercised with restraint, respect, and accountability. Parents have power over children; no sane parent would want to empower a two-year-old with the ability to control all her resources or make all her decisions. When David fainted and a heart attack was suspected, I did not want the power to decide whether he should be helicoptered to the hospital from our remote location. I wanted somebody else to be in charge and to make that decision for us.

In Reclaiming, we attempt to structure our groups and organizations to minimize power-over. Where it exists—for example, when we delegate to a spokescouncil the power to set a budget and spend our resources—it must be open, accountable, and temporary.

Power from within is our creative power, the power of spirit, imagination, courage, and will. Power from within is unlimited. If I have the power to write, it does not take that power away from you. In fact, you might learn something from my writing that will spark your own creativity. *Empowerment* is another word we use for power from within.

We teach from a model of empowered learning, in which we acknowledge that all of our students bring rich experience and their own wisdom to the work. Teaching is not just transferring knowledge and information; rather, it is about creating and sharing experiences, reflecting together on them, and arriving at insights. Our classes are interactive rituals designed to acknowledge and celebrate power from within.

Power-over and power from within are relatively easy to understand. But there is a third, more slippery concept of power. In my book *Truth or Dare*, I called it *power-with*. Since then, many people have begun using the term *power-with* to refer to collective power from within, the power a group can have when acting together, the power of solidarity.

That power is extremely important, but the type of power I want to look at is something different. Perhaps we should call it simply *influence, status*, or even *authority*, in the sense of the word that comes from *author*. Literally, authors have authority, the "last word" on the subject. So, too, someone who is perceived as having more experience or skill may be deferred to. Power-with identifies the differing level of impact we as individuals have in a group when our formal power is equal.

Power-with may be hard to recognize or acknowledge. We are uncomfortable with the very concept of status, because in the larger society it, too, often becomes linked to power-over as privilege. *Privilege* is the automatic assumption that some people's contributions are more valuable than others. Unlike true authority, it is not earned through experience or trial and error; rather, it is conferred by the control certain groups of people hold over common resources and confirmed by prejudices and assumptions that we may hold consciously or unconsciously. In fact, we are rarely conscious of the privilege we hold, and we are rarely aware of using it. The thoughtless exercise of privilege becomes oppression.

A Walk Through Town

The following meditation can help us become aware of what privilege feels like.

Breathe deeply, and imagine that you are about to take a stroll through town. As you walk down the street, notice that people similar to you in race and general appearance are the norm. The shop windows display goods that appeal to you and serve your needs and interests. The billboards display people like you as icons of attractiveness and success.

You pass a movie theater and notice that the lead character of the film is a person like you. Down the street is a place of worship, and as you walk by you notice that it is designed for the ceremonies you practice.

You turn a corner and feel lost for a moment, so you ask directions from a police officer who is a person similar to you and who treats you with courtesy and respect. Now you come to the town hall, where a meeting is in progress. You notice that it is presided over by someone like you and that people like you are making comments and being listened to with respect. You have no doubt that if you have something to say, you will be heard.

Now breathe deeply, let go of your vision, and prepare to take a walk through another town. As you walk down the street, notice that people very different from you are the norm here. The shop windows display goods that don't meet your needs or address your interests. The billboards display people very different from you as icons of attractiveness and success.

You pass a movie theater and notice that none of the characters in the film are similar to you. Down the street is a place of worship, but it is not designed for or open to your rituals or practices.

You turn a corner and feel lost for a moment. You start to approach a police officer but quickly turn away as you see the look of suspicion on the officer's face. But you don't escape before the officer, who is of a different race and gender, approaches and begins to interrogate you. Finally you escape and duck into the town hall, where a meeting is in progress, presided over by someone very unlike yourself. The people making comments are also not like you, and when someone similar to you speaks, that person is quickly passed over. You have something to say, but do you believe that you will be heard?

Breathe deeply, let go of the town, and return to ordinary space and time.

In a group, discuss your reactions to this meditation. Does your daily experience resemble one of the towns? Aspects of both? Did the experience push you off your core sense of worth?

Alone, write about these questions in your journal.

Privilege Inventory

Katrina uses the following exercise to help groups identify privilege and learn to be allies of target groups.

Take an inventory of the types of privilege you hold. These might include race, color, gender, sexual orientation, age, physical ability, education, class, and economic privilege, among others. Some of these can work differently in different situations; for example, sometimes elders are deferred to in our society, while in other situations youth is glorified.

When an issue, disagreement, or conflict arises in a group, determine which privileges are operating. If you hold the privileged position, breathe deeply, think of Rose, and keep silent. Check yourself, and allow the voices of the nonprivileged to be fully heard.

Sometimes the privilege operating is not what we'd expect. Katrina tells the story of the morning she was shoveling snow with her friend Russ, who grew up in Texas and had never before attempted to clear a sidewalk after a snowfall. Nine years older than Russ, Katrina grew up in Washington, D.C., and had shoveled many a walkway. "I was determined to teach Russ the right way to do it," Katrina remembers. "We were getting into an argument when I stopped and thought to myself, 'What's the privilege that's operating here?'"

An outsider driving by would have seen a white man arguing with an African-American woman. Surely the white man was the more privileged party. But Katrina recognized that the operative privilege at that moment was not race or gender, but age.

"I shut up," she said. "I went inside and let him shovel the walk, and you know, he did just fine. He might have been sore in the morning, but he learned.

"This practice can help move us away from automatically thinking we're always the victim. When we hold privilege, we shouldn't always need someone else to point it out to us. When we learn to check ourselves, we can become true allies for others."

Differences of structural power and privilege always affect communication. The exact same words may have an entirely different meaning depending on who is speaking and in what context. Following are two more awareness exercises about power and communication:

Power and Differential Exercise

In the group, divide into pairs. In the first round, imagine that each of you is a three-year-old. Partner A says to partner B, "I don't like that." Partner B notices how she feels and responds, telling partner A what emotions, energies, thoughts, and bodily feelings are evoked. Then partner B says, "I don't like that" to Partner A, who observes her own responses.

Repeat the exercise with the following phrases:

"You hurt me."
"I like you."
"I want to talk to you."
"You're wrong."
"You're right."

In the second round, partner A is a child, and partner B is the parent. Again, partner A says one of the simple phrases, and partner B notices how she as the parent responds. Then Parent says the same phrase to Child. Notice, again, all the responses evoked and all the implications. Repeat for the entire set of phrases, and then switch roles.

Repeat the same format with the following pairs:

Student to teacher/teacher to student
Prisoner to guard/guard to prisoner
Worker to boss/boss to worker
A pair of your choice, one that relates to your own experience

What changes as the power differential shifts?

Power and Speech Exercise

Partner A, think of a situation in which you faced someone with more structural power or privilege than you. Maybe you'll remember an incident from childhood or from school or work. Breathing deeply, go into your memory, and think of something you might have said in that situation. Try to distill it into one or two sentences. Say that phrase to your partner. Notice your inner dialogue, your energy, emotions, and bodily sensations.

Partner B, notice how you respond on every level and what implications are hanging in the air. Now, from your position of superior power, say the same phrase back to A. Again, both of you, notice your responses and all the implied consequences.

Switch positions, but work with the same roles in reverse and the same phrase.

Take time to discuss what you noticed. What changed as your roles changed?

Now return to your original roles, with B in the position of superior power. Ground, center, and anchor to your core state of being. In this state, A, consider what you might say to B in your situation. And B, from your core state, respond.

What changes?

Repeat the entire exercise with a situation and phrase from B's life experience.

Sometimes the worst abuses of our influence come about because we do not recognize that we have it. The behavior patterns that may have served us, well or poorly, when we were powerless can become destructive and abusive when we gain power. A voiceless victim who yells and screams is simply trying to be heard, but a person of status who yells at a newcomer will be intimidating and overpowering.

Shadow-Self Role-Plays

Remember the shadow selves we worked with in the Outer Path in chapter 3? Once again, introduce them and their characteristic phrases.

Now go through the following sequence of role-plays. (One person should keep time, moving the group along after ten or fifteen minutes on each one.)

You are a coven trying to decide whether to hold a public or private solstice ritual.

You are a university department trying to decide whether to support an affirmative-action policy.

You are a city council trying to decide whether to open a homeless shelter.

You are the top executives of a major corporation trying to decide whether to clean up a toxic waste site.

You are the Joint Chiefs of Staff trying to decide whether to bomb the Serbs in Kosovo.

When you are done, consider the following questions:

How did each person's dysfunctionality affect the decision-making process?

What changed as the stakes got higher and the group controlled more external power?

Which dysfunctions tended to accrue more power in the world? Which might have precluded taking positions of power?

————————

In spite of all the ways that privilege can be abused, power-with or true authority can be a positive force when it is earned through experience, service, and integrity. A group increases its collective intelligence and effectiveness by listening to the voices of those who have skill, knowledge, or wisdom. We can learn only when we admit that others might know more about a subject than we do.

I've seen true authority beautifully modeled by Keith Hennessy, a dancer, choreographer, and performance artist with an international reputation. At a workshop he gave one summer at California Witchcamp, he was suggesting a change in a movement to one young woman.

"Of course, I'm not *the* authority on this," he said, "but I am *an* authority, and that's something that is earned. It means that I do have something to offer you here. But ultimately, only you are the authority on how your body should move."

True authority is an offering, not an excuse for control. And it is earned, as Keith earned his, by training, practice, discipline, experience, and learning from our mistakes. Rainy, a Reclaiming teacher and geographer who is a child of hippie parents, quotes her father as saying, "I have the authority here because I'm older and I've been around long enough to have made more mistakes than any of you."

When Thorn and I taught a path together at mid-Atlantic Witchcamp, we created the following exercise to help our students own their true authority:

Stepping into Authority

In sacred space, take a few moments to think about the skills, knowledge, and experience you have. What true authority can you claim? You might be an authority on a subject the world recognizes: medieval drama or African percussion. Or perhaps you are an authority on something that emerges from your life: raising a disabled child or cooking on a welfare budget.

Stand in a circle in the group. Breathe, ground, and anchor to your core state of being.

One by one, each person steps forward, names herself or himself, and claims a true, earned authority. After each person has spoken, the group says, "We bless your power."

For example:

"I am Daniel, and I am an authority on growing wine grapes organically."
"We bless your power."

"I am Joan, and I am an authority on facing loss with grace."
"We bless your power."

"I am Angela, and I am an authority on my own healing."
"We bless your power."

"I am Rose, and I am an authority on weaving shirts from nettles."
"We bless your power."

When all have spoken, dance, chant, and raise power to celebrate the group's true authority. Open sacred space.

We have visited the Fata Morgana and taken up a true task, a big task, one that will require all our dedication, fortitude, courage, and will. We've identified our sources of strength and learned the power of silence.

Many tests still await us. We will need all our allies, skills, and strength to face them.

SIX

Holding Center

Comments on the Story

While Rose is spinning her thread outside the green cave one day, the king of the country rides by and, struck with her beauty, marries her. She bears a child, but his jealous mother steals the child and marks Rose's mouth with blood, accusing her of being a Witch and of eating her baby. She bears a second child, only to have the acts repeated.

Rose has learned to hold her focus in spite of pain and frustration. Now she must continue her concentration through love and loss. Rose is asked to live with the dedication of a priestess, but not to live as a hermit or an ascetic. She is able to love and be loved, to marry, to bear a child—all the life transitions that often distract us from our inner development and chosen tasks. But Rose keeps on weaving.

Her weaving is her center, her magical intention. By holding to her intention, Rose stays centered and withstands all the projections thrown at her, even her mother-in-law's jealousy.

Jealousy is a powerful force in fairy tales. Almost universally, it serves as the negative motivation and greatest threat in these old stories. Jealousy is a primal emotion: dogs feel it; young children certainly feel it. In small communities, people often go to great lengths to avoid evoking the jealousy of their neighbors, and negative magic is almost always perceived as motivated by jealousy.

A person of power must be able to withstand jealousy. A weaver of souls must be able to focus on the work without being swayed by other people's perceptions, whether idolization or vilification. When we find our voice and speak our truth, not everyone is going to like what we have to say, especially if we are truly weaving something new. We will meet criticism and attack. If we attempt to defend ourselves against every accusation, we divert our energies from the work—which, in the end, will be our ultimate answer to the critics.

In Rose's case, the jealous accusations and attacks result in heartrending loss. Still, she holds her ground and continues weaving. No words she might speak could carry the redemptive power that the completed work of transformation will hold when she finishes it.

Women are often accused of eating their babies in fairy tales, and puppies' blood is generally the substance of choice with which to literally smear the reputation of the heroine. Accusations of baby eating are often directed at religions that the establishment wishes to discredit. Witches were accused of child sacrifice, as Jews were accused of baking ritual matzos with the blood of Christian babies, as the early Goddess religions were accused of practicing human sacrifice by the compilers of the Bible.

Embedded in this image is some faint shadow of the ancient earth Goddess, to whom the dog was sacred, who births us into life and who takes us back into her body at death. We can also hear echoes of a more everyday mystery. Two-year-old Kore, admiring her Goddess-mother Juanita's swelling, pregnant belly, asks, "What's that?" "I have a baby in my tummy," Juanita says proudly. "Yuck!" Kore exclaims and proceeds to inform her mother that Juanita has eaten a baby.

Rose's own baby has not been eaten by her, but it is lost, thrown to the wolves, abandoned to the wild. Nevertheless, she must hold her ground and keep her attention on the work of creation, the weaving of souls. Like her, we must find the core of self we can hold to through both admiration and attack.

The work of this section is to know center: the center of the circle, the center of the ritual, the center of self that allows us to withstand projections and sustain our healing work.

The Elements Path

Now Rose returns to the human world, but this time she is the queen of her castle instead of the little daughter. She grew up as the princess in a castle, but she had to leave in order to come into her own as an adult woman. Now she is free and powerful, with allies she can rely on and with many skills and experiences to help her. She returns to the castle and moves back into the complex world of family relationships, in order to love and be loved.

Like Rose, we have left the familiar world of ordinary consciousness and walked out the doorway into the wild. We have learned to create our own sacred space. We have traveled to each of the directions, learning some of the magical techniques that belong to air, to fire, to water, and to earth. We have learned to rely on their powers and have pledged ourselves to protect them as well.

Like Rose, we must now return to the place where we started. We are back from our travels to each of the directions, back to the center of our own sacred space. But we return seasoned and powerful, with many new tools in our spiritual tool kit, confident in our ability to make magic and "change consciousness at will." The Elements Path work for this section of the story includes investigating some of the magical techniques that correspond to the center and revisiting our relationship with deity.

Element Path

Center

When we cast the circle at the beginning of any ritual, we begin in the north and greet each direction in turn, ending again in the north. Then, stepping into the center of the circle, we reach as high as we can with one hand and stretch the other toward the earth. We allow the circle we have drawn to spring up all around us, above and below, completing a sphere of energy that can hold us and our friends safely until our travels between the worlds are complete. We say something like, "Powers above, shimmering, shining ones, and powers below, magma heart of Mother Earth, welcome." Drawing the energy from above and below, we place our hands on our own centers.

A magic circle, like our own lives, has seven dimensions: the four directions, the sky above, the earth below, and the heart or center, because each of us is the self in the center of our own life story and in the center of our own consciousness. Just as Rose returns to the place she started, the castle, so we return to the center of our circles. In this chapter we will learn some of the magical tools, symbols, and techniques associated with the center.

Center: The Great Wheel

Any time of day or night, you can walk outside and look up. If you are in the Northern Hemisphere, the sun by day, or the moon by night, will be making its way across the sky from the east toward the south and then to the west to set. The sun and moon, and the planets, too, if you learn to see them, follow this basic path over and over against the bright cloud of the Milky Way. The constellations of the zodiac also make the same journey, always rising in the east and moving through the south and toward the west. During the day, if you watch the shadow of a tree or the shadow on a sundial, you will see the shadow swing from west to the north at midday, and then toward the east as the sun sets in the west. The shadows, of course, will always fall in the opposite direction from where the sun stands in the sky.

We discover a basic fact about life on our crazily tilted, spinning planet. The lights of the sky—sun, moon, and planets—and their shadows always move "clockwise" around us, as though we were standing at the hub of a great wheel. In magic we call the clockwise direction *deasil*, which means "sunwise."

The moon will show us a different pattern if we watch her through the course of a month. At the new moon, she rides with the sun, and we cannot see her in his brightness. But as she becomes a new crescent, she falls behind him just a little, and we can see her briefly immediately after sunset, following him down into the west. As each night passes, she falls back a step, as though he were walking a bit too fast for her. So as the waxing crescent grows, we find her higher in the sky by a hand's breadth each night, and by the time she is a quarter moon, she stands slightly in the south, at the zenith, at sunset. And so she continues falling behind a bit more with each passing day, backward through the sky, so that by the time she is full, she rises in the east just as he sets in the west. Now she has the sky to herself all night, and she sails free and full, setting only as the sun begins to rise.

As she wanes she continues to appear to move backward through the sky, until he catches up to her from behind, and she becomes invisible once again.

Although the moon always moves clockwise through the sky on any given night, in the course of a month she moves counterclockwise through the sky. In other words, if you look at the sky at sunset every night for a month, beginning at the new moon, the location of the moon *at the moment the sun sets* will move slowly from west to east, a little bit every day. This is a direction we call *widdershins* in magic, counterclockwise.

This directionality of the great movements of nature gives us another powerful magical tool. When we want something to grow and strengthen, we can weave it into the powerful clockwise movement of the great wheel. When we hope for transition, for the release of the old and the beginning of something new, we can weave it into the counterclockwise movements of the moon through the month, which always disappears and then regrows.

So a very basic ritual form we use is to begin moving counterclockwise around our circle, silently meditating on, or singing and calling and dancing out, something that we are ready to let go of, something that we are ready to let fall into the past. When we are ready, we change direction and begin going clockwise around our circle, raising energy for the new things that we want to bring into our lives and strengthen.

Center: The Cone of Power

In ritual, we often allow our energy to build up to a peak and climax. This is another basic tool of magic that we find in the center of our circle. We call it the cone of power.

When we create a spell alone at our home altars, we have to begin with a clear intention, strongly imagined in as much detail as possible. The same is true in a ritual working: the group needs to be agreed on a clear intention.

In a cone of power, we build an energy form as a group with our voices around a common image. We often allow the energy to rise with chanting, drumming, and dancing, but as the power of the moment begins to peak, the drums die away, and the chant becomes wordless toning and waves of sound. We build it to a peak and send it into the sky as a sensory, energetic prayer to the Goddess. Once we have released the cone of power, we ground ourselves again. We reconnect to our own normal energy, to our normal place between earth and sky, and touch the ground if necessary to drain off any excess energy we may feel in our own bodies as tingling, light-headedness, or dizziness. The energy form we have sent off will fall back to earth wherever it is needed, in whatever form is needed to achieve the desired outcome.

In the magic of Reclaiming tradition, we no longer consider it necessary for a high priestess to "lead" or "direct" the cone of power. In great sex one partner does not have to control the building of the energy; it builds quite naturally in its own rhythm if each partner is patient and sensitive to the energy of the other. In the same way, the cone of power builds naturally in a group if the members are patient and sensitive as well as exuberant. When a group works with sound together, it is important for each member to be a good listener as well as a good creator of sound. The group tone may try to die away a few times, or it may try to peak prematurely as members continue to discharge excess or uncomfortable energy with dissonance, howling, shrieking, or groaning. One member of a group may need to hold a strong, low tone to help the group's energy cohere, or various group members may take turns or work together holding this center. But eventually, as in a very hot fire, everything will be burned away except the clear, powerful tone of the group's energy flowing together, and it can build to a natural peak, which can then be released either quickly, like an arrow from a bow, or more slowly, like a soap bubble from a child's bubble wand.

Center: The Cauldron of Changes

When we look in the center of our circle, along with the great wheel of the sky and the cone of power, we also find the cauldron. The cauldron is a tool of the center, and it has an ancient lineage in Goddess tradition. Originally a great pot for boiling, the cauldron would have been a very important tool in the daily lives of our ancestresses. They would have used it for many purposes, such as rendering fat from slaughtered animals, dying cloth, making soap, or cooking nettles with wood ash for cloth making. Imagine how powerful the cauldron would have seemed, with its heat and violent boiling, and the strange steams and smells coming from it. Dead plants and animals would have gone into it, and something quite different would have come out, something delicious or useful, made by the art and craft of the mothers and grandmothers. So the cauldron became the symbol of the cyclic natural world and of rebirth. There are stories from many cultures of a fearsome boiling pot, sometimes of blood, in which the dead are revived and reborn.

In our story, Rose's mother-in-law accuses Rose of the monstrous crime of eating her own babies. The accusation rings with memories of the Great White Sow, one of the faces of Cerridwen, a Celtic Goddess of death and rebirth associated with the cauldron. Farm people knew that sows sometimes did eat their own young. Of course Rose, who is a human mother, has not eaten her babies; in fact, she is in terrible grief over losing them. But in the ancient mythology of the Great Goddess, the cauldron Goddess does ultimately eat all her children. This is an inevitable fact of mortal life; no mortal ever gets out of it alive. The Goddess of birth, death, and rebirth offers us no alternatives. Our lives will end in death, and we will be eaten, back into the dark belly of nature. And from that belly we will be reborn, in a new shape, into a new life. Into the cauldron we go, and when we climb back out, we are restored, reshaped, and young again.

So the people fear Rose, whose mouth is smeared with blood, because they fear the Goddess in her shape as Death. Ironically, they want to kill Rose, as if one could fight Death with death. And so Rose has to face her own fear of death, which menaces her as a stake and pyre are erected in the city square to burn her. The ensuing events bring Rose to the moment of truth.

In Reclaiming, we use our cauldrons, usually big cast-iron pots with three legs, as a tool for magic as well as a symbol of the Great Goddess of life, death, and rebirth. In our cauldrons we can build a safe, indoor fire that creates a physical center for indoor rituals when the weather doesn't allow ritual outdoors. We use Epsom salts and rubbing alcohol in equal parts to make this fire, and we always keep a tight-fitting top for the cauldron handy. In case the fire gets too rambunctious, it can be quickly and safely put out by simply putting the top on the pot. When the alcohol finishes burning and the flames die away, a blue and flickering glow remains in the salts, which can last for some time before it fades. This part of a cauldron ritual offers a wonderful opportunity for meditating and scrying in the mysterious, wandering blue flames.

If you want to try a cauldron fire at home, please place your cauldron on a fireproof surface, because the bottom of the pot will become hot. Try out a small amount of salts and alcohol first, and let the fire burn out completely before adding more. Each pot, because of its unique size and shape, will require slightly different amounts of salts and alcohol to make a good, safe fire, so experiment with a close-fitting lid close at hand, and find out what works in your cauldron. Alcohol fires will not generally set off smoke detectors, but if you burn other things in your cauldron indoors, like scraps of paper or string from a spellworking, you might set off alarms.

A cauldron can also be filled with water and dry ice to create a cold, mysterious mist that bubbles over its lips. This is also a great way to create a center for a dark, dreamy ritual.

So now we have learned three important tools of magic that we find in the center of our circle. We've observed the directionality of nature, the great wheel, which holds us at the hub and spins around us. We've learned the basics of raising a cone of power. And we have investigated the symbol of the cauldron, perhaps getting an opportunity to try out our own cauldron flame.

In the center of our circle we also find the invocation of deity, which we discussed briefly when we learned to keep an altar and create sacred space.

Charge of the Star Goddess

Hear the words of the Star Goddess, the dust of whose feet are the hosts of heaven, whose body encircles the universe: "I who am the beauty of the green earth, and the white moon among the stars and the mysteries of the waters, I call upon your soul to arise and come unto Me. For I am the soul of nature that gives life to the universe. From Me all things proceed, and unto Me they must return. Let My worship be in the heart that rejoices, for behold—all acts of love and pleasure are My rituals. Let there be beauty and strength, power and compassion, honor and humility, mirth and reverence within you. And you who seek to know Me, know that your seeking and your yearning will avail you not, unless you know the Mystery: for if that which you seek, you find not within yourself, you will never find it without. For behold, I have been with you from the beginning, and I am that which is attained at the end of desire."

Years ago, driven by a life-threatening illness to seek spiritual help, I first began to cautiously investigate the Goddess tradition. I found a woman who was willing to help me in my search, Pandora O'Mallory. It turned out that she was one of the early members of the Reclaiming Collective. I remember telling her that I couldn't be a *real* Witch, or I wouldn't feed my little daughter hot-dogs, which seemed to me like the opposite of what a *real* Witch would do. A *real* Witch would probably feed her children freshly picked, magic, organic vegetables from her own garden and homemade yogurt.

Pandora listened patiently and then set me the task of memorizing the Charge of the Star Goddess. She knew that I needed to stop evaluating my relationship with my Creatrix by comparison to any person or any image or any prejudice outside myself. I needed to learn to look within for my answers. On some of those dark days, all that kept me going was Pandora's faith that I could find everything I needed from the divine powers by a gentle, persistent search within myself.

As we work with stories and images and symbols of the Goddess, over years of seeking we each find our own way to the source of her power, her healing, her multiplicity, her joys and terrors. The Charge of the Star Goddess reminds us to direct that search within, for if we do not find her here, we will never find her without. If we want to be able to "change consciousness at will," we must each develop our own ways to approach deity through Younger Self. We need to find songs, gestures, images, meditations, stories, combinations of color, flavor, and smell, that evoke her power for us.

We seek deep alterations of consciousness, the ability to hear the voices of all life-forms, to live in sustainable harmony with nature, to respect and care well for ourselves and others. These abilities all flow from our certainty that each and every part of nature, including our sweet selves, is immanent deity, is holy. And the image of deity that enlivens and strengthens one person and fills her life with purpose may be meaningless or one-dimensional to another. We each have the right and the obligation to passionately pursue our connection with deity.

Gwydion's Opening to Deity Exercise

Gwydion Logan is a Reclaiming teacher who describes himself as "queer and a science geek." I asked him why he calls himself queer when that word has been used so often as an insult. Gwydion replied, "It's important to claim the power in words that have been used as epithets. *Queer* is inclusive, and it implies a spectrum of sexuality."

For Gwydion, invocation of deity is not a matter of reading or memorizing a safely scripted invocation. "Scripting," says Gwydion, "can leave the invocations feeling empty." Instead, he recommends stepping back from Talking Self and opening to Younger Self and Deep Self. He says we must "create a stillness inside to allow new things to enter, and see what comes."

Opening to Deity

In sacred space, begin by reconnecting to your grounding and feeling the energy of earth and sky moving through you. Breathe deeply, and call on the deity either by name or by qualities, Trickster or Mother or Opening Bud or Lady of the Wild Things, whatever you have need of. Without judgment, allow a stream of images and sensations and emotion to flow through your awareness in answer to your call. Pick out one or two of the more visceral images—the less abstract, the more powerful. If you are working in a group, express these images in words or sounds or movements, so that others can pick up on them, and soon the whole group will be doing a powerful invocation together. Gwydion says, "Take a risk and be vulnerable. Let it flow within you. The invocation is a way of honoring deity, and remembering this can help us get beyond performance anxiety and self-consciousness."

Gwydion tells the tale of how, one Winter Solstice night, Morgan Le Fay, a Reclaiming priestess, invoked the laboring Earth Mother: "She had a pillow under her dress, and she looked very pregnant. She squatted down in the center of the circle in the labor pose and began breathing and groaning like a laboring mother. Soon other voices joined her, women and men who had experienced the difficult passage of labor. Chills ran down our spines, and our hair stood on end, as an unearthly, powerful sounding arose. We really felt the Goddess arrive that night."

Calling Deity of Many Ancestries

There is a particularly tricky issue that arises when we look at the invocation of deity in our multicultural society. I've known many Witches over the years who were attracted to the stories and powers of a deity from a tradition different than that of their own ancestors. In fact, if I look around my own altar room, I find Quan Yin in the west, Willow Woman, the healer from the shady side of the stream. Around her feet are my homeopathic remedies and herbal tea bundles. In the north, Krishna, playful, sexy blue boy, raises his arms to play the flute while Radha, the most beautiful of the cow-herding girls, offers him a lotus with a mysterious smile. In the east stands the Venus of Willendorf, the greatbreasted, great-bellied Goddess of Neolithic Europe, with kernels of corn, grain of the Americas, scattered at her feet. And in the south, there's a photo of a California live oak, holy to the California first people, rising from a hillside with its amazing antigravity architectural limb structure.

By what right do I burn candles for these deities from cultures that would be strange to my own ancestors, make offerings to them, meditate on their stories, and pray for their assistance? How can I be sure my devotions are deeply respectful when I have no traditional teachers? And to what deities would I have the right, those of my British ancestors who were small and dark, or those of my tall, blond Saxon ancestors, who probably did their best to murder and rape the ancient Britons? In any case, the traditional teachers of those cultures are long gone into the earth.

These questions are particularly troubling in cases where some of my ancestors may have oppressed, robbed, disrespected, even murdered or enslaved the peoples whose deities and symbols I now invite into my devotions and onto my altars. I must take great care not to mirror these acts in my magic by ripping off or disrespecting any part of those cultures. If I take, I must give back, preferably three times.

In a recent article, Starhawk wrote an inspiring response to these questions, which trouble many modern Pagans and Witches. She wrote, "In the midst of my own wrestling with these issues, I ran into an old, wise woman in trance who simply shook her head and said, 'Forget about your ancestors, child. It's the children that I care about.'

"As I write," continues Starhawk, "three of my Goddess daughters are up in the loft giggling. Their ancestry includes English, Irish, African, Jewish, Native American and probably many others, but two of them look 'white' and one looks 'black.' I know that in spite of all our efforts to eradicate racism, their lives will be shaped differently because of that fact."

We long for the day when a child of color will never for a moment see her skin color or the texture of her hair as anything but beautiful, where every opportunity she craves will be open to her, where prejudice, racism, and slavery will seem as incomprehensible and archaic as the metallurgy tools of a Bronze Age culture. We want her to know that she is the Goddess and that the Goddess is black, brown, red, yellow, white; fat, thin; old, young.

To create that world for her, it's imperative that she see images of the Goddess that resemble her. We don't have the luxury to ask, "Do I have the authority to put African Goddess images in my home?" We need to have them, for her sake, and to know something about them if we are to fulfill our responsibilities to her.

But what about a European-American child? We want her, too, to see herself as the Goddess, as beautiful, as able to do anything she wants to do. And we want her to know that the Goddess is also black, brown, red, yellow, and white, thin and fat, old and young, and that deity comes in all genders and forms. Is it not equally important that she grow up surrounded by a multiplicity of figures and images?

And is it not important for the grown-up children we all are to also see a multiplicity of images of deity? First, so that we truly know that we are welcome whatever our heritage may be. But also so that we who live in a deeply divided, racist world remind ourselves again and again, in sacred space, that deity comes in all colors and that all of us are valued.

How do we do this without falling back into superficiality and cultural appropriation? And without losing or diluting traditions and connections that are dear to us? These are not simple questions, and each one deserves a longer discussion than we have room for here. But here are some guidelines we might begin with:

BE HONEST: Don't pretend to be what you're not or to speak with authority you haven't been granted.

MAKE ROOM: Conceive of the Goddess tradition as a garden big enough for many different kinds of beds. Make room for people to express their heritage, to sing in their own language, and to call on the deities and symbols they are deeply connected with.

DEFINE OURSELVES DIFFERENTLY, OR MAYBE REFUSE TO DEFINE OUR-SELVES: We can acknowledge that we are more like jazz or rock music, a synthesis of many influences. We can call ourselves an earth-based tradition without limiting our roots to one continent or one heritage.

DEEPEN OUR KNOWLEDGE: Truly learn and study the traditions that call to us. Take lessons on that drum, from a continent your ancestors would have found strange. Learn about the rich musical heritage it comes from. Don't just pick a name out of a book; devote real time and effort to developing an in-depth knowledge of both a deity and its surrounding culture. Moreover, learn about the history and present-day struggles of the people.

ASK PERMISSION: This one isn't always easy, because we don't always know whom to ask permission from or who has the authority to speak for a tradition. But sometimes it's clear; if someone teaches you a song they wrote or a story, ask permission to pass it on, and give credit where credit is due.

INTERRUPT OPPRESSION: Speak out when you hear insensitive, racist, homophobic remarks. Don't put the burden on the target group to confront attacks. If a culture has fed you, defend it.

GIVE BACK: If we are fed by symbols, stories, or deities of a particular people, we have an obligation to give back something to that community and to participate in their real-life, present-day struggles. This may mean doing political work or supporting cultural events. It might mean teaching what you know in that community or giving back generously with money or work exchange for teachings you receive there. It might mean visiting a friend in the hospital and entertaining him with a tale from his own culture that he doesn't know. It might mean giving back money; if you hit platinum with your recording of a Latvian folk song, you tithe back to that community. In practice, because everything is interconnected, giving back also means working on the global economic, social, and environmental issues that affect us all.

LOVE ALL THE CHILDREN: If we are nurtured and inspired by a tradition, we can worry less about who our ancestors are and start to think of ourselves as the ancestors of the future, taking on responsibility for the lives and well-being of the children of that culture and for creating the world we want all the children to grow up in.

Center: The Goddess

And so in the center of our circle, we find deep within ourselves the Goddess of many faces, many genders, many colors, many ages. We find her in every human being, in every living thing, in every act and mood of nature. Her shape shifts and blurs in the firelight; she appears first in my face, in my voice, and then in yours. And so a kiss is passed around the circle: "Thou art Goddess, thou art God." And as we gaze into one another's eyes and see ourselves reflected there, we know that there is no end to the circle and that its center lies in each of our hearts.

The Inner Path

Now Rose must take her magic spell out of her wild green life and back into community and family. She has learned how to live in her forest cave while spinning soul for her wild brothers, but now she must do the same in the king's castle. She experiences love and loss and faces jealousy. She must continue being herself and hold on to her core worth even when she is misunderstood, shamed, and slandered. Because she knows herself, she is able to keep weaving, keep spinning, and keep sewing.

Those of us who walk the Inner Path can take this opportunity to follow Rose. We will learn some meditations to illuminate our own loves and conflicts, and we will learn how to anchor ourselves firmly to our core worth.

At the beginning of our story, Rose also lived in a castle. That was the castle of family secrets, where Rose was never told the truth. She was the youngest and the least, living out a fate that had been determined for her by other, more powerful figures. But through the course of the tale she has broken free of her situation, passed many tests, and completed many challenges. When she returns to the castle this time, she is not a little girl, but a queen. She is no longer helpless when she steps back into the complex relational field of the family.

Whenever I read or tell this part of the tale, I always secretly think, "Don't do it, Rose! Stay in the green, in the shamanic solitary life of the mountain cave!" However, if I were eighteen or nineteen, I know I'd be up on that horse in a hot second.

It is love and longing for human companionship that draw her back to the castle, and so it is with us. As thrilling as the lessons of the wild—self-love, guidance, freedom, flight, weaving—have been, we are drawn back into the human world by love. It is a horseback ride with the young king, and the sexual love that is implied, that completes Rose's transformation to powerful, fulfilled adulthood.

In the story, this horseback ride is shared by a young woman and a young man. Bless their hearts! But in our own lives, mature, fulfilling love that powers us into full adulthood can be found between people of many ages and genders. There are many forms of love between people, and there are also those who have found an internal source of love power, in solitary delight with their art, or service to others, or devotion, or just plain joyful living. And there are those who are sexually active in joy, respect, and pleasure with many partners.

Yet in some way, in some form, love completes us. Like Rose, we go to the wild to free our souls, to learn to change our consciousness at will, and then we return to the human world to love and to do our living, strengthened by the skills and insights we have gained. We are drawn back into the human world by longing, by the deep intuitive knowledge that we can each express only part of what it is to be human. To experience humanness in all its richness, we need other people, and so we long to be close to them.

In Plato's *Symposium*, Socrates listens to Aristophanes, a comic playwright, describing human beings as creatures who formerly were physically joined with one another, woman to man, man to man, and woman to woman. We were very happy this way, in constant connection with one another, until our *hubris*, our disrespect of the Gods, caused the Gods to split us from one another. Now we wander the world searching for our other halves, clasping one another, trying to rediscover that primal state of connectedness.

There is something deeply resonant about this story, which still rings true twenty-five hundred years later. The search for an answer to the universal human feeling of longing is a mystery of human life that was old when Socrates was young, listening to Aristophanes' story and lusting after one of the young men at a dinner party. We humans come from a species that is polarized in many ways, gender being only one of them. And attraction and longing between lovers seem to fall into patterns of similarity and opposition. Often a dreamy, sensitive person will form erotic bonds with a practical, no-nonsense person, or a glamorous outgoing personality will be attracted to a strong, silent type. These lovers will have many similarities as well, maybe shared social values or artistic tastes. Love relationships seem to thrive on just the right mix of polarity and identity.

And whether we are involved in a twenty-year partnership, or are inflamed by the solitary longings of the hermit or artist, or are taking many lovers, we are all moved by love and longing that is ultimately powered from within. When we first began to grow in our mother's womb, we held the potential of all human qualities and of both genders. Through our lives, our bodies have grown into male or female bodies, and we have become distinct in character also, shy or outgoing, physically adept or awkward, visionary or practical, and so forth. Our gender expression, our "butch" and our "femme," are included in this list, because they represent just one of the ways we've learned to put ourselves forward in the context of our culture. But we have deep soul yearnings for the parts of ourselves that are not expressed, the opposites of our own expression. It is part of Witchcraft to develop a relationship in the Otherworld with a self, or a version of ourselves, that expresses the opposite qualities to the ones we've developed in this lifetime. We call this the Companion Self.

We try to seek and strengthen the connection, love, and longing for our Companion Selves in meditation. The Companion Self we meet in trance may or may not bear any resemblance to actual lovers in the "real" world. But the power of the attraction between ourselves and the Companion Self, and the love and respect and care we can offer one another in the Otherworld, completes a circuit in our own souls and teaches us to deepen our love and connection to the people in our "real" lives, who are always different than us.

Companion-Self Trance

In sacred space, prepare yourself for trance. Using whatever trance induction you prefer, go to your personal place of power. Greet each of the directions, casting a circle around yourself in your place of power. In the center of your circle, find a pool of water. Lean over it, and see your own reflection. Take a moment to exchange love, appreciation, and care with your double, your mirror image. Acknowledge the qualities in yourself that you value highly, and also your own mystery. Say, "Thou are Goddess."

Now breathe on the water, and sense how it ripples and shifts. The image in the water changes, too, moving one step away from you, becoming more like your opposite. Notice how your reflection begins to express qualities opposite of your own, polarizing, changing gender expression, from butch to femme, or from femme to butch, or ranging along some other very personal polarity. Maybe (s)he changes from shy to extroverted, from detached to passionate, or from practical to dreamy. Maybe (s)he grows breasts, a penis, or facial hair. Breathe again and again on the water, each time allowing a ripple to pass over its surface, each time allowing your reflection to change a bit more toward your polar opposite. When you feel ready, hold the image you've found, and begin to offer an exchange of love and appreciation and care. Say, "Thou art Goddess." Give yourself time to explore your reactions to your Companion Self, simply noticing what is there for you, without judgment. When you are ready, thank your Companion Self and say good-bye, knowing that the Companion Self is always with you and that you can return to this place whenever you wish.

Breathe again on the water, sensing the ripples spreading, clouding the reflection, and allow your double to reshape itself on the mirror surface of the pool. Exchange energy again with your double; exchange appreciation, love, and care. Thank your double and say good-bye, knowing that your double also stays with you always and that you can return here whenever you wish.

When you are ready, acknowledge each of the directions again, and thank them, opening your circle in your place of power. Return to normal consciousness, using the exact opposite of your trance induction. Slowly stretch all over, pat the outlines of your body, say your name three times, clap your hands. It is done. Eat and relax a little. If you are working with friends, you may want to discuss what you experienced, or if you are working alone, you may want to make some notes in your Book of Shadows. Open your circle only when you are ready.

The Jealous Rival

When Rose reenters the human world of the castle, she meets the challenge of human love, but she also must stand up to a jealous rival. Rose is working every day with nettle, one of whose magic powers is to break curses and to send other people's energy back where it came from. Rose is using this power, as she weaves the shirts, to break the curse on her brothers. But now she finds that this is a power she will need to protect herself as well, as she faces her mother-in-law's hostility.

Rose is no longer an unformed girl; she has become someone very special. She has traveled to other worlds, learned the language of intuition, and wandered the wildwood, where a little stream of self-love flows. She has found the salt shore, where she withstood her brothers' anger, and stepped into the basket for a wild flight beyond. She has walked in the dream castle of the Fata

Morgana and made a home in the hermit's green cave, where her spell was woven in mountain silence. Rose returns to the human world unique and whole, purposeful and silent with contained power.

Now these qualities make Rose attractive to the young king, but they also make her repulsive to his mother. And so it is with us, as we learn to move freely through all the worlds at will, changing consciousness, using the tools of magic. Our wholeness, our purpose, and our power will attract some and infuriate others.

This is one of the great lessons of adult human life—that not everybody will like us, that some will actually try to harm us. Once when I was working psychically with the myth of Persephone, who was raped by the Lord of the Underworld, I remember calling one of my Reclaiming teachers, Cybele, and weeping on the phone: "Why does there have to be a perpetrator?" I'll never forget her answer: "It's not so much that there *has* to be a perpetrator; it's just that there *is* a perpetrator." And in Rose's story, it is the old queen who wishes to harm her.

A Word to the Wise

This particular part of Rose's story, where she is cruelly attacked and cannot speak to defend herself, brings up powerful feelings and memories for many people. Women and men who have experienced abusive relationships, either as children or adults, know the feeling of being badly treated and being unable to speak up. Strong sensory memories and disturbing waves of emotion may come up for some people while working with this part of the story.

If so, there is a loop in the story for you. Please go back to the beginning, to the Castle of Family Secrets, and speak up, as Rose did, asking a million questions. Find the information you need and the courage to walk away from the castle. Reexperience the discovery of self-love and the ability to rely on guidance and help. Stand again on the salt shore, facing the truth about the wicked vow that never should have been made.

Many people who experienced abuse as children, and many people recovering from traumatic or violent experiences as adults, need the support of a therapist, recovery group, doctor, body worker, twelve-step program, or some other structured help in this process. If you identify with this paragraph, you deserve all the help you can get, and then some more. My prayers, and the prayers of many others, are with you.

Holding to Life Purpose

Meanwhile, Rose's challenge is to hold true to her life purpose regardless of how other people react to her. While Rose works, the old queen's cruelty endangers Rose, and Rose must continue weaving even when the old queen steals her babies and spreads hostile rumors about her. But we can just as easily be knocked off center by flattery, admiration, and praise. Rose also had to continue weaving when she married the young king and became queen of her own land. As our inner mastery (or mystery!) gleams through into our lives, other people will react strongly, and whether the storm is positive or negative, we need psychic tools to weather it.

So now let's practice a technique for anchoring and holding our center, our identity, and our life purpose amid the weather of the human world. First we will go over the concept of "anchoring" a psychic state so that we can return to it at will. Then we will create an anchored connection with our core worth. Our core worth is a centered, potent sense of identity, which we can return to when people or events, whether positive or negative, knock us off center. An anchored sense of core worth may be the end of an inner, healing journey as well as the beginning of the journey of the Outer Path.

Anchoring

As we walk between the worlds, enchanting ourselves with music and movement, trancing deep into the Otherworld, and reaching states of ecstatic embodiment, there come moments when we ask ourselves, "Why can't I box or bottle this moment, this amazing state of consciousness, so that I can return to it whenever I want?" Much of the art and craft of magic is exactly that: techniques that allow us to move from one state of consciousness to another at will.

When we create sacred space, we lead ourselves down a familiar and well-worn path with the repetition of familiar sounds, visual images, and physical sensations. We see the blue fire of our circle sister's sharpened knife cutting away the veil between the worlds. We hear the fluid, abundant sound of water being poured into the saltwater bowl. When we shake out and loosen our hips and knees and sigh out a deep breath to ground ourselves, we create physical sensations that become, with repetition, the key to a door that opens into an altered state of consciousness.

We can always choose to use auditory, visual, and sensory cues together to create a personal path or doorway to a desired state of consciousness. When we reach a state of consciousness we wish to be able to return to at will, we can choose a strong personal visual image, a word or sound, and a physical sensation that we can use together as our own magic "key" to the desired state. Then later we can re-create the sensation, image, and sound to take us back to the consciousness we seek. By using the vivid, sensual language of Younger Self, we create a swift and effective sensory prayer that asks Younger Self and

Deep Self to take us back to another state of mind, heart, and body. In Reclaiming tradition, we often refer to this technique as "creating an anchor."

Finding Our Core Worth

In order to be able to hold onto our identities and our purposes even when under attack, we need to find and anchor our basic sense of core worth. *Core* is a wonderful word that refers to the center, where the life force is held. The core of an apple is the center of the apple, but it is also the place where the seeds lie. From this center of potency, a whole new apple tree can arise. Coincidentally, Core or Kore is another name for Persephone, who goes down into the dark of the underworld to find her true self and to become a queen instead of a daughter.

The Goddess traditions recognize that at the core of each person, each animal, each plant, each natural event, the same mystery is revealed. We are each Goddess. She has many faces and many forms. She has infinite stories: the hungry shrilling of the baby birds in the nest, the crack of thunder and the lightning that races from sky to earth, the sunflower stretching toward the glory of sunlight—all tell the same story of her desire for herself. We are each an unfolding tale of her search for herself, for her longing for her own beloved soul. Our challenges, our miseries, our delight, our fruition are each the voice of a single instrument in the great symphony of her self-love. So at our core, we are each of the ultimate and highest value. There is no rank or comparison here, no striving or proving. At our core, we are each a deep and potent well of self-creation, through which the Goddess expresses herself; we are each her paint box, her orchestra, her dancers.

When we touch the deepest part of our own self, when we touch our true potency, we touch a place that is far beyond criticism or flattery from others, far beyond any defeat or accomplishment in the outside world. When we touch this place and anchor it, so that we can return to it at will, we have created for ourselves the strongest possible defense against the malice of the old queen. Like Rose, we will then be able to keep weaving, spinning, and sewing no matter what others may say or do.

Core Worth: Through Physical Sensation

The following meditation works by allowing us to experience the physical sensation of being pushed off balance and coming back to center. The first time we ever did this exercise was many years ago at the Vancouver Witchcamp. Cybele, from her knowledge of movement and bodywork and the depth of her own personal healing journey, led us through a set of exercises to find our centers.

In sacred space, find a partner. Stand opposite each other, ground yourself, and place one foot against the instep of the other foot, pointing out at right angles from each other, like fourth position in ballet. Now move your front foot forward about the width of your shoulders, and rock back and forth until you come to center. Make your knees soft, and center your breath in that power point in your belly about two inches below the navel. "In aikido," says Cybele, "this stance is called *hamni*."

Take a moment with your partner, and take turns pushing against each other's shoulders. Try to push or pull each other off balance, and see if that's easy or difficult to do. The receiver's task is to return to the centered stance and to study her responses to being knocked off center. Do I exaggerate the effects (drama queen)? Do I resist and not allow events to move me (stoic)? Do I have some other response? Allow each partner several opportunities to experience the sensation of returning to center. Allow yourselves to explore and deepen your sense of your own centers. Allow yourselves to experience the internal sensation of having a center that can you return to when you begin to lose your balance.

Now one partner should release the stance and stand beside the other. Relax and breathe deeply for a moment. Then say your partner's name. Ask, "How do you know that you are (name)?" If she is not comfortable using her name, you can simply ask, "How do you know that you are yourself?"

As the receiver, when you hear your name, let yourself notice where in your body that name resonates. Touch that place, creating a sensation. Notice what visual image comes to mind and what word or phrase you hear with your inner ear when you are centered and simply yourself.

Remember, being yourself is enough. You are already, in your nature, part of the living body of the Goddess. Focus on the touch, the image, the sound of the word or phrase. Breathe into them, let them deepen and take root as your anchor to your own core worth. Know that when you use these three things together—the touch, the image, the word or phrase—you will call yourself back into this sense of centered core worth.

Now let your partner push against you and try to knock you over. Has anything changed? Repeat so each partner has a chance to create an anchor. You can use your anchor anytime to bring you into this core state of being. Breathe into your anchor; tell yourself that the more you use it, the stronger it will become. Now let go of your anchor and come back.

Core Worth Spell: An Apple

You will each need an apple and a knife. With your circle at your group's altar, or alone at your home altar, create sacred space. Light your candles, and take a moment to look around.

Your altar is full of magic from Rose's story, from your own story. There are your lovely roses reflected in the mirror of self-love and self-care. There is food for you to share with deity, your commitment to accept guidance and teaching. There are ashes from the fire where you released your wicked vows, freeing yourself from any bitterness over past injustice. There is a bit of basketry, woven from the wild, and your drums, yoga mats, meditation cushions, or other tools for "flying." The nettle dolls rest there, your pledge to develop inner strength by nourishing yourselves with food, herbs, and the light, relaxing trance of repetitive work and exercise. Now we will add the mystery; our core worth.

You can each take an apple and cut it in half around the equator, the opposite way from how many people cut apples. In the center of the apple, observe the mystery, the seeds, surrounded by the pentacle, sign of the Goddess and of the cyclical life of nature. Know that the apple reflects you as surely as any mirror. You hold in your secret center the mystery, the Goddess immanent in your human life, with all its ambiguities. So do your sisters. Deep inside each of you lie the seeds of immortality and of deity. Let the apples stay on your altar for now, as a prayer to the Goddess to strengthen your sense of your core worth.

We have each had the opportunity to explore the feeling of core worth and to create an anchor so we can return to it at will. We have made a spell at our altars, a concrete prayer to the Great Goddess, for our certainty of our core worth. Now we will go on a trance journey to explore our own boundaries, to see how we are protected from attack. We will have an opportunity to make adjustments, strengthening and repairing our boundaries if necessary, and making sure we can get the information we need through them.

Trance: The Crone's Three Gifts

When facing jealousy or attack, we need protection as well as a strong sense of core worth. The following trance allows you to work with the boundaries you create to protect yourself, and with your ability to perceive the boundaries of others, in the safety of your own place of power and with the assistance of the Old Woman.

In sacred space, relax, go into trance, and go to your place of power. Take some time to explore your place of power to see and feel and sense what is here for you today.

When you've explored the inner realm of your place of power, take a moment and walk out to the boundary. Where is the edge of your place of power? What is that boundary made of? Is it thick or thin, solid or permeable? Are there holes or gaps in it? Is there a way for people or things you want to invite in to get through?

Now take a deep breath. Imagine that someone is standing close behind you, someone of great power and wisdom, the Old Woman of our story, the Crone herself. Slowly, slowly, turn toward her. As you turn, you begin to get a sense of her presence, how big she is, how she fills your space. Notice what you smell on the air, what you hear, what she looks like, what she is wearing and holding and doing. Open your ears, and hear what she says to you and to you alone.

And now, as you breathe deeply, you hear her voice again. "My child," she says, "I am going to give you three gifts, and the first is this: to have a boundary, to know where you leave off and the rest of the world begins, and to make that boundary be as you want it to be, strong enough to protect you, open enough to let through what can nourish and delight you."

Breathing deeply, you turn back to your boundary. Now you can mold it and shape it according to your will. Take time to form it into what you want it to be. Look for gaps or holes to repair, and notice what direction they are in. Choose the material you want your boundary to be made of, and know how you can let the people you choose into your place.

When you are ready, slowly turn back to the Crone. Listen to what she has to say to you and to you alone. Then take a deep breath, and hear her voice. "My child," she says, "I am going to give you a second gift, and this one is the tool you need to defend your boundaries and to repair them when they are damaged."

And you breathe deeply and look around you. Or close your eyes and just feel around you. What comes to hand? What does your tool feel like? What is its weight like to hold? What is it made of? Open your eyes and look at it. What can it be used for? And how do you carry it?

When you are ready, turn again to face the Crone, and listen once more to what she says to you alone. Then take a deep breath, and once again hear her voice. "My child," she says, "I am going to give you one last gift. Just as your skin is both a boundary to your body and an organ of sensation, so your boundary is also a sensory organ. The gift I give you is the ability to sense the boundaries of others and to know consciously when you are crossing them."

Turn back to your boundary. Feel it come alive. How will it gather information for you? How will it talk to you and let you know when you encounter another's boundary? What will you feel or sense or notice that will alert you?

When you are ready, turn back to the Crone. Thank her for her gifts, and know what it is you can offer to her. Then say good-bye. Look once more at your boundary, and see how it has changed. Take up your gifts, and return to the center of your place of power. Take whatever time you need there, and then return to your ordinary consciousness. Stretch all over, say your name three times, have a bite to eat, and make some notes in your Book of Shadows.

If you are working with friends, take some time to discuss what you've experienced and how it may affect your boundaries in the outer world. Only when you are ready, open the circle.

Like Rose, we are now anchored in our core worth. We know we can reach out in love, and we know we can protect ourselves from attack. Neither good nor ill winds will deflect us. Rose holds to her weaving, her sewing, and her silence whether she is loved or hated. She is a woman who knows her own name and the meaning of her life. And now the story builds to a final dramatic moment, sweeping us along with it.

The Outer Path

Rose has taken on a great task and has developed the courage, fortitude, and persistence with which to meet it. Now her work and her silence have made her an enigma. Clearly she is a person of power: both her lover and her enemies recognize that. But her silence allows each of them to project upon her their image of a powerful woman. To the king, she becomes an object of love. Perhaps he sees in her the silence and mystery of the earth herself. But to the mother-in-law (and, in some versions of the story, the archbishop), she becomes a threat. She is a rival for love and status. And she is also a woman of power in a world where women's power is feared.

Power is problematic for women. For men, increased power usually means increased attractiveness. For women, the opposite is often true. We are raised to fear that if we are too powerful, too smart, too successful, we won't be loved. Heterosexual women fear that men won't find us attractive, but even lesbians and queer women are not immune to the pressures of the culture. The wicked Witch, the evil stepmother, the overpowering mother, the bitchy boss—negative images of female power surround us.

Even for men, holding public power has become more difficult. Political campaigns are vicious. Celebrities are both adored and reviled. Power itself has become suspect—and rightfully so, as more and more of it is concentrated in fewer hands. But those who stand forth and hold power publicly and accountably must face all of our positive and negative projections, while the most dangerous power brokers operate anonymously behind closed doors.

To walk the Outer Path with integrity and effectiveness, we must be able to withstand other people's projections. We must be able to trust our power from within, be conscious of how we wield our influence, and be clear and accountable when we are entrusted with power-over.

To withstand projections, we must be aware of our own. To survive the jealousy of others, we must acknowledge our own envy. To find the partners, companions, and lovers who will cherish our true selves, we must know who we are beneath other people's assumptions of either our virtue or our malevolence.

As social beings, we are shaped by our reflections in other people's eyes. As infants, our sense of self is formed by how lovingly we are mirrored by our caretakers. As we grow and develop, our confidence and self-esteem are dependent on how others see us. How hard it is to feel like a competent adult at the family dinner when Daddy still sees us as a charming, helpless child!

One of the great gifts we can give is to strive to see each other fully and wholly. The following exercise is one I've adapted from a meditation taught by author and activist Joanna Macy.

Mirror

In sacred space, find a partner. Sit or stand opposite each other, in a position where you can comfortably hold hands. Take your partner's hands, and match your breathing.

Look into your partner's eyes, and allow yourself to see the child that is there. Keep breathing, and notice also how it feels to have your own child seen. Then close your eyes, and come back to yourself.

Open your eyes again, and allow yourself to see your partner's vulnerability and wounds. How does it feel to have your own vulnerability seen? Then close your eyes, and come back to yourself.

Now open your eyes, and allow yourself to see your partner's strength and power from within. How does it feel to be seen in your own true strength? Then close your eyes, and come back to yourself.

Open your eyes again, and see your partner as the Goddess, as the God, as deity becoming manifest right before your eyes. How does it feel to be seen that way? Then close your eyes, and come back to yourself.

Now use your anchor, and call yourself into your core state of worth. What shifts or changes? Open your eyes, and from your anchored state allow yourself to see your partner and be seen.

This exercise is one I often use to precede an energy-sensing exercise or to teach aura reading. If you use it in that context, go on directly to energy work without breaking the flow by talk. Otherwise, thank your partner, relax, and discuss what you experienced.

To acknowledge our own projections, we need to distinguish between observing, judging, assuming, and responding emotionally to someone. Part of our magical training is to learn not only what state of being we're in, but also what mode of awareness we're using. I first learned a variation of this exercise from Patricia Storm, of Diana's Grove. Patricia is a psychologist and a practical priestess, equally at home with a magic wand or a chain saw. She and her partner, Cynthia, studied in Jean Huston's Mystery School, where the original version of this exercise was taught. Later, Cynthia's daughter Kitty and I developed it further to make it conform more closely to the elements.

Five Modes of Awareness

In sacred space, find a partner. Sit comfortably opposite each other. Begin by taking hands and matching breath, though you may drop hands as the work goes on, since this exercise takes at least forty-five minutes to complete.

Begin with the element of earth, with physical awareness. Look at your partner and take turns describing what you see. As much as possible, limit your description to physical details; do not include knowledge or judgments. Although this sounds simple, it is actually extremely difficult, because as soon as we use words, we are entering the realm of judgment. "I see a face with many fine creases radiating from the eyes" is close to a purely physical description. "I see the face of an older woman" brings us into the realm of judgment.

As an alternative, let go of words altogether and make a drawing of your partner. To really draw somebody, we must see them clearly. The more we look, the more there is to see. I've spent an entire weekend painting two plums and an apple and only skimmed the richness of their physical form and color. But if the people you're working with are unfamiliar with art materials or in conflict about their abilities, drawing may raise issues that are a distraction from the focus of this exercise.

Next move to the element of air—to knowledge, insight, and judgment. What do you know about your partner from what you observe? Air brings in categories: woman, middle-aged, well-dressed. And categories can lead to assumptions: "Her hair is gray and she doesn't dye it, so I assume she is comfortable with her age and not trying to appear younger." Again, describe what you see.

Now move on to fire. What is the quality of energy you perceive in your partner? How does that energy flow? Where is it stuck? Use your hands to sense your partner's aura, if that helps you. Again, describe what you perceive.

Now move to water. What do you feel about your partner? What emotional state do you sense your partner is in? Again, describe what you perceive.

Now sit back for a moment. Tell yourself a story about your partner. If she or he were a character in a fairy tale or myth, who would they be? Share your stories with each other.

Ground, and anchor yourself into your core worth. Now move to the fifth element, spirit or center. How do you perceive your partner's spirit or essence? Again, describe what you see.

Then take time to discuss your experience with your partners and in the group.

Often we assume that our basic mode of awareness is physical perception. After all, we go around in the world mostly without bumping into lampposts or falling into ditches, able to navigate city streets and pick out groceries in the supermarket. But as we refine our awareness of perception, we may discover that we spend very little time in physical reality, that we walk through our lives surrounded by a fog of judgments and emotions that obscure much of what is around us.

I Notice/I Imagine

Katrina suggests a short, simple exercise she learned from anti-oppression trainers to help us distinguish between observation and judgment.

In a group, sit in a circle. One person begins and says to the person on their right, "I notice _____ about you, and I imagine _____."

Continue around the circle clockwise. The group is free to comment on the observations to help keep a clear distinction between the observations and the judgments that arise.

"I notice that you are wearing a red shirt, and I imagine that you support the Chicago Bears."

"I notice that you look tired, and I imagine you're working too hard."

"Wait a minute, 'tired' is a judgment."

"I notice dark circles under your eyes, and I imagine that you are tired."

Naturalists and trackers, detectives like Sherlock Holmes, and great artists are simply people who have learned to sharpen their physical perceptions. For us vague, absentminded, intuitive types, training in physical perception is an important counterbalance to all the work we do with internal imagery. I was an art student in college, and while my drawings and paintings showed less than stellar talent, the training taught me to see. I've also sought out programs such as those offered by the Wilderness Awareness School that teach observation of nature. Practice is key to sharpening our physical perception, just as it is a vital part of all magical training. Following is my daily meditation.

A Walk in the Physical World

Take a walk in nature, practicing wide attention. Stay in the physical world, observing as much as you can of what is around you. Notice when your own thoughts and internal dialogue take over your mind, and gently let them go.

If to be a leader or public figure in this society is to invite projections, then to stand forth and deliberately call yourself a Witch, a Pagan, or even a teacher of spirituality is like popping up on a shooting range wearing a target. The words, the role, and the personal power we may carry in our being evoke both positive and negative projections.

There are two basic tools that can help us fend off the arrows that may fly our way: shielding and anchoring.

To shield magically means to create an image that embodies a protective energy form. A shield may function like a knight's shield of steel and deflect weapons, or it can function more like the shields of the spaceships on *Star Trek* and absorb the energy of the attacks that come your way. Each has its advantages and dangers. Negative energies deflected are still bounding around the universe and may cause damage, just as ricocheting bullets do. But absorbing negative energies can be dangerous to your health unless you are skilled enough magically and secure enough personally to transform them. A shield may also function like a filter, a mirror, or camouflage.

"I visualize a solid oak barrier that comes up to about my chin," Melusine says. In her political career, she has had to learn many lessons about self-protection. "When my shield comes up, it makes the sound of a van door sliding shut. I can still talk over it, but nothing anyone says can get to me; it just bounces." Her image is visual and tactile and incorporates sound. The more senses we include in a visualization, the more effective it will be.

Pomegranate describes her shield as a priestess cloak: "In some contexts, it's a very thin, light cloak. With other people, I have a very thick cloak. It's important not to take too much personally when you are working as a priestess; it can be very ungrounding. I let the cloak take it. I spend a lot of time each week talking to people. One day I talked to two different people in my role as priestess. The first told me I had saved her life. Within a few hours I was consulting with a person who felt I was failing her. Because I was wearing my priestess robe, I was able to remember that both people were talking to the priestess archetype. The robe holds the big energies that are necessary for people to do their magical work and reflects the power that people bring to the work. Meanwhile, inside the robe, the human-sized me can stay grounded and focused on each person's situation and avoid getting pulled into their energy. In addition, I can take human-scale responsibility for people's progress."

Before doing the following working, do the "Crone's Three Gifts" trance, described in the Inner Path for this chapter.

Creating a Shield

In sacred space or at your altar, consider the situations in which you need protection. Invoke your particular allies, the Goddesses, Gods, or ancestors with whom you feel a special bond.

What tools did you receive from the Old Woman with which to defend your boundaries? Are any of them useful to you in this situation? What image of protection might you use? Do you want your shield to deflect or to absorb and transform energy? How will you let in energies that you do want and information that you need?

What protective image comes to you? Spend some time with it; get to know it. Create an anchor to it, one that you can draw up quickly and automatically.

Be aware that a shield takes energy to maintain. What source of energy will you use to maintain your shield?

Thank your allies, and devoke the circle.

Shielding Practice

With a partner, ground, breathe together, and take some time to explore each other's auras. When you have a sense of your partner's base state of energy, ask her to draw up her shield. Sense her aura again, and notice whether you can feel the change. Switch roles, and then discuss what you have observed. Practice together until each of you can call up a shield that can be clearly sensed by the other.

Shields do take energy to maintain, and they do in some sense keep us subtly removed from contact with others. They are necessary and vital in situations of attack. But when we are teaching, priestessing, or counseling, we need a different sort of protection, one that lets us remain wide open to energies and information but still able to separate what is truly ours from what is not. Rather than shielded, we need to be solidly anchored in our core worth and protected both by our allies and by the quality of energy we are running.

Perhaps by now you are weary of being told to anchor to your core worth. Nevertheless, if you haven't been regularly practicing with your anchor, make it a daily practice now. Your anchor is literally your lifeline and your link to sanity. I use mine constantly, whenever I need to stay clear and grounded in the face of intense energies, whether they are coming from a disagreement with my partner, an audience of five hundred people waiting to hear me speak, or a riot cop beating up the person next to me.

Anchoring Practice

Donate is one of our German Reclaiming teachers. A university professor in religious studies, certified body therapist, mother of two adult daughters, and ritual woman, she developed the following exercise to help us practice anchoring through intensity.

In sacred space, find a partner. Begin by sensing each other's auras first in ordinary, relaxed consciousness and then when anchored to your core state of being. Become familiar with each other's energies.

Now one partner becomes the receiver, and the other becomes the projector. Take a moment and discuss the type of stressful situations the receiver might encounter in her or his life. Then the receiver sits and anchors to her core state of being. The projector role-plays an attacker, sending out negative energy, jealousy—whatever the receiver might be facing. The receiver's task is simply to stay anchored and respond from the core state of being.

Reverse roles, and repeat the exercise. You might try it several times, with different sorts of energies and projections, positive as well as negative. Which are easier to resist? Which tend to knock you off your anchor?

How did it feel to stay anchored? How did it feel to be the attacker?

When you are done, be sure to shake out your hands, and do a brushdown on each other. Call back your anchors, and recheck each other to make sure you are back in your core state of being. If you feel it's needed, you might want to offer each other healing or positive energy as a counterbalance.

This exercise, with slight variation, can be used in nonviolence trainings for direct action. The attackers might role-play police, outraged workers blocked from their jobs, loggers prevented from cutting trees—whatever is appropriate to the situation.

Tunnel of Torture

Melusine and Pomegranate, who among their other sterling characteristics are two of the funniest human beings on the planet, came up with the following exercise together.

The group forms two lines, in the form of a gauntlet. The receiver walks slowly between them, holding her anchor to her core state of being. For the first half of the gauntlet, group members hurl attacks and abuse. For the second half, they lavish praise and adoration. Her challenge is to stay anchored and centered through both.

End with discussion, brushdowns, and whatever cleansing is necessary.

Constructive Critique

"There's a difference," Melusine says, "between a voter who thinks you've done wrong and is screaming at you, and a personal political attack. I have to listen to the voter because there may be a grain of truth in what he's saying."

For power to be accountable, leaders must be willing to hear criticism. As leaders, teachers, and priestesses, it is our responsibility to both give and receive constructive feedback.

As an artist, Donald is familiar with the need to give and receive constructive criticism.

"A true critique is a gift," Donald says. "It's a mark of your respect for the other person as an artist, to take the time and trouble to constructively criticize their work."

Donald has a set of guidelines he uses to distinguish constructive criticism from simply shredding someone's creative work. A constructive critique must be specific—not "I hate that chant," but "The words and the rhythm are fighting each other."

For criticism to be constructive, the intent must be to improve the work, resolve a conflict, or improve a situation: "I'm telling you what I don't like about your chant because I want it to be moving and beautiful and because I believe you have the capability of making it so."

The timing must also be right. Immediately after the ritual, when the priestesses are still in trance and exhausted, is not the moment to rip apart the drum trance.

Another helpful guideline put forth by the Bay Area Witchcamp teachers' collective is that a critique must focus on something the person can actually change. As in "Have you thought about taking some voice lessons to help you learn how to project in a group?" rather than "Your personality is too mousy for a priestess."

Finally, consider whether your criticism is best delivered privately or publicly. E-mail makes this consideration especially important, because it is very easy to press a button and deliver a critique to a whole list-serve.

A public confrontation almost inevitably will feel like an attack. When we are criticized in front of others, we lose face and feel humiliated. It's the difference between quietly telling your friend, "Your fly is open," and yelling loudly in a crowded room, "Hey, everybody, *Joe's fly is open!*"

Sometimes public confrontations are necessary and effective, as in the story of the young girl in the movie theater. When a man sat down next to her in the dark and began masturbating, instead of quietly moving away as so many women would do, she stood up and yelled loudly, "Hey, everybody—this man sitting next to me is *masturbating!*" He jumped up and fled.

In most circumstances, however, constructive criticism is best delivered privately. You owe the person involved a chance to listen, respond, and change before making the issue public.

To be teachers or leaders that empower a group, we must be willing to give and receive feedback. More than that, we must invite feedback and respond in ways that make others feel comfortable offering constructive critique.

The more power and influence you have in a group, the more a thoughtless or heavy-handed critique can hurt. When I feel a need to criticize someone, I give long and careful thought to what I'm going to say. I ask myself, "What do I really want this person to change?" I might mentally run through the mirror exercise described earlier, asking, "What can I reflect back to this person in a positive way that will call forth the qualities I'd like to see?" If possible, instead of a criticism I offer a suggestion or challenge or a tool that can help open up a new direction or insight: "Just once this week, I challenge you to step into the center of the circle, do something that gets everyone's attention, and enjoy it!" "Before you tend tonight, why don't you take some time, ground, use your anchor, and go over the boundary work we did today so that you stay centered in your own self and don't soak up other people's energy."

Offering and receiving criticism are not easy to do. Working with our anchor, becoming familiar with our own states of inflation and deflation, can help us learn to simply listen and to discern helpful feedback from attack.

Critique Practice

To listen actively is to make a commitment to really hear another person on all levels: content, emotion, process. For this exercise, work with a partner. Use your anchors, and call yourselves into your core state. One person speaks, offering some piece of real or imagined feedback. Their partner repeats back what was said, without commenting or disputing it, just reflecting. The speaker can correct the listener, if necessary, until both agree on what was said.

Reverse roles, and repeat the exercise.

Now consider and then discuss: Was the critique offered specific? Timely? Was the intent to improve the work? Did it focus on something you could actually change?

Did you get pulled into inflation or deflation? By what? Were you able to hold your anchor?

When we are anchored to our core state of being, we know that we are worthy and valuable people even when we make mistakes. We don't have to be right; in fact, our students may learn as much or more from our mistakes, if as teachers we have the courage to acknowledge them, as they do from our moments of brilliance. At Witchcamp, we often discuss the previous night's ritual over lunch. The most interesting rituals to critique are the problematic ones, where the students can question our judgment calls and ask why we made the choices we did. "Just when the energy was raising up, you jerked it around and made us do a spiral dance. Why?" "Well, the people close to the fire were raising energy, but everyone outside was cold, and no one would move back and let the rest of the group get it. So I started the spiral. But you're right: the energy was jerky, and it never quite came back up, so it may have been the wrong choice." Part of empowering our students is to let them see the gears and wheels, to let them understand the many choices involved in a ritual, to let them know not just what they experienced, but how the experience was created.

Criticism may be a gift, but it rarely feels like a gift. In fact, no matter how kindly it is meant, it often feels like an attack, or at least a blow to one's self-esteem. Rose's mother-in-law is not offering her a critique of her child rearing or helpful feedback on her nettle-gathering techniques. She is out to destroy Rose. A destructive attack is of a different quality than even the most blunt and ill-timed criticism. If we can learn to recognize an attack when it comes at us, we can also begin to recognize those times when we attack others.

Let us imagine that Rose's mother-in-law was genuinely concerned when she saw Rose enter the graveyard and was eager to resolve the situation. Instead of leaping to conclusions, making accusations to third parties, and trying to whip up anger against Rose, she might have come to her privately and said, "I'm concerned. I saw you going into the graveyard. Maybe it's none of my business, but my son's welfare is important to me, and I'd like to know what you were doing. I realize that you can't speak, but perhaps there is some way I can help you communicate."

An attacker doesn't usually bother to ask. Like the mother-in-law's accusations of evildoing, an attack is not based on specifics or on evidence, but on unproved assumptions. An attacker often involves third parties or speaks of anonymous others: "I don't feel this way myself, but other people have told me . . ." A complaint made publicly that has not first been made privately is an attack. One of the laws of mediation says, "The more people involved, the less likely an issue is to be resolved." A person who wants to resolve a conflict goes first to the person involved, presents the complaint, and gives her or him a chance to rectify the situation. An attacker, instead, wants an audience. She or he may try to draw the group into being a court of judgment; list-serves are especially prone to being used in this way.

An attack may also masquerade as concern: "You look tired" may be a genuine expression of caring, especially if it is followed by "So why don't you sit down and let me do the dishes?" Still, "tired" is a judgment, and a negative one. Nobody really likes to be told they look tired. When it is followed by "Maybe you should cut back and get off this committee," we might suspect a manipulation.

Attacks are often not made directly. Instead of confronting the person involved, the attacker may start a gossip campaign or organize a faction.

Rose meets her attackers with silence. Instead of defending herself, she focuses on her great work of healing, which will be her ultimate vindication. Sometimes silence is our most effective weapon.

"There was one woman on the council who was my political opponent and who was really vitriolic," Melusine says. "It was vitally important that I keep silent, that I not even look horrified or hurt, because the TV cameras are on me. I have to look quietly and curiously interested, as if I'm taking it all in and considering it, but in fact I'm just letting it bounce back. Another man was writing vicious editorials and saying that I was a Witch. (I'm not 'out' in my community.) There, too, I knew that if I kept silent he was just going to turn people against himself. But after I was elected, hah-hah, I took out a big anonymous ad that said, 'From the bottom of my broomstick to the top of my pointy little hat, thank you, Tom, for the free publicity.' I didn't sign my name, but everybody knew."

Matthew Fox, the former Dominican priest who for many stormy years has been the voice of the creation-centered, life-affirming stream within Christianity, likes to quote Abraham Heschel as saying simply, "I never respond to negative criticism." "Of course," he admits, "sometimes you do have to respond because they're nipping at your heels, but as a general rule, it works."

Rose has no choice but to remain silent. We, however, do have a choice, and sometimes silence is not our best defense. There are danger signals we can learn to recognize that tell us when the time to respond has come. When our health or energy level becomes compromised, when we start to suffer from depression or lose our sense of joy and enthusiasm for the work, we need to find a way to end the attack. When we are being treated in unacceptable ways or when we would lose respect for ourself as a person, we cannot remain silent.

And while we sometimes must ourselves respond to attack with silence, as good allies we may be able to speak up for our friends when they cannot. Rose is isolated: no one in the castle knows her true story. But we do not have to leave each other in isolation.

A good ally doesn't necessarily just leap blindly into the fray when someone is being criticized or attacked. Instead, a wise ally might ask, "What can I do to create a space where an effective dialogue can happen?" We are good allies when we simply refuse to listen to malicious gossip or when we ask that rumors be checked out before they are spread. Good allies might set the ground rules for a meeting or an on-line conversation or offer to mediate a dispute. And good allies also see and name the "ism" brothers when they manifest themselves in subtle ways: "Malefica, I can hear how much you dislike Rose. I just want you to look at the possibility that there may be some issues of social class operating here. Is it really what she's done, or where she comes from—a cave in the wilderness—that's bothering you?"

The most painful attacks are not those that come from our political opponents or evil mothers-in-law. Those we expect and can deal with. The attacks that hurt most deeply are those that come from within our communities, from the people we love and trust. And generally those attackers are not truly malevolent. They don't mean to destroy us; they are simply responding from their own old behavior patterns. And sometimes even the most furious, ill-timed attack can carry within it a grain of truth that is a gift, if only we can clarify what it is.

We honor ourselves and care for our community by not letting ourselves get thrown into inflation or deflation. If we can instead stay anchored to our core state of being, we can respond with interest and curiosity, practicing a sort of energetic judo that uses the opponent's own momentum to transform attack into constructive critique. Instead of defending our position, we can ask questions, soliciting the specifics that make criticism helpful.

"I'm curious, Malefica. What exactly is it about nettle crushing that disturbs you?"

"What could I do to help you feel more comfortable with all these nettles in the castle?"

"Malefica, I'm hearing through the grapevine that you're worried about my midnight trips to the graveyard. If that's true, I'd love to talk to you directly about it and hear what you have to say firsthand, because I value your opinion."

Gwydion reminds us that what may seem like an attack may actually be an expression of passion. He describes "that point where we become so impassioned about something, so idealistic, that we move into that 'us versus them' dichotomy, approaching or entering into self-righteousness and piousness. We become immovable in our position and stuck in this mode. We become unwilling to compromise, unwilling to back down, unable—perhaps even unwilling—to be compassionate, and blind to the impact of our actions. The energy of it looks like 'Get out of my way, or either my horse will trample you or I'll knock you down with my sword/club.'"

Wand Meditation

In sacred space, stand up and position yourselves so that you can move freely. Think of something that you truly and deeply care about, an issue that you feel passionate about. Imagine that passion as a wand, and hold it out in front of you. What does it feel like? Look like? Is it light or heavy? What energy does it take to hold it before you?

A juggler once taught me that to balance a stick on its end, you simply have to keep moving to stay under it as it tips and shifts. Imagine trying to balance your wand in that way. Let yourselves move through the space, feeling in your bodies the effort it takes to stay balanced with your passion. Is there anywhere in your life that your passion is pulling you and running you around like this? Have you ever bumped into the walls, or knocked people over, with your passion? Has it ever become a club to beat people with? Has it ever become a flaming torch and started a fire?

Slow down, and breathe deeply. Remember your grounding and your anchor to your core worth. Is there a way to dance with your passion instead of being run around by it? Is there a way to carry it so that its fire can also warm you and fuel your energies?

Slowly let your wand transform. What form does your passion take, and how can you carry it? How can you recognize the energetic state when passion runs you? What feels different when you can hold and cherish your passion in balance? Thank your wand, and bring yourself back into ordinary consciousness.

———————

Alone, write about this exercise in your journal. In a group, you might share something about your passion and where it has led you. End by blessing each person's passions. Open the circle.

Passion/Compassion Meditation

In sacred space, sit with a mirror. Consider the person you feel is attacking you. What if you believed their anger and energy stemmed from passion? Can you understand that passion? Look into the mirror. Can you feel that passion yourself?

What might shift in your interactions with this person if you could acknowledge their passion? Allow a space to open within you where the possibility of change can exist.

End by bathing in the love of the Goddess or one of your allies. Open the circle.

No group is pleasant to be in when people are attacking each other. A group can extinguish that behavior by not participating in it, by refusing to engage in malicious gossip, by having clear expectations for how critique is to be done and holding to them, by refusing to be used as an audience for personal conflict or as a court of judgment.

Madrone, who both teaches and organizes Witchcamps, likes to begin camp with a short statement about leadership. "There are people here in positions of leadership," she tells the group. "But what I want to do is invite you all to take leadership. That means taking responsibility for yourself, for everyone at camp having a good time, including yourself, and thinking well of each other. We all come from wounded places, and they manifest in different ways. It's important to give each other the space to be supportive and kind."

To think well of each other means not to make assumptions about other people's motives, not to listen to backbiting or negative gossip or third-party complaints. It means consciously holding the well-being of the community in mind before you speak or act, and choosing to treat each other with compassion and loving-kindness.

Clear, strong personal and group boundaries are also part of our protection against projections and attack. As the old woman tells us in the trance of the Crone's Three Gifts, our boundaries are both an edge that protects us and a sensory organ that lets us know when we are encountering other people's edges. To have good boundaries is to be able to acknowledge the limits of your power and responsibility, to respect other people's privacy, to know what is yours and what is not yours.

When we step into a position of leadership, our boundaries become crucial. We are entrusted with other people's vulnerabilities, and we must be able to practice silence, to keep their confidences within the circle. Our words can wound if we use them thoughtlessly or carelessly. We must know when to intervene and when to use restraint.

Other people's projections can easily throw us into inflation or deflation unless we have a clear sense of our own limits. "May I talk to you for five minutes?" a woman asks me. She is depressed, unhappy with her life, and she knows that if she can just speak with me, I'll help her. I am amazed at her faith in my power, which must be nearly miraculous if it can, in five minutes, cure a depression that ten years of therapy have failed to help. I wish that I could help her, but I know that five minutes or five hours of my time are no miracle cure. All I can do is be present with her for a bit and listen with compassion. If I get pulled into inflation, if I lose my boundaries and decide that yes, I can work miracles, not only will I not help her; I may prevent her from continuing to seek and find true help.

Projections can become extreme. On one trip to Ireland, the religious commentator on the national radio station actually went on the air and warned that my visit would "unleash a flood of black magic and terrorism." I had always assumed that Ireland was doing just fine in the terrorism department without any help from me, but I was rather charmed to think that, with just one speech in Dublin, I could undo centuries of Christianity and negate every priest in the country. I found that a long uphill walk in the rain was necessary to restore my sense of proportion.

Boundary Exercise

In pairs, take some time to discuss how people get through your boundaries. Is it with criticism? Neediness? Bossiness? Judgment?

Partner A, reflect on your tools for protecting your boundaries. Anchor to your core state of being.

Now, partner B, mount an assault on your partner's boundaries, using the techniques she's admitted get through.

Switch roles, and repeat the exercise. How hard was it to hold your anchor? What have you learned about how better to guard your boundaries?

Now take some time and discuss how you cross other people's boundaries. Are you aware of them? What techniques do you use to push past them?

Again, take turns trying to hold your anchor and your boundaries while your partner uses your favored technique for crossing boundaries. How does it feel to have your limits pushed with your own techniques?

Reclaiming is not a rule-bound tradition. With our anarchist roots, we tend to resist restrictions and to worship freedom. Yet when we become leaders and teachers, we sometimes need to hold stricter boundaries than we would if we were not in those roles.

Baruch, whose training as a therapist encompassed many of the experimental therapies of the 1970s and 1980s, recalls a saying from a neo-Janovian primal therapy group: "One of the instructions I received was that everything that happens between you and the client is relevant to the work. Part of the magic of the work is that amazing unintentional things happen that perfectly augment and support the work. The line was: 'As long as you don't fight with them, sleep with them, or do drugs with them, whatever you do in the context of the work will fit.'"

Those boundaries mirror the ones we keep as teachers. Our Witchcamps and public rituals are drug and alcohol free, in part to provide a safe place for those recovering from addictions, and in part to establish the clear base of energy we need for doing serious group magic. In our daily lives, we might enjoy a beer on a hot day or a glass of wine with dinner, but if we're teaching at a camp that is drug and alcohol free, we must respect that boundary. If a group of campers sneaks behind the outhouse and smokes a joint, they might get away with ignoring the agreement that makes the camp a safe place for those recovering from addictions. But if a teacher or organizer were to join them, it would demolish the integrity and trust of the circle.

We also set a boundary for teachers and student teachers around sexual intimacy with campers for the duration of a camp. Many of us also hold this boundary with our students in classes and workshops. In a Witchcamp, we feel that teaching a path in the morning, attending meetings in the afternoon, and putting on an intense ritual at night for a week at a time, as well as being on call to resolve crises and dealing with the interpersonal dynamics of ten strong-willed and psychic fellow teachers, should really be enough excitement for anyone without adding the thrill of a new affair. If a teacher has an ongoing relationship with a partner who comes to camp, the rule is of course relaxed.

In part, the boundary exists because we need the focus of each teacher to remain on the work. It also exists, however, because of the unequal power dynamics created when someone is in the role of spiritual teacher. Teachers acquire a glamour, and in camp we are out of our normal setting and extended community, so that glamour is not tempered by the demands of daily life or the presence of those who have known us at our worst for decades. The power issue does not apply for all campers, who are, after all adults, but it sometimes surfaces in unexpected ways, especially when other issues of gender or age are factored in. Many people have been sexually abused as children or adults. When a person in a role of responsibility and authority acts out sexually in a group, it can restimulate all the old pain and replay the destructive dynamics.

Teaching is a role of service. Part of the spell we weave is the creation of the group. When the teacher singles someone out for special attention or sexual favors or responds to someone's advances, the energy of the group no longer flows in a circle but twines into knots. "It's kind to acknowledge the energy," David says, "whether it's sexual or quasi-sexual or not sexual at all. But within the context of leading the circle, it's important not to play favorites, not to direct your energy, sexual or otherwise, to one or two, but to hold open the opportunity for everyone to connect with you, whether they see you as Dad or Mom or sexual object or whatever."

When the group dissolves, the camp is over and the spell is broken. At that point, we are free to act on our desires.

Teaching magic is a special role. We take on some level of responsibility for guiding and directing another person's spiritual life, the place where they are most vulnerable and tender. When Hilary and I taught a Teacher's Path together, we began with an exercise she invented:

Precious Object Exchange

Everyone is told to bring a precious object to the first meeting of the class. The class is divided into partners, who exchange their objects. As a symbol of the trust invested in us as teachers, each person must care for her partner's precious object for the duration of the course. At the end of the course, the objects are returned to their owners.

Jealousy Ritual

In our story, Rose's mother-in-law is deeply jealous of her. In real life, one of the major reasons we attack each other is out of jealousy, although we rarely admit to that motivation.

Part of our Outer Path work is to understand the jealousy that arises in groups, to look at our own jealousy, and to find ways to continue to come from love and compassion.

The teaching team for the German Witchcamp created the following ritual in the summer of 1998.

In sacred space, we lit a fire in the center of the circle. After giving the women (it was an all women's camp) time to ground and center, we asked them to take time to consider when in their lives had they felt jealousy and when they had been hurt by the jealousy of others.

We formed a large circle around the fire. The teachers modeled the ritual process for the students. One of us stood forward, spoke of something she was jealous of, and invited others who had felt that to also stand with her: "I am Starhawk, and I am deeply jealous of my neighbor's broccoli that always grows so much bigger than mine. And if you've been jealous of someone else's success, stand with me."

Whoever in the circle felt called to do so would swoop forward, stand in the center for a moment, and then step back.

Another priestess would step into the center: "I am Margot, and I am jealous of women who are young and beautiful. And if you have felt that, stand with me."

After a few of us had spoken, students began to chime in. When we had heard many varieties of jealousy, we shifted the focus to when we had been hurt by jealousy.

"I am Claudia, and I was hurt as a child by my sister's jealousy. And if you have felt the same, stand with me."

When all had had a chance to speak, we raised a cone of power to transform our jealousy, and then grounded it.

In the story we were working with, the beautiful Vasa Lisa's jealous stepsisters put out their hearth fire so she would have to go to the fearful Baba Yaga to get fire. Suddenly, at the end of the ritual, the loud, screeching voices of the stepsisters cried out, "Vasa Lisa, you stupid girl! You've let the fire go out!" Three buckets of water were tossed on the fire to douse it.

The fire smoldered and hissed for a long time as we stood around it in the dark and the cold. The act was a more powerful lesson than a thousand sermons on how jealousy can destroy the warmth of community.

When I find myself overcome with envy of my neighbor's vegetables, or her rosebush that blooms so heavily without any of the care I give mine, or any of the thousand other things I'm capable of working up a fit of envy over, I have to stop and shift my energy before I tumble into a destructive spiral that leads down into self-pity and blame. Jealousy arises from a sense of emptiness or lack. It is a sign of low self-esteem, an indication that we feel lesser than someone else. When I'm jealous, I lose sight of the gifts I have, and I can't see the beauty of my own garden.

Gratitude transforms jealousy. When we are grateful, we pay attention to what we have been given, not what we lack. In the Goddess tradition, we are always invoking the powers and elements, calling them in, asking for what we want. We would do well to learn from the Iroquois Nations, who begin every ceremony, council, or meeting with a Thanksgiving Address in which they express gratitude to the four elements, the sun, moon, and stars, the people, plants and animals, and the spirit. The prayer may go on for hours, as every aspect of the natural world is thanked. But when it is done, the people are brought into a sense of harmony and peace, filled with awareness of all the precious gifts of nature.

Gratitude Meditation

Create your own Thanksgiving Address. Ground and center. To create sacred space, instead of calling in the elements, thank them. Speak or write out your gratitude to the air and the birds and flying insects, to the fire and the sun, to the waters and all the water creatures, to the earth and all the plants and animals and the soil bacteria and fungi, to the center, to your human community and relations, to the moon and stars and the cosmos above us and to the depths beneath our feet, to the ancestors, to the Goddess and God. Take your time.

Make this part of your regular daily practice, especially in times of jealousy or stress.

———————

Up until now, we've been talking about withstanding other people's projections. In some situations, however, we may want to deliberately create a projection. Sometimes it's not enough just to be powerful; we also need to appear powerful, or beautiful, or wise. In *The Mists of Avalon*, Marion Zimmer Bradley describes priestess Morgaine le Fey as a tiny, dark woman who could, when she desired, appear larger than life and awe inspiring.

Thorn is a slightly built woman with a dancer's grace. For many years she has worked in a soup kitchen in San Francisco that serves the homeless. She often intervenes in potentially violent encounters. "Since I have years of experience, I can instantly ground myself," Thorn says. "And when I'm grounded, I can pull up energy to expand my aura. People have said to me after I've broken up a fight, 'You got so big!' That's what they're seeing. It helps when dealing with someone bigger than me. Some of these guys are over six feet tall; they could kill me, but they'll listen to me."

A glamour is an important tool for emergency situations, but it must be based on real power, or it can shift into inflation. A glamour works best when it represents a physical expression of a quality you actually have. Thorn may not be big physically, but energetically, emotionally, and spiritually she's one strong woman!

"I also listen," Thorn says. "In our tradition, we're so used to witnessing each other and really trying to listen to each other, giving each other space to speak. When I'm grounded and centered I can really listen to the person, look them in the eye, let them know that I'm present for them, and that helps calm them. To regain my equilibrium, I do deep breathing exercises, all the things I do in my daily practice. Practice makes magic instantaneous. You don't have to do a big ritual to make magic happen. I don't have time to stop and cast a circle every time I need help. It's magic on the go."

Pomegranate describes her glamour as "putting on the priestess robe that makes me ten feet tall." Practice the following meditation so that when you need a glamour, you can throw on your robe quickly and easily and remember to take it off again.

Creating a Glamour

Take time to reflect for a moment on a situation in which you might need a glamour. Maybe you walk home alone each night from the bus stop through a dangerous neighborhood, and you want to project an aura of physical strength and confidence. Or maybe you are a paramedic, and you want to be able to project calm, confidence, and competence at the scene of an accident. Whatever your situation is, let your imagination create a garment that embodies the qualities you wish to project. It might look like Superman's cape or resemble your uniform with magical symbols invisibly embroidered on it. Make your visualization clear and detailed.

Breathing deeply, use your anchor to your core self. Meditate on the qualities that your glamour embodies, and let yourself feel and sense where those qualities do indeed exist within you. Breathe them into your anchor.

Now, remaining anchored, imagine that you put on your garment. As you do, your aura changes. It may become larger or take on different energetic qualities. Let your garment shape your aura.

Walk around in the circle, letting yourself interact with others and feeling what your glamour does for you. Keep returning to your anchor, and notice the ways in which your glamour is different from a state of inflation.

When you are ready, take off your garment. Consciously let go of your glamour. Imagine a place where you can keep this garment, ready to serve you at a moment's notice.

Again use your anchor to your core state. Give yourself a brushdown, or request one from a friend. Then discuss what you experienced.

"I would add one caution regarding the use of glamour," Pomegranate says. "And that is the use of glamour to shore up the ego. When glamour is used, it should be used in a way that is empowering rather than ego gratifying. You might be tempted to use it when you're losing an argument or when you are having a bad-hair day, but it is far better to ask, 'Do I really need to win this argument, and why?' or 'Why do I feel bad about myself?' or 'Will this use of glamour enhance the situation for everyone or only for myself? Will it distract me from my personal work or help me with knowing myself better?'"

Character Work

In ritual drama, we may also consciously create a character, take on the persona of another being. We might portray a Goddess, God, ancestor, or character in the story we're working with.

Marnie, who brings her background in theater and mask work into ritual, tells us, "In character work, you keep all your brains and self-awareness working on many levels. You must have two things very clear in your head and your body: one is your intention for the ritual, and the second is to give yourself over, your body especially, to your character, to honor your character, aspect, Goddess, or messenger, and 'let them do it.'"

Properly done, character work can become a tool of self-awareness. Marnie continues: "You have to trust who you are so that you can 'become' another. You have to have the guts to experience your own true self, and not hold a cardboard 'pretend' character in front of you as protection. The more fully you can play your part, the deeper the experience. And you get to have a lot of fun!"

Following is an exercise she suggests for exploring character work.

Character Play

Ground, center, and anchor to your core state of being. Take some time, and choose a character you would like to explore, perhaps someone who represents an aspect of yourself, positive or negative, that you want to learn more about. You might want to experience Rose's dedication or learn more about the mother-in-law's jealousy.

When you're ready, begin walking slowly around the room. Let your body begin to transform, becoming heavier, lighter, older, fatter. End by transforming your eyes and seeing the world through your character's eyes. Step out of the way so that your character can have full swing, but don't go any further than you can get back from.

How do other people look to you? What changes in your body, your internal dialogue, your energy and aura, your emotions? How does this character perceive the world?

Your transformed body works as your anchor. If something challenges your concentration, focus on your transformed body. Interact with the characters around you.

When you are ready to come back, again walk slowly around the circle. Let your character go, and let your body and walk return to normal. When you've finished, again anchor to your core state of being, and exchange brushdowns. Take time to discuss your experience in pairs or in the group.

In character work, we retain full responsibility for everything our character does or says. Whopping someone over the head with a bone might be perfectly in character for the Angry Hag, but we must resist the temptation no matter how deeply we've gone into the role. We can't unleash a jealous tirade against a friend and then claim, "The stepsister made me do it." We are responsible for controlling our characters' impulses.

Aspecting

Character work borders on aspecting: embodying and giving voice to an aspect of the Goddess. Aspecting is a lighter form of trance possession, a ritual practice in which the priestesses open fully to the presence of the Goddess, Gods, or ancestors. Gardnerian priestesses Judy Harrow and Mevlannen Beshderen have gifted Reclaiming with their articulation of four levels of aspecting work:

ENHANCEMENT: The state in which your ordinary consciousness is deepened, your words flow freely, insights come, and creativity awakens.

INSPIRATION: When the words and images or sounds and movements seem to flow through you. Musicians, dancers, and even we word-bound writers often reach this state.

INTEGRATION: When you and the Goddess/aspect/character become one. You are the music, the dance, the characters in your novel. But you are still present, still capable of coming out of this state, and still responsible for your words and actions.

TRANCE POSSESSION: When you disappear, or retreat into a small corner of your consciousness, and the Gods take over. You are no longer responsible for your actions or for bringing yourself back into your normal consciousness.

In Reclaiming, we work in states of enhancement and inspiration. Indeed, most ritual training and techniques are designed to bring participants into those states. To do character work that borders on integration and beyond, we need to have a strong personal practice of grounding and anchoring. Deep integration and states that border on possession require personal instruction and a strong collective container. They cannot be learned from books. In traditions such as the Yoruban that practice full trance possession, years of study, training, and initiation are required, and priestesses live lives circumscribed by many taboos and elaborate rituals. In their ceremonies, the person who goes into trance is supported by others who care for her, who protect her and other participants from the Gods' wilder impulses, and who bring her back to human consciousness afterward. Without such a strong structure, trance possession can be extremely dangerous.

The lighter levels of character work can be deeply enriching precisely because we retain awareness and can gain insights available only through our human consciousness. "You learn the depths of what you are, as you learn from whatever is coming through you," Marnie says. She describes a ritual in which she played one of the daughters of Hel, the Norse death Goddess. "I was living in a cold gray place, caught between life and death, condemned to stay in this hopeless place forever. Now, this was a wonderful experience. I drew from my own life, from those days, weeks, months I had sometimes spent in depression and despair. I knew this place. It was not once removed from me, and so I went there, using that as my metal to form this character. I roamed all over the camp. As the daughter of Hel I would approach someone alone in the woods. They might wink and gesture to Marnie, but it was the daughter of Hel who looked back through a desolate space. One or two campers, after smiling at first, wailed for real. Some were shocked as Hel strode through the labyrinth, cutting all the paths willy-nilly. The intent and the transformed body kept the character in place, and the experience of living that despair out in service of the Goddess was truly an amazing gift."

As human beings, we each contain the potential for the whole spectrum of human qualities, from amazing compassion to incredible cruelty. Character work is most enlightening when we allow it to reveal those depths. We can experience parts of ourselves we do not want to enact in our lives. "You yourself know when a character is too 'hot' for you to play," Marnie says. "For instance, I may not have chosen to play Hel right after my mother died. You must be prepared to use parts of yourself you do not like, playing from your own unbridled jealousy and envy to be a successful stepsister to the pretty young maiden, for example. And to do this, you have to do deep personal work around your own negative emotions. If you do it well, your character may be hysterically funny in its naked hatred, and through this ripping open of energy the people in the ritual will really experience their own jealous emotions, bringing them into consciousness where they can be acknowledged and transformed."

Character work can also put us in touch with positive parts of ourselves that we want to nurture. Aspecting to the level of enhancement or inspiration lets us bring forth the depths of our wisdom, compassion, and love. We may even tap energies that go beyond the personal and bring through healing and knowledge from those great collective forces we call Gods.

We all, always, have a direct connection to the Goddess. We never require another person to stand between us and the Gods, to mediate or be their messenger. When we explore character work and aspecting, we must be careful to do it in a way that empowers the group, not just one or two people who become the Goddess's voice. When we receive information from someone in aspect, we need to question and evaluate it just as we would if it came in some ordinary manner. The message comes through a human channel and is colored and distorted by our own subjectivity. If we start taking the aspect's word as law, if we start excusing our lapses of behavior with "The Goddess made me do it," we can fall into a very dangerous sort of Pagan fundamentalism that contradicts our core values of equality and shared power.

But, approached carefully and respectfully, aspecting can truly expand our awareness and understanding of the mysteries. After aspecting the Green Man, I became conscious of trees in a new way, aware of their awareness of me. A priestess in aspect may intuitively ask us just the right question to spur our growth or give us the challenge we need to move beyond a block.

Beverly teaches an approach to aspecting that reminds us of the open flow of power and inspiration.

Pass-the-Cloak Aspecting

In sacred space, each person in the group meditates and writes out a question on a piece of paper. The questions are collected and placed in a bowl or a hat (Beverly has a wonderful foolscap that she uses). Participants should be warned that not all questions will necessarily be answered.

Three Goddesses or aspects are chosen. Often we might work with the three Fates or the Norns. From our story, we might choose Rose, the Old Woman, and the Fata Morgana. Three cloaks are laid out, along with the hat full of questions and a stack of the Major Arcana cards of the Tarot. One by one, each cloak is held up, and the aspect is invoked into it. We might call the Old Woman, describe her qualities, hold out our hands to the cloak, and imagine those energies swirling and flowing and weaving themselves into the fabric.

The group begins drumming as they move rhythmically in a circle around the cloaks. If possible, throughout the ritual, drummers and individuals move in and out of the dance as they circumambulate.

When the energy base is strong, someone who is moved to do so steps forward and pulls a question out of the hat and reads it aloud.

Participants listen to the question and to their own impulses. Three who are moved to do so come forward and take the cloaks. They spend a moment centering in the energy of the cloak/aspect, then pick a Tarot card and interpret it to speak to the question. It doesn't matter whether or not they have any knowledge of the Tarot; the idea is to let the inspiration from the aspect speak. When they are done, they replace the cards, take off the cloaks, and rejoin the circle to continue holding the energy. Someone steps forward to pick another question, and the process is repeated until all questions are answered or until the energy of the group begins to flag.

To end, the drums and chanting fade away. The aspects are thanked and devoked from the cloaks. Participants should give each other brushdowns and share food after the circle is opened.

Bringing Someone Back

As priestesses, we are responsible for bringing ourselves back from whatever state of consciousness we go into. But sometimes we do need a little help from our friends. At other times we may be called upon to help others. Whenever the energy base of a group is high, we can easily open further than we intend to. At a ritual or a Witchcamp, we are prepared for this possibility. One reason we work in teams is so that someone is always available for emergency tending. But in other situations, with high energy and no safeguards, people with lowered barriers may find themselves overtaken by energies and spirits, with no preparation and no framework of understanding. Rock concerts, demonstrations, even meetings and conferences can create such an energy base. Injury, pain, tension, and, of course, drugs and alcohol can all lower our barriers.

When performing an emergency soul retrieval, the first and most important step is to ground yourself and anchor to your core state of being. Again, the more you have practiced, the more easily these tools will come to you when needed. Then call in your allies of spirit and flesh. Ask for help on both spiritual and practical levels.

I next assess the person's overall state, to try to determine whether intervention is truly needed or whether the condition may correct itself after sleep or after the dose wears off. If there is a physical condition involved, I call for the appropriate help. At other times, I may need to fend off crowds of eager helpers who surround the hapless subject. Anyone whose own level of fear, guilt, or distress is higher than the patient's or who is draining energy rather than giving it should be asked to leave or sent on a helpful errand elsewhere.

I start with the simplest interventions: calling the person's name or whispering in her ear, breathing with her and encouraging deep breath from the belly, holding her hands or placing a hand on her abdomen to help her breathe. I might ask questions about where she is or what is happening, remembering that I am not her therapist and do not need to analyze or interpret her responses. I stay calm or, if I can't feel truly calm, wrap myself in a calm glamour. I tell myself, "The Goddess won't give me anything I truly can't handle." I have no objective evidence that this is true, and certainly history abounds with tragedies and atrocities beyond anyone's ability to cope with. Still, it's a comforting thing to believe in the moment.

I try to engage the person's senses. I generally carry bay leaves, one of my plant allies, and a good whiff of their pungent scent will often bring a person back into his body. Or I look for another herb, flower, or scented oil. I might offer food, although someone caught in trance is often reluctant to eat. In extreme cases, I might pour cold water on his third eye or crown chakra or bathe him in the nearest body of cold water. I also make myself available to hear whatever voice might be speaking through him.

When the person starts to return, we often ask grounding questions. Wilow likes to ask, "What's on top of your toilet tank back home?" or "How many different types of pasta do you have in your pantry?" Anything that causes the person to exercise memory and think about home will help her ground back into her identity.

Melusine used to go smoke a cigarette with tranced-out campers; however, she has since stopped smoking and has had to develop other techniques. Some priestesses simply use a strong will and a bit of the glamour of a no-nonsense schoolteacher who speaks in the voice of true authority: "Now, you get back here right away! We'll have no more of this!"

When someone is having an actual psychotic episode or actively hallucinating, you may still be able to set clear boundaries, which are actually very helpful to someone in that state: "You have a choice: you can stop screaming and be quiet and remain here with us, or you can keep on screaming and Maddie will take you outside." It is generally not helpful to let someone suck up all the attention and energy of a ritual, and we should never allow someone to attack or injure another person or herself.

We also find out what kind of support system the person in question has. Does he live with family or friends? Does she have a therapist, support group, or counselor she can turn to afterward? We might strongly recommend that she find someone, or we might even offer referrals.

Finally, we make sure the person eats something, however reluctant he might be. We should be sure he gets safely home, whether this means walking him back to a cabin in the dark or driving her back to her apartment. Someone may need to stay with the person overnight. And we should make contact afterward to make sure the person is receiving support and whatever help is needed.

Extreme cases such as these are rare. Should they occur, we can remember that all the magical tools we've developed are available to us. When we use them well, what appears at first to be a breakdown may actually become a powerful healing experience.

Rose's task nears completion. Through love, childbirth, and loss, in spite of lies, attacks, and projections, she has held to her healing task. The shirts are nearly done. But the spell is not yet over.

SEVEN
The Transformation

Comments on the Story

The citizens ready a pyre to burn the young queen alive. Rose cannot speak to defend herself but keeps sewing and sewing. As she is tied to the stake there is a rush of air, and her twelve swan brothers beat out the flames with their wings. She throws the shirts over them, and all are transformed into men. The Old Woman appears one last time, holding the unharmed babies. But Rose has not yet completed the last arm of the last shirt. Her brothers embrace her, but the youngest does so with one human arm and one swan's wing.

The culmination of an initiation is a symbolic death and rebirth. Rose, having faced down jealousy and survived both love and loss, now faces death. She must remain focused on her task in spite of fear, weaving even in the dungeon.

As we gather power, we must also face our fears of being a Witch, our fears of death, our fears of the consequences of taking action. Like Rose, we must learn to stay focused not on the terrors of a hostile world, but on our creative vision. When we do, the gray hues of the dungeon cannot discolor our weaving.

In some versions of this tale, Rose literally dies at the stake but is revived and brought back to life. The old Rose, the child, the seeker, the patient worker at an impossible task, is dead. A new Rose is born who has completed her work.

When we complete an initiatory process, we are different. The power we've gathered, the wisdom we've gained, the courage and fortitude with which we've faced our challenges have changed us. We now know that we need never accept untruth, denial, or ill wishes or comply with wicked vows. We are capable of working magic, healing ourselves, restoring balance to the world around us. If we are unsure of how to begin, we are bold enough to strike out into the unknown, for we know how to seek guidance, meet help with generosity, and follow a path to its end.

We've learned how to weave the structure that allows us to be carried away, and we are not afraid to take on a big task, a life-healing, world-renewing work. Nettles, silence, scorn, and jealousy cannot deter us, for we know how to focus, how to weave a vision even in the dark. Like Rose, we can die and be reborn, passing through the fire of transformation to create ourselves anew.

Rose returns to life and regains all that she has lost. Her brothers, her lost children, and the love of her husband are restored. She returns to human life, and her human speech is restored as well. In her transformative work of weaving, she has redeemed not only her brothers, but herself.

Our work for this section of the story is to face our final fears, to weave and sew in the dungeon, staying focused on our true task and grounded in our true self, no matter what our outer circumstances. Part of that work is also to celebrate even an imperfect transformation.

The initiation is complete, although the task is not completely done, as the work of healing and transformation is never ultimately finished. One sleeve still remains to be finished; one brother is left with one swan's wing. The others have been fully brought back into human community, but the youngest is still marked by the wild. Unable either to fly or to perform many human tasks, he is caught, half and half. His story might form another initiation tale: his shamanic task is to be the wild in the human world; his handicap may become a source of his power. But that is another story.

The Elements Path

Rose is almost finished making her shirts, and we are almost finished learning how to make magic. We have learned the basics of a spiritual practice based on nature. We have learned how to create sacred space and how to invoke the Goddess and the old Gods. We have begun to create a right relationship with the elements of air, fire, water, and earth and have practiced the magical techniques that correspond to each: breath and visualization, energy work, trance, and spellcrafting. We have investigated the skills and tools of the center. Now it is time to take what we have learned and find a way to celebrate.

In Reclaiming, when a new group of students finishes the "Elements of Magic" class, they have practiced more or less the same skills that we have covered in the Elements Path. The elements class ends with a final ritual, planned and created by the students. If you have done all the exercises in the Elements Path, you are also ready to create your own ritual. Creating your own ritual is a rite of passage. Rose is not a powerless young girl anymore; she is a queen, a lover, a mother, and a mistress of magic. She has passed through the fire. And you are not a novice anymore; you have covered the basic skills of a magical training, and you have the skills you need to begin practicing.

Creating Your Own Ritual

If you are working with a group of friends, you will need to follow a few basic steps to plan your ritual. If you are working alone, you can adapt this process to develop your own personal ritual. The Outer Path of this book provides many more in-depth discussions, meditations, and skill-building exercises for those who may go on to public priestessing roles. But if you are working in a small group that has bonded by studying the elements of magic together, you can create your own ritual by following a few simple steps.

In a group, begin by going around the circle, and let each person talk for a few minutes about what is going on in their lives and what their concerns are. After each person has spoken, allow some time for group discussion. Look for common themes in what people have said, things that could be drawn out as content for the ritual.

Don't forget to consider themes that go beyond the personal lives of your group. Is something big happening in the "weather" of your community? Do farmers need rain? Is there an exposé in your local paper about hunger in your town? Are you losing friends to AIDS? Breast cancer? Has your nation begun a war or a peace? What is the moon phase and the time of year? Has a story or dream captured your attention?

Do you wish to symbolize your completion of the work of the Elements Path by stepping through a doorway? Into the center of the circle? By being crowned? Allow your creativity its full range. Then try to pick one or two vigorous, concrete images to build your ritual around. Rituals can bog down if they include too many elements or intentions.

Next it is time to take responsibility for the roles in the ritual. Who will lead the grounding? The purification? Who will cast the circle? Do the invocations? It's fun to do at least some of these parts as a group, with a song or dance or with wordless toning. What chants or songs do you want to use? Decide how you want to bring in the content you've chosen, with a meditation, or chant, or group spell, or in some other way. Discuss how the energy of the ritual might move, and agree to take responsibility together as it unfolds. A good ritual has just the right balance of common intent and spontaneity.

Many rituals allow some quiet inner time for visioning and seeking and then begin to raise energy, which can rise to a peak with a cone of power. But once a ritual begins, it takes on a life of its own, and the energy may develop in a different way than you imagined it would. Our rituals are a form of religion, a form of art, a form of medicine, and a form of love all at once. So it would be naive to think we are going to be able to plan and control everything that happens once the gods of devotion, creativity, healing, and erotic love are loose in the room and in our hearts! It's often the surprising, or passionate, or funny turn of the energy in the ritual that holds the greatest teaching for us.

Once the ritual's energy has peaked and died down, it is time for a cooling-off period. Just as after a powerful and invigorating workout our bodies have to cool off and return to normal, so after a powerful ritual our souls need to do the same. And so we rest in the circle, share food and drink, talk a little informally about the ritual, and slowly begin to talk, joke, and gossip about other subjects. At some point we realize that the deity is beginning to withdraw and that the energy has shifted back toward the mundane.

Now it's time to open the circle formally, to thank and say good-bye to any powers that were invoked either in the creation of sacred space or later in the ritual, and, finally, to say good-bye to each other: "The circle is open, but unbroken. May the peace of the Goddess go in our hearts. Merry meet and merry part, and merry meet again!"

Once in a Month

"Once in a month, and better it be when the moon is full, shalt thou gather in some secret place, and celebrate Me, who is Queen of the Wise." So begins the Charge of the Goddess. The traditional, private celebration of Witchcraft follows the cycles of the moon, and when the moon is full, Witches gather together in living rooms, by seaside bonfires, on hilltops where drumming can go on all night, or under the lacy moon shadow of orchards. Together we cele-brate the great cycles of nature and of our miracle bodies and remember that we are all connected in the great web of life. We call down the gleaming, pearly, luminous moonlight into each and every one of us and remember to pass a kiss: "Thou are Goddess" . . . "Thou are God." The hard part is opening the circle and going home again.

For nine years, when my old circle met by moonlight, our rituals followed more or less the same structure. Each full-moon ritual was quite different from any other, depending on what was going on in our lives, in our health, in the weather, and in the world around us, but we always followed the same basic steps to create it. After we gathered and visited informally for a bit, each person would report briefly on what was going on in her life. As we got to know each other, these rounds became very powerful, intimate, and supportive, as we had a strong background on each woman's process, her dreams, her gifts, her troubles. As we listened deeply to each other, themes would emerge: resonance, dissonance, longing, joy. Soon we would know what we needed to do together.

Often the ritual magic we agreed on was something very simple: a trance together, a saltwater purification, a dance, a tarot reading. We would create sacred space together, taking turns with the invocations, and singing together, toning and raising power. Often, each woman would take a turn coming to the center of the circle. We would all work together with our voices, with movement, with visualization, to pull the beautiful moonlight down into our sister, blessing her as she made wishes for herself and opened herself to insight and inspiration from the Great Lady who sailed the sky.

Doing magical work in a circle of friends isn't always easy or only fun. As in any group, there are conflicts, misunderstandings, even tragedies. There are times when we feel we could have done better had we been wiser. But we wouldn't have become wiser if we hadn't tried. We dared to love one another and to celebrate our soul-lives in the way we longed to. We supported and strengthened one another for years and gained precious skills and insights, along with many ecstatic and transformative experiences, and deep love, support, and understanding. Finally the tides of our lives and of time carried us away from each other. Just as bubbles form and rise and break only to re-form in boiling water, circles form and rise and break in a community, only to reform and rise again.

Some circles and covens also meet at the moon's quarters (once a week, more or less). Because of the busy schedules of most modern Witches, these circles often meet on a particular night of the week rather than strictly following the moon. The waxing quarter moon is a good time for magic that strengthens and nourishes change that is already under way. The waning quarter is a good time for the release of things that are passing out of our lives or that we want to get rid of. The dark moon is an excellent time for dreaming, scrying, trancing, and visualizing of all kinds. In the dark lies the potential, the power of all possibilities. Here in secret a seed is planted deep within, which can grow to fullness as the moon turns and waxes again.

The Solar Holidays

In addition to the private moon rituals, Witches also create public, community ritual to celebrate the cycle of the sun. This is the background of many pre-Christian Pagan holidays that are still widely remembered. At Yule, evergreen boughs are brought inside to decorate the house and remind us that although nature seems dead in the winter, life is eternal. On Halloween, ghosts and spirits haunt the night, and at Eostar (spring equinox), eggs and rabbits remind us of the bursting fertility of nature and our own spring fever. The solstices and equinoxes and the cross-quarter days halfway between them mark the solar year into eight equal parts, each of which, for ancient agricultural people, had its own work, play, magic, and spirit.

The Waxing Year

The new sun is born on the night of Winter Solstice. On that night we vigil by bonfires and in living rooms, as we would with a laboring woman, and the dark winter earth gives birth to the new sun. At Brigid, February 2, we celebrate the first perceptible return of light and warmth by making pledges to the goddess Brigid. These pledges are seeds we plant inside ourselves for our growth during the year.

At Eostar we celebrate the Spring Equinox by decorating eggs and planning an egg hunt for the children, followed by community ritual focused on balance, as the night and day reach their perfectly even moment. Then comes May 1—May Day or Beltane—which we celebrate with a traditional maypole, weaving the magic of community as the beautiful ribbons wind the pole, and as we cross and recross one another in the pattern of the dance. We also leap over a bonfire together, in twos and threes, families, couples, friends, covens, work groups, as we renew and purify our vows to one another.

The Waning Year

At Summer Solstice, the sun crosses the threshold into the darkening time of year, and we celebrate his going by burning the Wicker Man. We weave and build a great figure out of natural materials and tie on old spells, completed work, symbols of things in ourselves that we are ready to let go of. When we are ready, we throw it onto a great bonfire. Now we are "walking the dark," turning inward toward completion and release, after the expansion and growth of the previous six months. At Lugnasad, August 1, we celebrate the wake of the Sun King, grieving for the waning year and offering him our prayers and our company as he walks the dark, going before us toward the Shining Isle, making a way for us mortals, who must, in time, follow in his footsteps.

At the Fall Equinox we celebrate harvest home with a community feast and the warmth of friendship. We draw inward toward our hearths, and the weather begins to turn. And finally, at Halloween, we celebrate the highest holy day of the Witches, when the veil is thin and the living and the dead can communicate easily in trance and dream. Now we can travel in trance to the Shining Isle, Avalon, to meet the beloved dead. We walk in trance with the Goddess in the apple orchard where leaf and bud and blossom grow together on the tree. For now, as the dark of the year triumphs, time runs differently, and past, present, and future meet, and all things are possible. Together we create our dreams for the coming time, casting wishes into the growing dark for healing for our spirits, for our watersheds, for our communities, for the earth herself and all her creatures. And we dance the Spiral Dance of rebirth, raising a great cone of power, that all life may thrive. So we dream the dark until Winter Solstice, and the rebirth of the sun again, on another cold morning as drums and songs awaken the earth and sky.

The Thresholds

Witches also celebrate the great life transitions with ritual. As a pregnant woman approaches labor, we circle and sing to her and to the baby, blessing them on their way. Many of our babies are born in circle, as coveners and dear friends hold circle around the laboring woman and celebrate as the child is born. A few weeks or months later, when mother and child are ready, the baby is presented to the community at a Wiccaning.

My circle always celebrated with a "flying up" ritual when a child made the transition from little kid to big kid at about ten or eleven years. Maturing girls can be supported with a first-blood ritual, and boys also receive the support of community as they stand on the threshold of manhood. Lovers are celebrated as they take vows with one another at a handfasting ceremony.

When mature women and men are called to take personal vows of service to the Goddess, we celebrate with an initiation rite. When a woman reaches menopause, her transition is celebrated in a croning ritual. And finally, we support our community members as they face the final threshold of mortal life with healing rituals for the ill or for the dying and memorial celebrations. Many rituals, songs, and meditations for celebrating these thresholds in the Reclaiming tradition can be found in Circle Round and The Pagan Book of Living and Dying.

Facing Fear

As beginners considering taking up a practice of Goddess religion, we may face considerable reluctance because of our fear of what others may say and because of legitimate fear of reprisals and repression. In our story, the whispered accusations against Rose grow, and Rose is condemned to death by burning. Facing death, and the fear of death, is a part of initiation rites for Witches, shamans, and medicine people all over the world. Rose's initiatory journey is no different; it is not complete until she faces the inevitability of her own death, the final step to adulthood for any mortal.

The Burning Times

People today who may wish to begin to celebrate in the Goddess traditions and who may wish to organize their lives to respect the earth and all forms of life must also face fear. It is no accident that we must try to resurrect the practices of Goddess religion from bits and shards of broken tradition, from fairy stories and Mother Goose, from unexplained habits of language, gesture, and superstition. In recent history, religious practices based on the earth and on respect for the web of life have been persecuted all over our planet.

From the burning of the Witches in Europe, to the murder of countless native people who would not "convert" to Christianity, to the outlawing of the drum voices of the kidnapped Africans under slavery, nature-based religions, along with their wisdom, their stories, their medicinal traditions, and their spiritual practices, have been repressed and, in some cases, driven underground.

Historians disagree about how many Witches were actually burned in Renaissance Europe. Estimates have ranged from 100,000 to 9 million, but today most historians tend toward lower figures. In a way, it doesn't really matter, because if even a single woman were tortured and then burned alive in front of her agonized friends and family for the crime of honoring the Goddess, it would create terror and horror that would long outlast her cries. The nature-based spiritual practices of many cultures became secrets, passed down along with vows of secrecy, or passed down only to family members, or not passed down at all.

Even now, at the turn of the millennium, when women and men try to revive the beliefs of their ancestors, they meet opposition. Today, there are still people preaching the medieval doctrine "Thou shalt not suffer a witch to live." Conservative voices claim that the first amendment of the Constitution protects only the right to practice "legitimate" religions. Witches have had to fight for custody of our children, for our jobs, and to defend ourselves from harassment and threats of all kinds in our communities.

And so Rose's story continues to be a template for the final step in our study of the elements of magic: continuing to practice while facing fear. As Rose is imprisoned and then carried to the stake in the executioner's cart, she continues sewing and sewing. And at the final moment, her allies appear "out of the blue," unexpectedly, from far away. The swans beat out the flames and surround her; the old woman has saved her babies; the wood of the fire itself rises up to her in leaf and bloom.

So, too, when we begin to reclaim the Goddess traditions that are our right inheritance from our ancestors, unexpected help appears and great forces arise to protect us. The last twenty years have seen a major shift in legal, religious, and media relationships with Witchcraft.

The Parliament of World Religions, and the United Religions Initiative, the two international, interfaith organizations begun and supported by mainstream religions, include in their membership and as signatories to their documents many Pagans and Witches. The first amendment to the Constitution, which has long guaranteed freedom of religion in the United States, was recently tested when the Witches in the U.S. military wanted to practice openly. Although there was an outcry from conservatives, the military stood by the constitutional right of the soldiers to a chaplain and religious practices of their choice. Even the penal system, which also allows inmates a chaplain of choice, has begun allowing Witches to do religious work in prisons in many states.

In all these areas, we owe a great debt to the Native American religions, which provided legal tests of these principles in the military and the penal system. We also owe a debt to other Pagan groups who've focused on these issues, such as Covenant of the Goddess, a legally recognized religious organization since 1975. Reclaiming is also a nonprofit religious organization, recognized as such by the IRS.

M. Macha Nightmare is a Reclaiming Witch who travels and speaks, doing public information outreach for Witchcraft. She has been approached by groups as wide-ranging as the *Wall Street Journal*, the hospice movement, and the biodiversity movement to represent Witches in discussions of religious and spiritual diversity.

There is now a strong nationwide community, connected through the Internet, watching for discrimination and unjust attacks on Witches. When these occur, public pressure and legal defense are immediate, with support arriving as it did for Rose from unexpected and distant places. On July 4, 1999, thirty-five Pagan and Witchcraft organizations cosigned a press release that was sent out all over the country, to media, legislators, and religious organizations, announcing our unity and our determination to protect our right to practice in the military. Even a few years ago, this would have been difficult to attain.

The Internet has been a tremendous resource for the Pagan and Witchcraft communities, making it possible for people who may be isolated to discover just how much support and community they actually have.

Witches and Pagans work freely in many open-minded church and environmental groups. People who are considering beginning a personal practice in the Goddess traditions may want to investigate their local Unitarian church. They may find Witches already practicing there. The Covenant of Unitarian Universalist Pagans (CUUPS) now has almost seventy chapters listed on its Web site.

But although there has been tremendous progress, each person still has to make a difficult decision for themselves about how open or discreet to be about their interest in, or practice of, Witchcraft. It may be frightening to begin a widely misunderstood and slandered spiritual practice. So take a moment to try these two meditations, alone or with your circle.

Exercise: Asking Your Fear Its Name

Create sacred space, and put a candle and a bowl of salt water in the center of the circle. As you gaze into the candle flame, allow yourselves to enter a light trance state. You can take turns asking the following questions.

   Is there fear in your body of being called a Witch? Where in your body is it? What color is it? How big is it? Ask it to tell you its name.
   Is there fear in your body of the intimacy and honesty in circle? Where in your body is it? What color is it? How big is it? Ask it to tell you its name.
   Is there fear in your body of your own psychic and intuitive abilities? Where in your body is it? What color is it? How big is it? Ask it to tell you its name.
   Is there fear in your body of powerful women? Of being a powerful woman? Where in your body is it? What color is it? How big is it? Ask it to tell you its name.
   Is there fear in your body of actual attack and reprisal from others? Where in your body is it? What color is it? How big is it? Ask it to tell you its name.

When you have asked all the questions, allow your fear to begin to make some sounds. Release the energy that came up during the exercise into the salt water as your voices rise into howls, groans, four-letter words—whatever comes. When these have peaked and died down, offer each other some love and care. A group back rub would be perfect, where each person gives the next a light massage around the circle.

Remind each other that no matter what life brings, you don't have to face it alone. Remind each other that the natural world and the spirit world and the human world are full of allies and of teachings and of powers that will help. Remember that sometimes we are most afraid of the things we most desire, like being powerful, intimate, and in touch with our intuition.

When you are ready, bless the food and drink. Help each other, fill each other's plates, offer each other tasty morsels. Feed each other. As you eat and drink, talk a little about what you found in the exercise. None of us need face fear alone.

Exercise: The Glass Half Full

For this exercise, you will need a favorite cup or glass and plenty of dark-colored juice or some other liquid that you would like to drink. Create sacred space, alone or with your circle. Fill your cups half full. Gaze into the cups, and look for your reflections on the surface of the juice. It may take a moment to find them. You may need to adjust the lighting or move the candles, but you can find your reflection in the cup.

When you have found it, gaze for a time, and let yourself enter a light trance. Take a moment to think about the empty part of the cup. There may be areas in your life where you are missing the support you would like to have for your spiritual practice. You may even face opposition and criticism. Ask yourself where in your life you wish you had more support or more security. Notice how, although the cup is half empty, your reflection still arises on the surface of the liquid.

Now take a moment to think about the part of the cup that is full. There are parts of your life where you do have support and understanding. Otherwise you would never have gotten this far. Although it may not be all you want, nevertheless, like the liquid in your cup, it is enough for you to show up in it. Ask yourself where in your life you find support and security.

Next, ask yourself where you could look to find a little more. How about that woman who does the herb garden at the zoo? Wasn't she wearing a Goddess pendant? How about the woman who teaches the yoga classes? How about the talkative man with the tattoos at the health-food store? How about those people who are restoring the pond and creek on Saturday mornings? If you open your mind, do you find a hint or clue of where you could look for a little more support? Keep watching your reflection.

Have you seen your face change as you meditated on what you're missing, on what you have, and on what you want?

Now take your cup and fill it as much as you want. How thirsty are you? Drink the juice. Drink in your acceptance of what you may be missing, your awareness of the support you do have, and your insight about where you might find more help. Drink in your insights about yourself. If you are working in circle, fill each other's cups, and toast each other. Celebrate yourselves and the work you have done so far. Only when you are ready, open the circle.

The Pyre Breaks into Leaf and Bloom

Rose has faced her fear, and so have we. The allies have arrived from far away, and she is not alone anymore. The shirts are cast over the swans, who change into men. The magic is complete; the transformation has occurred.

And so it is for us, on the last night of the "Elements of Magic" classes, when the students create their own ritual. They are no longer novices and beginning students; they are the priestesses, the artists, the Witches. They do all the preparation and planning; they lead the meditations and raise the energy; they help one another and take responsibility for any little snags that may arise in the ritual. The teachers are always surprised and often delighted by the ritual work the newly fledged priestesses create. Here are three examples of final rituals created by new Witches for the last night of their "Elements of Magic" class.

Everyone has brought some earth from their garden or compost pile and a green plant. The circle is cast, and we all put our earth together into a big pot. As we give our own earth to the center, we speak of what we have gained from the class, of the new friends and new skills, of the fun and the depth. When all the words and thoughts and feelings and earth are in the pot, we stir, blending, creating a new and fertile soil. Then each person takes a flowerpot and fills it with earth. We gift one another with the plants we have brought, and pot them up in the new soil. Now our new magical skills, and our love and connection for one another, will grow green in each of our homes and gardens. We finish with a spiral dance, and as the line dance coils into the center of the circle and then back out, it brings each person face-to-face with everyone else. We go slowly, singing songs of praise, and allowing each person to speak, exchanging appreciation for the energy and wisdom we each brought to class.

Everyone is dressed to the hilt, in silks and velvets. And everyone is carrying the little doll of themselves that they made at the last class. Like a group of exuberant but serious little kids, we sit in a circle and make our dolls create a ritual. A silly doll leads the grounding; a lovely doll does a saltwater purification in a tiny doll bowl. A big, powerful doll casts the circle, and all the dolls do the invocations together. The dolls do some trace work and raise a doll-sized cone of power. Then all the dolls have a party and say how much they enjoyed the class and make plans to keep seeing each other to do magic.

Everyone has brought a different herb or spice to the last class. We each put our spice into a central cauldron, speaking of why we picked that spice and what we hope for. With a stick long enough for everyone to get their hands on at the same time, we stir, and crush, and mix the spices. A strong and entirely new fragrance arises, giving out great powerful whiffs of a strange and exotic brew. We pass a ball of yarn around the outside of the circle, and we each hold it, symbolizing the circle we have all been part of during class. Then we pass a pair of scissors, and we each cut free our separate pieces of yarn. The class is over. But now, we each get a little square of cloth. We take herbs and spices from the central cauldron and put them into the cloth, tying it with the yarn to make a little spell bag that we can keep with us. Although the class is over, it has changed us and given us a new and powerful fragrance, made up of our combined energies, which we can use as we wish.

And so, like Rose, we have reached the end of the story. We have practiced in the face of fear, calling on our allies. We have stepped out into our power. No longer the seeker and the novice, we now know how to create ritual for ourselves. We know how to practice the art and craft of magic, and we can use it as we wish to enrich and deepen and celebrate our soul lives. We have picked up the broken threads left by the grandmothers and become the weavers of a fresh and shining pattern, based on the old and full of the new.

The Inner Path

Although Rose has been thrown into the dungeon, she continues sewing and does not speak. She holds true to her life purpose, even in the extremity of deprivation and fear. She's bound to the stake, and now she's done all she can. She's hit the limit of mortal life, the moment of surrender, when there is simply nothing else she can do for herself. In this chapter of the Inner Path, we will work with our own feelings about death and with our own allies.

Because in this extreme moment, the forces of the wild appear. They are Rose's allies between the worlds, and they are the ones who save her when there is nothing left that she can do for herself. She reaps in a moment the just rewards of all her efforts: her courage in seeking the wild to begin with, her generosity to the Old Woman, her ability to endure her brothers' anger, her fearless flight, her prolonged discipline. The great swan wings beat out the fire, the Old Woman has saved Rose's babies, the wood of the pyre itself—magic wood from the World Tree—rises out of the ashes of its own fiery death to break into leaf and bloom. In the exact moment when Rose's case seems most hopeless and all seems lost and she falls as if dead, instead all is found, all is gained. Suddenly, after quite a difficult and lonely life, Rose is surrounded by those who love her: twelve restored brothers, her husband and children, and her mentor, teacher, and guide, the Old Woman. Through her efforts, her family line runs now in unbroken love from past to future.

We are like Rose, too, although on the outside our changes may not look so dramatic. We have followed her every step of the way. We have broken out of our "old castle," learning to listen to the voice of Younger Self in our dreams, sensations, and divinations. We have walked out into the wildwood of self-love, and accepted guidance. We have faced the salt shore of grief, bitterness, and anger that bound us to past injustice, and we have woven a basket of trust so that we could take flight. We have accepted the tough challenge of our life purpose and have gone to the green and silent world of the hermit for strength. We have learned how to stay centered in the weather of the human world through love and scorn.

Our changes may have been subtle. We ourselves may be the only ones who know any change at all has taken place. But determined and persistent practice of the meditations, altar work, purifications, and spells described in this path will bring results, and even a scorched branch can burst into bloom.

Remember, the fairy stories do not recommend a spiritual way of life; they assume a spiritual way of life. Specifically, they assume the principles of earth-based spirituality, of an immanent nature Goddess. By following the story, we have learned respect for the voice of our intuitive, wild self, and respect for all life. We have practiced willingness to be part of the whole web of nature, and felt the passion for justice that comes when we know that what happens to the web of nature also happens to us. We have developed our ability to rely on the great forces of nature, on the green world of plants, on the luminous spirit world, and on the laws of our own human nature, where what goes around, comes around. And now for Rose and for us, what has gone around has come around, and there are rewards for courage, vision, compassion, inner strength, and the passion for justice. But first, Rose must face her fear of death.

Many women and men who have survived a life-threatening crisis, an accident or illness, or who have recently lost a loved one report feeling a new vividness of each moment of life, a new gratitude for each day. Sometimes, an experience like this will provide the impetus to make sweeping life changes or important new decisions. The perspective of near-death can change lifelong values or open a long-defended heart. However, there is no need to wait for an accident or illness to provide this perspective. The wise of many religious backgrounds have always sought this perspective in meditation. These are some meditations you can try, at your home altar or in circle with your friends.

Death Meditation: The Seamstress

On what might be the last night of Rose's life, she has been thrown into the dungeon under sentence of death. She is still sewing and sewing, working on the last shirt. Create sacred space at your altar, and light a candle. Take a scrap of cloth, a needle, and some thread, and begin to sew little stitches, allowing the rhythm of your stitching to bring you into a light meditative state.

If this were the last day of your life, what would be the eleven completed shirts in your workbasket? If this were the last day of your life, what would be the twelfth shirt, which you are still working on? Allow yourself to rest in the certainty that every life, including your own, includes jobs well done and challenges well met. Allow yourself to rest in the certainty that no life completes every task and lives up to every goal. When you are ready, open the circle.

Death Meditation: The Candle

Create sacred space, and at your altar, light a candle. Watch how the flame shape-shifts, dancing and flickering. Say, "By the fire of Her bright spirit." Know that your life is like the candle flame and that your shape has already shifted many times: baby, child, teenager, adult. Know that you are, even now, shifting and changing, that the "I" is no more static than the candle flame.

Just as the flame relies on the wick and the wax, our lives dance on deep sources unknown to us. If the flame is put out, it can be relit. Know that death will be one more shape-shift in the dance. Put out the candle. Rest in the not-knowing, the mystery of death. When you are ready, open the circle.

Death Meditation: The Allies

When Rose is bound to the stake, the great forces of nature and spirit appear to help her. The twelve wild swans beat down the flames; the Old Woman appears for the last time; the wood of the pyre breaks into leaf and bloom. In sacred space, bind your hands loosely together with soft twine or yarn. Allow yourself to know that there are things in your life that you cannot do for yourself—that, like all others, you rely on help from the natural and the spirit world.

Imagine your moment of need; call out for help. Who appears to help you from the animal world? From the spirit world? From the plant world? Thank those who appear to help you, and vow to protect them in turn. Loosen your bonds, and return to normal consciousness. If you are working in circle, you can experience how much easier it is to loosen someone else's bonds than to loosen your own. We each need a little help sometimes. Open the circle only when you are ready.

These three meditations, on death and on the allies, are not meant to be done only once. They are the basis of a lifetime of practice with these truths, which always appear when we, like Rose, face the final threshold.

In the Inner Path we have gained confidence in our ability to change consciousness at will. We have practiced many altered states. We've journeyed into the violet-black depths of the world of dream and trance. We experienced the ecstasy of our dancing, drumming, fire-lit bodies in the ritual circle. We've become the relaxed, superalert animal who walks open-eyed in the green world of nature. Each of these states brings us, in its own way, to a direct experience of the central mystery—that we are not alone and separate in this universe, that our lives and our awareness in all its forms are one with the rhythms of the great dance of universal energies. When we have experienced this basic mystical insight not once, but many times, and have come to rely on it even when we are not directly experiencing it, then we have a point of view from which we no longer fear death. We know from our own experience that our soul-life is boundless. Although we may not be able to explain or understand this experience, we are aware beyond words that our soul is infinite, divine, and immortal.

We offer this drum trance from Reclaiming tradition, which tells the story of immortality in a way that appeals to Younger Self. This trance was originally developed by a Reclaiming coven for a women's ritual about choice. There was an important electoral initiative on abortion rights coming up on the November ballot that year, and when we traveled between the worlds at Samhain (Halloween), we included our longing for freedom of choice in the intention of our ritual.

This drum trance will also allow us to accept the help of another of our allies between the worlds, the Old Woman. When the Crone appears in this drum trance, stirring the brew of her cauldron, remember that the Old Woman has guided Rose and has guided us from before our births and at every threshold and crossroads of our tales. Take the time to create sacred space, prepare yourself for trance, and enjoy.

Drum Trance: In the Orchard of Immortality

Take a deep breath. Feel your breath flow in and out of your body. Breathe down to your toes and out to your fingertips. Feel the life flowing through your body and how the energy moves with your breath. Feel how your body holds your history, all that you know and have experienced, and how that history shapes your energy and your breath. Breathe deeply, and acknowledge the places where you carry wounds and the places within you where you carry power.

Now we're going to go together to a special place, a place where we can walk through the history of our lives. Our breath can take us there. Let's take three deep breaths together, breathing in and out. In and out. Beginning to sink deeper, to feel this world dissolve. In and out. Feeling the ground of another world under your feet, and how your body feels here, and the weight you carry here. And, breathing deeply, open your eyes and look around.

You are in the apple orchard of the Goddess. And on your arm, you carry a basket. Feel its weight, how it hangs beside you. And around you are young trees, barely more than saplings, slender and supple and bending in the breeze. And as you walk among them, you begin to remember your child-hood, all the things that happened to you, all the choices you made. Look around you. On the trees hang the fruits of those choices. Look. Whom did you choose as friends? Did you love school or hate it? Reach up; feel the fruit in your hand. Did you love your body? Did you run fast; did you feel you were strong? Were there choices not offered to you? Some of the fruit hangs heavy, round and sweet. Some is bitter, some shriveled on the branch and dry. Breathe deeply. Pick the fruit, and put it in your basket, the bitter and the sweet. And walk on.

Walk on to where the trees grow thicker, a little older. And as you walk, you begin to remember your young womanhood, your young manhood. How did you feel when your breasts began to grow, when hair sprouted under your arms and above your sex? Were you joyful? Were you sad? Who honored you? Did you have a choice about who could see you? Touch you? Know the changes you were going through? See the fruit around you, hanging heavy on the branch. Reach up, feel it, touch it. Breathe deeply. Pick the fruit, and put it in your basket, the bitter and the sweet. And walk on.

Walk on to where the trees begin to grow in their full maturity, their branches heavy and graceful as bowers. Whom did you choose to love as you grew? Were you loved in return? What fruit hangs around you, sweet or bitter or rotten on the branch? Was your love honored? Joyful? Was it the right kind of love to please your parents, your teachers? Pick the fruit, the bitter and the sweet, the fragrant and the rotting fruit. Were you hurt by love? Put it in your basket; feel it heavy on your arm. And walk on.

Walk on to where the trees grow strong and fine, and around their feet are seedlings springing up. Breathe deeply. What are the choices you've made in your life about children? Did you, do you, want to bear children? Did you choose the time and the partner? And what choices did you have about how to make that choice? Do you carry in your body scars or echoes of those choices? Did you get pregnant with or father a child you didn't want? What choice did you make? Look, the fruit hangs heavy around us. Did you want children you couldn't have? The sweet and the bitter hang heavy on the boughs. Did you bear or father children in health and in joy? Did you bear a child and give her to someone else to raise? Did you lose a child in the womb? In childbirth? Or after? Pick the fruit, the bitter and the sweet, fruit of our choices and the choices we didn't have. Feel your basket grow heavy on your arm as you walk on.

Walk on to where the trees grow gnarled and old, bent by the wind and the force of winter storms. Look around you. Here are the choices you have made, will make as you age. How will you choose to be in your body as it grows older? What choices will you make about the ending of your monthly flow? What choices in your life will you look back on and celebrate? Regret? What losses will you mourn? The trees still bear fruit around you, ripe and rotten. How will you choose to face death when it comes? Will you pluck it from the tree, a final ripening? Will it taste bitter to you? Will it taste sweet?

Pick the fruit. Feel how heavy your basket hangs now. And walk on, until you come to a clearing in the orchard. And there she sits, the Old Woman, the Crone, stirring and stirring her cauldron. Take a deep breath, and look at her. Notice how she appears to you, for she looks different to each one of us. And look into her eyes, deep as the night skies where the galaxies swirl. Hear her voice.

She says, "My child, give me your fruits, the fruits of the choices you regret, of your pain and regrets, the fruits of your losses and your grieving. Give them to my cauldron, where they can be transformed."

And you search through your basket. Breathe deeply; find the fruits of your regrets. Notice what they feel like, look like, smell like. And give them to the cauldron. Use your breath, use your body, use your voice; let yourself make sounds that carry that regret into the fire and transform it.

And the Crone stirs and stirs her cauldron. Look deep into her eyes. Hear her voice as she speaks to you: "My child, give me your fruits, the fruits of happiness, creativity, joy, the choices you rejoice in. Give them to my cauldron; let them become part of my brew." And you search through your basket.

Breathe deeply; find the fruits of your joy. Notice what they feel like, look like, smell like. And give them to the cauldron. Use your breath, use your body, use your voice; let yourself make sounds that carry your joy and pride into her brew.

She stirs and stirs. Look deep into her eyes; hear her voice. She says, "My child, give me your fruits, the fruits of those choices you still aren't sure about, the fruits of your uncertainty. Let them, too, become part of my brew."

And you search through your basket. Breathe deeply; find the fruits of those decisions that carried no answers, where nothing showed you clearly whether they were right or wrong. Notice what they feel like, look like, smell like. And give them to the cauldron. Use your breath, use your body, use your voice; let yourself make sounds that carry these fruits into her brew.

The Crone stirs and stirs. Look into her eyes one more time. Hear her voice. She says, "My child, give me your fruits, the fruits of those choices you didn't have or weren't allowed, the choices made for you, the choices denied you. Let them, too, become part of my brew."

You search through your basket. Breathe deeply; find the fruits of those choices taken from you. Notice what they feel like, look like, smell like. And give them to the cauldron. Use your breath, use your body, use your voice; let yourself begin to feel your anger and rage. Let them swirl and rise within you, mingling within you as they do in her cauldron with your joy and your pain and your uncertainty. Feel her brew them into power, the power we share as women and men, the power of life itself with all its grief and ecstasy. Let that power build within you; let it begin to rise as the fire rises beneath the cauldron, as the brew transforms; let it rise on your voice, to rise through your body, to become a sound, rising with all our love and rage, swirling and dancing around her cauldron; let it rise . . .

Breathe deeply; breathe that power in, your power to choose, your power to claim your right to make the choices that shape your life. Take in what power you need, and give what's left back to the earth.

Look around you. One last time, look into the eyes of the Crone. Hear what she says to you and you alone. Reach forward, and let her give you a sip of her brew. Taste how rich it is, how fragrant with spices, how all of your pain and joy and uncertainty and rage have given it this flavor. Let it sink into your bones, and warm your body, and give you strength.

Say good-bye and thanks. And as you look around and lift your eyes from the cauldron, you see the trees of the orchard. And you realize that this orchard is a circle, with the cauldron at its center, and close beside the ancient trees are the youngest of saplings.

Now it is time to come back. Take three deep breaths, knowing that you can bring back the transformation you've made and the memory of all you've experienced here. In and out. Breathing deeply, letting the orchard fade. In and out. Coming back into your body, into this circle, this space and time. Pat the edges of your body; make sure you're all here. Say your name out loud. Clap your hands three times. And that's the end of the story.

Stepping into Our Power

Many women and men who have completed a healing cycle by learning to use the tools of magic wish to take the next step. When we have found liberation and inner power, when the soul energy that has been bound up in inner turmoil and self-doubt is released, the results begin to show quite naturally. For Rose this happens in a single dramatic moment, as she faces death and her allies appear. For most people it is a much more gradual transformation, as plateaus of healing are reached, to be followed by new challenges and breakthroughs. But over time we break into leaf and bloom as artists, healers, activists, home and family makers, responsible community members.

For some of us this means accepting a calling to healing, teaching, or creative expression. For some it may mean simply taking a new attitude toward a family or health challenge, while for others it means political and social activism and service. For Rose it means becoming the new young queen of her own castle, mother of her own future.

One person may volunteer as a Girl Scout leader; another may begin a long-deferred dream of going back to school or starting drum lessons. One woman may hang her artwork in a gallery or booth, while another might join with others to take responsibility for a community food bank or the local Sierra Club chapter. One person might step forward as a priestess and join with others to publicly celebrate the Witches' Sabbats. These could be dreams that have always been there, delayed as we struggled in the dense undergrowth of our personal process, or they could be brand-new dreams we have just now discovered or liberated.

But whatever progress we make toward stepping out in the world with our new strength and vision, we will always have to deal with other people's reactions to our changes. We will always face obstacles both inner and outer, and we will continue to be tested. We will need to continue to rely on nature, and the Goddess, and our own deep sources as we go along.

They Lived Happily Ever After

We have now walked the Inner Path together. We have chosen to live a Witch's life, seeking to know and love all of ourselves. We have bound our stories with that of Rose and learned, as she learned, the basic skills of living, intuitive and ecstatic, guided and grounded, wild and human, in harmony. We have gained the tools and the confidence to step up to our life goals, and now we have a whole lot of living to do. Following are three true stories about how Witches used the tools of magic, as Rose did, to create change in their own family lines.

Three Sisters

Three heads are bent over the saltwater bowl, blond, red, and black. The circle has been cast. The sisters are spending the last night in the house where they grew up. Tomorrow the keys go to the Realtor. The staircases of this house echo with the ghost footsteps of the little girls they used to be. The screen doors of their summer vacations bang in memory. There's the smell of long-ago lilacs. Here, too, they lost their father, who died young, and they lost pieces of themselves, trying to grow up with an overwhelmed mother. The sisters' voices are raised now, wailing, singing, grieving, a quiet story, then laughter. All through the night, they purify and release together, waves of grief, memory, love, and longing.

In the morning the Realtor comes with the sun, and it's time to go. But the bond between the sisters has never been stronger; they've never had so much family. They've helped themselves with the tools of magic and changed the history of their family line.

Two Cousins

Two cousins have called together a family meeting. Twelve family members from three generations are gathered together in the living room. They know that the time has come to talk about the family secret. The truth, so long avoided, is that Grampa was a child molester. Many of the women in the room have been deeply and directly affected; all the men and women in the room have been indirectly affected. All have carried this secret; some have never spoken out loud about it, although Grampa has been dead for years.

The cousins show the group the dry branch of an old beach rose, battered by storm and sea. This will be the talking stick. Each person in the room will have a turn to speak uninterrupted while holding the rose, and there will be no argument, just listening. As the rose wand passes, the power in the room builds. There are tears and anger, painful silences, blame and shame, and also hope and gratitude. Finally the last person has spoken. The cousins hold up the rose. "The silence is broken." They break the stick into twelve pieces, one for each participant, to take home, save, or burn as they will. They have used the tools of magic to change the history of their family line.

Mother and Daughter

A slamming door and the clomping of platform shoes announce the arrival of the teenage daughter. She flops down on the couch next to her mother: "I'm really depressed. Some things about this family really bother me."

The mother is startled and feels her defensiveness rising. But on a single, practiced breath she drops an anchor to the powerful core of herself. With an almost imperceptible movement, she touches the curve of her lower belly and says her secret word, *hearth*, to herself. Now she can open her attention toward her daughter and meet her confidences fairly.

"If you want to talk, I want to listen," she says. And so they do, breaking intergenerational patterns of mother-daughter pain and distance, changing all the worlds, changing the history of their family line with the tools of magic.

The Pyre Breaks into Leaf and Bloom

There are millions of stories, just as there are millions of souls seeking the fulfillment of their life purpose. We have reached for the tools of magic and become the main characters in our own fairy stories, the stories of the fair, the brave, the generous, the true. We have brought healing and inner strength into our lives, learning to rely on the spiritual wisdom of the Goddess's ancient cultures that slept under the outlines of our fairy story. We have teased that wisdom awake in ourselves, and in our circles, by building Rose altars and dancing Rose dances, casting Rose spells and trancing Rose trances.

Now we are beginning to let our internal changes bloom. And since a healthy priestess makes all things whole, our families and communities will never be the same. The wood of the pyre, wood from the world tree itself, rises up in leaf and bloom. We rise up with it, a new kind of woman and man, an ancient kind. We are powered from within, daring, passionate, joyful, free, and whole. The pyre, built for fear and death, breaks into a million Roses, and the whole world is changed.

The Outer Path

Rose's task nears completion just as the forces that would destroy her also reach their peak. She continues weaving and sewing in the dungeon, in the cart on the way to the stake, when tied upon the pyre itself. Even to save herself, she will not abandon her task and speak. Only by fulfilling her challenge can she be saved, for her task has become her own redemption as well as her brothers'.

Her focus, her concentration, her courage are an awesome model for those of us on the Outer Path. For when we undertake great works of collective healing, we are also called upon to hold our concentration, to overcome our fears.

A true healing, a powerful work of transformation, always involves a death and rebirth. To heal from a serious illness, we may have to change the patterns of our lives, dissolve and reconfigure our energies. To return to human form, the brothers must experience the dissolution of their swan bodies. To heal our torn social fabric, to restore justice and balance in the larger world, the patterns and institutions that exist need to change. For a structure or institution to change, it may first need to be torn down. Sometimes an old house can be repaired. But if it has deteriorated too far or is built on a bad foundation, we do better to rip it down and begin anew, or its rot will contaminate the new structure.

Everything alive resists death, whether it is an insect trapped against a window or an institution struggling to preserve itself. To challenge unjust institutions, to ask them in essence to die so that something new can be born, we must be willing to face resistance, to stay focused on our goal no matter what forces beset us.

We must also be prepared for what will happen if we succeed. When a structure dissolves, we may be left unsheltered from the rain and wind while something new is being built. After death comes decay, when the body is broken down into simpler and simpler forms until it goes back into its original elements, which then feed something else.

In times of chaos, weavers are needed who can restore the fabric of life, who can create new shirts, new souls, new values that allow us to live in our fully human selves without losing the freedom of the swans' flight or forgetting the language of the wild.

The work of the Outer Path in this chapter is to overcome fear, to learn to hold our vision and weave even in the dungeon, to walk into fire, to die and be reborn, and to heal.

Overcoming Fear

To act, to walk toward the fire while continuing to weave, to let go of control and let structures dissolve into chaos, we must overcome fear. We have already developed the tools we need to face and move through our fears: grounding, breathing, anchoring to our core state of being, calling in our allies. These skills and practices are what we need in moments of crisis and fear, whatever their source. Whether we're afraid of standing up in front of an audience to speak or of sitting down in front of a line of riot cops in a blockade, we can breathe, ground, center, anchor, and invoke help. And the more we practice these most basic magical skills, the better they will serve us in an emergency.

Sharing our fears can also help us move beyond them. Rose was not allowed to speak, and there was no one in her dungeon to comfort or reassure her. But we can speak and offer support to each other. Just knowing that other people are also afraid is a comfort.

Part of the discipline of magic is to choose the images in which we invest energy. Fear can make us obsess on all the undesirable outcomes we can imagine. We play them over and over in our minds, working ourselves into an exhausted, nervous state. But magic teaches us to release those images and instead to pour energy into a visualization of the outcome we desire. So, we might imagine, Rose shuts her mind to the horrors of the stake and continues to sew, holding before herself the vision of her brothers restored to human form.

When a group is preparing for a public event, a large ritual, a new stage in growth, or an action, fear may arise and become manifest in subtle ways.

Individuals try to control each other or express great anxiety about things that have never before seemed frightening. Energy may simply seem stuck, and creativity blocked.

The following ritual may help identify and release the fears that are undermining the group's trust and joy.

Fear Ritual for Groups

In sacred space, each person should have a candle, a pen, and a notebook nearby. Ground, center, and breathe deeply into your belly. Light the candle. Ask yourselves, "What am I afraid of? What are the images in my mind of the worst outcomes? Am I dwelling on them? What is the dialogue that goes with them? Is this fear telling me about something I can do or need to do?" Leave time to consider each of these questions.

Write down any information your fear is giving you or any tasks that emerge. Then become aware of your fear as pure emotional energy. Gather up your fear as you take a long, slow breath in. Hold your breath until you feel your body fighting for air, beginning to feel the physical panic of breathlessness. Then release your breath; blow out all your fear, and blow out your candle.

In the dark, renew your grounding, and breathe slowly and deeply. Ask yourselves, "What is the best possible outcome of this situation? What vision can I create of what I truly need and desire? What possibilities of hope and renewal can I entertain in this space I have now emptied?" Again, be sure to leave time to deeply consider the questions.

When your vision comes clear, light the candle. Breathe in the light and the energy of the fire to strengthen your vision. Anchor that vision into a place in your body you can touch or a specific image or phrase.

In the group, pass a lighted candle as a talking stick and share your fears and hopes, without interrupting or cross talk. Then discuss the information you've received. What is your collective picture of the worst possible outcome? The best? What actions can you take together that can alleviate your fears? How can you support each other?

Go around the circle one last time. Each person makes a commitment to something she or he will do to transform fear or support the group, and pinches out the candle flame to contain the fire within the wick.

"I will stop, breathe, and count to ten when I feel panicky,"

"When the energy is stuck, I'll remember to ask, 'What are we afraid of?'"

"I will listen without judgment when any of you want to talk about your fears, and I'll give you a back rub."

If you wish, you might chant and raise power to keep your commitments. When you are ready, open the circle.

When you find your fear returning, breathe your anxiety out. Use your anchor to recall your vision, and replace the negative images in your mind with your positive images of what you desire.

As we develop our psychic abilities, we sometimes receive information about the future in the form of premonitions or visions. Knowing that this is a possibility, we can become afraid of our own anxiety, mistaking it for precognition. True precognition does not come to us with anxiety attached. It arises from a clear, almost emotionless state and carries with it a sense of deep knowing rather than fear. Fear may come later, when we contemplate the message. Anxiety clouds our ability to receive true information, whether from the spirits or from the technical support person on the telephone trying to guide us out of a software crash. Breathing, grounding, and anchoring to our core state of being can help us take in the information we need, whether we're consulting the spirits through divination or asking for directions on a lonely road in the dark.

Trust is also a powerful antidote to fear. When we work regularly with our allies, spirit or human, they become figures of trust that we can hold to when we need courage. Trust can literally save our lives. Some years ago, I nearly died when I got caught in a riptide in Hawaii. What allowed me to stay calm enough to float and wait for rescue was my trust in my friend Ceres, who had gone for help; in the magical powers of my friend Teish, whom I was working with on the trip; and in the love and compassion of Yemaya, Mother Ocean. Had I panicked and struggled, I would surely have drowned.

When activists prepare people to do civil disobedience and risk arrest, we encourage the formation of affinity groups, small groups that can act together, get to know each other, and build trust. In circles, covens, and support groups, we can also find loyalty and comradeship that help us overcome fear.

Trust is a precious and fragile fabric in any group. Weaving trust is a process as challenging as weaving nettle shirts. In a sense, we are weaving the soul of a group with every act we take, everything we say or do. We can also easily rip the fabric apart with personal attacks, malicious gossip, or tasks left unfulfilled.

Revenge, jealousy, our own ill wishes, and wicked vows are like logs with which we build the pyre that will consume us even as we continue to try to finish our task of healing. But if we do the work in this book, the work of transformation, we can build a different kind of fire, a hearth fire that can warm and comfort us.

I've learned a lot about fire from living with a woodstove as my source of heat. When my relationship with the fire elementals is good (and/or the wood is dry), I can toss in a match and whoosh—the room is warm. On a bad night, when I'm impatient, when I haven't laid the fire correctly, it will fizzle out over and over again while I swear quietly and use up all my matches.

Fire is a teacher. It is no accident that the hearth is so much associated with the heart of home and community. Building a fire can teach us a lot about building a relationship, a family, a community, a movement. Following is a meditation—or, really, a sort of musing—I began working with at California, mid-Atlantic, and Vermont Witchcamps, with added inspiration from Kymistree, Baruch, Beverly, and Thorn.

Fire Meditation

Set up a fire pit, and ask each person in the group to bring something to build a fire. Be very careful not to specify what they should bring. (In the group Baruch and I led, people kept asking us, "What do you mean, 'Bring something to build a fire'?" "Just come up to the fire circle, and bring something to build a fire," we kept repeating patiently. Half the group brought wood, paper, or matches, and the other half turned up empty-handed. They'd brought passion, vision, courage, because they'd assumed we'd been speaking metaphorically.)

When the group gathers, look at what people have brought. Consider what we need to build a fire. Did anyone bring kindling? Small fuel to get it going? Matches? Did some people bring everything necessary in case others did not come through? Did some people forget to bring anything? Did some bring big logs?

Fire needs fuel, oxygen, and heat. What is the fuel that sustains your community? What is the oxygen, the breath of ideas, visions, concepts? What is the heat, the passion? And who or what is the spark, the catalyst to get things going?

To burn, a fire must have all these things arranged in the proper relationships. A fire has its own order. Before building a fire, consider what contains it. A woodstove? A fire pit? A cauldron? What boundary contains your community, defines it, and keeps it safe?

Begin with a small pile of something quick to burn. What catches fire easily in your community? Many times I start with garbage—used paper, old newspaper, tissues. Many times we begin to create community around our garbage: our old issues, our unhealed wounds. A fire needs just enough of that stuff to get it going. Pain can spark community into being, but to be sustained, we need to start adding sticks of hope and vision, small at first, then larger and larger. The big sticks, the grand visions, can't be added until the fire is going strong. Put them on too early, and you smother the fire.

What size log can your fire handle? What does it need? What do you tend to bring to the fire—kindling? The little sticks, the dealing with everyday details, that lay the groundwork for the big logs? Too many sticks at the same time can deprive the fire of the air it needs to burn. Sometimes we may bring a perfectly good stick to the fire only to find that the timing is wrong, that it is not needed and may even harm the fire if we insist on adding it at that moment. Have you ever done that? What might have happened if you had been able to hold your stick back?

A strong fire can burn up a lot of garbage—but garbage alone cannot sustain a fire. How does your community find the big logs it needs to keep going?

A fire, to be sustained, must be tended. How do you feed your fire? How do you tend your community? Think of everything you do in community, every communication you make, no matter how small it seems, as an act of feeding the fire. Timing is everything in sustaining a fire. The same log that may keep the fire burning if placed when the flames are hot may kill it if you wait too long. Returning a phone call, answering an e-mail, sending out the minutes of a meeting—all the thousand small acts of service we do feed the fire best when they are done at the right time. Have you ever undone your own work by procrastinating?

A hot blaze is wonderful for a bonfire or for quick heat, but if you want to cook, you have to cook on the embers. How do we learn to find the creativity in the ember times, when energy seems to be lower and the issue is sustaining, not blazing? What can we accomplish then that we cannot when the fire is high?

Some things will burn but create toxic fumes if we add them to the fire. Backbiting, vicious gossip, and unkind rumors are like plastic waste added to a hearth fire. We cannot trust a group, we cannot safely breathe, in their presence. Have you ever added them to your group's fire? Have you ever dumped explosives onto the hearth or dampened it with wet rags?

What are your own lessons from the fire? How do we sustain the hearth fire of this group?

When the group has had time to meditate, you can either open to discussion around the fire or move into more energetic ritual.

Weaving in the Dungeon

Rose holds her vision and continues to weave in the dungeon, on the way to the stake itself. When we undertake a great work of healing, we need a vision strong enough to carry us when we enter unfriendly or even hostile environments.

Harvard is not generally thought of as a dungeon, but to a Witch it is a learning environment built on assumptions about success and power very different from ours. Grove, a Reclaiming teacher who earned a Master of Divinity degree from Harvard, speaks of how she was able to continue to weave her unique vision in a highly competitive environment.

"Part of a Witch's training involves moving between different realms," Grove says. "At Harvard I translated that into moving between different schools. I was able to hold my own center and move between the Business School, the Kennedy School of Government, and the Divinity School, where the cultures and communities are very different."

Just as Rose had her nettles with her in the dungeon, we bring our magical skills and understandings with us, whatever environment we find ourselves in.

"It was all too easy to feel less than 'the best and the brightest' at the Business School," Grove admits. "I realized I needed to help myself very actively. Three crystals came to me, and I charged them with the red leaves of an autumn maple and the light of the full moon. Then I planted them around the Business School campus, one of them in full view in the bowels of the library, where I could see it every time I entered, and one in the chapel, and one along my path. I empowered myself through this spiritual action, increasing my sense of peace in being there, and decreasing the power of the illusions around me."

Grove used many magical skills and tools for support, from listening to the elements to spellcrafting and trance journeying. Perhaps most important, she was clear about her intention: "I was not there to change others or to inform them about Wicca. I was not there to be adversarial to the institution—rather, to be a part of it for a time and to learn as much as I could. I was very clear about my own spiritual path and commitment to the Goddess. Going to divinity school was an incredibly broadening academic experience, but not the spiritual searching that it is for some people. My own path is quite eclectic, so more exposure to other traditions was a gift rather than a challenge."

To anchor her intention, "the phrase that came to me was 'this bridge called my brain,' a variation of the title of a very important collection of writings by women of color: *This Bridge Called My Back*. I sensed that this education my brain was taking in was a bridge between many worlds."

Rose's intention was embodied in the shirts she was sewing for her brothers. Even in the dungeon, the shirts were a constant image of the human form, the soul she hoped to restore. As Witches, as workers of magic, we know the importance of directing our will through an image that holds our intention.

In political actions, we often focus strongly on what we are protesting against. We shout "No war!" or "Stop the bombing!" But our understanding of magic tells us that Younger Self doesn't understand no. Younger Self is like a dog: if we say, "Rover, I'm not taking you for a walk today," Rover hears "Walk!" and gets excited. To truly change consciousness, not only must we know what we don't want; we must hold a clear vision of what we do want.

That vision must be embodied in the actions we take, in the way we structure our groups and treat each other, and in the messages we put out to the world.

Margo Adair is a longtime activist, meditation teacher, and friend of Reclaiming. She and her friend Ruby Phillips created the following meditation for shared intent (which is taken from Margo's forthcoming book *The Applied Meditation Sourcebook*) as a preparation for political actions. It incorporates breathing, grounding, and creating an anchor to an intention for the action. As they put it, "This meditation creates a way for people to easily tap their own internal resources and feel collective purpose in the midst of chaos."

Shared Intent Meditation

Sit, stand, or lie in a comfortable position.

Bring your awareness into your body. Notice your body breathing.

Feel breath rolling through your body. Feel the rise and fall of your breath, relaxed and full.

Breath carries life. All that is alive breathes. Appreciate the simple miracle of breath. Breath renews life. As you breathe, feel your breath renew you now. Every cell of your body is bathed by breath.

Feel your feet. . . . Feel the earth. Feel yourself supported by the earth. Feel the stability of the earth. Grow roots down into the ground; draw strength from the earth.

What you breathe out, the plants breathe in. Breath weaves life together. Breath carries life.

Imagine that the earth is breathing with you, as though the earth and sky breathe, as though All That Is is alive. Remember the sacred. Life is sacred. Remember the beauty and uniqueness of human beings living in different places on the earth. All people on the earth are sacred. Remember the life of the forests, and remember the life of the seas. Breathe the powers of the forests, the animals, the seas, and deep in the earth. . . .

Now notice that all of us here are breathing.

Remember that we are all here to take a stand for life, for all living beings on the earth. We are all here together; together we are powerful. Breathe the power of life. Imagine that our breathing finds harmonic rhythms. Notice how the quality of energy here is changing as we focus on our common purpose. Bathe in this energy.

Breathing our unity, breathing our common purpose, breathing the power of our shared intention . . . breathing with the earth, breathing with each other, breathing the sacred.

Now create a symbol or a gesture that represents this energy, whatever feels right to you. Know that when you call this to mind, you evoke our shared intent. Know that every time you evoke it, its power increases. Tell yourself this now.

As you breathe out, send this power to where it is needed to help us work well with one another, to stand with all life. Imagine bathing the situation with this energy.

Tell yourself you will remember to call upon this energy. Tell yourself this now. Expect it to be true. Envision the success of our shared intent. Expect it to be true.

Vision Meditation

Finding a vision of what we want is often much more difficult than identifying what we don't want. The many issues we care about, the complexity of the problems we face, can seem overwhelming.

"I try to focus on just one issue at a time," says Oak, a Reclaiming teacher, therapist, and lifelong activist. "I imagine what a true victory would mean for that issue: 'What if all food were organic?' And what I find is that one victory changes everything."

In sacred space, think of an issue you feel passionate about. (You might reflect back on the wand meditation described in chapter 6.) Breathe deeply, and let yourself imagine what a victory around that issue would be like. What would change in your life? What would change for the poorest third of the people? What would change for the earth?

What would have to change to bring about this victory in the aspects of air, in the ways we think about things? Our ideals, our constructs of reality?

What would change in terms of fire aspects, in our energy systems, in who holds power and how that power is gained and distributed?

What would change in water aspects, in terms of our images of value or success or abundance? What would change emotionally?

What would change in terms of earth aspects, in our environment? How would our economic systems change?

How would we change in the realm of the spirit?

What's already changing to bring about this victory?

Breathe deeply. Is there a concrete image you can visualize of your victory? A symbol that you can weave into your magic and your actions? A word or phrase you can use to convey the essence of this vision?

Give thanks for your victory, and open the circle.

Headline Bonfire

Jeffrey Alphonsus describes a ritual performance in which he shouted out headlines from the newspaper while his partner Med-o told the real story of what had happened. To end, they burned the newspaper in a flaming cauldron and asked the audience to shout out the headlines they wanted to see.

Create a ritual, a performance, or a mummer's play around the headlines you would most like to see. Give some thought to phrasing them in positive language: "World Peace Declared!" instead of "All Wars Ended!"

In your journal, write the news story of your victory. Infuse it with magical intention, and keep it on your altar to be charged with energy.

When our vision is clear, sometimes the most powerful political statement we can make is simply to enact it. Rose May Dance was part of a group of Reclaiming Witches who also worked as counselors for drug users around AIDS issues. From their research, they determined that making clean needles available to drug users would help slow the spread of AIDS. Providing such supplies was illegal in our state. Nevertheless, they set up a needle exchange, beginning their action on November 2, the Day of the Dead, and holding both a magical and political intention. Instead of arresting the group, the police and later the mayor gave the group tacit support. Prevention Point, as the group was called, collected vital data that had a worldwide impact on AIDS-prevention programs, spurred the de facto legalization of the exchange, and eventually became a publicly supported program.

No matter how strong our vision, activism still often demands that we say no to injustice or destruction through all the usual forms of marches, petitions, and rallies. Demonstrations can also be joyful celebrations of life, and when we participate in them as Witches, using all our magical skills, we can have a powerful effect on the energy. We can use the symbols of our vision on posters, flags, and flyers. We can weave our phrases into chants. In many demonstrations over the years, we've learned the power of a song begun at the right moment or a spiral dance on a blockade line. At one Headwaters rally to save the old-growth redwoods, a group of us started a spiral dance when a planned civil disobedience was abandoned and the event needed closure. We had to fight a blaring sound system and a battery of thumping drummers, but by working the energy together we raised a cone of power as a double rainbow crowned the sky.

At the November 1999 protests against the World Trade Organization, giant puppets, flags, and balloons converged on the streets of Seattle. Sea turtles danced through the streets. Reclaiming Witches brought the banners of earth, air, fire, and water to represent the Elements of Life. Jeffrey Alphonsus was part of a group that drummed through the streets to hold the energy of hope and vision amid the tear gas.

"I had never felt such a real sense of urgency about the power of the drumming, how needed it was," he says. "People were coming to me saying, 'Will you come over here?' or 'Will you go over there?' They weren't just seeing us as entertainment; they could feel the power of the drums in keeping their spirits up."

We can weave a symbol into many aspects of an action. The I'll Drink to That affinity group, at the WTO demonstrations, went into a hotel bar where many delegates were gathered the night before the action. They bought a round of drinks for the house and began toasting the Elements of Life. They ended up drinking and talking with delegates until the wee hours, opening a dialogue that could not have taken place on the street in the heat of the action. And they continued to work with water and in-drinking as a symbol in many forms, from charged ginger tea to chants and libations.

When political action takes the form of nonviolent civil disobedience, it may afford us the opportunity to literally weave in the dungeon. Over the last twenty years, I've done many rituals in jail. After the WTO blockade, several Reclaiming Witches were held for five days for refusing to obey an illegal decree banning protest and free speech in the downtown area. We taught chants and sang songs, held morning meditations, and encouraged our fellow blockaders to share their skills and knowledge in everything from organizing strategies to folding paper cranes. We held a spiral dance in a holding cell and gave each other aura brushdowns before release.

"I found that what was most important was just working with the elements," Oak said afterward. "Again and again, that's what I would come back to. The guards took away my asthma inhaler, and I had to keep invoking the air spirits and stay focused on breathing. In that place where there was nothing but concrete, it was so powerful to know that we could still connect with the elements and be in touch with the powers of nature."

Extreme situations test the depth of our practice and compassion. We know we have worked a powerful spell when we can transform imprisonment into empowerment. But perhaps even more important is the weaving we do every day, the thousands of magical transformations that happen in our homes, our workplaces, our communities, whenever we enact our visions and truly care for one another.

When Juan Pablo was diagnosed with cancer, his friends transformed his hospital room with art and photographs and flowers. David came and told him the story of the Popol Vuh in installments to fit his energy level. Other friends brought poems, charms, spells, and the food he craved, making magic in what could have been a cold and sterile environment.

The many women and men who continue to create, love, teach, priestess, and serve their communities while fighting AIDS, chronic fatigue, or other serious diseases are weavers in the dungeon. Weaving might mean lending a compassionate ear to the woman next to you on the airplane who is going home to her father's funeral, or helping the young mother corral her unruly child in the subway, or offering to mediate in a fight between two friends. Cynthia and Patricia of Diana's Grove have established sacred land and good relations with their neighbors in an area openly hostile to lesbians and Witches. Thorn weaves magic in the soup kitchen, Paul in the public schools, Gwydion in a large corporation, Melusine in city government; Alphonsus weaves magic by drumming in the streets, Rose May and Flame by counseling drug users who have been tested for HIV or hepatitis. To be weavers, soul makers, healers, culture shapers means to gather the power and take on the responsibility to affect the energies around us, to focus on our creative task whatever the circumstances we find ourselves in.

Cultural healing is a collective effort. No one of us alone can fulfill Rose's task for our whole society. We need for all of us to be Rose, to weave the soul of a transformed world. In that process, we will also at times need healing. We must know how to receive as well as give. Reclaiming's Healing Ritual is a beautiful model of the fluidity we need to sustain great healing works.

The Healing Ritual

Our Healing Ritual has evolved over the course of four or five years, primarily at Witchcamps. In form it is different from most of our rituals, in that its power depends entirely on the whole community working together, and not on any individual's skill or inspiration. The structure of the ritual is simple: the community creates a strong, sustained energy base, and individuals or pairs may go into the center to give or receive hands-on healing, drawing on the power of the group. The explanation, preparation, and structure of the ritual require great care, but once begun, it runs itself. All the roles are fluid, and every participant is free to step into any role.

PREPARATION: Before the ritual, the group is given instruction in hands-on healing, in caring for their own health and energy, and in cleansing afterward. People with serious health concerns are encouraged to find partners to work with. Partners generally exchange healing, taking turns giving and receiving, but someone with an extremely grave condition may request several healers to take shifts and may remain in the center throughout the ritual. Generally, however, participants move in and out freely among the various roles.

Four stations are set up in the four directions. Groups commit to priestessing at a station in shifts, so that everyone is also free to experience the circle. The air station might offer smudging; the fire station might have candles and offer brushdowns or cleansing energy work; the water station should provide drinking water and waters of the world (kept clearly separate); and the earth station might have food, herbs, and stones or crystals.

The group creates sacred space, with a strong grounding and casting, and invokes the elements and Goddesses and Gods of healing.

Depending on the number of people involved, the group forms one, two, or three concentric circles around a large center. A fire may be lit in the middle. Three or four drummers sit in a clump in the center, but most of it is open. Drummers do not have to be highly skilled, only capable of keeping a strong, simple, steady beat. However, it is vital that they listen to the chant, stay in sync with the dancers, and do not speed up, which can be more difficult than you might think.

The circles begin a very simple chant and dance:

> Every step I take is a healing step,
> Every step I take is a sacred step,
> Healing, healing, healing my body,
> Healing, healing, healing the land.

—DONALD ENGSTROM

The dance moves clockwise: step, together, step, together . . . eight steps to the left, then four steps forward, and four back. It's folk dance reduced to the barest minimum. The chant and dance, together with the intention of the group, begin to build an energy field.

When they are ready, participants step into the center of the circle, drawing on that field to do healing work on each other. People may also bring objects to charge for someone who is not physically present. While physical healing is the core issue, some participants may choose to work on emotional or relational issues.

As the dance goes on, participants may move into the center and move out, or go to one of the stations for a rest, a drink, or a brushdown. Drummers relieve each other. The energy base builds until the whole group is in a state of timeless entrancement.

When the leading priestesses feel the energy begin to wane, they ring a bell or gong as a warning. The first gong tells the group that if they want healing and haven't yet gone into the center, now is the time. The second gong warns those in the process of healing to complete their work. The third gong is the signal for the drums to fade, the dance to stop, and the chant to become a wordless cone of power.

When the power is grounded, the group may choose to go on with other ritual acts or songs, but generally people are exhausted and ready to end. A priestess leads a formal grounding for the whole group, and people are asked to give each other brushdowns. The elements, Goddess, and Gods are devoked, and the circle is opened. Food must be available, preferably something with some protein, not just cookies and chips. Generally, one or two experienced priestesses make themselves available for anyone who still needs help fully grounding or integrating their experience.

In a setting such as Witchcamp where the group has been opening psychically and emotionally all week, the healing ritual can be very intense. Some true miracles have occurred: a woman diagnosed with hepatitis C reduced her viral load to zero; a long-term marriage on the rocks found its love rekindled. For others, the results are more subtle. The first time I went into the center of the circle, I found that the struggle to allow myself to ask for and receive energy was in itself the healing I needed.

We need many rituals such as this one, many ways to share energy and support, to sustain us on the Outer Path.

———————

As I write, Joan lies dying of cancer. An artist and lifelong activist, she has spent her life working for women and working for peace. Like Rose, Joan is weaving soul shirts down to the end of her life, making death into an art of courage and grace. Yet the work of peacemaking is far from done.

Ron, who was given four weeks to live by his doctors, writes in his last e-mail: "Development, be it international, community or human resource (and always sustainable), has been my passion from Peace Corps days and I wasn't quite finished with the job yet." Like Rose, Ron has lived with passion and commitment to his task and love for the people he has served. He will never finish that work now, not even his own piece of it. Someone else will have to take up his tasks, or they will remain undone.

We all finish each other's work. Just as Rose's task was begun by her mother's ill wish, someone else will have to untangle the consequences of her unfinished shirt. Our story teaches us that there is always one uncompleted sleeve, that no great work is ever wholly finished.

Yet an imperfect work may still be good enough. A partial transformation may still accomplish healing and change. A life lived in visionary passion is better than a life of cynicism and despair. So we must commit ourselves to the work and know when to end it and move on.

When we take action to change the world, we rarely see immediate results. We march for peace, but war rages on. We educate people about violence against women, but we have no way to count the rapes and beatings we've prevented, only the ones that are still going on. When we do achieve success, it often simply clears the way for us to see more extensive wrongs. Segregation was ended by the civil rights movement, but racism and poverty still blight lives.

We can be sustained by knowing we are doing the right thing, by trusting that our actions have impacts we cannot see. But to stay sane, we also need a few visible achievements. Our story teaches us not to expect total success, but to acknowledge and celebrate our partial victories. And magic teaches us to consciously act 'as if': live as if the world we want to create already exists. When we do complete a task, even partially, when we gain even a small victory, we need to celebrate. The pyre that would have burned Rose bursts into bloom.

Victory Ritual

Reclaiming classes often end with a ritual planned by the students. Now we have reached the end of the Outer Path. Our journey draws to a close. If you have done the work of this book, you have acquired the tools of magic, the skills of healing, and the vision and wisdom to change both yourself and the world.

Take time to think over your life, to think about the issues you've worked for, the great political struggles you've been a part of, the personal struggles you've waged, the work you've done in the process of reading and using this book. Know that however partial your successes might be, you have the right to declare victory.

Create a victory ritual for yourself, your group, or your community. Consider what you need to honor. What work is not being acknowledged? Who needs appreciation? Are there political victories you've never claimed? Magical feats or creative works that deserve acclaim?

How will you celebrate? A feast? A dance? A cake with candles? A ritual? An awards ceremony?

You know how to create sacred space, how to move, shape, direct, and ground energy. Use your skills, and honor the work you have done.

———

And so Rose's story ends as she is embraced by her youngest brother, with one human arm and one swan's wing. We have completed our initiatory journey. We have taken on the tasks of healing bequeathed to us by the mistakes of those who came before us. We have wandered in the wilderness and learned to follow a river to its end. We have stood steadfast in the face of rage and relinquished our own desires for revenge. We have learned to build a container for magic that can carry us away, and we have taken on a great task, a work of healing and transformation that requires all our passion and love. Our tools, our skills, and our allies have served us well as we have learned to withstand jealousy and projection and continued to weave even in the dungeon. We have overcome fear, died, and been reborn.

Initiation means beginning. We have traveled the paths of the elements, of inner healing and outer change. Now it is the youngest brother's journey we must follow.

The One-Winged Brother

You haunt the castle. When the feasting is over, when your sister has returned to the cares of her husband and her children, when your brothers ride out to hunt, you wander alone through empty rooms, your useless wing dragging at your side. Half of you is human, but half of you is still made for flight, and you yearn to soar on the updrafts and glide on the great currents, suspended, hovering, free. But you are earthbound, trapped. You will never fly again. And you will never ride with your brothers, for your wing catches in the trees and drags upon the ground. The maidens who chase after your brothers laugh at you, their hands covering their mouths to hide their mockery. And you cannot defend yourself. Your sister's voice is restored, but now you are doomed to silence, mute as a swan.

And when the loneliness becomes too much to bear, you steal away one night, to the cave where you lived so many years with your brothers, and with Rose always gathering, spinning, weaving. The cave is empty, silent, lonely, and you wander down to the shore. A small boat awaits you; see it on the shore, see how it looks to you and beckons until you step in, feeling it rock under your feet and steadying yourself with your one good arm.

Lie down. See the stars above you. Feel the breeze that you once could ride to beyond the ends of the earth. Reach for it with all the longing for freedom within you, and raise your wing to catch the wind. Your wing becomes a sail; feel the wind push against it and the boat glide through the water, almost as swiftly as once you could sail through air. Feel yourself rocking, rocking, rocking, cradled on the waves, carried away.

Sailing and rocking, rocking and sailing, the waves beneath you, the sky above. Almost free again, you hear the waves whispering, your journey a dialogue of sea and wind, rocking and sailing, sailing and rocking . . .

Until at last the boat comes to shore. Feel the bow scrape the sand; feel it move beneath you as you stand and step out and pull it up onshore after you. A mountain rises above you, a black shape against the pattern of bright stars in the sky. A path leads up the mountain, and you follow, beginning to climb. Feel the breath flowing in and out of your lungs; feel the muscles in your legs laboring to carry you up where once you could have risen light on the updrafts and soared. But now, step by step, you climb. The breath rasps in your mute throat; the night is filled with voices, the calls of night birds, frogs, beasts. All have a voice, but you are only a mute not-swan, not-human thing, climbing and climbing, the only sound you make the rasping of your breath, while around you the night chorus sings the song of the wild.

At last you reach the top. You pause for breath; you lay back and look up at the stars and cover yourself with your wing like a shroud. The stars are bright eyes in the night. Your ears are filled with the land's voice, and even the stars begin to sing—high, bright notes like bells that ring and ring through all the space that separates you.

Only you are mute. You long to sing, to join the chorus, to link your voice with those of the birds and the frogs. You open your mouth. You draw in breath and push it out again, painful and rasping. The stars are above you, but they could be below you, you could fall into them to dance and swirl and spiral in the dark. Breathe in; breathe out. No sound can force its way past your throat. Stop trying. Just breathe. And listen.

Listen deeply to the birds. Listen deeply to the frogs. Listen to the cat sounds, the howl of the coyote, the murmur of a stream, the stars singing. It all moves to the same rhythm, it all sings in a harmony that begins to fill you, until your body glows with it, and your wing shines pearly and iridescent as the moon. The wild sings to you, and you are of the wild, never wholly to belong to the human realm. Your wing marks you as a creature of the elements, soaring through air, reflecting the sun's fire, at home on the water, at home on the earth. Air, fire, water, earth—they echo through the voices that fill you, rising like an updraft to burst free from your throat, opening, opening, until your throat begins to pulse with sound and a great cry arises from deep within you, the cry of the earth, the wild, the song of the stars, ringing through you and awakening your silence into voice. And your voice rises and soars on the great currents of air, glides in perfect freedom over the far seas.

The wild is within you; you are its voice. You will never belong fully to the castle, the realm of humans, for yours is a different task: to be the voice of the land, the stars, the wild things, to speak for them in the councils of the castle, to live on the borderlands, not one thing or another but always moving between, shaman, magician, Witch.

And you lie for a long time, singing the song of the stars. Until you know it is time to return, return to the borderlands that lie near the castle, to take up your task, to use your voice.

Say farewell to this mountaintop, farewell to the stars. Thank them and take your leave. And begin to walk down, down the hill, around and down on the curving paths, hearing the night chorus around you, feeling the weight of your human body and the lightness of your swan's wing, and knowing how to balance between them as you walk. Down and down, until at last you come to the shoreline.

Find your boat. Feel its weight as you drag it down toward the water. Feel it float and sink under your weight as you step in and push off, hearing the sand scrape under the stern.

Lie down. See the stars above you. Feel the wind, and reach for it with all the knowledge of freedom within you, and raise your wing to catch the wind.

Your wing becomes a sail; feel the wind push against it and the boat glide through the water. You are rocking, rocking, rocking, cradled on the waves, carried away.

Sailing and rocking, rocking and sailing, the waves beneath you, the sky above. Free again, you hear the waves whispering; you sing a dialogue with sea and wind, rocking and sailing, sailing and rocking.

Until at last the boat comes to shore. Feel the bow scrape the sand; feel it move beneath you as you stand and step out and pull it up onshore after you.

The cave stands above you. The castle awaits you. You will never be fully human, never wholly swan, but you are something more and less than both: the translator, the one who knows the language of birds and interprets the wind, the constant reminder in human halls that to be human is not all.

Your wing is iridescent, pearly as the moon. It catches the wind and shines with its own light. Raise it high and proud; dance with it under the moonlight. Flaunt it. Admire its beauty. Cherish it. For what sets you apart is also what opens your ears and your heart.

Sing. Speak for the land; speak for the wild. Soar.

Bibliography

Our sources for the material in this book were mostly not written materials but rather the collective experience of our community over the last two decades of teaching. And there are so many worthwhile books on the Goddess tradition, and so many being published annually, that to produce a comprehensive bibliography is a major undertaking. We refer the reader to the twentieth anniversary edition of *The Spiral Dance* for a list of suggested reading. Here we include works we've referred to and books by authors mentioned in the text.

Adair, Margo. *The Applied Meditation Sourcebook*. Forthcoming.

Adair, Margo. *Working Inside Out: Tools for Change*. Berkeley, CA: Wingbow Press, 1984.

Cunningham, Scott. *Encyclopedia of Magical Herbs*. St. Paul: Llewellyn Publications, 1994.

Estés, Clarissa Pinkola. *Women Who Run with the Wolves*. New York: Ballantine, 1999.

Gimbutas, Marija. *The Civilization of the Goddess*. San Francisco: HarperSanFrancisco, 1991.

Gimbutas, Marija. *The Language of the Goddess*. San Francisco: Harper and Row, 1989.

Gimbutas, Marija. *The Living Goddess*. Edited and supplemented by Miriam Robbins Dexter. Berkeley/Los Angeles: University of California Press, 1999.

Harrow, Judy. *Wiccan Covens*. Secaucus, NJ: Citadel, 1999. (Out of print, but still available and hopefully soon to be reissued by another publisher.)

Macy, Joanna. *Coming Back to Life: Practices to Reconnect Our Lives, Our World*. Gabriola Island, B.C.: New Society Publishers, 1998.

Macy, Joanna. *Despair and Personal Power in the Nuclear Age*. Philadelphia: New Society Publishers, 1983.

Macy, Joanna. *Dharma and Development: Religion as Resource in the Sarvodaya Movement in Sri Lanka.* West Hartford, CT: Kumarian Press, 1983, 1985.

Macy, Joanna. *Mutual Causality in Buddhism and General Systems Theory: The Dharma of Natural Systems.* Buffalo: SUNY Press, 1991.

Macy, Joanna. *Widening Circles: A Memoir.* Gabriola Island, B.C.: New Society Publishers, 2000.

Macy, Joanna. *World as Lover, World as Self.* Berkeley, CA: Parallax Press, 1991.

Macy, Joanna, with Anita Barrows. *Rilke's Book of Hours.* Putnam Riverhead, 1996.

Macy, Joanna, with John Seed, Arne Naess, and Pat Fleming. *Thinking Like a Mountain: Towards a Council of All Beings.* Philadelphia: New Society Publishers, 1988.

Moraga, Cherrie, and Gloria Anzaldua. *This Bridge Called My Back: Writings by Radical Women of Color.* Watertown, MA: Persephone Press, 1981.

Palmer, Wendy. *The Intuitive Body: Aikido as Clairsentient Practice.* Berkeley, CA: North Atlantic Books, 1994.

Soule, Deb. *The Roots of Healing.* New York: Carol Publishing Group, 1995.

Starhawk. *Dreaming the Dark: Magic, Sex, and Politics.* Boston: Beacon Press, 1982, 1988, 1997.

Starhawk. *The Fifth Sacred Thing.* New York: Bantam, 1993.

Starhawk. *The Spiral Dance: A Rebirth of The Ancient Religion of the Great Goddess.* San Francisco: HarperSanFrancisco, 1979, 1989, 1999.

Starhawk. *Truth or Dare: Encounters with Power, Authority, and Mystery.* San Francisco: HarperSanFrancisco, 1988.

Starhawk. *Walking to Mercury.* New York: Bantam, 1997.

Starhawk, Anne Hill, and Diane Baker. *Circle Round: Raising Children in the Goddess Tradition.* Illustrated by Sara Ceres Boore. New York: Bantam, 1998.

Starhawk, M. Macha Nightmare, and the Reclaiming Collective. *The Pagan Book of Living and Dying.* San Francisco: HarperSanFrancisco, 1997.

Teish, Luisah. *Carnival of the Spirit.* San Francisco: HarperSanFrancisco, 1994.

Teish, Luisah. *Jambalaya: The Natural Woman's Book of Personal Charms and Practical Rituals.* San Francisco: Harper and Row, 1985.

Teish, Luisah. *Jump Up.* Berkeley, CA: Kinari Press, 2000.

Walker, Barbara G. *The Woman's Encyclopedia of Myths and Secrets.* San Francisco: Harper and Row, 1983.

Weed, Susun S. *Healing Wise.* Woodstock, NY: Ash Tree Publishing, 1989.

Resources

Teaching and Training

Reclaiming
P.O. Box 14404
San Francisco, CA 94114
www.reclaiming.org

Classes, workshops, Witchcamps, connections, and a magazine, the Reclaiming Quarterly, plus information on local communities and events. Reclaiming-affiliated communities exist in many areas across the United States, Canada, and Europe, and many Reclaiming teachers are available for teaching and community mentoring. Check the Web site or the Quarterly for the schedules of many of the teachers mentioned in this book.

Diana's Grove
P.O. Box 159
Salem, MO 65560
phone: 573–689–2400
dianasgrove@dianasgrove.com
www.dianasgrove.com

Diana's Grove is a 102-acre sanctuary in the Ozarks that hosts the Missouri Witchcamp, among many other wonderful events. Cynthia and Patricia lead an ongoing Mystery School that offers advanced training in ritual and magic. Gwenyth Brigit Dwyn also teaches at Diana's Grove.

VelaDanza Healing Arts
phone: 415–339–8313
Veladanza@aol.com

Beverly Frederick produced two compilations of Reclaiming's ritual music: Through the Darkness *and* In the Arms of the Wild. *She and Doug Orton offer classes, apprenticeships, and weekend retreats in the Reclaiming tradition.*

Anne Hill and Diane Baker
www.circleround.com

Anne and Diane are coauthors with Starhawk of Circle Round: Raising Children in Goddess Tradition. *They offer resources for Pagan parenting, teaching children, and creating rituals with children.*

M. Macha Nightmare
www.machanightmare.com

Macha is coauthor with Starhawk of The Pagan Book of Living and Dying. *She offers resources on death and dying from a Pagan perspective. She is also a resource for rituals, teaching, funerals, handfastings, and weddings.*

Margo Adair
madair@aol.com
www.toolsforchange.org

Margo leads workshops in Applied Meditation, anti-oppression and diversity work, facilitation, consensus, and organizational visioning and development through Tools for Change. Her "Shared Intent" meditation (see the Outer Path in chapter seven) will be published in her forthcoming book, The Applied Meditation Sourcebook.

Luisah Teish
5111 Telegraph Avenue
P.O. Box 305
Oakland, CA 94609
ibukole5@aol.com
www.jambalayaspirit.org

Teish teaches and offers workshops and storytelling in the Yoruba-based traditions of West Africa. She is starting a Mystery School: School of Ancient Mysteries and Sacred Arts Center (SAMSAC).

Wilderness Awareness

Wilderness Awareness School
www.NatureOutlet.com

Tom Brown Jr.'s Tracker School
www.trackerschool.com

Two great resources for deepening your awareness of nature and wilderness skills, with workshops, courses, and independent study programs.

Music, Chants, and Songs

Serpentine Music
P.O. Box 2564
Sebastopol, CA 95473
phone: 707–823–7465
fax: 707–823–6664
www.serpentinemusic.com/serpentine/

Reclaiming tapes and CDs available through Serpentine include Chants, Second Chants, *and* Let It Begin Now. *Tapes and CDs by Reclaiming teachers include* Circle Round and Sing, *by Anne Hill (music for children's rituals);* Face of a New Day, *by T. Thorn Coyle; and* Through the Darkness *and* In the Arms of the Wild, *by Beverly Frederick.*

Mary Ellen Donald/Mary Ellen Books
P.O. Box 7589
San Francisco, CA 94120–7589
phone: 415–826–DRUM

Drumming tapes, books, and lessons.

Layne Redmond
www.layneredmond.com

Drumming workshops, tapes, and book.

Pagan Organizations

There are thousands, but here are three to begin with:

Covenant of the Goddess
P.O. Box 1226
Berkeley, CA 94701
*www.conjure.com (Web page for the Northern California Local Council of the
Covenant of the Goddess)*

Covenant of Unitarian Universalist Pagans
P.O. Box 640
Cambridge, MA 12140

Pagans within the Unitarian Church.

Pagan Federation USA
c/o Michael Thorn
P.O. Box 408
Shirley, NY 11967-0408
PaganFedUS@aol.com
www.hexhus.a.se/pfint/

*International Pagan Networking. Please include small donation ($2) with requests for
info.*

Best Web Site Resource

The Witches' Voice
www.witchvox.com

*The most comprehensive Pagan Web site, with thousands of links, updates on events,
news, political struggles, and networking.*

Starhawk's Personal Web Site

www.reclaiming.org/starhawk

Index